In Defense of
Decadent Europe

In Defense of Decadent Europe

Raymond Aron

*Translated from the French
by* Stephen Cox

Regnery/Gateway, Inc.
South Bend, Indiana

For Laure, Alain and Pauline
who will see how the story ends.

Contents

Contents

Preface to the
American edition

In my introduction written for the French edition, I explained to the best of my ability the circumstances in which I wrote this book, during the year 1976. Published in February 1977, it answered questions which the French people were asking themselves one year before the March 1978 elections. It was part of the intellectual debate, from 1975 to 1978, between the Right and the Left or, perhaps more exactly, between the parties that had been in power since 1958 and the left-wing opposition, the Socialists and Communists who had joined forces for the electoral battle by presenting a single, unified platform.

Written by a Frenchman for a French audience, this book was at the same time adapted to readers in Spain, Italy, Portugal, and Germany, because translations were published in 1977 and 1978 in those four countries. It may come as a surprise to the British and American public to find ideological debate (in Part I of the book) combined with economic and social analysis (in Parts II and III). The British journal *Encounter* was sufficiently interested to publish, in the issues of September and October 1977, an extensive portion of my *Plaidoyer pour l'Europe décadente* (the title chosen by *Encounter* was "My Defense of our Decadent Europe").

The book is typical, in its format, of French and other European studies, but critics in America and England could be inclined to look upon the work as a mere "ethnographic" document, as a curiously French treatment of the political and historical problems of our day. I doubt it, however, for even though there are sufficient Marxists and Marxist-Leninists in Great Britain and the United States, not many of them speak about their Marxism openly. Nor is there the dialogue between Russian dissidents and Western Marxists, which, outside France and Continental Europe (as well as some other Latin countries), is scarcely felt. This possible criticism of the book aside, its central argument should also be of interest—and concern—to American readers.

Time and time again, European journalists, politicians, and intellectuals have asked themselves and their colleagues the question: "Is the United States also plagued with the 'British disease'? Have the causes that brought about the decline of the United Kingdom not become visible in America, as well? Faced with an increasingly powerful and militant Soviet Union, do the Americans still have the same resolution they did thirty years ago?" The current economic crisis, with its fluctuations, does not make the Western societies appear any less superior to the Soviet régime, but it does cast doubt on the international institutions of cooperation that were established after World War II. Will the United States continue to ensure their prosperity?

The juxtaposition of the words *In Defense of* and *Decadent Europe* in the book's title may startle the American reader, but the paradox expressed by these words is part of a theme that has long been debated. Our values, the youth movements, the struggles for women's rights—all are moving in the same direction: personal freedom. It will be up to historians and philosophers, one day, to decide what was extreme individualism and what was evolutionary historical vitality.

Having no small attachment to these older values, I do not deny them; I ask, instead, along with many others, what lies in store for this "Western rump of Europe," which has become one of the world's three or four centers of industrial prosperity but which is incapable of defending itself and, having no great plan in common, is reduced to the enjoyment of its own well-being and freedoms.

RAYMOND ARON
Paris
December 1978

In search
of a title

This book owes its existence to the publishers who suggested it to me, though I fear that it is not altogether in keeping with their intentions. The book they had in mind would have been meant for the general public, and its aim was to be the defense and elucidation of freedom, both economic and political. The superiority of the free societies seemed to them—as it does to me—so self-evident that any counsel for the defense would easily make the case stick; it would be enough to compare what life had in store for the individual on either side of the demarcation line which has divided Europe into two parts since 1945; the facts themselves would then become arguments, and irrefutable ones. It is not on the frontiers of the German Federal Republic but on those of the German so-called Democratic Republic that guards shoot on sight at suspects—meaning people suspected of wanting to exercise the right, recognized by the UN's Universal Declaration of Human Rights, to live in the country of their choice.

But the job turned out, on reflection, to be altogether more difficult than I had thought. Not that the facts or arguments which came to mind at the outset appeared any less obvious, but a defense is justified only by its effectiveness, which in turn depends on circumstance, on the kind of questions the reader asks himself, and on the true reasons behind his own position (quite apart from the justifications he may offer to himself and to others). Without listing the successive forms which this book has assumed in my own mind, if not on paper—a story of no interest to anyone—I need only say that *In Defense of Freedom* was replaced by *Europe, Beware of Losing Your Freedom*, and then by a lengthy hesitation between *In Defense of Decadent Europe* and *In Defense of Liberal Europe*.

I was first of all tempted to reply to a colleague from *Le Monde* who wrote me a personal letter deploring the fact that a "superior mind" should have allowed itself to be led astray by anti-Communist feeling. While today's intellectuals, great or small, scholars or hacks, may unrestrainedly execrate the cruelty of any despot of the Right, their conscience troubles them when it comes to ruffling the surface of a totalitarian régime proclaiming itself as left-wing, even if they do it with kid gloves.

Journalists provide any number of instances of this *sinistrisme*—the systematic application of political double standards. I happened to be listening to the radio on the day when Andrei Sakharov received the Nobel Peace Prize. "Une petite bombe," the commentator remarked in a superior tone, as if to remind the listeners that the defender of human rights honored by the Norwegian judges had played a major role in the manufacture of the H-bomb. So he had. But when Robert Oppenheimer, who had been head of the Los Alamos team, was persecuted during the McCarthyite "witch-hunt" period, the intelligentsia rose up in his defense all over the world. What did the "persecution" amount to? He was being refused access to U.S. secret documents on the ground that he constituted a "security risk." But the trustees of the Institute for Advanced Study at Princeton stood by him and retained him as director of that prestigious institution.

Sakharov has been fighting on behalf of human rights in the Soviet Union for years; he has sacrificed his peace of mind, his safety, and his privileges to a cause that concerns the whole world. Why should a tribute to a hero of nonviolent resistance be treated with reserve, as if with embarrassment? Sakharov was often to be found, the unidentified broadcaster said, in the "ranks of the professionals of anticommunism." Should those "professional ranks" include Nikita Khrushchev, who made his famous speech to the Twentieth Congress of the Communist party in February 1956, a speech which the "visceral" anti-Communists have never disavowed? Should it not be charged, instead, that these "professionals" were the only ones who, for so long, were telling the truth?

I know what the reply will be: what about the thousands or hundreds of thousands of victims of repression in Indonesia, the Philippines, and Chile, which belong to the *American* sphere of influence? Repression and terror flourish in the shadow of "American imperialism," too. I confess to being sickened by those arguments in which one side's horrors are brought up against the other's—Great Purge versus Indonesian massacres. I shall only say a few words here:

There has never been a state with clean hands. No great power has ever chosen its allies solely on the basis of the morality of their régimes. Churchill and Roosevelt did not require that Stalin account for his crimes, and they even delivered up millions of Soviet citizens to his mercy. (Today they are blamed for it: think how they would have been attacked in 1945, had they refused.) For thirty years, the United States has supported countries ruled by governments it must judge detestable, for economic reasons or because it has seen in such systems the only alternative to communism or to a régime with Marxist-Leninist leanings. American diplomacy has, more than once, been made to appear less than edifying or intelligent by its anti-Communist obsession. Having said that, to blame the

United States for the criminal acts which every country having direct or indirect ties with it commits, is to carry polemics beyond the rational.

Neither Brazil nor Indonesia nor the Philippines claims to be in the *avant-garde* of humanity. None of these countries possess a very powerful army, or a vast nuclear arsenal. But then, none of them impose their despotism on a hundred million Europeans. Crimes do remain crimes— whether committed in Indonesia or in Russia—but it is in Russia, and only in Russia, that crimes are *transfigured* by ideology and, thereby, become an integral part in the *building of socialism*.

It will not be long before I give up replying to accusations of visceral anticommunism, and for numerous reasons.

In 1954–55, when I wrote *The Opium of the Intellectuals*, Sartre and Merleau-Ponty dominated the philosophical life of Paris and, consequently, of France. The echo of their dialogue, and of the dialogue between Sartre and Camus, reverberated to the four corners of the country, and far beyond. The Twentieth Congress of the Communist party of the Soviet Union had not yet taken place. It was not unreasonable to look for the roots of "existentialist Marxism" in the myths of the Left—which dealt with the proletariat, and with revolution—and to bring to light the incompatibility between the Marxism-Leninism of Moscow and the historical philosophy of one of those existentialists.

Today, the ideological and political situation has changed. Dissidents from the Gulag are living among us, and no cool plea in defense could carry the weight of the testimony of a Solzhenitsyn, laden as it is with suffering and with genius. On the other hand, there is the surprise of these dissidents at the Marxism which they encounter in the West, and their encounter with Western Marxism has given rise to a *New Dialogue*, whose terms this book is intended to clarify. In spite of the experience of history, and of the hostility now common among intellectuals vis-à-vis the Soviet Union, it is as if Sartre's epitomization of Marxism as the "unsurpassable philosophy of our era" were still exercising its tyranny.

This conformism is so far-reaching that it even impresses its opponents. I have more than once noticed that, still today, there is no shortage of citizens, of intellectuals, nor of teachers who, out of sheer ignorance, feel inferior to the Marxists, as if the latter—and only the latter—possessed a general theory for the interpretation of the historical world, and an infallible doctrine of reformist and revolutionary action.

The first part of this book, consequently, has a number of tasks to perform: 1) to comfort those who are not Marxists without knowing *why* they are not; 2) to denounce Marxist-Leninist mystification; and 3) to explain how and why the messianism of Marx leads, on the one hand, to Soviet-style ideocracy and, on the other, to what I call the Marxist Vulgate: the set of ready-made formulas and prejudices which come to the fore whenever the liberal societies are undergoing a crisis.

This line of thinking led me to the title, which belongs to my old friend the Reverend Father Fessard, *France, Beware Your Freedom*. During the war, he had written a book called *France, Beware Your Soul*. After the Liberation, when the Communist party was using the pretext of a clean-out to colonize the trade unions and the administration, denouncing traitors—forgetting and concealing the fact that in 1939 it had chosen its ideological motherland in preference to France—he published a second book in which the word *Soul* in the title was replaced by *Freedom*. I wanted to replace *France* with *Europe* and to sound a warning that the danger he pointed out thirty years ago was back after a generation's sleep and closer than we think.

The second part of this book constitutes a defense of liberal Europe, in which I state some facts which could and should be common knowledge. In terms of productivity, technical innovation, living standards, scientific progress, and human freedom, it is the West, the United States and Europe together, which took the lead during the course of the last thirty years. Marxist-Leninist propaganda strives to devalue this accomplishment by identifying "capitalism" with "imperialism," as if Western prosperity were based on exploitation of the Third World and not on work and productivity. Without denying the part played by empires in the fortunes of Europe in past centuries, one must be aware that it is toward the European-American center of the world economy—not from the so-called socialist countries—that the Third World now looks for aid; it is the West, and only the West, which has the means to lessen, little by little, the gap between the rich and the poor countries. Spokesmen of the Third World derive some satisfaction out of railing at American or Western imperialism, yet when some Latin-American intellectual is driven out of his country by a military coup, where does he take refuge—in Moscow, or in Washington?

Throughout the centuries, the theme of the decline of the Roman Empire has obsessed men's minds. Even to this day, historians debate the cause, or combination of causes, which brought about the collapse of a political structure which had seemed capable of withstanding the challenges of centuries. One need only recall Churchill's refusal to preside over the "dismantling of the British Empire," or General de Gaulle's wish to raise the tricolor once more in every place it had flown before 1939, in order to understand one of the attitudes toward "decolonization." The fashionable vocabulary and value judgments implicit in the intellectual and moral conformism now reigning, from one end of this planet to the other, unreservedly condemn "colonialism" and exalt "liberation of the people." In the propaganda battle, though, the Europeans can at least claim merit for having "given up" their empires.

If historical conflicts were settled before a tribunal of law and morality, the defenders of Western Europe would have an easy cause to plead, and a winning case. Unfortunately, a different kind of trial, concealed by ideologies and set in language unhindered by universal conscience, is now going on.

The Soviet Union kept its empire, which now stretches from Weimar to Vladivostok;* the British and French have lost theirs. Whether or not they were *willing* to give them up changes nothing: does not renunciation, quite as much as desultory resistance, indicate decadence? In any event, propagandists continue to rail against "Western imperialism" from all points of the globe, at a time when all the empires of Europe have been consigned to oblivion.

Let us consider some not so pleasant facts. In spite of its wealth, in spite (or because) of its culture and its freedoms, Western Europe as a whole does not think it is capable of defending itself without assistance. In the face of the Soviet divisions that have been stationed in the heart of Europe for more than thirty years, it entreats the United States to ensure the political balance and its security by the maintenance of an American army—the symbol of nuclear deterrence.

Thus, in one sense of the word, the decadence of Western Europe is beyond doubt. To dispose of any objections, it is enough to replace the word decadence by the word decline. *Decadence* implies value judgments or a schema of development. *Decline* simply describes a power relationship. Britain's economic decline began in the late nineteenth century, not when its industrial production was overtaken by that of the United States, but from the moment that Germany assumed the role of pioneer of new (e.g., chemical) industries. The decline of France in the 19th century was, similarly, the inevitable outcome of the difference in population growth between France and the rest of Europe.

The "law of unequal development" (to use Lenin's phrase) applies to population, to the economy, to scientific and technical innovation, as well as to political-military power. The Britain whose navy ruled the oceans and which was the financial and industrial center of the world market, was condemned to decline because it could not conceal the truth about its

---

*The following are the territories annexed by the Soviet Union by virtue of its victory in World War II: Finnish provinces (15,897 sq. mi. inhabited by 500,000 people in 1938); Polish provinces (64,334 sq. mi. and 11 million inhabitants; North Bukovina, 3,757 sq. mi. and 500,000 inhabitants); the Baltic States (Estonia, 17,063 sq. mi. and 1,122,000 inhabitants; Latvia, 23,682 sq. mi. and 1,951,000 inhabitants; Lithuania, 20,045 sq. mi. and 2,957,000 inhabitants); East Prussia (4,196 sq. mi. and 300,000 inhabitants).

waning strength. Sooner or later, it had to resign itself to a position less at odds with the size of its territory and population.

In the same way, the Western Europe of pre-World War I days enjoyed a predominance which, sooner or later, had to decline. Democratic societies which pride themselves on their liberalism do not long retain the dubious virtues demanded by an imperial metropolis. The contradiction between the values proclaimed at home and the practice of domination abroad has an erosive effect on the values and the power of domination alike. Even in the absence of the two world wars, Europe would not have avoided decline, although it would not have been so rapid nor so dramatic. I only want to make it clear that the events of 1939–45 have brought Western Europe to such a point of decline that it no longer possesses even that share of political-military power to which it should be entitled by its economic resources, if not by its size.

Western Europe continues, in fact, to occupy a place on the world market and in international trade which is out of proportion to the size of its population. In the thirty years since the war it has gained on the United States in terms of production per capita and labor productivity. For better or for worse, it reacted to military defeat with an outburst of passion to rebuild: West Germany, France, and Italy surged ahead as leaders in the GNP race. A wiser (or more resigned) Great Britain, on the other hand, let itself be overtaken by the Common Market Six.

Let us suppose that the remainder of this century and the century to come belong to what the Saint-Simonians would have called "the producers" and not to the warriors: straight away the prospects change. What use are the thousands upon thousands of tanks which come out of the Soviet factories each year and which serve to restore orthodoxy to Prague (which did not require quite so many) or to fuel small wars in the Middle East or Africa? War between the nuclear-armed industrialized countries of the Old Continent would be costly: what would the victor—supposing you could pick him out from the radioactive ruins—have to gain? But the Soviet Union derives great profit from Western science and technology, which is more easily obtainable from Europe than it is from America. Despite their ideological convictions, the men in the Kremlin must suspect that their own régime discourages innovation and needs (for the time being at least) the creativity of "decadent" Europe.

This Europe sells the Soviet Union machines and factories, buying raw materials in return—an exchange typical of the relations between developed and underdeveloped countries. This puts a more optimistic complexion on things: military empires belong to the past; today, it is science, technology, and productivity that determine the rank of individuals and nations. In this hierarchy, the Soviet Union is lagging behind. If the whole of mankind is now on the path of scientific and technological advancement, it is not the Soviet Union that leads the field. Instead, it is only hanging on, by imitating and borrowing.

But—and here we are back to inquietude again—is it in fact this science and technology, which are now turning the conditions of our existence topsy-turvy, that determine the destiny of states? Is it not *virtù*, in the Machiavellian sense, the capacity for collective action and historic vitality, that now, as always, remains the ultimate cause of the fortune of nations and of their rise and fall? At once the perspective is different, completely turned around.

Marxism, of a more or less vulgarized, Leninist form, continues to be propagated in Western Europe, taught and inculcated as it is by the schools and universities in France, in Italy, and elsewhere. Of course, it is rarely Marxism-Leninism in strict observance. Communists are becoming Euro-Communists; Marxism, as Maurice Merleau-Ponty wrote twenty years ago (about Georg Lukács, oddly enough), is "Westernizing" itself. Left-wing intellectuals demand more freedoms, while dissidents, fresh from the Soviet Union, again and again cry out, Have they no eyes to see, no ears to hear?

Hence my hesitation between the two titles *In Defense of Decadent Europe* and *In Defense of Liberal Europe*. The defense would be only too easy, were it but a matter of comparing the freedoms of East and West; it is altogether more problematic if one examines the *virtù*, in Machiavelli's sense, of societies that call authority in question—in the church, the universities, in business, even in the army.

So I now appear to be a long way from my point of departure; this book—which remains a plea for the defense—is not to be compared with the literature that comes out of the Soviet world, where there is an altogether different conception of defense, minus the awkward ifs and buts: on the one side, the good and the future, on the other side evil and the past. Even had I wished to do so, I would not have known how to write that kind of defense and portrayal of the freedoms and liberal civilization of the West.

Marxists—but also liberals and progressives, in a more general manner—reject the notion of conflict between human aspirations and the course of history. Among the progressives, the Marxists stand out by their affirmation of the scientific nature of their confidence in the agreement between human values and social facts; also by their postulating of a catastrophic revolutionary transition between the now and the future, between hateful capitalism and peaceful socialism. I do not share their confidence. I cannot predict the future. I do my best, with pen and word, to make it resemble our hopes as closely as possible. I do not think it will ever eliminate antagonisms, or that it will take the shape of our dreams. Those who lived in the time of Hitler and Stalin know that the worst is always possible; keeping faith means believing that it is not always certain.

In this book, I will be blamed for following my customary procedure of asking more questions than I give answers. Nor have I altered my position, which is to say that liberal Europe, contrasted with ideocratic Europe, represents not only freedom, but productive efficiency; it embodies, less imperfectly than the other Europe does, the values proclaimed by Europeans from the Atlantic to the Urals.

My two objectives, in this defense, are to prove to Western Europeans that what I have been saying about liberal societies is true, and to convince them that they dare not seek salvation where they too would find only slavery.

The case is not yet won or lost. The struggle between the totalitarian temptation and liberal ideals goes on, and will continue as far ahead as we can see. The freedoms we enjoy in the West are humanity's most precious, and most tenuous, acquisitions.

In Defense of
Decadent Europe

part I
Europe mystified by Marxism-Leninism

Marx, critic and prophet

As economist and philosopher, historian and sociologist, political scientist and revolutionary, Marx left a considerable volume of work which has been discovered, little by little, and has not yet been fully explored. In the following chapters, there is no question therefore of sketching a general outline, still less of any discussion in depth. Personally, I am convinced that if Lenin and his colleagues had not seized the tsarist empire in 1917, Marx would be no more our contemporary than David Ricardo or Alexis de Tocqueville, but this proposition will remain forever undemonstrable, and I do not deny that historians, sociologists, and economists may find fertile ideas here and there in his writings, or a source of inspiration.

My intention is more modest. Since Marxists are fond of unmasking mystifications, I want to return the favor and unmask the greatest mystification of the century, that of Marxism-Leninism. I will not add yet another Marx to the versions already available to patrons of the "symbolic goods" market; instead, I will keep to the main elements of Marx's own thinking, which underlie the various activist branches of Marxism and which have done so much to forge the irons of our century. These elements are well known. As the inspirer or spiritual founder of the Marxisms, that is, the social movements and political parties claiming allegiance to him, *Marx is essentially–if not exclusively–a* critical analyst of capitalism *as he observed it in mid-nineteenth-century Britain and the* prophet of a catastrophe *which, after an interlude of dictatorship of the proletariat, was to usher in an end to exploitation of man by man and, therefore, socialism.*

Reduced to its kernel, the ideological history of the various Marxisms is a multitude of confusing hypotheses that have had to be tacked onto Marx's prophetic writings in order to make them correspond with events which apparently contradicted those original prophesies. Just as more and more epicycles used to be put forth to preserve, for as long as possible, the geocentric representation of the universe, so the Marxists are doing their utmost, come what may, to maintain a worn-out critique and an exploded prophetism.

The mystification I mentioned consists of presenting to the West a primitive catechism (the Marxism-Leninism of the Soviet Union) and calling it a science or, at least, a philosophy–like the great philosophies of the Western tradition–when, in fact, this "philosophy" is at present a direct path to Soviet ideocracy (under which a few ideological notions serve to justify absolute power of the party) or to a hodgepodge of prejudices which I call the Marxist Vulgate.

1

Marx's messianism
and its
misadventures

Prophetism and reality

Of all the socialist doctrines current in the last century, only Marx's became an official doctrine of the workers' parties. Historians have made many attempts to understand the posthumous fame of a writer whose lifework contains not only propaganda masterpieces such as the *Communist Manifesto,* but also works beyond the grasp of the ordinary reader. Perhaps it is the combination of simple ideas and difficult theories (the latter based upon the former) that explains Marxism's success. Everyone can understand the basic message, and the scholars, in their comments on the text of *Capital,* must temper the messianic faith of the activists with some words of caution.

The basic message is the *prophetism* that emerges from Marx's critique of capitalism. Each era of Marxism is defined by a particular version of the prophetism, ever at odds with the facts (which, as Lenin remarked, are stubborn). The first, the era of the Second International, extending to World War I, was marked by Bernstein's *revisionism,* which was a testimony of the contradiction between the prophetism and the actual course of development of European capitalism. The second era (which began in 1914 or 1917 and ended with the victory of Mao Tse-tung in China) demonstrated the fact that developed capitalism does not lead to revolution: it is

Marxism-Leninism that brings revolutions about. But are they in the image of the one prophesied by Marx? Do they lead to socialism?

The third era tends to furnish negative responses to these questions. Khrushchev's Twentieth Congress speech and the split between the Soviet Union and the People's Republic of China have shaken Marxism-Leninism, in much the same way the improvement of the standards of living in Europe and in the United States had done, and as World War I had shaken the Marxism of the Second International.

None of the three Marxisms—that of Kautsky, of Lenin-Stalin-Mao, or of the present day—have been able to reconcile the prophetism with historical reality. But none of them have completely disappeared.

The major themes

Marxism, *as interpreted by those who declare themselves Marxists,* presents itself first and foremost as a *philosophy of history,* an overall view of the "human adventure" from so-called primitive societies right up to the socialist society of the future. The capitalism immediately preceding socialism is the last "antagonistic" régime, torn as it is by contradictions and by man's exploitation of man. After capitalism, progress will continue, but social progress will no longer require political revolution. If this sort of interpretation of history can be called *historicism,* and if the expectation of a future society in which mankind will achieve its essential purpose can be referred to as *humanism,* then Marxism cannot be other than a kind of historicism and a kind of humanism.

For some years now, of course, there have been learned scholars with their own learned and esoteric languages who have stated, repeatedly, that Marxism is not a kind of historicism and not a kind of humanism. If the custodians of the faith do not interdict these new scholars' assertions, it is because they are addressed to only a limited public and do not disturb the pillars of the temple. Who would pardon the crimes of Stalin, who would fall under the spell of a bureaucrat like Brezhnev unless both of them—the monster and the Mister Average—bore within themselves the hope of mankind? It matters very little whether or not it is called historicist; Marxism remains a *prophetism.*

This prophetism is draped in scientific, or rather scientistic, fancy dress. In order for the prophecy of socialism—the end of prehistory; a classless society with no exploitation of man by man—to be different in nature from the various forms of Judeo-Christian millenarianism, history has to obey laws (this word, common in the scientific vocabulary, especially that of the nineteenth century, confers a sort of guarantee of scientific rigor). In other words, in one shape or another, the prophetism of the Marxist Vulgate is based on the laws of historical development, on the laws that determine the succession of the modes of production and of economic and social systems.

We are dealing here with macro-historical laws which apply to a society or civilization as a whole, not with laws such as the law of falling bodies, or Boyle's or even Gresham's Law. Take the latter, for instance: "Bad money drives out the good." It does not require the transformation of the entire economic system: it states that when two different coins are in circulation, the good one—the one which inspires people's confidence—will become rare because they will hold onto it, whereas the bad one, the one seen as likely to lose its value, will circulate in abundance.

Of the laws of historical development, one and only one is of intense concern to Marxists—the one which enables them to assert the necessity of a passage from capitalism to socialism. This law in its turn is subdivided into two propositions: that capitalism will give way to a different mode of production (just as capitalism itself took over from feudalism); and that the succeeding mode of production will be socialist—in other words, it will put an end not only to the particular form of exploitation implied by capitalism, but the exploitation of man by man.

To assure a proper mixture of prophecy and historical law, it is required that the capitalist system suffer a dual condemnation: it must be intrinsically unjust and, as such, it must be incapable of surviving. (Marx regularly expected its collapse, a century ago, with each new crisis of the cotton industry.)

Marx's stroke of genius was in having found a way of uniting these two condemnations and of basing one upon the other. Why is capitalism *per se* unjust? It is because of the surplus value which is basic to capitalism, and the mainspring of entrepreneurial activity. Why does capitalism proceed to its downfall of its own accord, like the sorcerer's apprentice? Because the frantic quest for surplus value tends of its own accord, toward paralysis: the quest for surplus value through the accumulation of capital finishes with the destruction of the conditions necessary to the creation of surplus value.

For the benefit of readers unfamiliar with the Marxist texts, let us recapitulate the principal stages of the proof. Starting point or *major premise: the theory of work value*. The value of each commodity (or object exchanged) is equal to the quantity of average human labor required to produce it.

Second stage or *minor premise: the theory of wages*. First of all, the capitalist mode of production is fixed by the private ownership of the means of production; the capitalist buys the workers' labor power in order to operate instruments of production which he himself owns. He does not buy labor but labor power; the wage is the price of labor power for a given time. What is the value of this labor power? Like any commodity, labor power has a value equal to the quantity of average human labor necessary to produce it. And producing labor power signifies providing worker and family with the indispensable means of subsistence. Is it possible to determine the *indispensable* level of these means? Marx replies that the level varies in relation to the "social conscience," but the working wage of his time was so close to the physiological minimum that he did not bother much about the oscillations around rock bottom.

Third stage and *conclusion: the theory of surplus value.* Given that the value of the commodity is measurable by the quantity of average human labor it embodies, and given that the value of the commodity (labor power) is measurable by the value of the commodities needed for the maintenance of worker and family, it is enough to assert that the labor power—the worker—produces more value than it receives in its wages, so that there exists a *margin* between the value of the wage (or buying power of labor power) and the value produced by this same labor power. This margin is called surplus value (profit).

This proof, which is an integral part both of Marx's Marxism and of the *vulgar* Marxisms, contains the same ambivalence as does the prophetism/historical laws combination: it joins scientific analysis and moral condemnation. Labor power is paid according to its value but, in a system of private ownership, this leaves the surplus value to the owner of the means of production. And what is nore obnoxious than a régime which treats human work as a commodity?*

How does one make the transition from the theory of surplus value, which brings to light the "intrinsic injustice" of a capitalist régime, to the confirmation of the historical law that guarantees the passage from capitalism to socialism? On this point, Marx and the Marxists offer several answers.

The simplest is that of pauperization. Let us suppose that, in their thirst for profit, the capitalists constantly increase productive capacity and that they distribute the lowest possible buying power to the wage earners. There will then be a growing contradiction between the development of productive forces and the return on production (whatever the precise meaning of the German expression *Produktionsverhältnisse* may be). And if the masses become poorer and poorer as society becomes richer and richer (or more and more capable of producing riches), the revolution that breaks out will no longer be that of a minority for the benefit of a minority, but of the majority for the benefit of all.

Another, more subtle, approach to the problem is derived from the law of diminishing returns. The rate of surplus value (e.g., the profit rate) is defined as the ratio beween labor and surplus labor or between the wage (or

---

*This argument illustrates the shift from the economic critique to the moral. Although this argument still impresses some people, it is meaningless. Any modern economy, whether socialist or capitalist, has to calculate the cost of labor.

variable capital) and surplus value.* On the other hand, profit is calculated in relation to the entire capital—not just the wages paid to the workers but the wages plus the fraction of the value of the machinery which is incorporated in the commodity. The profit rate will therefore be the ratio between surplus value and the total of the constant capital and the variable capital. Let us postulate that surplus value is levied exclusively on the variable capital (or labor power). The value of the machinery is incorporated in the commodity; each commodity incorporates a fraction of that value equal to the decrease in value (or depreciation) of the machinery. Therefore, the denominator of the "profit rate" fraction increases as the constant capital (or plant) represents a greater part of the total capital. Hence, by definition, the profit rate tends to diminish. (The idea that the profit rate has a long-term tendency to decline does not belong to Marx alone, but is borrowed from the economists of his time. His own special contribution is the explanation of the law by the *theory of surplus value.*)†

Besides pauperization and the law of the declining rate of profit, Marx and the Marxists afford other, more complex versions of the "law of the transition from capitalism to socialism." Without going into technical expositions, let us say that the Marxist schema of surplus value taken in combination with the agent of a free market, raises the question: How is surplus value realized? How are buyers found for consumer products? How is capital accumulated? What are the conditions under which surplus value is levied on the workers' labor so that more surplus value can be realized, ensuring, in other words, the perpetuation of the cycle? Rosa Luxemburg and Lenin (who, however, very strongly opposed Luxemburg's theory) both attempted to prove that a capitalist society cannot dispense with virgin territories to exploit. They located in the need for capital the root source of imperialism.

The theory of surplus value which is at the center of the Marxists' condemnation—moral and historical—of capitalism serves as a preface to a general Marxist theory of human development. In one of his most famous texts, the introduction to his *Contribution to the Critique of Political Economy*, Marx first of all distinguishes the three modes of production: slavery, serfdom, and wage labor; then an Asiatic mode, outside the West; and finally, in the future: socialism.

Marx's notions about slavery, serfdom, and wage labor suggest three

*In the numerical examples which he gives in illustration of his proof, Marx always assumes equality between the variable capital (or cost of labor power) and surplus value ($v = s$). This gives a rate of exploitation (the ratio between labor and surplus labor) of 100%—a rate which is implied but never proven.

†The profit rate is written as follows: $\frac{s}{c + v}$. Since the surplus value (s) is levied exclusively on v (variable capital or labor power), the growth of c (constant capital or plant) in its relation to v inevitably involves the decline of the profit rate.

ways of obtaining surplus value. The slave owner puts to work the labor power belonging to him, and he gains because it produces more value than it consumes in the form of the food provided by the master. In like manner, the feudal lord, owner of the land, keeps for himself the whole share of the crop except for what the serf uses for sowing and for consumption. Wage labor is revealed as the *ultimate form* of exploitation: the proletarian is free, but forced to sell his labor power; for this, he receives the proper price, the value, in other words, of his own reproduction. But this free economy—in which the owner exchanges the worker's labor power for wages—remains based, under capitalism, upon the exploitation of man by man: the surplus value, once levied by slavery and later by the military strength of the feudal lords, is obtained and accumulated with no open violence or violation of laws, but through the supply-and-demand relationship between a seller who possesses nothing and a buyer who possesses capital.

In the dim past, imagines Marx, there existed a primitive community; on the horizon ahead: a non-antagonistic society. Between the two, three modes of levying surplus value represent not so much three ages of history as three models of the relationship between owner and worker. In the Asiatic mode of production, it is the state bureaucracy—playing the part performed by the owners, in the West—which exploits the village communities.

The opposition between owners of the means of production and workers is all the more central a theme because it provides a "scientific" basis for class struggle and because it also characterizes all of society:

. . . a certain mode of production, or industrial stage, is always combined with a certain mode of cooperation, or social stage, and this mode of cooperation is itself a "productive force"; further, . . . the multitide of productive forces accessible to men determines the nature of society; hence, the "history of humanity" must always be studied and treated in relation to the history of industry and exchange.*

Productive forces, social relations, classes, and class struggle belong to what Marxists call the "infrastructure," although without ever clarifying the position of the state, of law, or of science within the infra- and superstructure. If science counts as a productive force, does it not belong to the infrastructure? And where are the ideas, which are inseparable from science? The state which maintains the "antagonistic" society is *ipso facto* in the service of the class that exploits the other classes. But the state, which controls the "instruments of violence," possesses, hence, a certain autonomy with respect to the owners of the means of production. It does not have the same function as the owners nor does it exercise its function in the same way, in the various modes of production.

*Marx/Engels, *The German Ideology, pt. I* (London: Lawrence and Wishart, 1977), p. 50.

I have presented the themes of Marxist prophetism, commencing with its overall view of history. I might have done as Marx does in the Communist Manifesto and taken classes and their struggles as the starting point:

The history of all hitherto existing society is the history of class struggles. Freeman and slave, patrician and plebeian, lord and serf, guild-master and journeyman, in a word, oppressor and oppressed, stood in constant opposition to one another, carried on an interrupted, now hidden, now open fight, a fight that each time ended, either in a revolutionary reconstitution of society at large, or in the common ruin of the contending classes. . . . The modern bourgeois society that has sprouted from the ruins of feudal society has not done away with class antagonisms. . . . Our epoch, the epoch of the bourgeoisie, possesses, however, this distinctive feature: it has simplified the class antagonisms. Society as a whole is more and more splitting up into two great hostile camps, into two great classes directly facing each other: Bourgeoisie and Proletariat.

This famous text suggests an historical issue: What classes composed a particular historical society? It also raises other questions. Is it true that capitalist societies tend towards a simplified dualistic structure with "the bourgeoisie" on one side and "the proletariat" on the other? On a higher level of analysis, how does the analysis of the development of capitalist society as described in *Capital* fit in with the vision of history in terms of class struggle?

The historic task of overthrowing "the last antagonistic society," the last one to contain classes in struggle, falls to the proletariat. Why? The slaves did not overthrow ancient society, nor the serfs feudal society. In the works of his youth, when he had not yet studied political economy, Marx uses philosophical arguments to justify proletarian messianism:

Where, then, is the *positive* possibility of a German emancipation? In the formation of a class with *radical chains,* a class of civil society which is not a class of civil society, an estate which is the dissolution of all estates, a sphere which has a universal character by its universal suffering and claims no *particular right* because no *particular wrong* but *wrong generally* is perpetrated against it; which can no longer invoke a *historical* but only a *human* title; which does not stand in any one-sided antithesis to the premises of the German state; a sphere, finally, which cannot emancipate itself without emancipating itself from all other spheres of society, which, in a word, is the *complete loss* of man and hence can win itself only through the *complete rewinning of man.**

I repeat that this is a text of Marx's youth, predating his research into economics. But it is no less interesting to note that proletarian messianism and the historic mission of a proletariat responsible for revolution and for

*This famous text dates from 1844, in the *Introduction to the Critique of Hegel's Philosophy of Law.* How might this class, with no position in society, become the ruling class? The question has no answer except for the Leninist or Stalinist solution which substitutes the party for the proletariat, and a mythical proletariat for the real one.

human liberation were already in the mind of Marx the philosopher before he consulted reality to prove them. A revolution that puts an end to all antagonisms is a radical innovation compared to past revolutions, just as the proletariat viewed as an *emancipating class* resembles none of the classes which in past times have made mankind progress from one mode of production to another.

Between the two modes of production, capitalist and socialist, Marx mentions an intermediary and indispensable link—the *dictatorship of the proletariat,* an expression which recurs several times in his work, from the letter to Weydemeyer of 1852 to the days of the Commune in 1871, and later still in the *Critique of the Gotha Program.* What meaning did Marx himself assign to this expression? All polemics aside, there are grounds for various interpretations.

According to one interpretation, which certainly contains an element of truth, Marx starts from the revolutionary experience. In light of the French Revolution, he reaches the conclusion that absolute power—the only power capable of achieving the transformations involved in the shift from one mode of production to another—must inevitably undergo a transition. And capitalist societies *may* have a democratic type of state, with formal freedoms, with governmental representatives elected by universal suffrage: need it be said, nevertheless, that the bourgeoisie is "exercising its own dictatorship"? If the answer is yes, the form of the state which would assume the dictatorship of the proletariat is not fixed, particularly since the proletariat must not take possession of the bourgeois state in order to manage it for its own benefit, but in order to bring it down, the final goal being the "withering away" of the state.

Similarly, in the economic area, Marx visualized successive phases. The passage which is most often cited as the standard authority on the subject occurs in his *Critique of the Gotha Program.* During the first phase, that of socialism, each individual producer is to receive a quantity of value proportional to the value created by his work. Equality will consequently not prevail, because not all individuals can contribute in equal measure to the common wealth. It is only in the second phase, that of communism, that each individual receives an income proportional to his needs.

Yet beginning with the phase of socialism, Marx seems to imagine that, generally speaking, the market—the sale and purchase of goods—will disappear. Everyone is to receive not money but purchasing certificates. The "associated producers" are to manage the economy, determining the share of the national product to be devoted to public expenditure, the upkeep and replacement of the means of production, and the investments necessary to expand those means. As for the allocation of the share of the national product destined for consumption among the various spheres of industry and agriculture, Marx seems to look on this as a simple matter corresponding to known and pre-established needs.

Whatever the nature of his profound cogitations on the working—firstly of the socialist, then of the communist—economy, it seems to me that Marx never did renounce his *prophetism,* namely, his radical cleavage between the antagonistic régimes and the future, nonantagonistic, régime of mankind. Certainly there are any number of texts by Marx, and especially by Engels after Marx's death, which condone a reformist version of the doctrine. But there remains in my view a contradiction between Marx's prophetism and the candid adherence to a reformist, nonrevolutionary line of action. (It is to me a revealing fact that a socialist so typically social-democratic as Léon Blum, who only felt at ease in a parliamentary society little prone to violence, should never—except perhaps after 1945—have given up the theme of the definitive split. I can still hear him telling an audience of students, fifty years ago, that the day would come when the creaking, worm-eaten old tree of capitalism would have to be brutally cut down or uprooted. Between the wars he stubbornly clung to the distinction between the *exercise of power* in a capitalist society and the *seizure of power* that would symbolize the revolutionary split. Unlike the Bolsheviks, he refused to admit the contradiction between professing a revolutionary outlook and temporarily being at the head of a capitalist society. And unlike revisionists of the Bernstein variety or today's social democrats, he would not resign himself to defining socialism as the sum of the reforms achievable without abrogating legality.)

All Marxists proclaim the unity of theory and practice. This equivocal attitude is, in at least two ways, significant: as adherents of a prophetic system, they set their actions in the framework of a "vision of history" and do their utmost, for better or for worse, to avoid sacrificing the future to the contingencies of the present; theirs is long-term thinking. In addition, they model their world after their theory; the world they see, and in which their actions take place, fits into their theory: hence their practice fits, of its own accord, into their theory.

The Marxism of the Second International

The Marxism of the Second International—by which I mean the ideology proclaimed by the Marxist parties, especially German social democracy—has its origin in the prophetic themes as I have summarized them. The books of Friedrich Engels, in particular the most famous of them, *Anti-Dühring,* simplified and popularized the thinking of Marx in order to facilitate its use as a doctrine of action and as the ideology of a mass movement.

The economic interpretation of history is transformed, first, into historical materialism and becomes an integral part of a metaphysical materialism, with the movement of matter and history alike obeying laws baptized as "dialectical." The simplest or, if you like, the crudest expression of these laws is to be found in *Anti-Dühring*. Reality, both inorganic and organic, is a state of constant flux, of transformation. Echoing Heraclitus, we might say that "no one bathes twice in the same river." But if the cosmos, life, and mankind are in a state of *becoming*, this does not occur as a series of infinitesimal changes but by sudden mutations. Between matter and life, plants and animals, animals and mankind, feudalism and capitalism, there subsists a homogeneity of substance—the basis of materialism—but, from one level or one type of reality to another, there appears a discontinuity.

The discontinuity or rupture implied by the shift from one species or one economic system to another is in harmony with a Hegelian idea adopted by Engels as a law of the dialectic: the transition from quantity into quality. After a certain point, quantitative change brings about a qualitative mutation. This law could lead toward an evolutionary or reformist interpretation of history. In fact, in Friedrich Engels's writings the law of the transition from quantity to quality and the law of mutation are mutually supportive. Taken in tandem, they confirm the revolutionary, prophetic interpretation of Marx's thinking. Capitalism will not give rise to socialism by gradually reforming itself; at some point there must be a break, a revolution.

The second contribution of Engels, which I call the *schema of the historical development of our epoch*, tends to overcome the possible contradictions between the various laws of history. On the one hand, that which fixes the direction of capitalist development is the development of the forces of production—which signifies, in the Marxists' analysis, both capital accumulation and the rising productivity of labor. On the other hand, within the capitalist society, the working class organizes, creating its own institutions and wringing advantages out of the capitalist class. So it must be supposed, firstly, that the development of the productive forces matures the process of mutation (or revolution), and secondly that the working class, by organizing itself within the capitalist régime, prepares itself for revolution and the seizure of power.

Unfortunately for the orthodoxy of the Second International, these two visions are incompatible: the first assumes that the productive forces can no longer fit into the structure of the "relations of capitalist production"—a dictum lacking in precision, but which suggests either that the creation of enterprises vast enough to ensure the necessary capital accumulation is impossible,* or else that the purchasing power distributed to the masses is

*The Soviet taste for giantism seems to derive from this idea that private ownership is incapable of accommodating the necessary concentrations of productive forces.

inadequate. Neither idea lends itself to serious discussion. The first disagrees with the Marxist polemic against monopolies; the second disagrees with the facts. The pauperization theory was contradicted toward the end of the nineteenth century by the rise in the living standard of the working class, the power of the German trade unions, and the creation of cooperatives and other socialist-inspired institutions. Did the proletarians of Wilhelmine Germany have nothing to lose but their chains? Anyone who would believe that particular proposition would believe anything.

Friedrich Engels—unlike Marx, who died too early—took an active part, both personally and through the medium of his direct disciples, Karl Kautsky in particular, in the "Marxifying" of the socialist parties and of the workers' movement in the continent of Europe. By this I mean he caused the leaders of the socialist parties and, to a lesser extent, the trade union leaders to adhere to Marxism (as interpreted by Friedrich Engels). Engels retained, in essence, Marx's prophetic themes; positing them within a materialist metaphysic, he proclaimed the dialectic to be both a method and a doctrine, he combined Marx's economic interpretation of history with materialism and—using the *schema of historical development*—he linked reformism and revolution: revolution ripens as a consequence of the development of the productive forces; the socialist parties and the working-class movement, in becoming stronger, play a part in bringing about the "creative split" leading to Marx's vision of a new world order.

The last quarter of the nineteenth century, during Marx's own lifetime and after his death, posed a number of problems which, although theoretical at first, later came to dominate the practice of Marxism. How far can the analysis of capitalist society undertaken by Marx in *Capital* be regarded as universally valid? Will all societies follow the path of England and the Western European countries? Marx had too great a sense of history to categorically deny the possibility of different roads to socialism. But the question did arise: What is left of the prophetism, the schema of historical development, what is left, even of the economic interpretation of history, if just any professedly Marxist party—no matter what the degree of development of the productive forces—can build socialism?

In Wilhelmine Germany, the great Marxist debate matched Karl Kautsky against Eduard Bernstein (later, they both wound up in the same "revisionist" camp). Friedrich Engels and his disciple Kautsky had "Marxified" the Social Democratic party of Wilhelmine Germany, which resulted not only in the party's adherence to a few ideas stemming from (or declared valid by) Marx, but in the establishment of a philosophical-historical doctrine into which the members of the party were initiated. Every party congress proclaimed, in its final motions, *not so much the immutable truth* of the theory *as the correct interpretation* of the events or, rather, of history-in-the-making. In this respect, the Bolsheviks and the parties of the Third International continued the practice of the Second. The congresses of the Second could pronounce excommunication (although this did not mean execution or even necessarily expulsion). They followed the same procedure, the same political-intellectual routine. Due to its historic mission, the party did not confine itself to setting immediate goals but set its duties in the framework of a broad interpretation of history. Practice—the party line defined at every congress—was not separated from theory—the diagnosis, bearing on the circumstances, and in relation always to the class struggle and the socialism of the future. Eduard Bernstein and the revisionists were condemned for doctrinal reasons, not because they were suggesting a practice significantly different from the one actually being followed by the Social Democratic party, but because they cast doubt on the cardinal feature of the prophetism: the radical disjunction between capitalism and socialism and the revolutionary hiatus that divided the two.

In this debate, Kautsky remained in the prophetic camp and believed himself faithful (and probably was so) to the teachings of Friedrich Engels. The major argument against the trade unionists and revisionists—an argument which salves the conscience of socialists whenever they act against the apparent will of the majority—was formulated by Kautsky before Lenin made it the foundation of bolshevism in *What Is To Be Done?* It holds that, left to themselves, the workers do not get beyond trade unionism: they aspire to improving their own condition in the here and now, and overlook their duty toward mankind, namely, the destruction of capitalism and the building of socialism, the classless society. Who reminds the workers of their destiny? Who holds onto the awareness of the historic mission of the proletariat in the face of the temptations of "bourgeoisification"? It is the *intellectuals*. Marxism, a doctrine of intellectuals, attracts intellectuals because of the historic role it confers on them, which heightens their status in their own eyes. The intellectuals go to the proletariat to provide guidance, not to learn.

Marxism-Leninism

What did Lenin add to the Marxism of the Second International? Four books, each of which contained one or two of the essential ideas (or ideological themes) marking the shift from the original Marxism to the succeeding version (or, if one prefers, from Marxism to Marxism-Leninism): *What Is To Be Done?; Materialism and Empiriocriticism; Imperialism, the Final Stage of Capitalism;* and, lastly, *The State and Revolution.*

The first book is basically a reply to the objections put forward by working-class reformism against Marxism. The idea that the workers, left to themselves, lean toward trade unionism (the wish to improve their life in the here and now) and that Marxism is brought to them from the outside, by intellectuals, comes from Kautsky, but in *What Is To Be Done?* Lenin gives it what in retrospect appears to be an altogether different application by joining it to a principle of organization—democratic centralism—whose outcome is only too well known.

After citing with approval an article by Kautsky in *Die Neue Zeit,* Lenin goes on to say that, as soon as the working masses are incapable, in the course of their movement, of working out an independent ideology for themselves, the *sole* question is whether to choose a bourgeois ideology or a socialist ideology. There is no middle ground (because mankind has not forged a "third" ideology; besides, in a society torn by class antagonisms it is impossible for there to be any ideology outside or above the classes).

Hence, to belittle the socialist ideology *in any way,* to *turn away from it, in the slightest degree,* means to strengthen bourgeois ideology. There is a lot of talk about spontaneity, but the *spontaneous* development of the working-class movement leads to its becoming subordinated to the bourgeois ideology, *leads to its developing according to the program* of the *Credo,** for the spontaneous working-class movement is trade unionism . . . and trade unionism means the ideological enslavement of the workers by the bourgeoisie. Hence, our task, the task of Social Democracy, is to *combat spontaneity,* to *divert* the working-class movement from this spontaneous, trade-unionist striving to come under the wing of the bourgeoisie, and to bring it under the wing of revolutionary Social Democracy.†

Lenin, in contrast with any number of French sociologists, never thought that his own Marxism was the spontaneous ideology of the working class. On the other hand, he did stress the idea, which goes back to Marx, of the simplification of the class struggle to a contest between the proletariat and the bourgeoisie. Hence, unless trade union action binds itself to revolutionary social democracy (in today's terms to Marxism-Leninism), according to Lenin it drifts into the camp of the bourgeoisie. Thus, at the beginning of this century, the foundation was laid for the polemic against the social democratic parties.

Class political consciousness can be brought to the workers *only from without,* that is, only from outside of the sphere of relations between workers and employers. The sphere from which alone it is possible to obtain this knowledge is the sphere of relationships between *all* the classes and strata and the state and the government, the sphere of the interrelations between *all* the classes.‡

The clash between working-class trade unionists (or "economists") and social democrats gave rise to the role of the professional revolutionaries.

---

*This was a text produced by the so-called economist group, to which Lenin was opposed.
†Lenin, *What Is To Be Done?* (Peking: Foreign Languages Press, 1975), pp. 48–49.
‡*Ibid.,* p. 98.

A workers' organization must, in the first place, be a trade organization; secondly, it must be as broad as possible; and thirdly, it must be as little clandestine as possible (here, and further on, of course, I have only autocratic Russia in mind). On the other hand, the organizations or revolutionaries must consist first, foremost, and mainly of people who make revolutionary action their profession (that is why I speak of organizations of *revolutionaries*, meaning revolutionary Social Democrats). In view of this common feature of the members of such an organization, *all distinctions as between workers and intellectuals,* and certainly distinctions of trade and profession, must be *utterly obliterated.* Such an organization must of necessity be not too extensive and as secret as possible.*

Lenin sees this secret organization of professional revolutionaries as "a small, compact core of the most reliable, experienced, and hardened workers."† It is the core of professionals that runs the specifically political struggle and controls the local sections and mass organizations, and it is this same core, armed with the Marxist prophecy and armored against working-class spontaneity (always inclined toward trade unionism), that will lead the revolution. As Rosa Luxemburg wrote, criticizing Lenin's *One Step Forward, Two Steps Back,* he is defending the ideas of the *ultra-centralist* tendency:

. . . on the one hand, the selection and constitution as a separate body of the most eminent active revolutionaries, as distinct from the unorganized, though revolutionary, mass around them; on the other, severe discipline in whose name the other leaders of the Party intervene directly and resolutely in all the affairs of the Party's local organizations.‡

Democratic centralism (the first example of the institutionalized lie) means the opposite of democracy, the absolute power of the Central Committee over the party as a whole.

It was a structure adapted to clandestine action but conceived, also, as a continuing prerequisite of effective action. The critique formulated by Trotsky at that time—that the Central Committee takes the place of the party, the Politburo of the Central Committee and, in the last analysis, the secretary-general of the Politburo—found shattering and tragic confirmation in reality. By a chain of serial delegation, the first link was the substitution of party for proletariat in the name of the Marxism of the intellectuals, and the final link was the substitution of one man for the party. In those days, the thesis made no stir: although German social democracy respected a democratic constitution, Kautsky himself, the leading thinker of the

*Lenin, *What Is To Be Done?,* p. 138.
†Ibid., p. 146.
‡Rosa Luxemburg in *Iskra,* July 10, 1904, quoted by K. Papaioannou in the anthology *Marx et les Marxistes,* (Paris: Flammarion, 1972), pp. 269–71.

Second International, assigned intellectuals a prominent role vis-à-vis the workers and the trade unions.

Lenin made a second contribution to the body of belief known as Marxism-Leninism in the short book called *Imperialism, the Final Stage of Capitalism,* written at the start of World War I. Like other theorists of the Second International, he had referred, long before 1914, to colonial exploitation by the capitalist countries as a way of explaining history's apparent contradiction. He denied the rising standards of living in the capitalist countries and introduced the notion of a working-class aristocracy which took the bourgeoisie's thirty pieces of silver—in other words, relatively higher wages—as the price of its own betrayal (meaning the rejection of the class struggle in favor of class collaboration). According to him, it was this that explained revisionism, the inclination of some social democrats to rely on economic progress and piecemeal reforms to improve the life of the proletariat without a break with capitalism. The attitude of the different socialist parties at the moment when the European war broke out caused him more indignation than surprise: the whole of the Second International was treasonous, not just the revisionists alone. He and his followers became, finally, the sole embodiment of the world proletariat and of socialism.

Marx himself was not unaware of the tendency of capitalist societies toward external expansion; he saw that the capitalist mode of production— the most advanced mode—would overthrow traditional societies and cover the entire globe. Nor did he at all regret the expansion of capitalism and of Europe hand in hand: while he denounced its cruelties, he also discerned the promise inherent in the "looting" of the planet by the colonialists. In India, the British would break up the remnants of an Asiatic mode of production, the age-old organization of the villages under the arbitrary power of an inefficient and predatory bureaucracy. Marx, too, has an occasional tendency not to distinguish between the *concept of capitalism*—an economic system defined by private ownership of the means of production and by commercial exchange—and the *concrete historical entity* constituted by those countries in which a system of this order is more or less imperfectly realized.

On the other hand, he did not systematically account for the causes of European wars in terms of economic rivalries between countries but usually explained them, following the ordinary method of historians, in terms of clashes of national interest and the ambitions of great powers. He was exceptionally strong in his condemnation of the imperialism—in the commonplace sense of the urge for conquest or for territorial expansion—of tsarist Russia.*

*Cf. chapter 6, below. See also Miklos Molnar's book, *Marx, Engels et la politique internationale* (Paris: Gallimard, 1975).

In his judgments of the wars of the nineteenth century, Marx took sides according to 1) the type of domestic system maintained by the states concerned, 2) the foreseeable consequences of the victory of one side or the other, and 3) the accountability of the belligerents—he sided with Prussia in 1870 until the fall of the empire, and then with France once it had turned republican. Lenin started with the simple assumption that Marx's subtle analyses belonged to a bygone era: Marx was compelled to choose from *among* various imperialisms, whereas he himself was at liberty to choose *against all* imperialisms—the socialist movement, newly come to power, being their successor and grave digger. Lenin counted on a revolution which would emerge from war itself and which he would lead. The Bolshevik party would deal with the behavior of the working masses—misled by traitors or other surviving groups—by proclaiming the truth of history to them.

Lenin could have interpreted the war of 1914 as Marx had interpreted the war of 1870. The European states had warred among themselves for centuries before they acquired capitalist economies, as Lenin knew quite well. But the authors R. Hilferding and, in particular, J. A. Hobson provided him with another possible way to interpret the war: to demonstrate not only that the French, British, and Germans who had carved up Africa among themselves all deserved to be called *imperialists* (as was undoubtedly the case), but that they were destroying each other in an unforgivable struggle *because of their imperialism*. The establishing of a link between the monopolistic structure of the capitalist economy, the role of the banks, and the concentration of capital on the one hand and colonial conquests on the other, and then decreeing that the competing expansionism of national capitalistic systems did not allow any friendly division is all it would require.

He decreed that the war was imperialistic on both sides, a diagnosis he supported by referring to Clausewitz's classic description of war as the "continuation of state policy by other means." All the states involved had carried on imperialist policies before 1914; the war through which they had been pursuing their policies had not changed in nature: it remained imperialistic. Socialists who did not use all possible means, each in his own country, to oppose imperialism (and thus also the war) were betraying their faith and their earlier commitments.

The theory of imperialism accomplished several objectives: it enabled Lenin to explain the rising living standards of the working aristocracy without casting doubt on the Marxist interpretation of the development of capitalism; it placed wars within the historical framework of capitalism; it accounted for working-class revisionism and the social democratic betrayal; it made plausible the eventuality of revolution even in Russia, in spite of Russia's lagging so far behind the more advanced capitalist areas. The theory had everything—it lacked only truth.

It can be said therefore that Lenin awaited and expected a world-wide revolution, from 1914 on, with no concern for the specific conditions prevailing in this or that given country. Before 1914, loyal to the historical schema of Engels, he had discounted any hypothesis of a socialist revolution in tsarist Russia or of permanent revolution. It was events—World War I—that led him to renew his historic vision and to judge possible and necessary—*because of the combination of world events*—what had seemed to him in the Russian context incompatible with Marxism and, therefore, impossible.

Before 1914, Lenin's Marxism did not differ visibly from the Marxism of the Second International. Or, at any rate, the book that revealed the underlying originality of Leninism, *Materialism and Empiriocriticism,* had not been read with attention—nor did it deserve to be, except for documentary purposes. In one sense, Lenin confined himself to pursuing the thinking of Friedrich Engels in *Anti-Dühring.* The economic interpretation of history as outlined, without systematic interpretation, in the writings of Marx, becomes inseparable from a metaphysical materialism. Man and human societies form part of natural reality and are subject to its laws, as are all inorganic and organic phenomena. Lenin presents Engels's metaphysical system by referring to the alternative of realism (or materialism) and idealism. External reality exists, it is primary in relation to awareness or thought; knowledge *reflects* this reality and, by its progress, comes closer and closer to the truth, to a faithful reproduction of reality.

No one attached any special importance to Lenin's philosophy, to his junction of objective laws and dialectics—which resulted in the dialectical laws of development by mutation, the transformation from quantity to quality, and the negation of the negation. In retrospect, what is striking when one rereads *Materialism and Empiriocriticism* is the presence, throughout, of the thesis that *any metaphysical deviation implies political deviation.*

German social democracy, although deeply inspired by Marx's atheism, imposed no philosophical orthodoxy; it tolerated Kantians, Hegelians, positivists. Before he came to power, Lenin was unable to impose orthodoxy, but he excommunicated deviationists with the pen before expelling them if the opportunity presented itself. His system of thought established in advance the system of total discipline he later practiced.

The fourth book mentioned above, *The State and Revolution,* make no original contribution to the thinking of Marx himself, but it combines realism and utopianism in a style made all the more striking by Lenin's apparent unawareness of the contradiction. The subject is: the conception of the state guiding the Bolshevik party's plan of action in July 1917, some months before its victory.

Lenin comments on Marx's letter to Weydemeyer of March 3, 1852.* Marx borrowed the thesis of the class struggle from the bourgeois historians, but he himself showed that it is linked only to certain phases of the historical development of production, that it leads necessarily to the dictatorship of the proletariat, and that this in turn leads to the abolition of all classes and to a classless society. The proletariat wants to seize the state, but only in order to destroy it:

. . . the next attempt of the French revolution will be no longer, as before, to transfer the bureaucratic-military machine from one to another, but to *smash* it . . . And this is what our heroic Party comrades in Paris are attempting.†

Thus, two ideas are brought together: the substitution of the dictatorship of the proletariat for the dictatorship of the bourgeoisie; and the commencement of the dismantling of the state's administrative, military, and police machinery with a view toward hastening its withering away and eventual extinction. By what ideological trick can the dictatorship of the proletariat simultaneously constitute the first phase of the withering away of the state? In a primary sense, this "hocus-pocus" is a built-in part of the definition of the state, considered as an instrument utilized by the ruling class to preserve its own power and to exploit the masses. Political or parliamentary democracy makes no essential difference in the application of the trick.

Democracy is a *state* which recognizes the subordination of the minority to the majority, i.e., an organization for the systematic use of *force* by one class against another, by one section of the population against another.‡

The dictatorship of the proletariat would also constitute a kind of force, but the fact that this force would be exercised by the vast majority against the tiny exploiting minority would already represent a "democratic step forward."

Lenin offers the Paris Commune as the model of a state in transition, with the standing army replaced by the people under arms, all officials elected, subject to recall, and never paid more than workmen's wages. He quotes from Marx's *The Civil War in France:*

*Lenin, *The State and Revolution: The Marxist Theory of the State and the Tasks of the Proletariat in the Revolution*, written in 1917, (Moscow: Progress Publishers, 1977), pp. 34–35.
†Letter to Kugelmann, (April 12, 1871).
‡Lenin, *The State and Revolution*, p. 79.

The judicial functionaries lost that sham independence . . . ; they were thenceforward to be elective, responsible, and revocable.*

These are some of the reforms which Lenin says would alter the nature of the state created by the dictatorship of the proletariat, and would reveal its transitory character.

Looking beyond this mutation, Lenin proceeds to offer a truly utopian account of the state apparatus of the future:

Capitalist culture has created large-scale production, factories, railways, the postal service, telephones, etc., and *on this basis* the great majority of the functions of the old "state power" have become so simplified and can be reduced to such exceedingly simple operations of registration, filing and checking that they can be easily performed by every literate person. . .†

Incredible as the statement may seem, Lenin really believed that capitalism would bequeath to the proletariat an economy comparable with a public service, and that the armed proletariat would take this over by using the few necessary experts, since the jobs of the vast majority of officials would have been so simplified that anyone could do them. He had given no greater consideration than did Marx himself to the radical difference between managing a business and managing an entire economy.

All citizens become employees and workers of a *single* country-wide State "syndicate " All that is required is that they should work equally, do their proper share of work, and get equal pay.‡

In this utopia, memories of Saint-Simon (the administration of things replacing the government of people) mingle with the Jacobin myth (the people in arms under the guidance of its vanguard) and the radical misappreciation of the economy and the state. Dialectical sleight of hand enables the ruthless dictatorship of the proletariat to be announced as preceding the withering away of the state itself, by switching the pros and cons from extreme dictatorship against a tiny minority to total freedom for everyone. The world is still waiting for the realization of that switch.

Of course, Lenin also takes up the distinction between the two phases which are to succeed the revolution: the phase of socialism, during which everyone will receive a reward equal in value to the amount of labor produced (in the form of a noncirculating certificate), and then the phase of communism, when everyone will receive a share of the social revenue proportional to each person's needs. Reading *The State and Revolution* and

*Ibid., p. 42.
†Ibid., p. 44.
‡Ibid., p. 96.

recalling the prophesy of socialism and communism after the proletarian revolution, one cannot doubt that the Bolsheviks really were convinced that eliminating private ownership of the means of production, along with the market—and thus abolishing surplus value and exploitation—would be of incomparable benefit to mankind.

Here again, history—the supreme tribunal, according to the Marxists themselves has given its verdict. Just as the development of capitalism before 1914 had refuted the *schema of historical development,* so the experience not only of the Soviet Union but of all the socialist economies has refuted the Marxist-Leninist utopia.

We can leave the economists to argue over the merits of Marxist conceptualization—the distinction between surplus value and profit, and the origin of profit only in living labor (variable capital). What reality makes crystal-clear is that the meaning currently assigned to the theory of surplus value, namely, that of an immense reserve of wealth "stolen" from the workers and available immediately after the revolution, does not hold up to experience any more than it does to reason.

After the 1917 Revolution: the present situation

What is left of those two pseudoscientific myths: Marxism (the destruction of capitalism by its internal contradictions) and Marxism-Leninism (the transfiguration of society—or even *la condition humaine*—by the abolishment of private ownership of the means of production)? At the risk of inciting the irony of Parisian Marxists, why not quote here the passage from Solzhenitsyn's *Letter to Soviet Leaders* in which he shows the bankruptcy of Marxism (or of Marxism-Leninism)—a "decrepit" and "hopelessly antiquated" doctrine which

. . . even during its best decades . . . was totally mistaken in its predictions and was never a science . . . *

[Ideology] was mistaken when it forecast that the proletariat would be endlessly oppressed and would never achieve anything in a bourgeois democracy—if only we could shower people with as much food, clothing and leisure as they have gained under capitalism!

It obviously cannot be argued, except absurdly, that the working class did not gain benefit from the economic development in capitalist societies.

[Ideology] missed the point when it asserted that the prosperity of the European countries depended on their colonies—it was only after they had shaken the colonies off that they began to accomplish their "economic miracles."

*This and the following excerpts are from Alexander Solzhenitsyn, *Letter to Soviet Leaders* (London: Index on Censorship/Fontana, 1974), pp. 42–43.

There again, contrary to all sophistry and false subtlety, Solzhenitsyn is right. The thesis put forth by the Marxists, particularly by Lenin, that the rise in living standards of the upper level of the proletariat came as a result of exploitation of colonies is untenable when compared, for example, with the experience of a country such as the Netherlands, which drew considerable revenues from Indonesia and which nonetheless has succeeded in raising the living standards of its population after the loss of its empire.

[Ideology] was mistaken through and through in its prediction that socialists could only ever come to power by an armed uprising.

Marx did not say this explicitly, and it may be that he did not always think it. All the same, the Marxist-Leninists the author has in mind protect their dogmatism by decreeing that the socialist parties which have come to power peacefully have "betrayed socialism" and "reformed capitalism without destroying it." Their messianism causes them to make that judgment: if it is postulated that the transition to socialism requires a violent break, it follows that, without such a rupture, the socialists in power have not fulfilled the socialist mission.

[Ideology] miscalculated in thinking that the first uprisings would take place in the advanced industrial countries—quite the reverse. And the picture of how the whole world would rapidly be overtaken by revolutions . . . ?

A classical argument, impossible to refute by what I have called Marx's *schema of historical development*. Certainly it is possible to find texts by Marx or Engels stating that other countries will not reproduce the English experience as such, or envisaging revolution elsewhere than in the most industrially advanced countries. The fact remains that in neither Great Britain nor the United States is the endogenous development of capitalism leading toward revolution. Yet capitalism's self-destruction as "the victim of its own contradictions" was one of Marx's central theses, one which his disciples always held onto until events proved it wrong.

And the picture of how . . . states would soon wither away was sheer delusion, sheer ignorance of human nature. And as for wars being characteristic of capitalism alone and coming to an end when capitalism did—we have already witnessed the longest war of the twentieth century so far, and it was not capitalism that rejected negotiations and a truce for fifteen to twenty years; and God forbid that we should witness the bloodiest and most brutal of all mankind's wars—a war between two communist superpowers. Then there was nationalism, which this theory also buried in 1848 as a "survival"—but find a stronger force in the world today!

This text contains a debatable proposition: ought the fifteen or twenty years of Cold War to be referred to as war? Was it only the Soviet Union that refused negotiations and a truce? For the rest, socialism did not curb nationalism, but always reinforced it. The rivalry between the Soviet

Union and People's China has proven, if proof be required, that inter-state conflicts which existed *before* capitalism did, will continue to endure after capitalism's demise.

The Marxism of Marx and Engels ceased, after 1914, to fulfill its function as the ideology of the Second International and the various socialist movements. After 1917 it became the justification of "the Soviet experience." Its subsequent destiny was determined, all in all, by the Marxist-Leninist faith and by a society wanting to conform to that faith. There exists a country, according to the sacred phrase, where capitalism has disappeared because the proletariat—through the medium of the Communist party—has taken over the state and its means of production.

Between the two world wars, the exponents of Marxist ideology fell into two camps: the Bolsheviks and all those who adhered to the Third International, and the socialists or social democrats who refused to see in the Soviet Union the fulfillment of the prophesy. The debate between Lenin and Karl Kautsky, on looking back, is symbolically significant to this day. It was Kautsky who pointed out the disparity between the labor movement and the socialist vision; it was also he who conferred on the intellectuals the task of bringing socialist doctrine to the proletariat and imparting to it the sense of historic mission. On the other hand, German social democracy retained democratic procedures within the party, and it called for democratization of the institutions of Prussia and of Wilhelmine Germany.

The period which opened in 1929 was at the same time that of the Great Depression, the Great Purge, and the Great Temptation. In the West, millions were unemployed, as everybody knew; in the East, millions of *kulaks* were being deported or exterminated during the years of agricultural collectivization, as no one knew—or wanted to know. Moscow triumphantly published bulletins of victory, of unrivalled growth-rates; in the West, even after recovery of the economy, production was not going at full capacity. In 1933, Hitler moved into the Chancellery and, in the face of liberalism and socialism, he established the Third Reich, the Nazi hierarchy, and Aryan racial supremacy. He brought the universities and the press to heel and connected the state with a single party. "Fascism" as a political genre and "National Socialism" as a particular example came to represent absolute evil in the eyes of the Left (which grew to include liberals and moderates).

The Great Purge—the liquidation of the Leninist Old Guard after what were witchcraft trials, and the imprisonment of millions of Soviet citizens, deported or liquidated—all this the majority of the Western intelligentsia refused to see and, sometimes, even when seeing it, refused to mention. Hitler gave Stalin an all-absolving excuse. To question the guilt of Zinoviev or Bukharin was to accuse Stalin, thus to act in the same way as Hitler, thus to become his "objective ally," and thus to act as an "agent" of the Gestapo.

Out of the Great Depression there came *la grande tentation*—the temptation of the Soviet Union as model and promise. And only the Big Lie, which concealed the Soviet archipelago of concentration camps, made the Great Temptation possible.

The socialist parties, all of them more or less compromised in the management of capitalist society in time of crisis, no longer held out any transcendent hope. Even if they still kept references to "socialization of the means of production" and to the "dictatorship of the proletariat" in their statutes, they acted in accordance with Eduard Bernstein's revisionism, inasmuch as they were integrated in capitalist society as well as in representative democracy. Crisis was affecting both of these institutions: the democratic system lacked majority government, the capitalist system was faced with hundreds of thousands of unemployed. Most of those who still called themselves "Marxists" without going over to Marxism-Leninism were not unaware of some of the features of Soviet despotism and, if they wanted to base their actions on history, they could no longer seem to find a place for themselves.

The third epoch of Marxist ideology started after 1945 and, for the first time, it was no longer Germany but France that became its center and home. In Paris, philosophers—and first among them Jean-Paul Sartre— declared themselves Marxists, but without endorsing the dogmatism (which should more properly be called Soviet than Marxist-Leninist).

During the Cold War years, from 1946 until Nikita Khrushchev's speech in 1956, the historical circumstances were radically different from those previous to 1939. The German *Reich* no longer existed, the British empire was tottering. When the fighting ended, the division of the Old Continent was being drawn on the map. By the summer of 1945, the expression "Iron Curtain" was coming into common usage. The Soviet Union was not so much *une expérience socialiste,* be it dreadful or glorious; rather it was the Red Army, bringing with it occupation régimes together with revolutions sanctioned by the authority of the state.

A good many intellectuals who had belonged to the Communist party or had worked with it in the struggle against fascism, aligned themselves now with the opposite camp. The socialists of the old tradition, and even the liberals, had detested fascism more than communism, and had supported, if not applauded, the Popular Front. With fascism eliminated and conservatism weakened, they found themselves willy-nilly in the anti-Communist coalition. It was a coalition which, embracing as it did all non-Communists, from the socialists to the Right (only ex-Fascists were excluded, out of hostility), was now best defined by its hostility toward Marxism-Leninism and in particular toward its ideological claim of being the exclusive guardian of the Absolute Truth. Hence the spread of the concept of *pluralism:* acceptance of *several* parties and of *rival* doctrines became the hallmark of liberal Europe. Yet this identification of pluralism with liberalism is not free of risk. Should the same rights be granted to parties who do not abide by the rules of the game as to constitutional parties? What a swindle to fall for, if the loss of one battle meant losing the war.

We all know now—and the Communists themselves do not deny it—that in the Soviet Union the years 1945–53 were no less stern and cruel than the years of Collectivization and of the Great Purge. The concentration camps were filled with civilians and prisoners, handed over to the Soviet authorities by the Allies. Never, except in the days of the Great Purge, was Stalinist terror so omnipresent, never did it stretch out so far, nor strike with more apparent irrationality. The state, appointing itself as the judge of truth in biology, excommunicated genetics. In the satellite countries, resistance fighters with democratic convictions soon were returned to the camps they had just left.

Yet, in those days, Communists and their fellow travelers were passionately defending the "achievements of the first socialist revolution in history." If one were to believe them, there was not a single concentration camp, but only camps for "reeducation through labor." Maurice Thorez proclaimed that the French people would never fight against the Red Army. Political-ideological debate tended to come down to a duel between the Communists, flanked by their fellow travelers, and the rest, which included the socialists. The elimination of the socialist parties in the countries of Eastern Europe fueled the anti-communism of socialists of the Jean Jaurès and Léon Blum persuasions.

Khrushchev's Secret Speech put an end to this delirium. No question now of a socialist paradise: millions of innocent people had died in the camps, and millions of innocent people had confessed under torture to crimes they had not committed. Collective property, planning, economic power, the Red Army—these remained. But what remained of the essential link, according to Marxism or Marxism-Leninism, between the social restructuring of the economy and the communist prophesy? Was it the proletariat that wielded power, or was it the party? If the proletariat, then how could it tyrannize itself, dispatch millions of its own to the camps? When had the "deviation" begun? With Lenin? With Stalin? What was the Marxist explanation for the "cult of personality"?

The events of 1956—Khrushchev's speech, the Hungarian Uprising— caused the desertion of a section of the intelligentsia and weakened the Western Communists' unconditional devotion to the Soviet Union. They also had the effect of restoring some vitality to Communist parties, by provoking them to criticize themselves and compelling them to stop blindly repeating the orders from Moscow. The Soviet Union after Stalin—under Khrushchev and, after him, Brezhnev—appeared more and more "normalized" (i.e., authoritarian and bureaucratic), and minus its revolutionary aura. The specter of the Red Army had taken over from the specter of communism.

Twenty-three years later, where do we stand? One is tempted to answer, Back where we started. The revelation of the crimes of Stalinism has made no lasting impression on the *apparatchiks* in the Soviet Union, nor even on bureaucrats beyond the Russian borders. Quite a few of them, especially in the USSR, had little to learn from what Khrushchev made public. The condemnation of Stalinism by the Marxist-Leninists remains partial and equivocal. Khrushchev regretted the excessive repression which had *accompanied* collectivization, not collectivization itself. He blamed Stalin for having turned terrorist methods against the party; he did not criticize their use against other elements and classes.

At the same time, the condemnation of Stalinism favored the diffusion of divers brands of Marxism (which I call the Marxist Vulgate). With a good conscience, intellectuals and activists again took up Marx's messianism and one or the other of his arguments, at the same time dissociating themselves from the Soviet experience. And, swearing by all they hold sacred that their own Marxism has nothing to do with the one which Solzhenitsyn attacks, they continue to "Marxify" the universities, the social sciences, and the political and literary magazines—naively convinced that *their* revolution will not end in the same despotism, too eagerly bent on destroying capitalist-liberal society to ask themselves what society they would build on the ruins.

In the Soviet Union, Marxism (Marxism-Leninism) is still the official ideology of a bureaucratic despotism of totalitarian character. In the West, various kinds of (more or less imaginary) Marxism abound, building up prejudices in favor of state planning and collective ownership of property, and condemning the "imperialism" of a West which no longer has any colonies.

2
Ideocracy: Marxism as state ideology

The opium of the people

In the Soviet Union, Marxism-Leninism is used to justify a régime which is far from resembling socialism as envisaged by Marx himself or by the Marxists of the Second International. But there is nothing to prevent the use of Marx's own thought and vocabulary from being used to expose the real nature of the Soviet régime. One has only to replace the word "religion" with the words "Marxism-Leninism":

Marxism-Leninism *(religion)* is the sigh of a creature weighed down by misery, the soul of a heartless world, just as it is the spirit of an age without spirit. It is the opium of the people. The real happiness of the people demands that Marxism-Leninism *(religion)* be suppressed as the *illusory* happiness of the people. To demand that we give up the illusions about our own situation is to demand that we renounce a situation that rests on illusions.

One might also cite the following remarks, taken from the same early text (the Introduction to the *Contribution to the Critique of Hegel's Philosophy of Law*): "Criticism is no longer an end in itself, but only a means. The essence of its moving style is indignation, and its main task is denunciation."

What is still surprising is that so thoroughly Western a doctrine, standing at the crossroads of the German, English, and French traditions, identifying itself with liberty and equality and looking forward to a society without exploitation and without state authority—that such a doctrine could become the official ideology of the most total state known to history. Why was a faction which early in this century represented only one of the tendencies within the Russian Social Democratic party, affiliated to the Second International, able to seize power? And, once having seized power, why did it build the kind of state that makes a traveler crossing the Soviet border have the physical sensation of entering a different, distinctly "other" zone of civilization?

The revolutionary sect

The Bolshevik strategy for conquering the tsarist state fell into two phases and sprang from what are really rather commonplace notions. Phase one runs from the tsar's abdication to the November *coup d'état*. With Lenin's return, the Bolsheviks took up extreme theoretical positions. They demanded and obtained all possible freedoms, straight away; they supported popular power, power to the soldiers', workers', and peasants' soviets against the provisional government (composed of bourgeois or moderate socialist elements); they launched the slogans Land and Peace, which corresponded to the aspirations of the masses; they did their utmost to penetrate the soviets, to occupy the key positions, to mobilize the masses and rally them to their cause. Phase two begins either with the successful November *coup d'état* or, if one prefers, with the abortive July coup. The Bolsheviks set themselves the aim of seizing power; in accordance with ideology, this was equivalent to the seizure of power by the proletariat or by the worker-peasant bloc.

In January 1918 the Bolshevik government tolerated free elections with universal suffrage. The constituent assembly produced a majority of Socialist Revolutionaries, and the Bolsheviks—who had received about 17% of the votes—proceeded to stage a second coup which was as easy as the first. It required only a few dozen troops, to enforce the carrying out of the decree disbanding the assembly.

The two coups of November 1917 and January 1918 call to mind some historical precedents. The English and French revolutions had revealed the force of revolutionary sects, ruthlessly efficient and drawn toward terror by their own intransigence and suspicion. No freedom for freedom's enemies, but who, other than the Jacobins or the Bolsheviks, defines the enemies of freedom? How can freedom be preserved by refusing it to those who are considered its enemies? In *The Phenomenology of Mind*, Hegel elevated the connection between revolution and terror to the level of sheer necessity.

The following phase, that of civil war, also fits into the classical schemas. The group which is now the master of the state represents only a small minority of the population. A product of the majority section of the Social Democratic party, it resembled the small armed parties which, according to the old Greek authors, take possession of the government of the city in times of trouble and proclaim themselves the law and the state. An inexpiable civil war followed, which, by the time it ended, had succeeded in restoring discipline in the factories and in the army. The latter contained a dual hierarchy which survives to this day, one technical, the other political: the political commissars were responsible for the loyalty to the new régime of the officers of the old régime whom the revolutionary powers had to employ; nowadays, they police the ideological loyalty of officers brought up under the revolutionary régime itself.

Unrest, coups, civil war—none of these three phases (nor their successors) announced or implied a régime incompatible with the ruling values of Western rationalism or liberalism. A Jacobin party, and not a General Bonaparte, had dismissed an assembly that never would have restored order by dint of its speeches. A fanatical party, controlled by a small general staff—as demanded by the exigencies of clandestine action—played the role of saber bearer. Only a few observers—such as Karl Kautsky, the leading light of German social democracy and of the Second International—realized the implication of the event: the *dictatorship of the party over the proletariat,* and not the dictatorship of the proletariat. Even observers whose far-sightedness has been confirmed by subsequent history never foresaw anything that could be compared with Stalinist Collectivization, or the Gulag Archipelago.

Why did a section of a social democratic party usher in a new era of European history, in the space of a few days, and pave the way not only for the murder of millions of people but for a state which is still today a total one, absorbing or attempting to absorb civil society within itself? Why has an essentially Western doctrine removed Russia from the West, even though giving it the industrial and technological equipment characteristic of the Western countries? To this question, historians offer two answers (each of them hedged with reservations and variations): some refer to the Russian context or the tradition of the tsarist system, others to the party and its ideology. The Russian dissidents, whether of the school of Sakharov or of Solzhenitsyn, subscribe to the latter account.*

The Bolsheviks built the perfect revolutionary party on the lines of the ideal type created by the twentieth century. Possessed by the conviction of a necessary break between what is and what shall be, they doubted neither the corruption of the prevailing system nor the promise of regeneration by the system of their dreams. Hitler's National Socialist propaganda also played on this duality: the damning of the Judeo-Marxist republic was the

---

*I shall come back to the first theory in Part II.

basis of the certainty of salvation through the party (or through the man who embodied it). But the *prophetism* of the Bolsheviks, more fertile than that of the Nazis, continues to exercise an influence over political doctrines throughout the world, an influence which no amount of reason or empirical evidence has been able to successfully combat.

The content of the prophetism explains, partly, its durability and its power: it is the dialogue between liberal and socialist thought—an integral part of Western culture—from which Marxism-Leninism derived its promise of a régime rid of the evils of capitalism, with no more social injustice, an end to the exploitation of man by man and state oppression. A formal framework taken from Christian millenarianism and a dialectical system of contradictions and their resolution were borrowed to structure a vision of world history that strives to reconcile the moral aspirations of man with the necessary flow of events.

This account of the "final régime" or the end of prehistory is not the sole monopoly of the Bolsheviks. In one shape or another, all revolutionary parties cultivate such myths (in Georges Sorel's sense of the word). What marked the efforts of the Bolsheviks, even before 1917 was their intransigence, their Manichaeism, and their version of the role to be played by the party. When war broke out in 1914, nearly all socialists hesitated to advance beyond a certain point, most of them rallying in one way or another to their homeland. Lenin, who was the prisoner of a single idea, the Revolution, did not hesitate: the war was imperialistic on *every* side; it created a favorable conjuncture for revolutionaries, not a justification for socialists to spring to the defense of their nation. Lenin's single-mindedness—which assured him a special position among the Social Democrats—was strengthened by another character trait: the conviction that he was right which he maintained even when isolated within the Second International). To put it another way, wherever Lenin was, the Revolution and socialism were also. The idea, incarnated in the party, was there, if need be in a single personality.

But the idea, in the mind and in the writings of Lenin, had already hardened into a metaphysical as well as a political dogma. In this respect, the break between Marxism-Leninism and the Marxism of the Second International had been consummated before 1917. Lenin's polemic against philosophical deviation—which he viewed as inseparable from political deviation—was of a piece with his revolutionary single-mindedness and his embodiment of the idea in one party, or even one man. Out of this combination sprang Marxism-Leninism and, through it, the ideocratic régime which still holds sway today. The party structure, the democratic centralism, the discipline imposed upon activists, all became fused as elements of a single system, linked unconditionally to a doctrinal faith. Yet half a century ago, no one had any idea that such a system of thought and action as Lenin's would endure and impose its mark on Soviet civilization itself.

As soon as they seized power, Lenin and his followers began fabricating lies in all good faith (the faith of the true believer). They did not represent the worker-peasant bloc* but an armed minority which felt chosen to bring about a radical transformation of society. What was it, if not the doctrine which they professed and which legitimized its own embodiment, that made this "chosen"?

During the first phase, the Bolsheviks expected revolution to take place in Germany, if not throughout the world; they knew the empire of the tsars was in no condition, by Marxist theory, for socialist revolution. Yet one only needs to read *The State and Revolution*—written on the eve of the November coup—to discover the most disconcerting evidence of the capacity for self-delusion in a man who has rightly been considered a genius for the realism of his tactics in the political struggle.

In other words, the Bolsheviks, and most of all Lenin, took power in the name of an ideology and without the slightest experience in governing nor in managing an economy: they derived, *from their ideology,* the condemnation not only of large-scale owners, but of all tradespeople, of all freedom of private commerce.

Even when Lenin—in recognition of the despair of the peasantry and the exhaustion of the working class—wisely decided to launch the New Economic Policy (NEP), he did not sacrifice the slightest scrap of his dogma. There was no question of accepting peasant landowners:

The teachings of Marx show that once the small proprietors become owners of the means of production and land, exchange between them necessarily gives rise to capital and, simultaneously, to the antagonisms between capital and labor. The struggle between capital and the proletariat is inevitable; it is a law manifesting itself all over the world. This must be accepted by anyone who refuses to fool himself.†

After the large landowners and the capitalists of the cities, the next target of bolshevism was therefore the mass of the peasants.

According to that same thinking, all tradespeople belong to the universe of capitalism: "So what is freedom of exchange? It is freedom of commerce; and freedom of commerce is the return to capitalism." In the name of Marxism and the dictatorship of the proletariat, the Bolsheviks eventually found themselves fighting practically the whole population except for a small fraction of the proletariat or, rather, of a *mythical* proletariat.

When Stalin made the decision to collectivize agriculture, he was re-

---

*Except for the popular longing for peace and land.
†Lenin, speech at the Transport Workers' Congress, March 27, 1921, *Collected Works*, 32:272.

maining much more loyal to Lenin than Leninists will admit. To this day, the men in the Kremlin are resigned to allowing the peasants their own plots of land, because they cannot avoid this concession to the demands of productivity. But they have not given up the struggle, and they cling to the goal dictated by their interpretation of Marxism: the abolishment of private ownership and, as far as possible, of commercial exchange. They would rather have less production than the strengthening of private ownership and of capitalism which, in their eyes, are inseparable.

Characteristic of the Communist régime is the hiatus between the practice (its reality) and the theory (its meaning, as determined by the custodians of the official word). But this gap does not date from Stalin and the "most humane constitution in the world" which Bukharin drew up (at a time when he already foresaw his own fate—namely, his death). In retrospect, at least, it can be said that the era of the Big Lie began with Lenin himself. For the event—conquest of the state by an armed faction— became, viewed ideologically, a proletarian revolution. The nationalization of all the means of production was decreed as the first stage of socialism, yet between the power of the party and abolition of private ownership, on the one hand, and a stateless society without exploitation, on the other, only a mythology ordained any necessary link. It was the prophetism of Marx that postulated, first, the dictatorship of the proletariat, then, management by the producers in association and, finally, socialism in the sense of an egalitarian and liberal society. But once the ideological version of events identified "all power to the party" (or its central committee) with the dictatorship of the proletariat, what was to prevent concentration camps from being baptized reeducation-through-labor camps? What was to prevent the party's opponents, even the Socialist Revolutionaries and Mensheviks, from being tarred with the same brush as the White Guards? Or, why shouldn't all deviationists, left or right, Trotskyists or Bukharinists, be equated with "objective accomplices" of the Gestapo? A super-reality was born.

The function of ideology;
Solzhenitsyn and Sakharov

More than half a century has elapsed since the taking of the Winter Palace. A third generation of Bolsheviks is now in power in the Kremlin; in appearance, these men of the Politburo are very little different from other bureaucrats: satisfied with their exceptional success, they exhibit above all a wish to avoid any risk of losing what they have attained. Must the Soviet reality be understood in terms of the Marxist-Leninist ideology? Does the super-reality denoted by the official word remain the Bible of the régime and its guide to action? Is the Marxist-Leninist ideology so threadbare that it no longer provides anything but slogans like the *liberté-égalité-fraternité* of the French Republic? Does the régime remain an ideocracy, or is it shifting toward an administrative despotism less cruel and less fascinating than the régime of the Stalinist period?

On this point, the diagnoses of the two most famous Soviet dissidents are directly opposed. According to Sakharov, Solzhenitsyn faithfully describes—but misinterprets—certain phenomena typical of the Soviet régime.

Solzenhenitsyn very aptly describes various anomalies and costly absurdities in our internal affairs and our foreign policy, and he does so with justified indignation and compassion for his countrymen. But his view of them as directly generated by ideological causes seems to me somewhat schematic. I see present-day Soviet society as being marked rather by ideological indifference and the cynical use of ideology as a convenient façade: expediency and flexibility in the manipulation of slogans go along with traditional intolerance toward free-thinking "from below." Stalin committed his crimes not from ideological motives but as part of the struggle for power, while he was building a new "barrack-square" type of society (as Marx called it); in the same way, the present leaders' main criterion, when facing any difficult decisions, is the conservation of their own power and of the basic features of the system.*

A few lines later he completes and corrects the analysis in these terms:

What Solzhenitsyn says about ideological rituals and the intolerable waste of the time and energy of millions of people on drivel which only accustoms them to fatuity and hypocrisy—all this is undoubtedly true and makes a strong impression, but the point is that, in our situation, this hypocritical drivel is merely taking the place of an "oath of allegiance": it binds people by mutual responsibility for the shared sin of hypocrisy.†

By saying this, is Sakharov not admitting that despite "ideological indifference," ideology continues to perform an essential function? It binds people by mutual responsibility. No one believes in it, but everyone talks as if he did.

Are we all that far from Solzhenitsyn?

... that same antiquated legacy of the Progressive Doctrine ... endowed you with all the millstones that are dragging you down, ... the need to inflate military development for the sake of making grand international gestures, so that the whole internal life of the country is going down the drain and in fifty years we haven't even found the time to open up Siberia; then the obstacles in the way of industrial development and technological reconstruction; then religious persecution, which

*Andrei Sakharov, "On Alexander Solzhenitsyn's 'A Letter to the Soviet Leaders,' " *Konti-nent* (New York: Anchor Press, 1976), pp. 5–6.
†Ibid., p. 6

is very important for Marxism, but senseless and self-defeating for pragmatic state leaders—to set useless good-for-nothings to hounding their most conscientious workers, innocent of all cheating and theft, and as a result to suffer from universal cheating and theft. For the believer his faith is *supremely* precious, more precious than the food he puts in his stomach.

Have you ever paused to reflect on why it is that you deprive these millions of your finest subjects of their homeland? All this can do you as the leaders of the state nothing but harm, but you do it mechanically, automatically, because Marxism insists that you do it. Just as it insists that you, the rulers of a super-power, deliver accounts of your activities to outlandish visitors from distant parts—leaders of uninfluential, insignificant communist parties from the other end of the globe, preoccupied least of all with the fortunes of Russia.*

The same Solzhenitsyn combines the thesis of ideological tyranny with the apparently contrary thesis of ideological scepticism:

This ideology does nothing now but sap our strength and bind us. It clogs up the whole life of society—minds, tongues, radio and press—with lies, lies, lies. For how else can something dead pretend that it is living except by erecting a scaffolding of lies? Everything is steeped in lies and *everybody knows it*.

These two themes, ideological indifference and the tyranny of ideology, are thus common to them both. Solzhenitsyn reconciles them by asking: does an ideology have to remain powerful, even after people have lost faith in it, in order for it to continue being tyrannical? But is this an actual—or only a verbal—reconciliation? Perhaps the truth can be decided by breaking down the content of what both the physicist and the writer call *ideology*.

First question: do certain Marxist-Leninist dogmas continue to influence the managerial practice of the Soviet leaders, or do they not? To this question, the answer is a resounding yes: Soviet leaders refuse to make concessions to the peasant landowners whenever they can because, once and for all, they have damned private ownership and blessed collective ownership. They are not unaware of the greater productivity of labor on the private plots of land; but in this regard they subordinate economic rationality to ideological rationale or, to put it another way, they prefer their ideology to their economy, their dogma of collective ownership to the spiritual boosting of the individual which private ownership affords.

The persecution of believers is, similarly, a product of Marxism-Leninism. Atheism was, from Marx's early writings onward, at the heart of his vision. Western Marxists (or call them liberal or civilized Marxists) have welcomed Christians into the party and have gone over to laicism, religion being to them a private matter which only concerns the individual, not the party nor the state; Lenin, however, never consented to reduce his own

*Solzhenitsyn, *Letter to Soviet Leaders*, pp. 43–44.

ideology to a social-political program. In the Soviet Union, Marxism-Leninism still sets out to be a total faith.

Lenin's book *Materialism and Empiriocriticism* contains the germs of this dogmatism. If revisionism begins in metaphysics, and if philosophical deviation necessarily leads to political deviation, how can believers be tolerated? To leave each activist free to believe or not to believe in God means admitting the sovereignty of the individual conscience, and relegating the political viewpoint and the proletarian movement to the second rank, to the level of "likely opinions."

Perhaps those Catholics now developing a theology of violence or of revolution have realized, dimly, that the Marxist-Leninists have not been content with the elective affinities between socialist and evangelical values. The rallying of Catholics has satisfied them only if it culminates in genuine conversion, with the proletarian mission and the revolution becoming an integral part of Christian faith, and with Christian dogmas being integrated into those of Marxism-Leninism. The Marxist-Leninist dogmas are thus not merely an application or illustration of the former; Christian theology consecrates, rather, the Marxist prophetism: through the proletariat and the revolution, mankind is able to find a fulfillment on this earth.

By inviting the Soviet leaders to give up militant atheism, Solzhenitsyn is asking—and knows he is asking—for ideological surrender. The leaders would gain millions of good citizens, but not good *Soviet* citizens. There cannot be two metaphysics of salvation. Stripped of its atheism, Marxism-Leninism would lose the principle of authority on which its visionary super-reality rests and on which it relies for its judgments upon profane reality.

How does one reconcile faith and scepticism? How does ideology manage to tyrannize minds which have stopped believing in it? The Soviet leaders are not unaware of the true relation between the Western and Eastern standards of living, the superior productivity of the Western economies, and the more rapid advance of American science and technology in most fields. In this sense, they accept the "profane reality" of the statistics. But that does not mean that they have abjured the super-reality—the identification of the party with the proletariat and the necessity for public ownership of the means of production—in other words, the prophetism of Marx himself. Reality and super-reality coexist in their minds. Capitalism is still damned as such, whatever the experience of the so-called socialist régimes may be. And is that so surprising, when we in the West can meet people any day who acknowledge the failure of Soviet-style socialism, yet who cling to the basics of the Marxist vision? In the Soviet Union, the opposition condemns this attitude, criticizing it as "institutionalized lies." The opposition is right, if the super-reality which defines the prophetic vision compels the denial or falsification of profane reality. But if—like Sartre immediately after the Hungarian Uprising—the faithful write that this blood-sodden monster is socialism all the same, are we to conclude (with Sakharov) that nobody believes in it, or (with Solzhenitsyn) that, although corroded by scepticism, the ideology continues to tyrannize people's minds?

If the Soviet régime has created in the Russian empire a civilization different from our own, a share of the blame at least must fall on ideology or, more precisely, on the way the Bolsheviks have interpreted—and continue to uphold—the Marxist prophetism.

Marxist Ideology is the fetid root of present-day Soviet life, and only after we have cleansed ourselves of it can we begin our way back to humankind.*

Other opponents of ideology besides Solzhenitsyn, the most famous of them being Sakharov, have reached the point of condemning socialism itself. Since ideological indifference does not suffice to heal Soviet society, then perhaps it is the "public ownership" of all the means of production, and authoritarian planning, which must be called in question.

Forty years ago, there was a great deal of debate in the West about the compatibility of public ownership, central planning, and political democracy or respect for individual rights. How is it with these matters in the Soviet Union? The Soviet régime is not the result of constraints which the exigencies of planning placed on those in power. The Bolsheviks took power by a coup, without the consent, or at best with the temporary consent (on the basis of peace for all and the land for the peasants) of the mass of the population. Their ideology—an account of the world and a prophetic vision—prevented them from seeing the world as it was and urged them to "build socialism." Agrarian collectivization, the financing of the Five-Year Plans by ruthless reduction of the standard of living, particularly that of the peasant class—all those measures justified in their opinion, possibly, by economic arguments—would never have assumed so extreme and almost monstrous a character if the men responsible had not given them an ideological meaning. There were other means of collecting a proportion of the harvest to feed the towns; the development of heavy industry, which is quite detached from socialism, did not require such sacrifices. The normal resistance of the victims would not have been identified with treason or counter-revolution, had it not been for the influence of ideology.

One might debate forever about the respective roles of ideology (such as the rejection of private ownership) and of economic necessity (the need for food in towns crowded by the influx of peasants into factories) in Stalin's

*Alexander Solzhenitsyn, "Sakharov and the Criticism of 'A Letter to the Soviet Leaders,'" *Kontinent* (New York: Anchor Press, 1976), p. 18.

decision to force collectivization. That kind of decision, it seems to me, is inconceivable in the absence of what both Solzhenitsyn and Sakharov call "ideology" and I call ideology as well—a word which, in the language of Marxism-Leninism, has no pejorative overtones. Since 1917, in fact, the Soviet Union has been run by a sect of "true believers" and remains unintelligible if the stress is laid only on one of the faith's two fundamental ideas—fanaticism and scepticism—whose connection is an enigma, although the dissidents and their commentators sometimes stress one and sometimes the other of the two ideas.

Why did it never occur to anyone, even for a moment, that the leaders of the USSR would listen to Solzhenitsyn's appeal? Yet it was this man, who has been accused of exaggerating the influence of ideology, who wrote:

For a long time now, everything has rested solely on material calculation and the subjection of the people, and not on any upsurge of ideological enthusiasm, as you perfectly well know. This ideology does nothing now but sap our strength and bind us.

He too, in his own words, recognized the ideological indifference, but he gave it a unique interpretation:

All these arsenals of lies, which are totally unnecessary for our stability *as a state*, are levied as a kind of tax for the benefit of ideology—to nail down events as they happen and clamp them to a tenacious, sharp-clawed but dead ideology: and it is precisely because our state, through sheer force of habit, tradition and inertia, continues to cling to this false doctrine with all its tortuous aberrations, that it needs to put the dissenter behind bars. For a false *ideology* can find no other answer to argument and protest than weapons and prison bars.*

This brings us to the core of the debate among the Russian exiles (within or outside the USSR), or rather in each of their minds. How and why does a "dead ideology" retain the power to tyrannize the living? What would remain of the Soviet Union if it were no longer what it is now? Sakharov answers:

It is only an extreme form of that capitalist path of development found in the United States and other Western countries but in an extremely monopolized form.†

Without ideology to justify some unspeakable crimes, without ideology as the basis of the legitimate power of the Communist party, the USSR would

---

*Solzhenitsyn, *Letter*, pp. 46–47.

†Andrei Sakharov, from an interview with Olle Stenholm, Swedish radio correspondent, July 3, 1973, in *Sakharov Speaks* (London: Collins Harvill, 1974), p. 167.

be shown up in its profane reality: as an arbitrary industrialized nation, unbalanced by a military budget that—according to Sakharov—absorbs as much as 40%* of the national product, with planning methods that the best servants of the régime judge costly and inefficient, a standard of living low for a superpower, brilliant space and defense technology (but inferior to that of the United States). It is a nation which sells raw materials to the West and purchases whole factories, ready-made, in return, and which has an agricultural system that is unable, in one year out of three, to feed its population. So how can such a system renounce its ideology, in other words, its transfiguration of profane reality into a super-reality, into a higher stage along the way toward human salvation? The prophetism makes it possible to present Marxist-Leninist society as superior, as better *per se* than other, different societies. The Soviet system is, indeed, profoundly different from Western societies, but not different in the way claimed by the ideologues.

It would not be overstretching my own thinking to say that, among the Soviet leaders and the anti-Communists (among whom I include myself), there is a measure of agreement on interpretation. Once ideology and the sanctioning of the super-reality is eliminated, Sakharov is right: all that is left is a bizarre, irrational, expensive industrial structure (which has nothing to do with building socialism) which, in the past, was only excused by isolation and, in the present, is barely explained by its lust for power. But eliminating ideology and super-reality means making it impossible to understand the USSR's prestige among leftists all over the world, and the allegiance of so many revolutionaries on every continent to the Kremlin leaders, as the heirs of "the first socialist revolution." Soviet society is differentiated, it contains inequalities: what it *must not* contain is classes. The disparity between the living standards of the "privileged few" and the workers is considerable: this discrepancy *must not* imply *exploitation*. So much is clear: more and more in the USSR, and still more in the satellite countries,† sociologists are analyzing the profane reality. But such analysis occurs either on the fringe of the orthodox analysis of the super-reality, or else it has to adopt a circuitous, sparing approach in criticizing the super-reality.

Of course—and on this point Sakharov and his followers are right—the Soviet leaders are utterly uninhibited in their use of the ideological

---

*This figure, which is also quoted in a Samizdat text drafted by some Leningrad economists, is certainly wrong. "Disinformation" has wound up by deceiving a scholar to the point of accepting an absurd figure. Cf. Appendix, Note A.

†In the West too, of course. Cf. for example in *Soviet Economic Prospects for the Seventies, A Compendium of Papers Submitted to the Joint Economic Committee*, Congress of the United States (June 1973), pp. 87–123.

weapon. They dub Tito a heretic because he has manifested some schismatic leanings, and then rehabilitate him when the need arises, with a total absence of coherence. In the Middle East, they make use of Communist parties or let them be liquidated, according to their own great-power interests. To a degree, they cling to their ideology as a means of policing thought. But they would be changing radically if they renounced all theology. In the language of Solzhenitsyn: they need ideology to justify their own villainy. In the language of Sakharov: they need ideology to bolster a régime which does not stand up to comparison with the societies of the West, even (or perhaps especially) if that comparison refers to the criteria accepted on both sides of Europe—namely, welfare, freedom, and economic and technical efficiency.

Why should the Soviet leaders' refusal to break the ideological yoke surprise anyone? The press and the intellectuals in the USSR are powerless to effect a change: without reference to dogmas or, to be more precise, to an ideology (a conceptual system of interpreting the world and history), their activity never can compete with an ideological system which makes criticism invisible by filtering out both the expression of thought and the information itself. There is no need, as can happen in ordinary dictatorships, to ban a newspaper, suppress an article, or jail an editor. Each publication is an offshoot of one of the official organizations and participates in any internal conflicts which may affect the régime—which does not prevent them all from being cast in the same mold and using the same language while working within the tolerated margins of expression. But if ideology were officially abandoned, a radical modification of the administration's mentality would follow. What would be left? Nothing but an oligarchy based on bureaucratic preferment and appropriation from above.

Neither in the Soviet Union nor in Hitler's Germany was the management of the economy responsible for bringing about tyranny; on the contrary, it was the absolute power of a single sect or movement which, after the seizure of power, caused the economy to be subordinated to a vague and grandiose plan aimed at history's far horizon—a plan that demanded the mobilization of resources for the purpose of war or, in the case of the Bolsheviks, for the radical overthrow of all social ties. Ideology "legitimates" the party's political monopoly, transfigures its achievement, plugs the gap between the reality and the objective, and excuses the crimes of yesterday. A régime of this order cannot easily do without a spiritual point of honor. Pluralist democracy accepts its own imperfection by accepting scrutiny of itself. The USSR does not accept scrutiny, because it is based on an ideology; it will not give up its ideology, because it would then be compelled to tolerate scrutiny. And the power elite does not know whether the régime (and their own power) could withstand that.

Scepticism and faith

Is there any lesson or prediction to be drawn from the Soviet experience? Would a Communist or Marxist-Leninist party exercise power in Madrid, Rome, Lisbon or Paris in the style adopted by its brother parties in Moscow, Warsaw, Budapest or Prague? After all, today there is no longer a single church of Marxism-Leninism but several offshoots, all paying lip service to it. What would Italy be like under Berlinguer, or France under Marchais?

It has to be admitted that this question has little application to the already Communist countries of Asia. There, no matter what sort of feelings are inspired by the régimes of the People's Republic of China, North Korea, Vietnam or Cambodia, no one would claim to detect any trace of liberal civilization. Marxism-Leninism "Sinified" or "Vietnamified" is like a tool of power, a way of mobilizing—and molding into conformity—the minds of the population. It allows but one of the hundred flowers to blossom and, in accordance with the progress of events, it lets loose its Red Guards against revisionists and bureaucrats; then, when the hurricane has passed, it confirms the bureaucrats' authority and encourages them to keep an eye on each other, so that one after another is condemned to public self-criticism. Nowhere does the scientific and technological Westernization, sought after by the leadership, bring with it or preserve those values which, for want of a better word, we call liberal: intellectual freedom, free debate, and free communication.

By making a distinction between liberal values and democratic procedures, we are able to arrive at a more discriminating diagnosis. Pluralist democracy, it seems, does not lend itself to "transplantation" outside its original seedbed, the Anglo-American societies. In fact, by its very nature, it contains a number of features incompatible with the traditions of most of the political entities recorded in the annals of past centuries. The separation of the political class into a party of government and a party of opposition rules out the *unity* or *unanimity* which, whether simulated or authentic, forced or spontaneous, seems to most of the world's governmental systems to be the normal or desirable condition of the society. Not that those governments are unaware of group conflicts or rivalries among their candidates for the highest positions, but the "institutionalization" of conflict or debate has, for them, a quite different meaning according to their divers circumstances.

In one ideal type of government—best illustrated, for a long period, by Great Britain—parties which regularly compete with each other remain aware of their common interest in safeguarding the society. Their rivalry does not lacerate the national fabric—quite the reverse, it favors its preservation by disclosing the points at which it might be rent. The parties channel grievances, organize objections, and maintain the ever-precarious equilibrium between group self-interests and the greater good of the community.

At the other extreme, the same governmental procedure results in a permanent civil war: the parties hostile to the government exploit discontent in order to weaken it, to prevent it from effecting needed changes, to burden it with unsatisfiable demands. No government will risk passing reforms which all the parties know to be necessary but also unpopular; in order to return to power, the opposition will condemn a policy which it will continue to practice itself, once it has won. Even in Great Britain, the Labour party obliges the Conservatives to support it even after the party itself, or the trade unions, have prevented the Conservatives from governing. In other countries, conservatives act the same way toward the labor party, and the system becomes definitely paralyzed.

Almost everywhere, the reality is growing to be more like the second type of government, not the first: numerous parties, badly organized, with too little awareness of the common interest of the society or the community, with grievances permanently on parade, and with the political class either too close to the privileged or the revolutionaries—and no respect for the rules of civilized competition, for the "peaceful duel."

Any speculation on the future of the West in the event of increased Communist participation in Western governments must take account of the distinction between liberal values and democratic procedures. Does retaining the procedures necessarily imply respecting the values?

Here again, the dialogue of the Russian dissidents provides insight. Most of them discount the possibility of a change through revolution—not only because it is extremely unlikely, but because the lesson they draw from our century of terror is that violence breeds violence, and a revolution against one dictatorship, even in the name of liberty, would only create another one. Some of the dissidents, and Solzhenitsyn most of all, go further: they would put up with an authoritarian régime providing it agreed to separate religion—which is to say ideology—from the state and, at the same time, to re-establish the freedom not to have to tell lies. I have already explained why the Soviet leaders will not agree, even though the régime may be evolving in that direction of its own accord. If the countries of Eastern Europe were rid of the pressures from Big Brother, would they not move, of themselves, toward secularization? (Already, unofficial thinking about social reality, in Poland and in Hungary, is developing much more freely than it is in the USSR.) It is conceivable, at least, that the Communist party might keep its monopoly of political power yet also tolerate debate at home and abroad—among its own members regarding the reforms to be undertaken, and with the pluralist societies on the respective merits of the two kinds of economy and government.

Yet, even if one subscribes to this optimistic hypothesis, the short-term outlook depends on the world situation, in other words, on specific developments in the Soviet Union, the great-power diplomacy of the Kremlin, the duality of the world markets, and the problems which a Communist or part-Communist government would have to resolve.

A Communist party has a brand image; it belongs to an International composed of fellow parties many of which have installed régimes radically different from anything known to Western Europeans. On the day when it finally comes to power, if not on its own then at least as an influential member of the ruling coalition, the party will unleash waves of enthusiasm among its own faithful, and of fear among those who feel their property or lifestyle threatened by these revolutionaries who are so near and yet, occasionally, so far away. No one knows whether they belong to their native land or are coming in from the cold.

For thirty years, Europe has been divided into two different zones of civilization: the one ruled by the Red Army and Marxism-Leninism, and the other, where parties loyal to Marx and Marxism-Leninism take part in the struggle for power (except in the Federal German Republic). In Hungary and Czechoslovakia, Soviet or Warsaw Pact troops have intervened to restore authority and orthodoxy. No one imagines that American or NATO troops would step in tomorrow to overthrow Enrico Berlinguer or Georges Marchais. So the two Marxisms of East and West now stand side by side. What chance is there that the ideology proclaimed by the Italian and French Communist parties—namely, Marxism-Leninism, which is presently being used against the liberal order—will become tomorrow, what it is in the USSR: the state ideology?

Twenty years ago the answer would have been clear beyond all doubt. Communists—as individuals, with all freedom of speech and action—submitted themselves, then, to Soviet-style discipline of their own accord. Reputable doctors had few qualms about admitting the guilt of their white-jacketed colleagues. The European Communist parties did not hesitate to follow the Moscow line, even if they sometimes deplored it. In 1978 that is no longer the case, at least as far as one can tell. But the future of freedom in Western Europe is largely dependent on the answer given to the question: has there been a fundamental change in the Communist parties within the "Western zone"?

The fact that these parties criticized the invasion of Czechoslovakia by Warsaw Pact troops or the persecution of Russian writers, and the further fact that they no longer slavishly echo the Moscow line are public displays of independence, but they prove nothing, one way nor the other. The

Western Communists can repel political attacks and gain votes by keeping their distance from the country of the Gulag, which compromised them in the eyes of the voters.

While we wait for the only valid finding, the one based on experience, let us examine the facts available for analysis. The first, because it is the most visible, is the internal organization of the parties themselves. The first distinguishing feature of Communist parties is their *democratic centralism*. To be sure, this appears in a variety of forms between the limits set by Lenin's practice and the practice of Stalin. Lenin was in the position of having to convince his colleagues, and he did not exclude those who had opposed him during the phase of debate. The fact is that, even to this day, decisions in the Italian and French Communist parties are taken at the top by a small group of co-opted activists and that, once the decision is taken, all party leaders and militants must forget their disagreements and present a unanimous common front. The formation of groups or sub-groups within the party is still forbidden. This kind of organization may promote efficiency, but it is different in nature from the organization of the socialist parties and of the other democratic parties.

What is the objective of the general staffs—which are ultimately responsible for the policy of their "troops"—beyond the immediate one of getting elected into positions of power? Is theirs the socialism of Leonid Brezhnev or of Olof Palme? Abandoning the formula of the "dictatorship of the proletariat" means nothing, or rather it has several meanings. When Klement Gottwald threw the formula overboard in 1945–46, when Czechoslovakia was governed by a coalition of parties, he justified working in coalition with several parties. In the Eastern European countries, other parties than the Communist party have continued a theoretical or fictive existence to this day.

When Alvaro Cunhal stated, in 1974, that the dictatorship of the proletariat no longer squared with the circumstances, he was doing no more than to eliminate a word with inconvenient overtones. The word dictatorship had been used for the régimes of Mussolini, Franco, and Hitler; it wasn't a good idea to retain it to designate the phase of transition between capitalism and socialism.

What remains essential to Marxism-Leninism is Lenin's assertion that, socially, there is always a class dictatorship, bourgeois or proletarian, whatever political form this dictatorship may assume. This formula makes it possible to envisage a dictatorship of the proletariat which would tolerate a representative form (just as the dictatorship of the bourgeoisie sometimes takes the form of a representative democracy). But the bourgeois/proletarian alternative reveals the ultimate intention of Marxism-Leninism, which does not accept either the plurality of social groups whose interests are sometimes opposed and sometimes in agreement, nor the institutionalization of conflicts between groups; it postulates the existence of a dictatorship of one class behind the pluralism of the interest groups, and it seeks to abolish this supposed dictatorship—and thus to replace it with another—before the building of a classless society.

There is nothing to suggest that Western Europe's Communist parties have renounced this vision of the historical world, this notion of the eventual advent of Soviet-style socialism (not in the extreme Stalinist and Gulag form, necessarily, but at least as a one-party monopoly). The Soviet ruling power of today professes to be the government of *all* the people. Neither Enrico Berlinguer nor Georges Marchais have explicitly rejected this claim. When they comment on world events, neither strays very far from the Moscow line. It appears that they still view socialism as defined by the accession to power of a Marxist-Leninist party, with nationalization and state control of the means of production.

Later on, I shall examine the risks incurred by Western nations in sharing power with the Communists. For the moment, I merely point out that the desired conversion of the Communist parties, in countries such as France and Italy, remains to be shown. It may be that this is what the Russians are afraid of, despite our scepticism. Indeed, a society which claimed allegiance to Marxism-Leninism while preserving the liberal values and/or democratic procedures would come as a shock to the Soviet ideocracy, if not to the Soviet empire. The more a self-styled Marxist-Leninist régime diverges from the Soviet model, the more that model loses its exemplary character, and consequently its authority. The conversion of the Western European Communist parties to a practice of social democracy would be a significant turning point in world history. As long as Eastern Europe remains subject to the law of Moscow and as long as the big Communist parties of Western Europe maintain their voluntary association with the Kremlin, the present balance between the Warsaw Pact and the Atlantic Treaty will remain the only possible way of keeping the peace. The conversion of the Italian Communist party to Western civilization would weaken the Soviet presence in the West and strengthen the Western presence in the East. It might perhaps be a step along the road to the reunification of Europe—a long-term speculation, certainly, but, in this respect, why not imitate the Marxist-Leninists, whose Russian patience goes hand in hand with a faith immune to refutation?

Soviet societies and their distinctive features

The thesis outlined in the preceding pages all at once seems commonplace, because it is self-evident, and also unlikely to be generally approved. The objections both from the Left and the Right will be aimed at the "idealist" character of the interpretation. Do ideas and, in this case, a certain interpretation of Marxism and its prophetism bear such a "historic" responsibility? Before proceeding, let us remind the sceptics, by way of a preliminary observation, that Marxist-Leninists have as yet found no better way to explain Stalinism than the cult of personality; in other words, they indict a single individual—which, in the Marxist context, is even more ludicrous than indicting ideas.

Let us consider the régimes that claim kinship with Marxism-Leninism in themselves, in accordance with the ordinary concepts of sociology. They contain the same socio-professional categories as the industrial societies of the West, although in different percentages, and are even at a comparable stage of economic development. The services and trade employ a relatively smaller fraction of the labor force; Soviet agriculture shows itself as being exceptionally inefficient—with 25 to 30% of the labor force, it does not manage to keep the population regularly fed. The portion which goes to consumption—in other words, the amount left over after armaments and investment—appears to come to less than half of the GNP (although the calculations involved are open to argument). Differences between one occupation and another are revealed in terms of salary, which makes possible a comparison between the inequality of the so-called socialist societies and the salary situation of the so-called capitalist societies (or, at any rate, it would make this comparison possible, if statistics in the USSR were not still shrouded in mystery and, occasionally, in state secrecy). A comparison of that kind—like a comparison of the stadiums in the Olympic Games—would not always put the so-called socialist régimes at a disadvantage. Yet they reject it on principle, as if there were some sort of sacrilege involved in comparing societies which are essentially heterogeneous.*

The Soviet Union too has a political class which, as in the West, is recruited from among the various privileged social categories, by which I mean those with qualified, usually non-manual, occupations. The first ruling generation contained a sizable number of former manual workers, but the party, in power, has a different way of recruiting than the party in revolution; the Church triumphant differs from the Church militant. The party hierarchy constitutes a hierarchy parallel to those of the military and the economic administration. The political class is organized as a single party with a monopoly on state activity (broadly defined as the determination of society's values and goals, and the allocation of resources among the various occupations). Organization of the political class into a party and

*The countries of Eastern Europe, where the régimes are imposed from without and have no national legitimacy, are often ready to accept this comparison. The vast majority of Polish and Hungarian intellectuals belong to the Western universe—which is not always so even with the dissidents in the USSR.

monopolization of state activity by this minority of the population (itself subject to the discipline imposed by the ruling agencies) constitute the specific features of the Soviet régime—the features by which it transfigures and, in our eyes, condemns itself.

I have used the concepts of sociology—political class (or the ensemble of those taking a direct part in the rivalry for the exercise of power) and monopoly of state activity—so as to highlight the fact that this rivalry is carried on within the party. I am aware that this monopoly does not rule out influence or pressure from social strata or organizations outside the party: one author has devoted two books to the various kinds of opposition in the People's Democracies (church, trade unions, sections of the intelligentsia).* In the countries of Eastern Europe where the régime was imposed from above, without the mass killings of civil war and agrarian collectivization, the unity and political monopoly of the political class allows a kind of pluralism to survive, and even the prospect of a legal pluralism. The fact remains that this alleged detail, the monopoly of politics by a single party, defines the essence of the régime as a whole.

Once again, the Soviet régime—interpreted in the neutral terminology of modern sociology, minus its excesses and delusions—does not call for the passions it arouses. If the leadership were to tolerate minor individual trade, give the peasants back their freedom, and pay reasonable prices for farm produce, then straight away they would palliate the most crying and also the least necessary defects of their system. Let them accept comparison with Western societies, and the historical conflict would tend to draw closer to the economic and constitutional debates which Westerners so enjoy. Yet they do not and will not accept this comparison, even though it is in keeping with the logic of the times.†

Do they refuse this comparison because it would not work to their advantage? That was indeed the classic argument thirty years ago. Wait, we were told, until the Soviet standard of living overtakes and passes the West's: the Iron Curtain will be shifted from one side of the frontier to the

*Ghita Ionescu, The Politics of the European Communist States (1967) and Comparative Communist Politics (1972).

†European sociologists do make this comparison, which I outlined about twenty years ago in three books, Eighteen Lectures on Industrial Society, The Class Struggle, and Democracy and Totalitarianism. A good example is David Lane's The Socialist Industrial State (London, 1976), which tends to underestimate the abnormal character of certain aspects of the régime. Other examples may be found in Russian sociological literature. Cf. Soviet Economic Prospects for the Seventies, op. cit.

In particular, certain Soviet sociologists have undertaken to complete the official theory of classes in the USSR, which bases class structure on the relationship to ownership of the means of production, by an analysis of what the West would call social stratification. Cf. the quote from Prof. Arutyunyan in Lane's book, p. 96. They adhere to the thesis that no classes are created in socialist society, but they admit the differentiation of groups and roles, and of the positions of individuals within groups.

other. We are still waiting. What can we do about it? It is not the West which closes its borders; it is not our side of the demarcation line that bristles with watchtowers and barbed wire; it is not the West which has cut a town in two with a wall fit for a prison. But this still does not bring us down to essentials, because it might be argued that those attempting to emigrate to the West are recruited mainly from among the privileged, and that the West gives its privileged citizens more advantages than does the East (which is not true, at least for the Soviet Union). One thing the Marxist-Leninists will not tolerate is the elimination, by hypothesis, of the Marxist notion that a radical break must occur between capitalism and socialism, nor the elimination of their myth of an historical development oriented toward a happy, classless society. Who decided that the party alone should wield power, if not the proletariat? And by what right did the proletariat make that decision? Did history not single out the proletariat, with a view toward bringing about the salvation of mankind?

In the opinion of Oswald Spengler, liberal democracy and bolshevism do not stand in opposition to one another; rather, an "elective affinity" exists between them.

Bolshevism's home is Western Europe, and has been so ever since the English materialist world-view, which dominated the circles where Voltaire and Rousseau moved as docile pupils, found effective expression in Jacobinism on the Continent. The democracy of the nineteenth century already amounted to Bolshevism: it lacked only the courage of its logical conclusions. It is only a step from the Bastille and the equality-demanding guillotine to the ideals and street-fighting of 1848, the year of the Communist Manifesto, and only a second step from there to the fall of Western Tsarism. Bolshevism does not menace us, it governs us. Its idea of equality is to equate the people and the mob, its liberty consists in breaking loose from the Culture and its society.*

With his genius for terse formulation, Spengler wrote in the same book:

. . . effective Communism is *authoritative bureaucracy.* To put through the ideal requires dictatorship, reign of terror, armed force, the inequality of a system of masters and slaves, men in command and men in obedience—in short: Moscow.†

He at once adds that there are two kinds of communism: the brutally realistic version which leads to the Moscow régime, with its camouflage of Marxist religion, and the version which leads to ascesis, the cloister, bohemianism, foot-looseness and vague utopias. Certain forms of leftism have a resemblance to this second version, the nonviolent form of bolshevism.

Thus, stemming from the same sources, subscribing to the same ideas,

*Oswald Spengler, *The Hour of Decision,* trans. C. F. Atkinson (New York: Knopf, 1963), p. 97.
†Ibid., p. 129.

containing all sorts of analogous and homologous institutions, the régimes of liberal democracy and Marxism-Leninism can be compared by sociologists by means of neutral concepts; as hostile brothers, they are damned by all those who are nostalgic for hierarchic, religious, aristocratic societies; and pessimists, with perverse pleasure, assert that the liberty and equality proclaimed by democracy must culminate in Stalinist tyranny, gradually to be routinized into Brezhnev-style authoritarian bureaucracy. The fact is that, in the Europe of today, a choice will have to be made between having a single party that exercises a monopoly on politics, or else a situation in which free debate precedes the election or appointment of those who will govern.

For the time being, at any rate, these alternatives designate two models of civilization, despite all the features they hold in common. As long as the commentator, in the East or the West, only looks at the surface of the phenomenon, the economic institutions, he can acquire a reputation for hard-headedness quite cheaply. Sakharov writes that state capitalism represents only the ultimate outcome of capitalist concentration. How do the capitalist conglomerates differ, basically, from the Soviet trusts? The directors of the conglomerates have a function analogous to that of the Soviet planners.* There is nothing more false or superficial than propositions of this kind, seemingly drawn from similar but rival systems. The *spirit* of the two societies is deeply opposed; the similarities impress those economists who are naive enough to believe that American society is made up, essentially, of conglomerates.

Even on the level of institutions and the manner in which they operate, the two systems are opposed in spirit, because central, authoritarian planning differs *qualitatively* from indicative planning or the conglomerates' manipulation of prices. Centralized authoritarian planning is inseparable from the Marxist-Leninist ideology as professed and imposed by the Kremlin leadership. Moreover, greater autonomy for the Soviet enterprises, which in itself would fit in with rationalization (in the sense of managerial efficiency), would bring the Soviet régime closer to the market mechanisms (whose condemnation is part of the original Marxist catechism). Lastly, reforms of this kind would run counter to the ultimate objective, namely, the abolishment of the economic principle itself—an abolishment implied by the notions of "management by the associated producers" and "to each according to his needs."

If we approach the problem from this angle, interpretation which takes ideology into account becomes integrated with interpretation based on comparisons of economic mechanisms. Any number of planning methods are and will continue to be compatible with democracy or liberalism. But

*J. K. Galbraith also puts forward ideas of this kind.

total, centralized, authoritarian planning is not and cannot be compatible with it, because such planning is directed at an impossible target and necessarily resorts to tyranny. In some countries of Eastern Europe, where the European tradition survives, relaxation of Soviet pressure is already giving rise to a sort of liberalization; if these countries regained their national freedom, in a few years the régime would be transformed.

Out of this century of wars and revolutions, at least one lesson emerges: in essence, the Soviet régime is the combination of an authoritarian bureaucracy and a sociological gnosis, twin offspring of revolution and ideology—of a revolution misunderstood by the revolutionaries and of an ideology which distorts reality.

What kind of régime does the majority of people prefer when it can give its answer in the secrecy of the polling booth or the confidentiality of the opinion poll? Answers have come from Portugal, since April 1974, and from Spain, since the death of Franco. After the sudden or gradual disappearance of authoritarian right-wing régimes, the "silent" majority has voted for the institutions characteristic of Western Europe. Portugal and Spain want to join the liberal civilization of the Common Market. In these two countries, only the nostalgic Right stands out against this aspiration: the majority of the bourgeois and capitalist Right is in favor, and in Spain even the Communist party associates itself with the common front of the democratic opposition and takes care not to profess the orthodox doctrine of Eastern Europe.

Those aspirations seem to me authentic: imperfect as they are, the governments of France and the Federal German Republic are helping by giving immigrants from Spain and Portugal (or used to give them) decent wages and the example of free trade unions and freedom to put forward demands. (The GDR did proclaim a policy of *Abgrenzung* after the treaty between the two Germanys, but only because the temptation of this Western European example also applies to the socialist countries.) Despite the recession in the Western economies, it is the East that keeps the Iron Curtain lowered.

3
Western Marxism, or the Vulgate

From ideocracy to the Vulgate

In the East, Marxism has assumed the character of a dogma, even if on some points, like all dogmas, it involves slightly divergent interpretations. Soviet philosophers expound on the very definition of philosophy, on the laws of the dialectic, on categories, and so on. In the West, only professional Sovietologists take any interest in these expositions. Western philosophers, whether or not they call themselves Marxists, are not the least bit interested. In the Marxist literature of Eastern Europe, only the fringe schools—that of Georg Lukács in Hungary, and of *Praxis* in Yugoslavia, both of them derived from Hegel and the writings of the young Marx—have found an echo in France, Italy, and the Latin-American countries (where thought is supposedly "Marxified").*

So there exists between the Marxism-Leninism of Moscow, or the dialectical materialism stemming from the materialist metaphysics of Engels and Lenin, and the Marxism of those Western thinkers worth taking seriously, an initial and fundamental difference: apart from a few rare intellectuals—members of the Communist party—no one attempts to rescue the philosophy of Lenin. Not that Western scholars are not for the most part materialists, in the vague sense of the term—which means making the assumption that psychic phenomena are also subject to a physiochemical

*The Anglo-American countries have generally escaped this process of Marxification.

explanation not as yet capable of being developed at our present state of knowledge. Between the materialist philosophy and the economic interpretation of history there is, at most, an affinity of inspiration, certainly not any necessary link.

Once having eliminated the orthodoxy of dialectical materialism (although it is still taught in party schools in France and Italy), there remain several sects or schools* claiming allegiance to Marx inside, outside or on the fringes of the Communist parties. What do they still have in common, apart from the ritual obeisance toward the author of the *Communist Manifesto* and *Capital?* They continue to accept some major tenets of Marx's critique of capitalism, as well as his prophetic vision (more or less modified). *The inveterate Marxists are those who persist in condemning the liberal or mixed economy as evil incarnate, and in advocating planning and collective ownership of the means of production as necessary stations along the way to the humane values of the free and egalitarian society dreamed of by the founders of socialism*—a condemnation and advocacy which go right back to Marx, and which constitute the nucleus of what I call the Vulgate because, nowadays, it is not so much a living system of thought as an amalgam of prejudices and off-the-peg ideas.

Philosophical reinterpretations

In the time of the Second International, Marxists made liberal use in their debates of the distinction between vulgar and true (or discriminating) Marxism. One man's Marxism would be seen as vulgar by another Marxist who, in turn, suffered the same dismissal. Maurice Merleau-Ponty used to call Arthur Koestler a bad Marxist, but Koestler paid very little attention to existentialism, and remembered the Marxism he had absorbed in his days as a party activist.

Then again, any Marxist accused of being vulgar will find texts deserving of the same description in the writings of Marx himself. Even in his historical books, such as *The Eighteenth Brumaire of Louis Bonaparte*, the prophet's voice alternates with the scholar's. Why does he assert—after showing with the conviction of an Alexis de Tocqueville the growth of the state machine—that it will be the task of socialism not to take possession of that machine but to destroy it? For the inhabitants of the twentieth century, Marx's promise to eliminate the market while destroying the state machine sounds not so much like utopianism as it does sheer ignorance. In the short term, at least, how does one replace the market, except with a

---

*Not to mention the Marxologists who enjoy more freedom and consider themselves to be more inventive than their colleagues in the East.

bureaucracy? In fact, in the first phase of the Soviet régime, it took more than the bureaucracy to relieve the peasants of their wheat: it took the army.

Marx, with his rebellious temperament, had shown some sympathy for the Commune. Look, he cried, the dictatorship of the proletariat is at hand. Depending on the situation, he talked like a Jacobin or like a libertarian. On the other hand, he never did face up to the problem which today seems basic: finding the connection between a policy intended to be libertarian rather than merely liberal, and an economy which rejects commercial exchange and the "anarchy of the market." It is as if he thought that "management by the associated producers" were an answer, and that the determination of "needs" and the allocation of the collective resources in accordance with these needs could arise out of general discussion among the "producers," enlightened by the common sense of a cook.

The oscillation between prophetism and scholarship would not have produced the same consequences if the scholarship itself had not contained ambiguities—which are the delight of philosophers in the Hegelian tradition and the despair of would-be analysts. The fascination of Marxist thought derives from the synthesis of a Ricardian economics, a sociology of classes and a philosophy of historical contradictions. Through this synthesis, Marx was attempting to embrace the functioning of the capitalist system and the laws of its self-reproduction and self-destruction at one and the same time. His system of thought tends to combine synchronic study (analysis of simultaneous phenomena) with diachronic study (the study of change) and to deduce from the former sufficient reason for what is disclosed or foretold by the latter.

In non-technical terms, Marx claims that the capitalist system will progressively create the causes of its own paralysis, making either self-reproduction or enlarged reproduction (reproduction with investment of part of the surplus value) impossible. All theories of imperialism, including both Rosa Luxemburg's and Lenin's, proceed from the supposed contradictions between given elements of the system. For example, the idea that if there were no non-capitalist (or non-industrialized) countries, the owners of the means of production would be unable to "realize" surplus value. There is assumed to be a contradiction (or rather incompatibility) between the quest for profit (involving keeping wages down) and the purchasing power necessary in order for profits to be "realized." According to this schema, capitalist society is bound to be driven into overcapitalization and the maintenance of low wages. In fact, only the Soviet régime provides anything like an illustration of this picture, namely intensive accumulation of the means of production (and of military power) with low distribution of purchasing power to the masses.

Marx's thought thus combines analysis based on a model with an exposition of the model's development. Philosophers, studying Marx, find his works replete with the fundamental ambiguities of historical perception, which deals with human lives, with what human beings have felt, suffered, loved, and achieved. Need it be said that individuals alone constitute the *reality* of history? Neither capitalism, nor the state, nor imperialism are real in the sense that Hitler and Stalin were real. But the kind of history that sees itself as scientific does not stop at this microscopic reality of individuals and their actions, even if it does refer back to them in the last instance; it strives to grasp the systems that individuals create and support by their actions—partial administrative systems, partial economic systems or, finally, the global social system. So there are two kinds of possible theoretical approach, one based on the dictum that it is men who make history (even if they are not aware of the history they are making), and the other based on the substantial character of systems, even if these systems do result from individual actions, human beings appearing as no more than representatives or bearers of economical-historical categories. The first kind is a continuation of the Hegelian philosophical inspiration, which led to a particular version of historicism in the late nineteenth century. The second enables the objectification of human actions to be presented as if a reality derived from human beings became autonomous and conformed to laws, with individual responsibility disappearing into the general determinism of which the myth of the sorcerer's apprentice is an illustration.

The first philosophy—call it historicist or humanist—is expressed in any number of texts by Marx and Engels. It dominates the early writings and appears, also, in the *Grundrisse* and the parts of *Capital* dealing with alienation and commodity fetishism.* It accords with the interpretation of history in terms of class struggle, and with the anticipation that prehistory will end in a society without antagonisms. But class struggle as Marx presents it in the *Communist Manifesto* and the historical texts *(The Class Struggles in France, The Eighteenth Brumaire)* does not make an explicit appearance in *Capital,* although the theory of surplus value and of rent leads to a sociological analysis of class at the end of the manuscript of *Capital.* The synthesis between the economic interpretation of capitalist development, determined by the falling tendency of the rate of profit, and the socio-political interpretation governed by the class struggle came about in what I have called the *historical schema* on which the actions and orthodoxy of the Second International were based. Since then, events and philosophical doubts have cut this synthesis to shreds, causing the profusion of Parisian brands of Marxism, with Jean-Paul Sartre and Louis

---

*In plain language, the theme of commodity fetishism comes down to saying that people make the mistake of seeing commodities as realities substantial in themselves, whereas they are only commodities in and for the régime, resulting from concealed relationships between people.

Althusser (if I may venture to compare an authentic philosopher with an academician having no true originality) as its two protagonists.

Sartre *as a philosopher* owes practically nothing to Marxism. With some hesitation he has taken up its prophetism and offered permanent indulgence to *sinistrisme,* which is to say that he displays extreme complaisance toward crimes committed in the name of "the right ideas." More than once, he has given evidence of a primitive Manichaeism, holding that, although the Left may perhaps betray just causes, outside the Left there is no salvation. He does not borrow its materialist metaphysic from Marxism-Leninism: on the contrary, immediately after the war he wrote an article intended to convince Communists that a philosophy of freedom would do more to further their struggle and justify their plan than the materialism of Engels or Lenin. Later on, in *The Communists and Peace,* he speculated about the relationship between class and party, and the right of one to represent the other in thought and deed. This unfinished series of articles is more akin to political activism than philosophical formulation.

It is in the *Critique of Dialectical Reason* that Sartre speaks as an authentic philosopher. Yet, although he makes his act of obedience to Marxism there, he does not enrich Marx's thinking insofar as it is applied to analysis of the capitalist society, its functioning, and its future. He states in a few words that he considers the economic theory of *Capital* to be self-evident, and he takes up Engels's remark: "Men make their history,* but on the basis of given material conditions." Sartre's contribution is on quite a different level: he is trying to demonstrate the compatibility between existentialism and Marxism, between the primacy of the "for-oneself," of lived experience and freedom on the one hand, and the reality of classes and their struggle on the other.

In the Marxist context, Louis Althusser—despite the limited nature of his contribution—is or is alleged to be the anti-Sartre. He posits the human or social world as being an "objective reality" containing within itself an inner organization—or, if you wish, structure—and he rejects the formula that men make their history, on the grounds that it verges on humanism and historicism. Hence, in order to make a definitive break with the latter, he cuts the umbilical cord between the theory of self-reproduction and that of self-destruction. Revolution does not spring from the falling rate of profit nor from the pauperization of the working class, it results from a particular conjuncture created, if not by all instances, then at any rate by the interaction of several (or, in ordinary parlance, by a combination of economic, social, moral, and political circumstances). It goes without saying that this rectification of one of the articles of the dogma also enables the latter to be reconciled with history as it has actually happened.

*One rudely commonsensical British critic commented on this formula as follows: "Who the devil else but men could possibly make history?"

Sartre had put an existentialist gloss on Marxism, but because he was not at all interested in Marx and economics, he continued his own work, not by adding new variations on Marxist themes but by rethinking the philosophical foundations of these themes.

In one sense, Louis Althusser wanted to do the same job, in other words, to give the philosophers (or professors of philosophy) an acceptable formulation of the dogma. Instead of an existentialist or historicist version, an objectivist, materialist one. It is no longer man, or men, that constitute reality, but systems. Each system—or social formation—is made up of a plurality of instances, with economics as the determining factor in the last resort. In certain systems the very nature of the economic instance necessitates the use of physical violence to ensure the extortion of surplus value. Other concepts now current in fashionable Paris circles, such as *over-determination, epistemological break, structure,* and *combinatory,** lard Althusser's vocabulary without throwing any further light either on the capitalist societies, the so-called socialist régimes, or future prospects. This scholasticism does not question either the prophetism or the dogma; basically, it aims to rescue Marxism-Leninism by adapting it to modern taste, in this case by translating it into the vocabulary of a theory currently in favor with the Parisian intelligentsia.

In a sense, the rival translations of Marxist thought in postwar Paris recall the debates which raged among German and Austrian Marxists before World War I. Instead of the rivalry between Kantian and Hegelian Marxism, we find an existentialist versus a structuralist variety.

This brief analysis may serve to outline the limits of what has come to be known as the "Marxification" of Western thought. The main philosophical schools are developing quite apart from Marxism and, *a fortiori,* from Marxism-Leninism. But because certain philosophers or quasi-philosophers still adhere to socialism or Sovietism, they try to combine their thinking with their faith. The various exercises in translation succeed or oppose one another without renewing the socio-economic content of Marxism itself.

In other words, the seeming Marxification has to do with a dual phenomenon: a sizable fraction of the modern intelligentsia stands more or less assuredly or reservedly by the Marxist prophetic vision and the parties claiming allegiance to it; arising out of this political commitment, these "Marxifying" intellectuals make the effort either to find a philosophically acceptable expression of Marxism (if they are philosophers), or to utilize one or another of the Marxist concepts in their work.

*Unfortunately it is impossible to explain these rather mysterious expressions for the non-philosopher in a few lines. I venture to refer the reader to my own *Histoire et Dialectique de la violence,* and also to my *D'une Sainte Famille à l'autre.*

Opponents hailing from the USSR cannot quite put their finger on the basic misunderstanding, which is that the same doctrine which (in the hands of Marxist-Leninists) will produce a critique of the West and a justification of the Soviet régime can easily, and with no excessive subtlety, be turned against the power elite that pays lip service to Marx and Lenin. If the same doctrine has a self-critical function here but a self-justifying one there, this paradox finally comes down to a simple deception: we are asked to believe that the proletariat rules when the Communist party has taken power, or that public ownership of the means of production constitutes the necessary, if not the sufficient, condition of freedom. Eliminate these myths or sophistries, and dialogue between Eastern dissidents and Western Marxists will once again be possible.

Marxism as critique and as dogma

These preliminary analyses may put us on the right track toward answering Pierre Daix's question: is Marx still our contemporary, even in political economy? And if so, in what sense?

We can start by looking at Marx as a philosopher of history. The idea that dominates the materialist (or economic) interpretation of history as put forward by Marx in *The German Ideology* or in the Preface to the *Contribution to the Critique of Political Economy* might be described as stating that human beings must not be taken at their word, that they are not what they believe themselves to be, and that in general they do not act for the reasons they invoke. Marx therefore causes historians to examine social life, and especially what Hegel called civil society (the system of needs, and economic activities) for the effective, even if not the consciously lived, reality. A human society is first of all a natural society, an animal species in rapport with nature, both organic and inorganic. Never mind the conquerors and philosophers, the first and most important factors to look for are the way human beings procured their means of subsistence in different epochs, the tools they used, the relations they established between rich and poor, oppressors and oppressed, owners of the means of production and workers, and the use made by the privileged of the surplus which becomes available after the minimum living requirements of the masses have been met.

The theme of the "infrastructure" only becomes dogmatic when it is inserted into a catechism and when scholarly initiates solemnly begin to ponder about what constitutes the infrastructure (science? the juridical rules of property?) and what is part of the super-structure. The infrastructure itself places the scholars in a dilemma: What *determines* social relations? Is it the technique of production? Are tools and equipment the final determinants? The concept of "relations of production"* designates the organization of labor without making any distinction between the respective responsibilities of the class struggle and of technical constraints.

When Marx applies himself to the study of the past, he never goes into the question of the limits of the infrastructure, or even that of the respective causality of technology and social relations. What he constantly uncovers are enemy classes, rich and poor, slaves and masters, serfs and lords, proletarians and proprietors, and abstract examples of the extortion of surplus value (none of these abstract types suffices in itself to define a mode of production, the economy of ancient times not being reducible to slavery). This enumeration itself leaves the reader uncertain. It does indeed suggest that all societies have been torn by conflicts between social classes and that the "relations of production" are expressed in these conflicts. But it does not in any way suggest the idea which Marx holds dearest of all, namely, that history's one driving force is class conflict, and that the oppressed class triumphs over the class of oppression, unless both classes disappear together. Neither the slaves of antiquity nor the peasants of the Middle Ages triumphed over their masters or embodied a society of the future. Nor did they bring with them a higher form of social organization, adapted to more fully developed productive forces.

In a famous letter which I have already mentioned, written to Joseph Weydemeyer and dated March 5, 1852, Marx wrote that the theory of classes did not belong to him, but that he had borrowed it from the historians, in particular the French historians. Marx claimed:

What I did that was new was to prove: (1) that the existence of classes is only bound up with *particular, historical phases in the development of production;* (2) that the class struggle necessarily leads *to the dictatorship of the proletariat;* (3) that this dictatorship itself only constitutes the transition to the *abolishment of all classes* and to *classless society.*

No text provides a better illustration of Marx's own responsibility in the development of Marxism: he actually *states as a fact* that he has *proved* a historical *prophecy.* He proved—as many others have done—that all societies are divided into classes. But that the class struggle leads to the dictatorship of the proletariat and that the dictatorship of the proletariat leads to classless society, he did *not* prove. The very claim to have proven statements of that order is logically absurd. One cannot *prove* the *inevitable* advent of an *unprecedented* type of society.

Any *dogmatic formulation* of Marxist themes—and this dogmatism crops up here and there in Marx himself—is easily refuted. But *critical use* of these same themes—class relations, classes and modes of ownership,

---

*The German *Produktionsverhältnisse* is vague in meaning. The word *Verhältnisse,* which is translated as *relations,* also means conditions, or state.

modes of ownership and technology—which is just as open to non-Marxists as to Marxists, remains as immediate today as it was a century ago. What I call the critical use of Marxist themes constitutes the common wealth, part of the mental apparatus of all economic historians.

The oscillation between a *dogmatic use* which relegates Marxism to the past and a *critical use* which keeps it alive in the present is also to be found in economics.

Let us take the two theses intended to provide scientific proof that capitalism contains the seeds of its own destruction: the fall in the rate of profit and pauperization. The scientific instinct impels Marx, as if in spite of himself, to refine the analysis to the point where the original thesis becomes at best not proven. Since the proportion of constant capital in the total capital grows, and profit is produced exclusively by the variable capital (or human labor), the rate of profit must show a long-term tendency to decline. Marx is too good an economist to tie himself to this crude formula. He lists the variables operating in the reverse direction: increased degree of labor exploitation, reduction of wages below the value of labor, declining cost of the elements of constant capital, relative overpopulation, foreign trade, the joint-stock company, etc.*

Once given that a number of causes operate on the rate of profit in opposing directions, the strength of each cause has to be measured. In fact, all that remains of this thesis is an idea found in the Marxist Vulgate (although it appears in all the bourgeois economics textbooks): that capitalism will work only if businesses are willing to invest, and that they only invest if they can expect a profit from their investment.

More striking still is the nonproof (in fact the nonaffirmation) of the thesis of pauperization. The theory that, as the productive forces develop, the misery of the masses grows, is commonly attributed to Marx and to the Marxists. See, for example, the end of the chapter entitled "The Historical Tendency of Capitalist Accumulation" (*Capital,* vol. 1, chap. 32).

Marx first describes the process of "expropriation" of what he calls the "immediate producers," the craftsmen and peasant proprietors—in other words, the transformation of independent producers into wage-laborers or proletarians. In a second phase: "What is now to be expropriated is not the

---

*Analysis of the causes which counteract and slow down the action of the law is still of interest today. Marx correctly saw that selling abroad often makes "surplus profit" possible. The less developed country provides more labor materialized into kind than it receives, but this does not prevent it from obtaining commodities more cheaply than it could produce them itself. The basic difficulty for the Marxist thesis seems to me as follows: the increased intensity of capital, the accrued value of the constant capital operated by the worker, does not rule out the diminution of the share of capital used for the production of a commodity. "We must be careful, therefore, not to identify the reduction in the relative cost of an individual commodity, including that portion of it which represents wear and tear of machinery, with the rise in the value of the constant in relation to variable capital . . . " Marx, *Capital* (London: Lawrence & Wishart, 1974), 3:239.

self-employed worker, but the capitalist who exploits a large number of workers. This expropriation is accomplished through the action of the *immanent laws of capitalist production* itself, through the *centralization of capital*" (my italics).

No comment here: the forecast of a centralization of capital was current and indeed commonplace in Marx's day. It has been largely confirmed, although small businesses have survived in various forms both in agriculture and in industry.

There then follows a gripping, exaggerated and partially true description of capitalist expansion:

Hand in hand with this centralization, or this expropriation of many capitalists by a few, other developments take place on an ever-increasing scale, such as the growth of the cooperative form of the labor process, the conscious technical application of science, the planned exploitation of the soil, the transformation of the means of labor into forms in which they can only be used in common, the economizing of all means of production by their use as the means of production of combined, socialized labor, the entanglement of all peoples in the net of the world market, and, with this, the growth of the international character of the capitalist regime.

The world market, the application of science to technology, and the communalization of the means of production, all these do in fact constitute the long-term tendency of what Marx calls capitalism, even though the common usage of the "means of production" does not, juridically speaking, imply any particular system of ownership.

The text continues with the following much-quoted passage in which the prophetism of catastrophe erupts:

Along with the constant decrease in the number of capitalist magnates, who usurp and monopolize all the advantages of this process of transformation, the mass of misery, oppression, slavery, degradation and exploitation grows; but with this there also grows the revolt of the working class, a class constantly increasing in numbers, and trained, united and organized by the very mechanism of the capitalist process of production. The monopoly of capital becomes a fetter upon the mode of production which has flourished alongside and under it. The centralization of the means of production and the socialization of labor reach a point at which they become incompatible with their capitalist integument. This integument is burst asunder. The knell of capitalist private property sounds. The expropriators are expropriated.*

Here we are in the realm of myth.

By what miracle could the development of the productive forces come about without the proletarians, the masses, consuming more? How could

*Marx, *Capital*, trans. Ben Fowkes (Harmondsworth: Penguin Books), 1:928–29.

industries mass-produce if their commodities were inaccessible to the buying power of the greater public?

Marx understood better than most of his contemporaries the mechanism by which the productivity of labor is increased. Through the use of machinery and organization, the worker produces more in the same amount of working time. How else is the real wage to be prevented from rising, unless by an increase in the rate of profit (the amount of exploitation)? If a worker's labor produces the value of the goods necessary to maintain him in four hours instead of five, either he will receive extra goods (his standard of living will rise), or else the number of surplus-labor hours will increase and the rate of surplus value will rise.

When commentators are asked about the characteristics of socialist society according to Marx, they usually hesitate: some point out the unpredictability of the future, others correctly think that the specifically capitalist forms condemned by *Capital* disappear in socialism, while others cite the fairly numerous texts where a utopian naivety shows through.

Marx presents the market as typically capitalist, yet this simply means that the products of labor go onto the market and are exchanged for cash, which then enables the vendor to buy other goods. It does seem as if Marx often had in mind the disappearance of the market economy and of money. Thus, in the *Critique of the Gotha Program,* he states:

Society gives [the worker] a certificate stating that he has done such and such an amount of work (after the labor done for the communal fund has been deducted), and with this certificate he can withdraw from the social supply of means of consumption as much as costs an equivalent amount of labor. The same amount of labor he has given to society in one form, he receives back in another.

The Bolsheviks at first tried out this kind of moneyless calculation by the amount of labor.

But in the absense of the market the means of production still have to be allocated among the various spheres.

. . . society, as if according to a plan, distributes its means of production and productive forces in the degree and measure which is required for the fulfilment of the various social needs, so that each sphere of production receives the *quota* of social capital required to satisfy the corresponding need.

Or again:

In the case of socialized production the money-capital is eliminated. Society distributes labor-power and means of production to the different branches of production. The producers may, for all it matters, receive paper vouchers entitling

*Marx, quoted by K. Papaioannou in *Theories of Surplus Value* (Moscow: Progress Publishers), p. 529.

them to withdraw from the social supplies of consumer goods a quantity corresponding to their labor-time. These vouchers are not money. They do not circulate.*

Having got this far, why not also envisage abolishment of the distinction between intellectual and manual labor, town and country, society and state? Total man finds his realization in a society without classes, and therefore without antagonisms and without a state, the latter always tending to hold the oppressed or exploited class in servitude. All Marxists, Marx included, lend a scientific character to the final utopia, or to the forecast of the historical movement that leads up to it.

Let us dismiss this allegedly scientific prophetism. Ought it to be said that Marx's historical and economic philosophy are still relevant, or that they are null and void? The answer is implicit in the preceding pages. It is possible to find the themes of the socio-economic analysis of societies and the economico-cultural critique of modern societies in the works of Marx, who is our contemporary so long as we ascribe these themes to him. But they do not belong to him alone: those who profess the Marxist Vulgate ascribe sole paternity to him (which doesn't matter much), but above all they slip more or less explicitly from themes to dogma, dogma to prophetism, and they generally refrain from applying the same methods of analysis and criticism to the socialist régimes as they do to the capitalist systems of the West.

Whereas some sociologists tend to represent society in the form of a complex and harmonious whole, held together by the adherence of the majority to the same values, another school, which goes back to Machiavelli as much as to Marx, finds the opposition of oppressors and oppressed, the privileged and the masses, the great and the common people, in every society. The problem requiring research is not the existence of a minority holding the wealth and power, but the nature of that minority's composition, the means it uses to maintain itself in power, the number of intermediary groups, and the opportunities given to the greater number of the people. Yet on all these points one would search in vain for what could be called a Marxist theory.

Would-be Marxist sociologists keep repeating, as if it were a great discovery, the trivial proposition that the dominant ideas or ideologies of a society are in fact those of the upper class. Where else do the ideas of any era come from, one might well ask, if not from those who have both the leisure and the power? In any case, this trivial proposition has less bearing on our own era than on any other, because our culture has a specifically scientific sector relatively little influenced by the ideologies of the ruling class. There is only one biology, whether the ruling class is Marxist or not.

*Marx, *Capital* (London: Lawrence & Wishart, 1974), 2:362.

Even to this day, the concept of surplus value also lends itself to polemical uses. Whatever the type of government, part of the value of production goes toward amortization, plant modernization, expansion of production facilities, general business or state costs, and higher wages. But the concept of surplus value—the theory according to which it can only be taken from living labor—makes it possible to replace the comparison of rates of productivity, of the various methods of allocating resources, or of forms of inequality, with the vague but insinuating notion that there is an intrinsic unfairness in the Western economies, even though the Soviet economy, too, contains a mechanism equivalent to surplus value (and one which gives the consumer a far smaller share of the GNP).

Finally, the early writings, some passages from *Capital,* and in between them the *Grundrisse* put forward not so much an economic or sociological critique as one which instead is moral or existential. To an economist, commercial exchange means nothing more than production for the market, and monetary wages quite simply mean payment for work. In a more or less Hegelian context, the commodity becomes a "fetish" perceived as having an autonomous, material reality which "mediatizes" men's relations (prevents them from communicating with each other directly). Because wages are figured into the costs of production (just as plant and raw materials are), they are supposed to transform the worker into a commodity. Max Weber's judgment was that the anonymity of relations among individuals, mediation by money, and the constraints exercised by the cost of production, competition, and rationalization were characteristic of all modern economies (and history has so far borne him out). Along this line of thought come the Frankfurt school, Herbert Marcuse, and Freudo-Marxism.

This critique of human alienation in the process of production belongs to the Marxist Vulgate, but it is just as much a part of the spiritualist or religious reaction against the productivist society. An offshoot of romanticism, it only remains an integral part of Marxism given two assumptions: that the human condition would be profoundly changed by collective ownership of the means of production, and that collective ownership is an integral part of socialism, the chosen successor of capitalism, and a necessary stage along the way to salvation.

Despite all objections, Solzhenitsyn is not mistaken when referring to the Western "wish to believe" in order to account for the Western obsession with Marxism.

Economy, industry, democracy: the Western belief in progress

Westerners continue to believe in Marxism or Marxism-Leninism because no other doctrine allows for belief in "another world" on this earth and not far away. Since the early nineteenth century at least, modern societies have thought about themselves with the help of three kinds of concepts— concepts of *economics,* of *science and technology,* and of *democratic and revolutionary politics.* The individual is identified sometimes with *homo oeconomicus,* the trader and calculator, sometimes with the toolmaker, *homo faber,* and sometimes with the *citizen,* who both participates in the state (or, in philosophical terms, the universal) and retains a sphere of personal freedom.

Marxist millenarianism leaves no room for *homo oeconomicus* but it does retain the two other ideal types, the technician and the citizen, whom it sees united and fulfilled in the shape of the socialist "man of the future." Even if the worker votes every four years, can it be said that he achieves any sort of full citizenship when he sells his labor power to the owner of the means of production, and takes no part in the organization or management of the enterprise? To bring about a society of free and equal men, of technicians and citizens, "management by associated producers" must be envisaged. Whatever the meaning of this formula, it postulates the exclusion of economic calculation, otherwise we are back with *homo oeconomicus,* the trader, and, with profit, inequality. Present at the birth of Marxism and Marx (and also of the Vulgate) are Jean-Jacques Rousseau and Saint-Simon, democracy as the truth of all politics,* and industry as the vocation of modern society. The aim is to restore a genuine community of free and equal men by taking industrial development to its ultimate conclusion, to the solution of the economic problem by abundance or, if need be, to abolition of the division of labor.

At different times in his life, and in different texts, Marx appears to have believed in abolishing division of labor;† in the union of man and nature (man naturalized, nature humanized); in the possible transfiguration of labor into a voluntary and pleasurable exercise or, contrarily, in freedom existing only outside of labor and so in the reduction of the latter's duration (*Capital,* 3:820). What we have to do here is find an answer to Solzhenitsyn's question: why this desire to believe? And the first answer is that Marxism, and Marx himself, provides us with an irreplaceable, unsurpassable synthesis, one which joins together Saint-Simon and Rousseau, industrialism and political democracy. Unsurpassable because, since the first half of the nineteenth century, modern society has sustained the twofold

---

*"Democracy is the truth of monarchy; monarchy is not the truth of democracy." "Christianity is the religion par excellence, the *essence of religion*—deified man as a *particular* religion." Similarly, "democracy is the *essence of all state constitutions*—socialized man as a *particular* state constitution." Cf. *Contribution to the Critique of Hegel's Philosophy of Law,* in Marx/ Engels, *Collected Works,* (Moscow: Progress Publishers, 1975), pp. 29–30.

†Marx, *The German Ideology,* p. 54: " . . . in communist society, where nobody has one exclusive sphere of activity but each can become accomplished in any branch he wishes . . . "

desire for Prometheism and equality, knowledge and community, and because only the myth of their reconciliation satisfies the *need to believe*. Irreplaceable because, with Marxism, it is not the destiny of mankind which is at stake, as Merleau-Ponty wrote, but that of the secular faith in the supra-rational.

Marx conceived the key themes of a secular faith—in other words, a belief in another world radically different from the one we live in, yet destined to grow out of our world at the end of a long process of development. In the same breath, he added to *industry* and *democracy* the third concept, *history*, which is indispensable to a modern faith.

In Europe, the crumbling of *l'ancien régime* after the discovery of civilizations on other continents created a historical awareness that was torn between pride and doubt. The planet-wide spread of European culture promoted pride hand in hand with a craving for power and conquest. But as time went by, observation of the variety of the world's morals, customs, and manners was bound to give cause for inquiry. In the *Persian Letters,* Montesquieu lent this a politely ironic expression—how could you possibly be a Persian, which was the same as asking, how could you be a Frenchman? Jean-Jacques Rousseau, who was both more radical and more inspired, utilized one of the possible images of the primitive, that of the "good savage," to arraign the progress of the arts and sciences and also to outline the plan of a secular history of salvation, a way for civil society to regain the virtues and rights of man before the Fall. Engels and Marx also drew the broad outlines of a history assumed to have begun with primitive communism, then to have taken the Via Dolorosa where each of the antagonistic societies is a station along the way, but whose final destination is the communist society.

In the last analysis, Montesquieu and Rousseau each chose one of the possible solutions, and together they symbolize a basic alternative: either human diversity, enlightened by reason and the constants of human nature, or else a terminal achievement—either *décadence irrémédiable* or *accomplissement final* (depending upon whether the hope is cherished of "winning back" man's corrupted and—through centuries of social struggle—alienated nature).

People prefer that version of historical awareness which gives a direction to the social process and makes it possible to hope for a future consonant with their declared values. American thinking has been very little influenced by Hegel or by German historicism, but it has not been any the less thoroughly dedicated to the belief in progress, in the broad sense of the word: faith in a future better than the present is embedded in the consciousness of the American nation. That consciousness is unhistorical, in that the Americans broke with the old Europe; turning their backs on it, they embarked on a venture without precedent. However, they did not take with them only the technical equipment of a civilization; they took also its optimistic vision of the future, a vision which harmonized with their longing to leave a corrupt past behind them.

Between the liberal progressive Americans and the collectivist progressive Soviets, it is the latter who hold the best cards, by which I mean the best arguments for convincing the many, if not the wise. The American progressive attitude does involve a breach with corruption, but it locates this breach in the past. The immigrant, crossing the Atlantic and sighting the Statue of Liberty, breaks into the *other world,* into a community freely created, in a sparsely populated land, by people proclaiming the sovereign rights of the individual. No other society of today is the product of such a breach. By that very fact, the United States does not stand as a model for the *historical* societies of the world to follow, those which have sprung from a long past and continue to carry history's mark. A society of pioneers in a land of boundless space does not think of itself or dream of its future in the same way as do societies which know their own origins only through myths and which look upon themselves as rooted in their soil.

A "pioneer society" finds it easier to think in terms of *equal rights* and *opportunities* than of equal conditions. If American sociologists are nowadays surprised to discover that, despite the spread of secondary education and the multiplicity of universities, children do not all start off with the same chances of getting ahead, this is a recent phenomenon which weakens, but does not eliminate, the inherited ideology. In any case, whether or not American society retains its faith in competition and in justice based on competition, this ideology is not suitable for export, particularly when it is waning even in its own country. In an era when justice and equality are considered to be inseparable, the varying conditions of competition in an established society are too far from producing equal opportunities for the resulting *de facto* inequality to be considered fair. Besides, American philosophers have now reached the point where they rank actual equality of conditions second only to the rights or freedoms of the individual among the criteria of justice.*

In other words, Marxism-Leninism owes some of its persistence to the content of its prophecy, which is definitely millenarianism, but not just any brand of it. Typical of modern society, it promises the completion of the immanent vision in terms of the values of an industrial-democratic society.

Yet the strength of the temptation should not be overestimated. The history of the past century does not confirm the thesis that Marxism or, after it, Marxism-Leninism has worked any irresistible attraction upon the masses or even upon the working class. The organizations or institutions

*I have in mind John Rawls's book *A Theory of Justice* and the considerable impact it had.

closest to the working class—the trade unions, friendly societies, cooperatives—have never been fully "Marxified" (by which is meant their degree of allegiance to the Marxist prophecy and not merely their mode of describing reality with a vocabulary borrowed from Marxism). Certainly, factory workers do have an awareness of the gap between "them" and "us," between manual and non-manual work, and they do feel the alienation of being "extensions of the machine," or of being subordinated to a rationalization process which "they"—the managers and engineers—have devised and imposed upon them. But this state of mind does not necessarily give rise to faith in Marxism or Marxism-Leninism.

Kautsky and—after him—Lenin seem to have been correct in their belief that, in the late nineteenth and in the early twentieth century, the labor movements in the bourgeois democracies were more inclined toward what the theoreticians called "trade unionism." In 1914, working people both in France and in Germany turned out to be citizens and patriots first, Marxists and revolutionaries second. Lenin accused the social democratic leaders of treachery, but the "traitors" were obeying the wishes of their rank and file and acting in accordance with their democratic convictions (and perhaps even with the example of Marx himself).

Technology tends to devalue manual work simply because this becomes an appendage of the machine, whose accumulated energy mocks, as it were, the strength of human arms. Today, machines in many cases even possess more intelligence than the men who serve them. In fact, nothing could be further from working-class psychology and social reality than the glorification of manual labor at this time, when it is becoming more and more discredited in the factory. The specialized worker, trained on the job in the space of a few weeks, can no longer see himself as the "salt of the earth," the *démiurge* who fashions dung into riches. He regards production as a collective activity in which his own contribution is still indispensable, but where the managers and engineers have an essential part to play. If a feeling of opposing interests between workers and bosses, between *them* and *us,* persists in nationalized industries, then the fault for such opposition does not lie solely with the so-called capitalist or bourgeois system. Experience proves that, once the "lyrical illusion" has faded, even in supposedly Marxist and proletarian régimes, the rift shows through again, and the re-establishment of discipline after its breakdown sometimes requires more brutality from the new master than the dead régime ever produced. In smaller businesses owned by a single person or family, the vulgar interpretation of Marxism—those who create versus those who possess and enjoy—occasionally retains some plausibility. In big businesses, that which contributes to the persistence of a sort of Marxism is not the pride of the craftsman confronting a boss whose hands never held a tool, nor the producer vis-à-vis the man of leisure; rather, it is the feeling among "blue collar" workers that productivity does not depend on them, and that their only strength lies in their acting all together.

I dispute the notion put forward by one non-Marxist, Daniel Villey, who says that Marxism is the spontaneous philosophy of the proletariat itself. This idea is correct if, by Marxism, he means the "dichotomous" vision of the industrial world, with the managers (proprietors and bosses) on the one side, and the toilers on the other. It is wrong, however, if no distinction is made between this approach to the problem and the prophetism of Marx. The Marxism whose vicissitudes I am following results from a synthesis of analysis and prophetism, a brand of Marxism which in no way constitutes the natural expression of proletarian thinking and attitudes. German social democracy and the Second International preserved the hopes of the prophetism, while at the same time it restored the working class, gradually, into European society (from which Bismarck had excluded that class in Germany, and the repression of the Commune had done so in France). One kind of Marxism gave workers pride and an awareness of their own contribution, while compelling the privileged to make reforms; another kind bred in them a sense of unquenchable hostility toward the established order and, even more, toward the men who constituted that order—capitalists, monopolists, bourgeois.

The "wish to believe" of which Solzhenitsyn has written is particularly prevalent in Italy and France, but it is difficult to talk about this problem—of the Communist leaders and of those who follow them—because of the strange nature of the Communist parties there, which are national and foreign at the same time, basing their methods in part on the example of a post-revolutionary party now in power, and in part on adapting themselves to quite a different socio-political system. To a Soviet dissident, the Marxist-Leninists of France and Italy pose a problem which Solzhenitsyn's phrase "the wish to believe" does more to point out than it does to resolve.

What did a Communist party's leadership believe in 1950, and what does it believe today? And what about the permanent cadres, and the ordinary activists? There is no lack of evidence, since the basis of our knowledge about these close—and yet so distant—men comes from the writings of former party members. Many of the leaders outside the USSR knew all or part of what Khrushchev made official in his famous speech yet, for all that, they did not renounce the Soviet Union as the embodiment of their faith. The Church corrupted remains the Church, as long as no schismatic church springs up. The troubled activist has any number of available explanations to enable him to maintain his faith.

The initial experience was staged in an underdeveloped country: it was necessary "to fight barbarism with barbarism" (Isaac Deutscher). The West drove the Bolsheviks to extremes, first by intervening militarily, then by applying a "sanitary cordon." The isolation of the first socialist country and the menace of fascism induced an accelerated industrialization. Russia, a military empire, had never known political freedom, in the Western sense of the term. Administrative hierarchy, the obsession with treason, the cult of secrecy, government by fear, all are features of the eternal Russia which the Marquis de Custine (in his *La Russe en 1839*) observed a hundred and fifty years ago. The Bolsheviks claiming kinship with a Western ideology were simply swallowed up by the environment. Soviet Marxism—the bastard offspring of the Marxism of the Second International and the empire of the tsars—does not refute the faith any more than does Maoist Marxism (another bastard of a European ideology and an age-old Eastern empire). Socialism in Italy or France will not reproduce the socialism of Moscow or Peking. Particular national experiences do not justify the definitive condemnation of a universal faith. The believer will never run out of arguments to explain his disappointments, for, if he could no longer explain them, he would have to give up his dreams. And all these arguments do have a certain plausibility, perhaps even an element of truth but, together, they destroy the foundations of the prophetism's claim to universal validity: after so many experiences, what version of communism could possibly resemble that legendary "régime without antagonisms" administered by the "associated producers"?

The final balance sheet

What remains, then, of Marxism, either in Western Europe or in countries where thought is allegedly Marxified? Allow me here to summarize, in a scholarly style, the conclusions to which the foregoing anaylses have led:

1. No one outside the party schools takes dialectical materialism seriously anymore. The materialist system of metaphysics and the dialectical laws of cosmic, organic, and human development fully deserve the contempt or indifference they now receive. These ideas, furthermore, do not belong to Marx himself: Engels takes a little of the responsibility, and Lenin a great deal. The history of philosophy as interpreted by Lenin—a permanent, inexorable struggle between materialism (the primacy of reality) and idealism; the theory of consciousness as a reflection of being—is of no interest to any Western philosopher, apart from those whose membership in the Communist movement obliges them to go through the motions of Marxist scholasticism. (Even in the USSR itself, if they had their way, Russian philosophers would prefer to debate with their Western colleagues rather than annotate the sacred texts, though they are still ready to insert a few ritual doctrinaire phrases at the beginning and end of what they write.)

2. Three of the principal themes of Marx's prophecy have been rejected, one after the other, by history.

a) Neither the pauperization of the industrial proletariat, nor the self-destruction of capitalism, nor the contradiction between the forces of production and the relations of production* have stood up to the judgments of experience. No revolution came about upon the development of the forces of production as the result of mass impoverishment and the concentration of revenue within an advanced economy, as Marx himself had envisioned.

b) Collective ownership of the means of production has not elicited any potential wealth which would enable workers to transform their condition. On the contrary, it first became necessary to restore discipline—which involved, under Trotsky (and under Fidel Castro), militarization of labor in the factories (and in the sugarcane fields). After that, the equivalent of what Marxist-Leninists call surplus value was siphoned off by the state or by the bureaucracy.

c) The seizure of power by an allegedly Marxist party does not preclude conflicts between states. All the versions of socialism are edging toward nationalism, or paying lip service to it, as a counter to Soviet domination. The maintenance of proletarian internationalism in Eastern Europe requires the presence of hundreds of thousands of Soviet troops.

3. In place of the prophetism of Marx—the passage from capitalism to socialism, brought about by contradictions aggravated by the development of the forces of production—an altogether different vision has arisen: the régimes which Marxist-Leninists call socialist are the ones they themselves construct upon their seizure of power. Nowhere—not in the USSR, nor Cuba, nor China—has revolution been the work of the proletariat or the "immense majority" against a tiny majority of profiteers. The collapse of the tsarist régime after three years of war created a power vacuum which the Bolsheviks were able to fill by applying a technique of action. Mao Tse-tung waged a civil war from the countryside with an army of peasants officered or led by intellectuals, by professional revolutionaries.

4. Most Third World nations declared themselves to be socialist to one degree or another, but the word has no precise meaning: it implies state intervention on behalf of economic growth, nationalization of a more or less extensive sector of industry, and a certain kind of planning (usually reduced to the establishment of priorities). The would-be modernizing state is monopolized by an elite which may consist of the old privileged class, young revolutionaries, proprietors, and soldiers, and may sometimes be organized into a Marxist-Leninist party. This acts as a servo-mechanism

*This formula has no exact meaning at all.

between rulers and people, encourages total planning and the necessarily resulting inefficiency, and practices a verbal radicalism (see chap. 5).

5. All régimes which claim allegiance to Marxism-Leninism, and even to Marxism, remain more or less despotic in Montesquieu's classic sense of the word. None of them has preserved the personal freedoms, free debate, and free competition among parties. They all have in common not monolithism—for they do have to deal with internal conflicts—but the theory and practice of a leading role being accorded to the party, its central committee, its politburo and, finally, its secretary-general. The struggle for power takes place according to a combination method of conspiracy and voting.

6. That being so, why should one not discard into the oblivion of history the theory and practice of Marxism-Leninism—a theory for the use of fanatics and dunces, a practice at best for the use of underdeveloped countries, neither theory nor practice having any value at all for Western Europe? Centralized authoritarian planning of the Soviet type would be disastrous if applied to the advanced economies. The Leninist interpretation of Marxism would cause even Western Marxists either to laugh or to howl, if ever their country's leadership were to make it a state truth.

7. Why, then, does Western thought appear so "Marxified," especially in France and in Italy? Why this obsession with Marxism (or with a version of Marxism)?

a) Marx's basic concepts—forces of production, relations of production, classes, class struggle, dominators and dominated—are useful as a vehicle for analyzing *any* modern society, whether it be called capitalist or socialist.

b) The mature Marx never clarified the philosophy which inspired his socio-economics. Reinterpreting Marx's philosophy therefore offers believers in quest of a rationale an inexhaustible theme of speculation. Most so-called Marxist literature in Italy and France adds nothing to our economic or sociological knowledge, but confines itself to translating the supposedly correct theses of Marx into another language. This applies to Sartre and Merleau-Ponty, for example.

c) The neoclassical or Keynesian economics taught in departments of economics neglects, by epistemological assumption, the social context—or the social variables—of economic activity. In times of crisis, therefore, Marx exerts a kind of fascination over economists,* because his models do include a version of sociology, the private ownership of the means of production, the dominator/dominated opposition, and even the theory of

---

*In the last analysis, the serious economists belonging to the tradition of Marx are more numerous in the Anglo-Saxon countries. In the Latin countries, conversely, it is philosophers who "Marxify."

surplus value and exploitation. The idea of the declining rate of return on capital (which does not originally belong to Marx at all) is traced, by those economists who are considered radical, to *Capital*.

Those who reject the market economy, impelled more by pre-capitalist nostalgia than the dream of a post-capitalist new world, gather beneath the banner of Marx, who links his specifically economic critique of the capitalist system to a moral (money worship) or existential (alienation) critique. Thus, any critique of modern civilization has a Marxist veneer.

8. To the extent that it shelters intellectuals from "terrorism" in Italy or France, this seeming Marxification would not warrant any lengthy commentary, if it were not for the fact that it propagates false ideas. It protects Soviet-type societies from the necessary criticism, and popularizes the twin influences of what I call the Vulgate, and *sinistrisme*.

The Vulgate involves the condemnation of the market *per se* and a bias towards collective ownership of the means of production. One only has to use certain words, and to point out certain structural features common to all societies, in order to belong to the camp of the progressives and benefit from the indulgence of the "right-minded." The absolving excuse which Marxist-Leninists claim for themselves—namely, their pretext of aspiring to a classless and stateless society—is gradually extended to everybody who can parrot the Marxist jargon. So, at long last, our intellectuals—great unacknowledged simplifiers—find in the Marxist Vulgate what they are looking for: an all-embracing explanation for all hardship and all injustice.

East-West dialogue

Marxism remains "the unsurpassable philosophy of our era," according to Sartre, who repeated this dictum even at the time of his break with the Communist party. Alexander Solzhenitsyn's reply to the man he ironically describes as the "master thinker of the West" is:

Marxism has fallen so low that it has become simply an object of contempt. In our country, not one serious person, not even the pupils in the schools, can talk about Marxism without smiling.

So Pierre Daix was not mistaken when he concluded a series of articles on Marxism for the *Quotidien de Paris* with a statement of reciprocal incomprehension:

Whereas Marx has become an object of contempt for intellectuals in the socialist countries, in France he remains essentially our contemporary, and that includes his own particular field of political economy.

With whom do we side, the Russian exiles, or the European (French or Italian) intellectuals? Why these contradictory judgments? What is it about this doctrine, or body of ideas, invoked in turn or simultaneously by executioners as well as victims: Bukharin on trial for his life, Stalin with his deep-seated cunning, Sartre the philosopher of freedom, Suslov the guardian of the orthodoxy labelled Marxist-Leninist? The three preceding chapters give some answers to these questions, which I would like to bring together and clarify.

The Russian dissidents put forward an initial reason for the incomprehension they encounter among Western Marxists, including those who do not belong to—or are even sternly critical of—the Communist party. We have lived under it, the dissidents say, we know about Marxism in practice, tried and tested. You in the West are speculating about Marx's thinking, his words or his dreams. Experience has taught us what you refuse to admit.

Another reason, which occurs to Westerners themselves, is that Marxism plays different roles in the East than in the West. Its function there is to justify the status quo; here, it is to criticize it. The one side attacks the doctrine in the name of which it is oppressed; the other side takes up certain elements of this same doctrine because it seems to best indict capitalist society as such. But this does not mean endorsement of the practice claimed by Lenin and his successors to have been deduced from the theory.

Whatever the reason, Marx must take some of the blame for this use of his own thinking as both the ideological basis of a totalitarian despotism and as a ruthless critique of what is, after all, a liberal society. His responsibility comes from having linked together an analysis/indictment of capitalism on the one hand, and a prophetism cum socialist utopia on the other. The instruments of the analysis—surplus value and exploitation—are equally applicable to any system known today, whether ownership is private or collective, and whether the surplus value is in the hands of private businesses or individuals or of the bureaucratic class. The prophetism, which has been refuted both by the evolution of capitalism and by the experience of the so-called socialist régimes, remains as vacuous as it was from the first. How was the proletariat supposed to become a ruling class? Why should collective ownership suddenly display unprecedented efficiency? What magic wand could reconcile centralized authoritarian planning with individual freedom and democracy? What substitute is there for commercial exchange, other than bureaucratic planning? *The mystification started wtih Marx himself, when he called his prophetism science.*

If Marxism can still be considered a living force and Marx our contemporary, it is due to the West, not the Soviet world. When Westerners set the target of accelerated growth, they quote Marxism as their authority. When they denounce pollution and want to protect the environment with words, Marxism becomes ecological. When they prefer the quality of life to the GNP, again they produce texts by Marx. Sometimes the Western economy is "Malthusian," and Marx hit the nail on the head; sometimes it "overproduces," and that he said, also; if it produces unnecessary goods (who can define necessity?) and favors ostentatious consumption, enter Marx once again.

Are inflation and higher wages, which the trade unions have provoked, causing capital return to be reduced? One scurries back to the sacred book (or makes a show of doing so). The researcher studying multinational corporations' investments in the poorer countries, criticizing certain unfortunate consequences, feels protected under the London exile's broad umbrella.

In the final analysis, the Marxist Vulgate tends to merge into "the myth of the Left." What jeopardizes the message of a man like Solzhenitsyn, tending to limit its dissemination, is that this writer of genius cannot be contained within the standard framework of the Western intelligentsia. Not that I myself subscribe to his indictment of modern civilization since the sixteenth century, nor to his approval of the extreme proposals of the "club of Rome," but others, in the Western Left, have committed such heresies without being excommunicated. He is not forgiven for his refusal to think out his politics in terms of the Left/Right alternative.

Of those intellectuals viewed as belonging to the Left, only André Glucksman and Claude Lefort, from their very different positions, have roundly attacked this conformism. Glucksman:

Le Monde ironized about the ramblings of this peasant from the Volga. The "Left" proved more traditional: like a good tourist agency, the French Communist party launched its umpteenth publicity campaign about "the mother country of socialism" and presented Solzhenitsyn as a carrier of Nazi germs because he did not dare taste the unequaled charms of the mother country of the proletarians. . . . Most newspapers of the far Right sacrificed to the same atavism, pondering about whether Solzhenitsyn should be located "leftward" of Raymond Aron, the Sorbonne professor and *Figaro* editorialist, thereby indicating that they had no trouble locating Brezhnev to his left.*

And Claude Lefort:

Aren't we already hearing one man whispering, "Solzhenitsyn's a rightist," and another murmuring, "Aren't you worried by this love of Old Russia and religion?"†

Lefort rightly points out the anti-authoritarianism expressed, continually, in all of Solzhenitsyn's writings, in particular the passage in which Solzhenitsyn, speaking of his arrest, passes an unindulgent judgment on himself for having refused to carry his suitcase, and reveals—on looking back—how far he had gone toward exercising his *own* authority, acting as if

*André Glucksman, *La cuisinière et le mangeur d'hommes* (Paris, 1975), p. 34.
†Claude Lefort, In *Textures* 7:10–11.

"the chief" belonged to a superior world. Solzhenitsyn does indeed write as a libertarian.

Lefort has made the best reply of all to those who call Solzhenitsyn a conservative or look down on his religious faith.

Solzhenitsyn to the right? But where is the Right in the USSR? Where are the conservatives, the reactionaries, the holier-than-thous, the right-minded (as he so aptly calls them)? Where are the people who want no justice—except for themselves, when they feel threatened, who are assured of the superiority of superiors and the inferiority of inferiors, who tolerate no criticism, still less any instituted opposition, and who see their own order as sacrosanct? Where are the chauvinists and racists, the ones who make other people suffer, not only for an action, but also for a supposedly nonconformist thought? Well, they reign, they are at the summit of the state, in the party, occupying the top ranks of society, everywhere.*

*Lefort, *Textures*, p. 21.

part II
Europe unaware
of its own superiority

The confrontation of the two Europes

Thirty years have elapsed since Ivan met John on the Elbe, since Europe was split into two zones of political civilization and into two military blocs. Through successive phases—the Cold War, the death of Stalin, Khrushchev's Twentieth Congress speech, détente—the two worlds have coexisted peacefully. The wars in which American troops participated occurred a continent away—in Korea or Vietnam. It has been as if the Old Continent contained too much TNT for anyone to dare bring a match too close. In Europe, peace is indivisible.

The historic rivalry between Marxism-Leninism and liberal pluralism—not as military as elsewhere for, once begun, hostilities in Europe seem virtually impossible to limit—assumes here what might be called a pure form. The doctrines motivating the régimes of East and West both belong to Europe. Marxism represents one of the critiques, which sprang up in the mid-nineteenth century, of the capitalist version of society. Whether or not one agrees with its basic assumptions, it constitutes an integral part of European thought, exerting more influence on the Continent than in the United Kingdom and in the small countries influenced by Anglo-American philosophy, and is still a source of inspiration for social research, quite apart from politics.

In the East, Marxism—which has become Marxism-Leninism and a totem of national pride in the Soviet states—underwent the test, perhaps the only decisive one, of experience. So it is not enough to lay bare the processes of Marxist-Leninist mystification, as I have tried to do in the preceding three chapters; the facts and figures must also be examined. For Westerners (falling sometimes into the trap of ideas and imagining that Lenin's or Stalin's heirs possess an infernal machine capable of blowing capitalism sky-high or else some virtually infallible instrument for guiding their strategy) lose interest, at times, in an ideology they cannot be bothered to study and allow themselves to be impressed by yesterday's growth rate or today's hundreds of millions of tons of coal and other energy resources, or billions of kilowatt-hours.

It is not a question of going from one extreme to another and denying the achievements of what the Russians, with their Marxist-Leninist vocabulary, call "building socialism," and we call "industrialization." Our wording, it seems to me, is more precise than theirs. In its humane vision, and in the vision of Marx himself, socialism does not tolerate the Gulag nor, sixty years after the seizure of power, a standard of living for peasants and workers which neither the French nor even the Spaniards would accept. The Communist party has paid an exorbitant price for building its large-scale industry, but the USSR continues to depend on the United States for its food, on the West for its technological innovations, and on its ubiquitous police for keeping order and orthodoxy. If the virtues of an economic régime are measured by its capacity to answer the wishes of the population, organize the rational allocation of resources, and efficiently produce the goods necessary to the physical and moral well-being of individual people, the Soviet experience remains to this day the most spectacular failure in history.

Do the Politburo members recognize the superiority of the economies of liberal Europe over those of the Europe which calls itself socialist? And if so, do they acknowledge it? Once again, these simple questions can have only complex and qualified answers. Stalin and Khrushchev used to speak of catching and overtaking the Americans; Leonid Brezhnev hardly ever men-

tions it anymore. The Soviet leadership has never been ignorant of the statistics it keeps from the public. Perhaps they have taken a step further and admit to themselves that individual ownership leads to higher agricultural productivity; ideology, however, justifies for them their doctrinal preference.

Today, they insist on keeping up in only one field, that of armaments. The priority given to heavy industry since the time of the first Five-Year Plans remains, immutably, in the results if not in the targets set, in retrospect if not in anticipation. The Soviet Union now enjoys the status of a superpower with military forces of the same order of magnitude, globally, as that of the United States—superior on land, perhaps still inferior at sea. The technical innovations—the MIRVs, the cruise missiles—are usually developed in America, but within a few years the Soviet technicians are putting the finishing touches on the same sort of sophisticated weapons demonstrated as possible by their U.S. rivals. It goes without saying that this resultant military parity is achieved at the cost of an effort at least twice and more likely three times as great as that of the United States, measured as a fraction of the GNP.

Whereas ignorance or intellectual indolence often keeps Western Europeans from being aware of their success as compared with that of the other Europe, the leaders of the Third World, with a few exceptions, are even more resolutely contemptuous of the lessons of experience. Marxism-Leninism has certainly scored some propaganda victories, but at the expense of truth. *The propaganda message is that the Europeans owe their prosperity not to their own work but to the exploitation of the poor; imperialists, even when they withdraw from all their possessions, are still the opponents of the developing world. The Russians, however, by ideological decree—and because most of the needed industrial raw materials are held in their own soil—are not imperialists.*

4
Socialist capital accumulation

The ideas and the circumstances

The Soviet régime did not spring fully armed from the mind of Marx or Lenin, nor was it the outcome of any determinism of events stronger than men and their intentions. Lenin and his companions believed in the Revolution when they seized power; they believed in a particular kind of socialism when they abolished money. For anyone seeking to pin down the role which ideas and circumstances played, the best method is to trace the building of socialism through its main stages, starting with the book *The State and Revolution* to the taking of the Winter Palace, thence to War Communism, the New Economic Policy (NEP), the Five-Year Plans and agrarian collectivization, and winding up with the USSR in its maturity, which expels Solzhenitsyn and obeys a bureaucracy of old men.

Capitalism as Lenin saw it; the soviets

In the works of Marx, the analysis of capitalism is the only part which can be called scientific. On the other hand, the Marxists have regarded as scientific the element which I have called prophetic, namely the inevitable transition from capitalism to socialism, the self-destruction of the mode of production based on private ownership of the means of production and on market forces, and the advent, after the revolution, of a socialist régime.

What were the concepts that inspired the Marxism of Lenin and his fellow masters of power? Marx himself did not clearly establish what is now the commonplace distinction between the functioning of an economy, economic calculation, and the allocation of resources, on the one hand, and the institutional characters of a mode of production, in particular the private or public character of ownership, on the other. So neither Marx nor the Marxists afforded Lenin any usable theory of the allocation of resources among the various sectors. The texts most often cited, *The Critique of the Gotha Program,* for example, assumed that the strictly economic problems had either been settled or had disappeared. The determination of needs, the allocation of means of production to the various sectors to satisfy such hypothetically worked-out needs, was treated as a simple matter. Lenin thus took power with a mental utopia in search of a model.

Added to the absence of a model for a socialist economy were circumstances which historians have unceasingly expounded on. The revolution labeled socialist by its own authors came about in a country where capitalism had not reached its mature phase. Originally, Lenin had hoped and waited for a revolution in the advanced capitalist countries, particularly in Germany. He then resigned himself to the formula of "the weakest link in the chain"—which required going beyond the simplistic thesis of the correspondence between production and profit. It was an altogether theoretical difficulty, and he solved it, by using a little ingenuity, but his solution—in the Marxist tradition—tended to give precedence to revolutionary determination rather than economic determinism. This willingness to use power has continued into our own time.

The nonmaturity of the homeland of the revolution also enlarged the gap between what Marx envisaged as the necessary conditions for socialism and the real conditions of tsarist Russia. But there was an even greater gap between what Lenin meant by "capitalism" and the real thing. Take, for instance, the following passages from *The State and Revolution,* which Lenin wrote in Finland on the eve of the revolution:

To organize the *whole* economy on the lines of the postal service so that the technicians, foremen and accountants, as well as *all* officials, shall receive salaries no higher than "a workman's wage," all under the control and leadership of the armed proletariat—this is our immediate aim. This is the State and this is the economic foundation we need. . . .

Accounting and control—that is *mainly* what is needed for the "smooth working," for the proper functioning, of the *first phase* of communist society . . . The accounting and control necessary for this have been *simplified* by capitalism to the utmost and reduced to the extraordinarily simple operations—which any literate person with a knowledge of the four rules of arithmetic can perform—of supervising and recording, and issuing appropriate receipts.*

The most striking thing about Lenin's remarks is not so much what is, after all, the commonplace idea that the large-scale enterprise is the form common to the death of capitalism and the birth of socialism, but rather the idea of industry becoming organized *within* the enterprise as well as in the enterprise's dealings with the market. The economic tasks of *running* the enterprise are simply ignored. How does one conserve scarce resources and yet increase productivity in all areas? How does one distribute the manufactured goods? These and many other questions are not asked, nor was any awareness shown of them. All Lenin provides is a military and administrative model of management, coupled with a naive vision of the tasks to be accomplished. A central bank, monopolies like the postal service, cadres working under the control of a mythical armed proletariat, battalions of bookkeepers—these suffice to define the *economic base of socialism*. Marx used to refer to management by the associated producers; Lenin imagined that the economic base for socialism was already in existence. It was ignorance, even more than hope, that kept the revolutionary faith alive.

The first phase of the Soviet economy, from November 1917 to the summer of 1918, differs from all the others because the target set by Lenin was not building socialism but consolidation of the new power. Yet right from the start he made four decisions which he viewed, correctly, as fundamental: nationalization of land, and of big enterprises, control of power by the soviets (also known as the workers), and creation of a Supreme Council of National Economy.

The first decision resulted both from circumstances and doctrine. The land decree of November 8, 1917, sanctified public ownership of the land, which meant dissolution of the Old Order in the countryside. The peasants, occupying land belonging to the large landowners and the church, began parceling it out without consulting the capital. The Bolsheviks were hostile on principle to small or middle-sized peasant landholdings and had intended, before the revolution, to use nationalization to encourage industrial farming on a large scale. Lenin, finding himself unable to impose his own conception immediately and bound by his alliance to the Socialist Revolutionaries, bowed to the inevitable, but he made provision for the future: the land reverted, for the time being, to the peasants, but the state retained ownership.

The first wave of nationalization affected only about 500 enterprises, banks, railways, and foreign businesses. Their transfer to the state was

*Lenin, *The State and Revolution* (Moscow: Progress Publishers), pp. 50, 96.

sometimes determined by military considerations (the railways), sometimes by the new power's cruel lack of financial resources (the banks). At
that time, Lenin behaved with greater caution than Bukharin, who favored
nationalizing the entire economy. But he conformed to doctrine by turning
control of enterprises over to workers' councils or soviets, as well as to the
state, which was on its way toward becoming a party monopoly.

The workers' councils, which were distinct from the trade unions, received greater privileges: they had the right to supervise not only the
organization of labor but management itself. In this first phase, the new
masters did not go into the questions of freedom of the market, the function
of prices, the use of money, and decentralization of decisions. The Supreme
Council of National Economy set up departments divided in accordance
with industries, which gave rise to the present Soviet bureaucracy now
responsible for planning.

This first phase (preceding, so to speak, the building of socialism) produced a result now seen as logical and inevitable by historians of every
shade—namely, chaos. There was chaos in the private businesses, whose
proprietors—formerly managers—lost all authority. And in the *nationalized* enterprises, the workers ceased to accept labor discipline and the
decisions of the people at the top, be they former owners or bosses newly
appointed by the party. The nationalized sector was not broad enough to
allow the state to plan the entire economy, too broad to allow private
enterprise to operate.

Solzhenitsyn recently republished* a pamphlet first issued in Petrograd
in March, 1918, reporting the proceedings of an extraordinary meeting of
delegates of factories and plants in the city of Petrograd. This document
reveals both the deterioration of the productive apparatus, the decay of
labor discipline, and the gradual transformation of the soviets into organs of
the state. The delegates voted to make the following statement:

The factory committees . . . have become obedient tools of the Soviet government.
The trade unions have lost their autonomy and independence and no longer stage
campaigns in defense of workers' rights. The Soviets of Workers' and Soldiers'
Deputies seem afraid of the workers: they are not allowing new elections, they have
thrown up a wall of armor around themselves and turned into mere government
organizations that no longer express the opinions of the working masses.

The experiment to decentralize economic power, attempted under the
most unfavorable circumstances, gave way now to an experiment in the
opposite direction. In the workers' councils or soviets, real flesh-and-blood
workers had run the enterprises; brought to heel by the party, they became
cogs in a machine transmitting the will of a mythical proletariat embodied

---

*In *Kontinent 2* (London: Coronet Books, 1978), pp. 211–41.

in Lenin and his associates. This alternative was inscribed in Marx's own
Marxism, for what could be meant by his utopian vision of a proletariat
excluded from society, then magically transformed into a ruling class, but
anarchy and despotism? The choice was: either the workers' councils
spawned by the revolution—prolonging, briefly, the lyrical illusion—or a
proletariat represented by a power *declaring* itself to be proletarian and
subjecting proletarians themselves to the pitiless rule of necessity.

War Communism and the NEP

The phase known as War Communism was the logical successor to the
phase which can be called moderate, in the sense that it comprised the
soviets (participation of the workers in running the enterprises), *de facto
private ownership* in agriculture and in a part of industry, and the retention
of *money* and the *market*. The outcome of the "mixed régime" was chaos: of
the measures adopted in retaliation, some—essentially Jacobinistic or
despotic—contributed to the restoration of a sort of order, while others—
ideologically inspired—laid economic foundations, which are still maintained, but unleashed, at the same time, a kind of war between the
Bolshevik power and civil society, in particular the peasantry (then the
mass of the population).

Among those measures of War Communism to have survived, essentially, all the ups and downs of state policy, collective ownership is at the top
of the list. Collective acquisition of the means of production became the
rule: all enterprises, great or small, foreign or domestic, right down to
shops and cottage industries, were nationalized. Another perennial article
of dogma, in a more or less attenuated form, is the idea that workers'
councils, being critical of the socialist scheme of things, were responsible
for the state of anarchy, and that they must either disappear or change their
function by becoming the expression of the will of the proletariat in
power—and not of proletarians at work. The choice made in 1918 between
self-managing or communard Marxism and Jacobin or despotic Marxism
has never been revoked.

The 1918–21 period, on the other hand, up to the NEP, was characterized by the abolishment of money and the suppression of the market,
which occurred upon the setting up of a régime of centralized, authoritarian planning. In the absence of money, wages were paid in kind, public
services were free, and food was distributed by a general rationing system.
A central planning organ sent out precise directives, in physical terms, to
all enterprises. This initiative, which even to this day seems aberrant,
almost incredible, was an effort to respond to an urgent conjuncture, but it
can only be explained in terms of ideology, and of the way Lenin and his

companions thought. The best proof of this is that the NEP, to which Lenin resigned himself in 1921, could in fact have been adopted earlier. The NEP arose from the force of circumstances, War Communism from the force of false ideas.

Lenin had been deeply impressed by the German experience with its wartime economy, in which he had seen a prefiguration of the socialist economy. He had not grasped the difference between a peacetime economy—whose object is to meet the needs or desires of the population—and a wartime economy—whose main objective is to meet the material and manpower needs of the military machine and which shares out to civilians, as best it can, the resources remaining available.

Elie Halévy attributed a decisive importance to Rathenau's influence on Lenin. Indeed, some characteristics of the German wartime economy can still be found in the Soviet economy: the prime objectives of heavy industry are nearly always achieved or exceeded, while light industry (and, therefore, private consumption) lags behind. In this sense, the Soviet economy prolonged the wartime economy and became "*a siege economy with a communist ideology* . . .; sleepless, leather-jacketed commissars working round the clock in a vain effort to replace the free market" (my italics).* Of course, there is no overlooking the other source of that tragic experiment: the replacement of reality by a state of semi-delirium.

Money, the root of all evil, and the market, in which nothing is seen but capitalist anarchy, are destroyed, and every operation of the economy is centrally planned by physical orders, from the worker's choice of his job through all inter-enterprise transactions to the consumer's choice in the shops. Indeed there are no longer any such choices: all choices are made by the center. *The whole economy is one single big enterprise* [my italics] and the management of the economy is identical with the government of the country; there are no quasi-independent public boards, regarded as the non-political trustees of particular industries or enterprises. On the contrary, central power must participate and penetrate everywhere. Indeed, the whole country is one single big Commune, since the consumer and the worker are fully included in the plan; and the model can only be understood as a futuristic attempt to establish full Communism on the spot.†

Military organization in the factories, iron discipline throughout society, and absolute party unity—all these traits of War Communism emerged from the same amalgam of chaos and utopian ambition. The ambition took other forms but the chaos grew worse; the more the legal market was forbidden by law, the greater became the black market. Having nothing to barter, the government imposed obligatory levies on the peasants. These levies, in the absence of any goods given in return, soon took on the

*Alec Nove, *An Economic History of the USSR* (London: Penguin Books, 1972), p. 74.
†Peter Wiles, *The Political Economy of Communism* (Oxford: Blackwell, 1962), p. 30.

character of requisitions which, in turn, assumed a fully military character. For the first time, the army militia became instrumental in the struggle being waged against the peasantry by the Bolsheviks. Lenin's realism, tottering on the edge of the abyss, got the better of utopia.

Would the economic failure of War Communism have sufficed to convince Lenin, had the revolt and bloody repression of the Kronstadt sailors not revealed to him a threat far greater, in his eyes, than any statistics, namely, the risk of an ultimate split between the masses and the party? Obsessed by the lessons of the French Revolution, the Bolsheviks came up with the notion of *Thermidor*, which they used as an ideological label for this revolutionary step backward. Some years later, Trotsky would apply the same notion to the Stalinism of the Five-Year Plans. But unlike the French Thermidor, the Leninist Thermidor was initiated by Lenin-Robespierre himself, anticipating his revisionist or counter-revolutionary opponents; he gave way on economic orthodoxy in order to maintain complete political power.

The NEP was neither a systematic whole nor yet a model of a régime. Basically pragmatic, it marked both a return to reality and a truce between the Bolshevik party and the peasants. In February 1921 it was Lenin himself who proposed that requisition—the seizure of so-called peasant surpluses—be replaced by a tax in kind. Step by step, the peasants regained the right to sell their products on the market; they cultivated nearly all the land. Small businesses and trade reverted to private owners; the decree of May 1921 denationalized small-scale industry. Handicraft production regained a privileged status. Money wages were restored, and money resumed its former role while the central bank was being restored. The trade unions ceased participating in the management of enterprises; foreign capital was welcomed. The Bolshevik state retained a monopoly on foreign trade, and it continued its ownership of large-scale enterprises, together with some apparatus for planning—which was not yet used, between 1921 and the first Five-Year Plan, as a substitute for the decisions of agents, enterprises, and consumers.

The results of this policy—imposed as it was by the circumstances, and in spite of doctrine—confirmed its success. In 1928, industry was producing slightly more than in 1913, and agriculture nearly 20% more. The people enjoyed living conditions and an intellectual freedom which, even to this day, have since been refused them. More than thirty years elapsed before workers' and peasants' wages overtook the 1928 standard of living. The policy which the party accepted by force of circumstance, and which it saw as a temporary retreat or setback, came to the people as a relief and a source of hope. Civil society was breathing again, people were taking pride in themselves, and the state was relaxing its pressure; utopia was "just round the corner."

Lenin and his colleagues did not renounce the fatal error of confusing the market with capitalism: to Lenin, they were still one. In his speech at the Tenth Party Congress in March 1921, he asked whether it was possible to restore freedom of trade and a degree of capitalism to small farmers without undermining the political power of the proletariat. He answered his question in the affirmative, but the assumptions he made are doubly revealing. Being the prisoner of an elementary kind of Marxism, he wondered whether the power of the proletariat could stand up to a rising class of peasant proprietors, or small tradesmen, as though state power emanated directly from the economically privileged class, and as if the police and the army would not be able to guarantee stability. In all good faith, Lenin called this state power (that of the party) the "power of the proletariat," though not without some unintended irony, for each time "the proletariat" took a step backward, the flesh-and-blood proletarians went ahead one step. The transfiguration of reality by means of ideology, analyzed in Part I of this book, began with the taking of the Winter Palace and persists to this day.

The challenge to Marxist-Leninists created by the NEP successes was augmented further, after 1923, by the fading of hopes for a revolution in Germany (or anywhere else in Europe). The party economists and leadership discovered problems which are treated, nowadays, in thousands of books, but whose elements and possible solutions then were unknown. *Capital* contained a schema of what we call growth, together with the outline of a macro-economy, an account of the circulation of wealth (borrowed from the French Physiocrats), and the distinction between sectors I and II, producer and consumer goods. Once they became aware that they were not going to build the communism of their dreams overnight in a country which they themselves called backward, the Bolsheviks debated the growth model appropriate to the situation. The Five-Year Plans represent the outcome of that debate.

Why did the party put an end to the NEP, which had favored raising the standard of living, recovery in agriculture and industry, and slackening of despotism and terror? None of these "successes" were in tune with the Bolshevik ambitions and, in a sense, each of these economic successes meant a doctrinal setback and, therefore, a political defeat. Yet the historians still hover between two interpretations, either rationalizing party policy in the framework of *our own* system of thought, or trying to locate its rationality *within the terms of Marxist-Leninist ideology.*

The NEP reached the culminating point of freedom in 1925; freedom was gradually eliminated, between 1926 and 1928, through the reduction of the role allotted to the free sector in industry and trade, through the levying of taxes on trade and agriculture, and through the introduction of prices fixed by decree. It was in 1928 that Stalin finally adopted, and carried to its extreme, the Trotskyist program of out-and-out industrialization, accompanied by the elimination of private ownership in the countryside, as well as within the distribution apparatus.

During the years of the NEP, the leadership constantly debated the then famous question of the "price scissors," the terms of trade.* When they decided against collecting a share of the crops by military means, they lowered industrial selling prices in order to raise peasant incomes—through the medium of a relative increase in agricultural prices —and to give the farmers an incentive to sell a greater portion of their produce.

But this relative drop in industrial consumer prices gave rise to such predictable effects as scarcity, the black market, and waiting lines outside the shops. When the party tried to correct the error by closing the price scissors and decreeing a relative increase in industrial prices, agricultural production—or, at any rate, the share of it which reached the market—fell. One interpretation holds that because the Soviet bureaucracy had failed to master the market forces, they once again chose the hard line, in other words, outright suppression of commercial exchange and a return, with a few changes, to War Communism.

However important they were, the price scissors are not viewed by anyone today as the true cause of the decisions made in 1928–29. Even the "deep, blind distrust of the market" mentioned by one of the best analysts of the Soviet economy is insufficient to explain the Stalinist policy of extreme industrialization and agrarian collectivization.

Capitalism according to Marx, fulfilled the historic function of capital accumulation ("Accumulate, accumulate, that is the law and all the prophets"). Moreover, a number of Marxists, including both Lenin and Rosa Luxemburg, thought capitalism was incapable of distributing sufficient purchasing power for the absorption of production. In *Imperialism, the Final Stage of Capitalism,* Lenin made the incidental observation that expansion abroad would cease to be necessary, in both senses of the word, if capitalism would introduce technical progress into agriculture and raise the purchasing power of the peasants and workers. Since the party had taken power in a "backward" country, it had to undertake the task which elsewhere fell to capitalism, in other words, to accumulate capital in sector I—that of the goods of production—and to allow sector II—consumer goods—only the resources remaining after the secteur I priority needs were met.

In this way, the two schemas uppermost in Marxist-Leninist thinking, those of *Capital* and of the German wartime economy, came together: sector I became the equivalent of the priority needs of wartime, even

---

*This expression is used to designate the ratio between the prices of imported and exported goods in international trade. The same category can be applied to trade between town and country.

before Hitler's rise to power and the massive arms drive which it imposed. The reduction of sector II and of the purchasing power of the masses, both factors seen by Marxists as characteristic of capitalism, became the means of forced industrialization. Stalin and his henchmen thought of industrialization in strictly quantitative, almost physical terms. Invest; build dams and factories—these slogans took the place of the all-pervading "guns and munitions" slogans of fifteen years before. The same Stalin, who had resisted this leftist program for so long, now took it over, and went still further.

We are fifty or a hundred years behind the advanced countries, and we have to cover that distance in ten years. We will do it, and we will do even better.

Simultaneously, Stalin gave the order for agrarian collectivization, involving the liquidation of the *kulaks* as a class. After June 1929, he decided to double the number of peasants on the collective farms, and in February 1930, 50% of the peasants were regrouped onto the collectives. After March 1930, the peasantry had a period of respite and the collectivized manpower was more than halved in three months (from 55% to 23%). But movement soon resumed, and the percentage of collectivized peasants was close to 90% in 1936. By the eve of World War II, collectivization had been extended to all land under cultivation.

It is well known—although the news has not yet reached all the writers of school textbooks—that agrarian collectivization involved unspeakable atrocities: Stalin himself once told Churchill that collectivization had been an ordeal greater even than that of the "Great Patriotic War." Human history affords probably few examples of a war waged by a state—fallen into the hands of a band of semi-intellectuals, fanatics, and know-nothings—against its own population.

Millions of *kulaks* were deported. The peasants slaughtered their animals rather than contributing them to the collective farms; heavy livestock decreased by 50%, light livestock by 70%. Grain harvests fell at first, then, between 1928 and 1935, they stagnated. The party levied a greater proportion of these harvests (probably between 30 and 35%), adopting the same technique as was used during the War Communism period. *Sovkhozes* and *kolkhozes* tied the peasants to the soil, paid them as little as possible and sent the necessary food supplies to the towns. With doubled levies being siphoned out of reduced resources, a countryside "freed" of its *kulaks* underwent one of the rare famines attributable to the folly of men and not to the indifference of nature.

Without going back on collectivization, the party legalized the peasants' right, after 1933, to their own private plot of land—a right which has alternately grown and dwindled in the forty-five years since then. A substantial fraction* of the country's milk, meat, eggs, and poultry comes from these private plots, which occupy a ridiculously small fraction (1%) of the total area under cultivation. Since 1933, a truce has reigned between the rulers and the peasants, but never a peace.

The making of the Soviet model

Whatever progress the Soviet economy has achieved since World War II—and especially since Stalin's death—the system and régime that we see today date from the years 1929–39, from the growth model adopted, only halfway consciously, in 1929, thence adapted, gradually and partially, to the pressures of human beings and the constraints of circumstance.

Compared to War Communism, the authoritarian, centralized planning system makes two concessions to "formal freedom": the wage earners are paid in money; and, although their freedom of movement is limited by internal passports, they are not tied to an enterprise in the same way the peasants are tied to the *kolkhoz* or *sovkhoz*.

Historically speaking, money wages represent a kind of liberation, although the utopianism derived from one stream of Marxist thought tends to give them the opposite meaning. Once he has rubles to spend, the urban worker or the *kolkhoznik* selling vegetables on the official free market (or the black market) can choose what he wants to buy, though naturally within the limits created by the decisions of the planners. Up to the present, consumer preferences have influenced only slightly the use of the means of production (or the allocation of the collective resources among the various sectors). The amount of freedom on the labor market is controlled; if the authorities find it necessary, they send workers to the regions where some "priority project" is being launched, or else evict them from towns where overcrowding is a problem. And yet, statistics indicate that there is both a fair degree of labor mobility from one enterprise to another, as well as a differentiation of wages within enterprises according to the nature of the job, the particular industrial sector, or the province.

Neither the existence of money nor a monetary wage modify the actual character of the Soviet model. Its characteristics do not depend exclusively upon the wholesale collectivization in industry, trade, and agriculture, but also upon the switching of the relationship between means and ends and upon the Soviet planners' acceptance and accentuation of the defect attributed by Marx and the Marxists to capitalism—namely, perpetual accumulation at the expense of consumption.

An economic *régime*—as opposed to the *system* defined by institutions,

---

*Private production accounts for between 25 and 30% of total agricultural production.

especially those of ownership—consists of a particular way of allocating the collective resources among the various types of production, and among the different classes. In the abstract, economists conceive of two "ideal" extreme types of socialist planning. The first is full-scale planning, where the central authority makes all the decisions and these determine the general conditions of society; here, the allocation of resources, revenue distribution, and the nature and quantity of goods produced—from capital to intermediate and consumer goods—all reflect the will of the party, the arbiter of efficiency and justice. Civil society, "absorbed" by the state, becomes, so to speak, transparent, allowing the thinking of the leadership (incarnated in a society in which the role played by each person is open to the scrutiny of all) to be revealed.

At the other extreme is the socialist market economy, whose broad outlines were laid down by Joseph Schumpeter. The consumers regain the part they play in a market economy. In theory, if planning goes according to indices of the market of end products, the demand of the consumers is less frustrated than in Western-type "mixed economies." The state's central planning agency owns the means of production, but allots these in response to the wants made known by the choices—that is, the purchases—of the economic subjects. Money and prices continue to play their part, however: it is through the medium of prices, as the expression of relative scarcity, that the planners are informed of the populace's requirements. According to this theory, there is even "freedom of prices" for intermediary and capital goods, thus enabling the central body to respond to its economic subjects' demands by the rational use of resources. The state retains the right to fix the percentage of investment in relation to the GNP, as well as the level of expenditure for collective needs. With these two reservations, the central authority—which owns the means of production and is responsible for the allocation of all resources—submits its powers of choice and reason to the will of the consumer, as revealed by the fluctuation of prices.

Neither of these "pure" models has yet existed and never will exist, at least not in the foreseeable future. They both come up against people's natural resistance and the resistance of matters in general: the complexity of the economy, the number of different goods, the ingenuity of individuals to defy the competence of planners, even though they be equipped with computers. A centralized planning power never does put itself at the service of the public, because the public is not a unified body; the planning power—or rather the few who control it—makes its power serve the ends which it deems appropriate to its own, and to the collectivity's, interest. There is no *logical* contradiction between collective ownership of the means of production and the sovereignty of the consumer, yet there does in fact exist a social and psychological incompatibility between them. Why should we expect history to provide us with the (as yet unprecedented) spectacle of a powerful minority so virtuous that it bows to the wishes of a majority which it can effectively constrain?

Which of these two ideal types is closer to the utopia of Marx? Strange though it may seem, no one can answer that question with certainty. Usually, it is assumed that Marx knew the needs of mankind and of classes—an assumption requiring either absolute abundance (Trotsky's myth) or a more or less stationary economy. For the socialism (and, even more, the communism) envisaged by Marx does present itself in terms of abundance, not of penury.

In their doctrinal hostility toward money and prices, the Soviet planners were forced to ignore the consumers' wishes in 1928–29, when their priority was the accelerated accumulation of capital as described by Marx himself. The example of the wartime economy was well suited to this method of growth: the producer goods which, in a Consumer Society, count as intermediary goods became end products in a Production Society. Steel as end product and bread as intermediary product—this was the grotesque outcome of placing priority on the rapid accumulation of capital in heavy industry—an accumulation first regarded as the condition of growth, and then as the means of rearmament.

Three characteristics of the Soviet economy during the era of the Five-Year Plans are traceable to this ordering of priorities. Since 25 to 30% of the national product had to go into investment, and since most transactions were made with money, the planners lowered the salaries granted to workers and farmers. Right up to Stalin's death, this method meant payment of very low prices for the produce of the *kolkhozes* and *sovkhozes* which, as state institutions, had to provide the required amounts come what may. The difference between the price paid to the producer and the final price to the consumer was fixed by the state as a means of taxation and reverted to the state. Through this *indirect taxation* of consumer goods, the state fulfilled two objectives at once: 1) it collected a share of the national product proportional to the needs of investment, and 2) it established a price system which reflected not the relative scarcity of goods, but the *political will* of the planners.

By means of the tax on all transactions, the state modified the price system. But, for purely doctrinal reasons, the planners fixed the prices of producer and intermediary goods by an "arbitary" process. Opposition "on principle" to the market persisted in the form of the rejection of market prices. It was the central body which set the rate of exchange between goods, in the context of the overall plan. (If statisticians find it hard to arrive at a precise figure for the share of the national product devoted to armament, it is because all it requires to artificially reduce that share is to artificially underprice arms products.)

Hostility to the anarchy of the market, which involves the establishment of an arbitrary price system, leads also to regarding the planning body as omniscient, and to making it all-powerful. Theoretically, the annual Plan—the sole effective instrument for control of the economy—is reflected in a myriad of plans for all the various enterprises, and for transactions between enterprises (each having to meet targets expressed as a rule in physical quantities, although there exist uncertainties regarding the nature of these quantities*). The planners are cognizant of, and tolerate, a certain "grey market"† in transactions between one enterprise and another, in order to facilitate fulfillment of the Plan and to help enterprises avoid supply problems which develop when materials and machinery are not delivered in accordance with orders and forecasts.

This kind of régime imposes a radical division between the domestic and the foreign market, with the state taking responsibility for importing and exporting. If there are two national economies of this type, they normally have two price systems—equally arbitrary, perhaps, but not identical. Hence—the conditions of international trade conforming to neither national system—a third one has to be devised. Indeed, ever since the development of a "world socialist market," the necessary third system has been borrowed from the capitalist economies, and expressed in convertible currency (the dollar). For political reasons, as well as for reasons of prestige, the Soviet leadership would like to make the ruble convertible and, within COMECON, to go beyond bilateral exchanges and create a multilateral compensation system. This objective could be achieved only if the convertible ruble were used for international transactions and constituted a substitute, a conventional equivalent, for the dollar.

In theory, the purchasing power distributed through remuneration given to peasants, workers, and civil servants should be equal to the value of the consumer goods made available for them to buy. In practice, this balance is never achieved and, from the very beginning of the Five-Year Plans, inflation has been endemic in the ordinary sense of there being too much money going after too few practically-priced goods. Striving for parity between the two quantities would not be enough: since the prices do not react to overdemand, the planners do not know, or find out only after a long delay (and refuse to take any notice when they do become aware), how consumers are spending their wages. Overdemand does tend to push prices upward, all the same; the waiting lines by the shop doors are their

---

*To take an everyday example, is a given weight of nails required (in which case the factory will only produce big ones), or a given number (whereupon it will only turn out small ones)?
†This free market, tolerated both through its illegal and its legal periods, has been indispensable for palliating the deficiencies of planning.

own proof of the disparity between the goods available and the ways individual households would rather allocate their income. Neither inflation nor shortages nor supply problems, however, have the same effect on a Soviet-type as on a Western-type economy.

One must never forget the underlying idea of Soviet priorities. Granted, a "black market" does exist for theatre tickets, for works of art, even for meat, and there is a "grey market" for building materials, yet, in reality, these "flaws"—some wanted, others tolerated—do not impede the accumulation of capital, the growth of heavy industry, and arms production. The danger which weighs upon this politicized economy is of a political nature: resistance of the peasantry, absenteeism and idleness among the workers. During the first Five-Year Plans, Stalin increased both moral exhortations (Stakhanovism, or socialist emulation) and material incentives (salary differences became greater during the 1930s); the Leninist principle that party members should be paid no more than skilled workers was discarded and condemned as "petit bourgeois."

In the Soviet satellites, after 1945, the revolts in East Germany (1953), Hungary (1956), Poland (1956, 1970, 1976), and Czechoslovakia (1968) spontaneously assumed a political character, since the national power seemed to be Moscow's prisoner, but also because the protests (against low living standards and rising prices) were aimed at the party leadership and its decisions. With strikes being forbidden, all strikes become rebellions.

In 1945, the Soviets took the model of the 1930s seriously enough to impose it on the Eastern European countries liberated by the Red Army where Marxist-Leninist parties had seized power. They tolerated, and even encouraged, methods less inhumane in agrarian collectivization. (In Poland, private ownership still predominates to this day.) Nevertheless, they acted, on the whole, as if they wanted to convert each of the "people's democracies" into a small-scale Soviet Union, with total collectivization, centralized authoritarian planning, priority for heavy industry, arbitrary pricing, reduction of purchasing power, and collection of resources necessary to the state through taxes on all consumer goods. The Stalinist régime—which had been a compromise between utopia, a war economy, and experience—was transfigured into a model for socialism.

Such a régime does not rule out quite a number of "reforms" dealing with matters such as investments and consumption; the relations between individual enterprises and the central planning bodies; the price system; and trade with the West. All the same, in the Soviet Union the system remains basically unchanged, and the principles of the régime resist every reforming initiative that touches on essentials. But the East European countries have all more or less modified, made more flexible, and improved the Stalinist model.

Interpreting Stalinism

The debate on Stalinism which Marxist-Leninists avoid by placing the blame on one man (despite their own depersonalized theory of history) is full of confusion, even in the West. The problem, first and foremost, is to define what Stalinism is, or, to be more precise, what the phenomena are that were observed in the Soviet Union from the time when Stalin began to enjoy absolute power and that have been attributed exclusively to his personality.

From 1930 or 1931 (or, to reduce the Stalinist phase to a minimum, from the time of the Great Trials and the liquidation of the Old Guard) to the death of Stalin in 1953, the power of the party—essentially collegial, even at the time when Lenin imposed his will upon his comrades—was subject to the unquestioning authority of one man. He—as the Marxist-Leninists, his colleagues, and his successors all agree—acted as a tyrant, ruled by fear, violating the laws of heaven and earth. At the same time, he hid behind a curtain of lies and organized a cult of his own greatness and beneficence.

Thus, the Stalinist phase of the Soviet experience undoubtedly displays certain special features, compared with the periods that came before and after. Neither Lenin, nor Khrushchev, nor Brezhnev terrorized their comrades in the Politburo as Stalin did for more than twenty years. None of them, neither the founder nor the heirs, accused *those close to them* of treasonable conduct to the benefit of the secret services of London, Paris, Berlin or Washington. Imre Nagy was shot without a public trial, after 1956; Dubcek survives in the shadows, since 1968. The Politburo Bolsheviks detest Stalinism in retrospect and justifiably fear it, for what it did was to apply *to the Marxist-Leninists themselves* those methods which they regarded as being quite proper for use against the Socialist Revolutionaries and the Mensheviks.

Should it be concluded that Lenin contained within himself the seeds of Stalin, that 1917 led *of necessity* to collectivization and to the Gulag? The opposite thesis can be argued, within strict limits. The centralization of authority in the Politburo of the Central Committee gave the secretary-general the opportunity to place his own men in key positions and gradually build up for himself an automatic majority in the Central Committee, then in the Politburo. At the same time, he possessed legal authority which he could exercise in tyrannical fashion through the police. The vengeance wreaked against the former comrades-in-arms, the confessional ritual, the condemnation of genetics, the songs in praise of No. 1, all these are peculiar to Stalin—although such a bureaucratic despotism could at any time have created another such tyrant.

Once this concession has been made to the partial abnormality of Stalinism, the continuity of Sovietism is even more apparent. War Communism did not treat the peasantry much more humanely than did Collectivization. Foreign engineers, accused of "sabotage," also confessed to crimes they had not committed, even though they could not be suspected of any *kamikaze* devotion to the party. Lenin considered himself, just as much as Stalin did, to be the embodiment of "the proletariat"; and he just as ruthlessly attacked those who did not endorse that paranoid faith. The baneful nature of commercial exchange, the "exploitation of man by man" as implicit in all private ownership, the obsession with industrial giantism, the hatred of the peasantry—all these Bolshevik dogmas, sustained by a mixture of fanaticism and ignorance, are present in Lenin quite as much as in Stalin. As for militarization of factories and labor discipline, it was Trotsky who initiated them, just as it was he who sang the praises of accelerated industrialization.

In other words, without saying that Trotsky would have done the same, had he been in Stalin's place, the fact remains that the plan for forced industrialization, the refusal to tolerate private ownership, and the mistreatment in the area of agriculture are part of the main thrust of bolshevism and Leninism. Even if the Five-Year Plans did not logically imply collectivization, they sprang from the same inspiration, the same ideology.

At the time of the fiftieth anniversary of the 1917 revolution, certain journalists of the "bourgeois press" competed with one another to exalt the greatness of the man who had lived for nothing but the Revolution, in the hope of completely destroying liberal capitalist society. The death of Mao Tse-tung occasioned the same grotesque tributes of adulation. And indeed, if "great" is the word for men who have left their mark on an era, then both of them do belong to this category, both should be numbered among history's "heroes." Stalin, too, unquestionably. After all, Mao was continuing the line of those who had liberated and unified the Chinese empire. Whatever one's judgment of the way Mao exercised power—the Great Leap Forward, the Cultural Revolution—no one speaks slightingly about the epic Long March, the revolutionary mobilization of the peasants, the restoration of the Imperial Unity of the Central Kingdom in the name of a doctrine borrowed from the West and adapted to Chinese needs.

In the Russian empire, the Bolsheviks' seizure of power,—favored by the state of disorganization caused by World War I and by the abdication of the tsar—altered the course of history. The popular conception is that prewar Russia did not count as one of the industrialized countries. There is more falsehood than truth in this assertion. Although relatively "underdeveloped" compared to Western Europe and the United States, Russia had been developing rapidly, especially after 1880. It has been calculated that the annual rate of growth of industrial production rose to around 5% a year between 1888 and 1913, which was a high rate for that period, and greater than the growth rate of Great Britain or even Germany. Agricultural production grew by 2% annually between 1861 and 1913, which meant only a slight rise in per capita food resources, given the growing Russian population. The GNP is calculated to have risen by about 2.5% a year between 1880 and 1913, which was below the American and German growth rates, but above that of the French and British. The prediction that Russia would be dominating Europe by the mid-twentieth century was a common theme among economists.

Had there been no war, could tsarist Russia have modernized the economy and the state without a revolution? It is pointless to speculate about history that never happened. But it is contemptible to worship success: to decree that what did happen was written in advance and in conformity with reason. Those professional revolutionaries, the Bolsheviks, may have astounded our century, but that does not mean that Lenin was a great spirit. His hatred and ignorance cost his people tens of millions of dead. Even to this day, sixty years after he seized power, it is still necessary to struggle against his aberrations. When French socialists like François Mitterrand and Michel Rocard pretend to discover that collective ownership does not mean suppression of the market and the price mechanism, the commentators cry out at the miracle, at this cultural revolution.

None of the Soviet leaders belonged to the Russian intellectual elite, even if they were a part of the *intelligentsia* in the Russian sense of the word. To take only one case, that of Lenin, it takes the masochism or the *mauvaise foi* of a Parisian professor to rehabilitate Lenin's philosophical works. His so-called theoretical books, *Imperialism, the Final Stage of Capitalism* and *The State and Revolution,* are just propaganda literature. The first ranks next to the *Communist Manifesto,* or a notch below. The reader has seen a few excerpts from the second, and may draw his own conclusions about the extraordinary distortion of reality instituted by that great simplifier, so praised by his admirers for his realism in the political battle.

The "giants" of the French Revolution, men such as Danton, Saint-Just or Robespierre, also lived through events that were greater than themselves. Their written works are of interest to nobody except a professional scholar, and not one of them is noted for originality of thought. From the members of the Constituent Assembly of 1789–91 to the Jacobins, from the reformers to the extremists, the level of political reflection declines, while passion and violence rise. The Jacobins have benefited from the French nation's admiration for *la grande Révolution;* they possessed many of the qualities required for despotism, camouflaged by invocations of *la liberté.* The Bolsheviks far outdid the Jacobins, in their absolutely unwavering faith, their determination to conquer, even if it meant committing the utmost violence.

The objection could be raised that I have not mentioned the civil war and the foreign interventions which drove the Bolsheviks into violence and isolation. The seizure of power by a minority party—hastening to take back from the peasantry what it had just given them—could hardly lead to the setting up of a new régime without bloodshed. The Mensheviks *foresaw* the inevitability of civil strife and despotism.

In any case, the vicissitudes of the civil war and the foreign intrusions do not account for the Five-Year Plans, Collectivization, the Gulag, and the Big Lie. Whether in regard to War Communism or collectivization, the same combination of causes is evident: the town dwellers and soldiers had to be fed; the leadership detested the landed peasantry; and the leaders did not believe in the effectiveness of material incentives—which they rejected for ideological reasons, as well. Twice they sent the army or militia to collect the grain, for which they refused to pay a proper price—once because of a lack of money, another time because they had earmarked all their resources for industrialization.

Once more, we must clarify what it was that made the Stalinist period exceptional. First, it exaggerated some procedures dating back to Leninism: the camps, the secret police, the terror (on this point, the truth is finally emerging)—all sprang into existence after the Bolsheviks gained control. But after the relaxation of the NEP, Stalin revived and accentuated the rigors of War Communism because he wanted both to skim off a sizeable fraction of the harvest and to create, in the countryside, a production system that would guarantee the state the amounts it required. For the peasantry, collectivization appeared to be not so much a retreat from War Communism as it did a systematic organization of requisitions masquerading as "collective ownership." All those who resisted this "second revolution" became "enemies of the state" in their turn.

The originality of Stalinism is apparent also in the Great Purge, in the liquidation of thousands, tens of thousands, of party members (particularly Lenin's closest comrades), in the arrest of millions upon millions of Soviet citizens, both civil and military, in the swelling population of the labor camps. Stalin's collectivization—and the accompanying deportation of the *kulaks*—is no different, essentially, than Lenin's requisitioning of harvests. On the other hand, if Bolshevik terror *can* lead to Stalinist terror, I do not regard it as necessarily doing so; Lenin made Stalin possible, but not inevitable. Once again, the real history of bolshevism refutes the theory of history which the Bolsheviks proclaimed. Trotsky later wrote that, without Lenin, the revolution never would have happened; in the same way, it may be that, without Stalin, the Russian people would have been spared the extremes of the Great Purge.

Stalinism is neither characterized nor explained by the "cult of personality." It is defined only by the concentration of the party's power in the hands of *one* man, who used the secret police in turn against everyone, even his own followers. The glorification of this one man is not the cause of illegality and terrorism, but a cover for it, an extreme example of the ideological camouflage or lying which began with the seizure of power. Inasmuch as the proletariat—alleged to have taken power—does not exist and amounts to but a myth, anybody, even a Stalin, can become the proletariat's embodiment.

The persistence of the model

One may ask: why go back over the past, a past that is bygone? It is understandable for Solzhenitsyn to call on the leaders of the Soviet Union to admit the crimes of those who bequeathed them their power: the Zek is expressing the sufferings of the victims, the appeal to human justice, the patriot's indignation, and the Christian's compassion. Politically, Brezhnev—or whoever comes after him—has no interest in raking over events which are hardly compatible with the myth of the "infallibility of the party." What matters is the present-day reality of the Soviet Union, and what it will be like in the future. The Bolsheviks, who started out with a double utopia (dictatorship of the proletariat, and total planning with no exchange system or private ownership), have finally built an industrial society, which may be called "state socialism"—a powerful economy supporting a military establishment of the same magnitude as that of the United States.

One must think back to that Russian exile, watching in Switzerland, day by day, for the signs of destiny, then returning to Russia after the tsar's abdication. One must then consider the interstate system of today: the Soviet Union, now a superpower, ruling over Eastern Europe through the Marxist-Leninist parties; the Communist parties of Western Europe may be keeping themselves at a distance from the Red metropolis, but they remain linked to it by a common faith. All over the world, millions of people still admire the Promethean feat of 1917 and the Heroes of Bolshevism. How can one challenge the verdict of history, a tribunal which judges not according to morality, but by success?

In the Soviet Union today, more coal and all other forms of energy resources are being produced than in the United States. Steel production is more than double the 60 million tons set by Stalin in 1945 to ensure the country's independence and security. On the other hand, the average monthly pay, (excluding those employed on collective farms) rose to 135 rubles in 1973, according to an American estimate fairly favorable to the Soviet régime. If one converts this (at the official rate of just under a dollar to the ruble), it still represents an average pay well below the level of the minimum French pay. In either case, the contrast between the power of the Soviet state and the poverty of its subjects is glaringly apparent.

The Soviet model, or "Sovietism," as it is called, has three main features: 1) the reduction of private ownership to the minimum in all sectors, including agriculture, crafts, and trade; 2) authoritarian centralized planning, with strictly limited concessions made to the autonomy of enterprises and to managerial initiative; and 3) the use of the planners' absolute power to ensure priority provisioning for the number one sector, the rapid accumulation of capital—mass consumption being reduced by the high level of investment and armament production, and taxation on turnover serving to reduce overall consumption.

In the USSR, these three features constitute a system, in the sense that they were formed simultaneously, in the era of the first Five-Year Plans—the first two by a sort of unstable compromise between ideology and experience, the last in response to the Marxist-Leninists' own ends, and also in answer to an external threat.

What are the advantages, in the abstract, of such a model? There are two that are apparent: a) it permits concentration of resources in what the planners calculate to be priority sectors, and b) it raises the necessary capital for investment by taxing turnover or enterprise profits, instead of individual savings. In the West, savings play only a minor part in investment financing. Self-financing, however, in the case of private businesses, creates the risk of confusing "profits" budgeted for modernizing or expanding the means of production, and "profits" which increase revenues, and consequently the consumption and patrimony of private individuals. As far as large-scale enterprises are concerned, only the ill-informed are confused on this issue: distributed dividends represent only a very small percentage of the company turnover and even of the gross profit (before depreciation and reinvestment). The fact remains that to argue in favor of business "profitability," in a mixed economy, inevitably gives rise to suspicion; investment does depend on business profits—but so do the fortunes of the rich.

At the extreme, a Soviet-type economy could make all revenues go back into salaries, and the planners could reduce wage inequality for the urban population as a whole, while retaining substantial advantages for minorities selected for political reasons. But the reduction of all revenue to wages is not carried that far in the USSR, because of the private plots of land of the peasants, the openly tolerated grey markets, and the black market. And, in the *sovkhozes* and *kolkhozes*, there are wage differences which may be attributed to geographic and climatic variations, as well as to differing degrees of soil fertility, or to organizational inefficiency. But widespread public ownership obviously does prevent the accumulation of vast fortunes and does make it possible for the planners—if they have the will to do it—to decrease the gap between higher and lower wages.

The simple—and, so to speak, primitive—character of this model does not safeguard it against either inflation or fluctuations. But inflation does not reduce enterprise profits to the point where it would affect productive investments; and fluctuations do not give rise to any visible decline in production or obvious unemployment. Enterprises can employ excessive numbers of workers without running the risk of bankruptcy. Unemployment becomes apparent,* in the West, because businesses have to balance their accounts and make a profit, in order to keep their equipment and machinery operating. The French government, which in 1974–75 encouraged French businesses to pay supernumerary employees, mortgaged economic recovery; businesses lost their financial means to invest and became hesitant to take on more workers.

As to the omnipotence of the planners in a régime of the Soviet type, agrarian collectivization showed how fatally dangerous that is. Capital accumulation and rapid industrialization appear to justify all-powerful planning power, in the eyes of the Third World; but the two arguments, for and against, overlook the real questions, which are:

1. To what extent has experience shown this model to be economically efficient? I shall try to answer this question in the next chapter.

2. Does this economic model necessarily involve single-party government and ideocracy? The Soviet experience does not permit us to give a categoric answer. It is true that the model was set up on the basis of an ideology that claimed a monopoly. The less the reality conformed to the builders' intentions, the more they ruled out dissent or criticism. It is not Soviet-style planning as such that is hostile to individual and intellectual freedom; it is the Marxist-Leninists themselves, who practiced this kind of planning at the same time they imposed their dogmas on a population at first rebellious, then passive, and, at last, skeptical.

Must it be stated that Soviet-type planning today makes liberalization impossible? In the USSR, relaxation of authoritarian centralization would probably improve the performance of the economy. Some of the East European countries—particularly Hungary—have been discreetly flirting with a market economy. Others, like the East German Democratic Republic (which has relations with the West German Federal Republic), have managed to make the system work tolerably well. Making the economic system more flexible would not endanger one-party rule, even though there is a kind of "elective affinity" between a consumer's freedom of choice and a citizen's independence.

On the other hand, no Western country could adopt such a model without undergoing a lengthy phase of despotism. Centralized planning within the national framework, with its arbitrary price system, requires a breach with the world market. French industry works a day and a half per

---

*Unemployment exists in all societies, especially in all complex societies, but it comes to light only under certain conditions.

week for export; the same goes for Italy. Italy and France cannot leave the European-Atlantic community, either to join COMECON, or to turn inward on themselves: in either case, they would suffer ordeals incompatible with the survival of their liberal institutions.

3. Are collective ownership and/or planning compatible with civil liberties? Friedrich Hayek, in *The Road to Serfdom*, argues that they are not. Joseph Schumpeter says they are. But Schumpeter envisages a rational planning based on the price of the end products on the market—a system more easily imagined by an economist than by a sociologist. He does not assume the elimination of private ownership in the spheres of crafts and trade, where it is probably irreplaceable; in any case, the question goes beyond the framework of this book.

4. Does the Soviet model have a general—if not universal—value for the Third World? Before answering this last question, I must point out that no one argues that the Soviet model is suitable for already industrialized countries. And this book is addressed to the Western world, not to India or Angola. It would be the height of absurdity to take a method which favors forced accumulation of capital as a model for a country which already enjoys a high standard of living.

And yet, even in the Third World countries, the Soviet model has spread more false ideas than true ones. As it is, the rise of this one state to the rank of one of the world's two superpowers inevitably seems to prove the merits and efficiency of the Soviet method. The minorities which hold the power in the new states hardly bother about "liberal values" anymore, partly on account of the Soviet experience. They conclude that the main requirement for growth can be met by accumulating capital in heavy industry.

This imperative, in turn, is expressed in three formulas: 1) the priority of industry over agriculture; 2) of heavy industry over light industry; and 3) large-scale projects over modest ones. This order of priority—which may possibly be justified in countries that put power before welfare—loses all meaning in most Third World countries, where agricultural development and the transformation of the countryside afford the sole means of preventing the flow of manpower to the cancerous cities (that cannot provide employment). Despite the lack of capital and the abundance of labor, ideological conviction and imitation cause the planners to choose investments which create very few jobs and consume a great deal of capital.

Lest there be a mistake about the meaning of these remarks, let me say that the only thesis I support, with respect to "development strategy," is that no model can have universal validity. The priorities implied in the Soviet model do not seem to me to be suitable for any of the sub-Saharan African countries, and they seldom meet rational requirements for Asia or the Americas. Most importantly—like the Western countries, which retain from Marxism only a sort of Marxist Vulgate—the Third World borrows from the Soviet Union not a method in all its elements (party, police, ideology), but a Vulgate of the strategy of development, a conglomerate of one fourth half-truths and three fourths errors.

I must acknowledge that Marxism-Leninism has made a decisive contribution to the imperial fortunes of Moscow, whose rulers, subscribing to a universal ideology, have been able—in the eyes of the world, of the "decadent West," and perhaps their own—to transfigure a violent revolution and, thereby, a military protectorate into a socialist community.

5
The undiscoverable socialism

Maurice Duverger and socialism

Everyone calls himself a socialist now, or so says Maurice Duverger at the start of his *Lettre aux socialistes* (Paris, 1976). And I might be tempted to agree with him, since even Jean-François Revel (in his *La Tentation totalitaire*) declares that he is a socialist, too. It seems that this word now stands for a system that accords with the hopes of men of good will, with the so-called modern values: welfare and justice, rights of the individual, purposefulness of work. But in the area of economics, socialism has come to mean the gradual substitution of planning for the market, and of collective for private ownership. It designates, in other words, an institutional system and a régime about which there is nothing to prove that these values are guaranteed (or even permitted). The postulate of a preordained harmony between collective ownership and planning, on the one hand, and democratic aspirations, on the other, has no foundation except in the Marxist Vulgate. I therefore see no reason for linking my own profession of socialist belief with that of everyone else.

What are Duverger's reasons? Here are a few:

The cultural models dispensed by the cash-dominated media impose habits, behaviors, ideas, and ways of feeling and understanding in conformity with the fundamental aim of capitalism: consumption by the many for the profit of the few.

It would be difficult to express more nonsense in so few words. How could buying by the many possibly restrict profit to only a few? If everyone buys, then at least everyone is enjoying a higher standard of living. Would they use their purchasing power any differently in the absence of the media? The East Europeans, sheltered from the noxious influence of the "cash-dominated media," appear to favor a model of consumption very much like that of their Western counterparts. The waiting lists for would-be car owners are constantly getting longer in the Soviet Union. And a few pages further on—with no concern about the contradiction—Maurice Duverger blames our society for its poverty among the masses:

The majority of workers remain cooped up in a life that is grey and hard, well below the possibilities of industrial society.

What possibilities? Of which industrial society? Anyone who complains about the excess, and then the insufficiency, of buying in the West must either not be reading his own words or must have some other kind of buying in mind—one which has not yet been defined.

"Why socialism?" I ask my colleague, who was so anxious to instruct the socialists, then apparently on the brink of power in France.

Only a socialist economy can be organized fully in a rational fashion—which assures its technical superiority over capitalism. It alone can guarantee that production will be directed in the future toward social utility, and not toward business profits.

What does "full organization" mean? The expression does not convey any precise meaning and for that reason it evades, so to speak, any criticism. It does suggest, however, a more or less attenuated form of overall planning, either 1) Soviet-style planning aimed at replacing the market and the independent decisions of private business but in fact ending up by fixing the priorities in favor of certain sectors, in the vain hope of controlling, from the top, the whole of economic life, or 2) planning whose sole task is to keep the general situation under control and maintain a balance among the various factors, while at the same time conducting an active policy on behalf of this or that industry: the broad type of organization being practiced by the Mixed Economies of the West. As for the question of social utility versus profit, that is a kindergarten topic. Who determines "social utility" if not the holders of power? And the Soviet experience ought to have proven, once and for all, that the will of the planners does not coincide, through some sort of divine dispensation of the state, with that of ordinary mortals. There is no scientific measure, by democratic process, of the common good. In the USSR, "social utility" requires devoting what Sakharov considers a monstrously high proportion of the national product to armaments. And business profits—as distinct from speculative or accidental profits—are testimonies of either greater productive efficiency or agreement on the part of consumers. Everyone is free to prefer the decisions of planners to the choices of customers, or vice versa. In varying proportions, they both influence the allocation of resources. But to decree that socialism embodies the "rationality" of being "fully organized" and is *ipso facto* superior to capitalism, can only produce a smile or a howl, according to whether the hearer is in a good humor or happens to recall the Gulag.

This brings us back to the theme of this chapter: everyone claims to be a socialist, but no one sides with Sovietism anymore. How are these two statements to be reconciled? In the light of the experiences of this century, how can one distinguish between Sovietism and social democracy? Does the socialism professed by Mario Soarès in Portugal and by François Mitterrand in France exist at all? And has it a chance of ever existing?

Western productivity;
inefficiency and the Police State

Growth-rate comparisons used to occupy a central position in the ideological—or should one say rhetorical?—rivalry between the Soviet régime and Western-style societies. Now they have almost dropped out of sight. Westerners have stopped terrifying themselves by working out GNP ratios for ten, twenty, thirty years' time. The Soviets, however, although not with much enthusiasm, are beginning again to praise the growth of Soviet-style economies, comparing crescive Eastern Europe to stagnating Western Europe.

A number of circumstances account for the change of attitude among the Soviets. During the 1960s, in the United States and France, a sizeable fraction of what was thought of as leftist thinking started condemning "productivism"—the illusion that the Good Life, or Equality, would automatically emerge from a higher GNP. At the same time, first-hand evidence about real conditions in Eastern Europe was rapidly accumulating. Public opinion refused to believe, at this time, that the West could ever be threatened by the wealth of the USSR. But the revelation of the horrors of Sovietism—War Communism, Collectivization, the Great Purges, the Gulag—finally went part of the way toward dispelling such an illusion. It is now common knowledge that tributes of admiration and gratitude were washing over Stalin just when he was committing his most vicious crimes. Even the Western cult of Mao was somewhat stifled by reminders of the Stalinist "cult of personality."

All calculations of growth rates involve technical difficulties which I cannot go into in this book. In the USSR and the Eastern bloc, further difficulties arise, some due to the unreliability of statistics, others to the different way of defining the national product in the Soviet Union (services and transportation are eliminated), and above all to the price scale. If growth is calculated on a *constant* price base, then if calculations are figured on the prices current during the early period of the Soviet economy—when industrial products and new products were scarce and, therefore, costly—the national product in the later period will be higher. Choosing the prices current in the *later* period gives a smaller national product and, therefore, a lower growth rate. Only expert Sovietologists who combine a knowledge of Russian and of statistical techniques with critical minds and plain common sense can produce any valid findings and, even then, there is bound to be a certain margin of approximation.

In this deliberately summary account, the relevant facts appear to be as follows. The growth rates of the Soviet national product since the 1917 Revolution exceed the achievements of the Old Régime, at least if those of the latter are calculated for the entirety of the period that began in 1860. For the 1950-72 period, characteristic of postwar times, the Soviet growth rate of 5.8% is also higher than that of the United States for the same period (3.7%). But it declines from 7% between 1950 and 1960 to 4.7% between 1960 and 1972.* In any case, the drop in the Soviet growth rate reminds us that, if the comparison is to mean anything, it must apply to more or less homologous phases—in other words, for the United States, to the phase of rapid industrialization during the nineteenth century.

Since World War II, the United States has taken relatively little part in the "race for growth." The percentage of the national product channeled into investment has been consistently lower than that for other Western countries (about 15-17%, as against 23-25% in West Germany or France). Last, and most importantly, it is the GNP per capita and the efficiency of production factors that determine the long-term relative wealth of nations. According to the World Bank, the current growth rate of the Soviet GNP per capita for the period 1960-73 amounts to 3.6%, as against 3.7% for the German Federal Republic and 4.7% for France.

Even more significant, in my opinion, are the figures relating to the productivity of the various factors of production.† All observers agree that the rapid growth of the Soviet economy from 1928 to 1940 and again from 1945 to 1973 is due essentially to *forced* industrialization (the accumulation of capital in the producer-goods sector), a steady increase in the work force, and the ruthless reduction of the living standards of the population as a whole—and especially of those bound to the soil, the *kolkhozniks*. Although formulas of this sort do not carry much weight with the statisticians, the USSR's 1928 standard of living was not equaled again in Stalin's lifetime: it was not until the 1960s that consumers once more realized the level prevailing on the eve of the Five-Year Plans.

*All these figures are lower than the official Soviet figures, and are taken from the most reliable Western statistical sources.

†Cf. Appendix, Note C.

The "law of priorities"—the principles of which I described in the previous chapter, with sector I being accorded preferential treatment over sector II—goes along with an obsession with production goods. It is as if Soviet planners saw no distinction between *growth, capital accumulation,* and *mobilization of the work force.* The targets set for the priority sectors are achieved only by using more manpower than the plans allow for. The result is overcapitalization and a decline in the growth rate of the apparent productivity of capital. Table 3 in Note C of the Appendix to this book sums up a number of experts' findings. It shows that the apparent productivity of capital declined by 1.9% per year between 1928 and 1966 and by 3.9% between 1950 and 1962. During the latter period, the annual growth rate of reproducible capital comes to 10.1%, of labor to 1.4%, of output per unit of total factor input to 2.6%. The apparent productivity of labor shows a rise of 4.7% per year (revenue 6.2%, labor 1.4%), but capital productivity drops from year to year.

Let us turn from these academic facts and figures to the facts of experience. Western businessmen who visit Soviet factories report that Western-style equipment requires two or three times as many workers to operate there. André Fontaine, in his recent book,* records:

> The unconcern of the average Russian, who is well known for not being exactly obsessed with productivity, does not seem all that assumed. But there is food for thought in the reply made by one Intourist guide to a French businessman who remarked that clearly "people in Russian factories did not overstrain themselves." "And what if that is the advantage of socialism?" she asked.

May I respectfully suggest to André Fontaine that he should pass on the good news to his fellow contributor to *Le Monde,* Maurice Duverger, who claims that the obvious superiority of socialism is based on rationality? To applaud *hidden unemployment* and *overstaffing* (when the planners are bemoaning the depletion of the total manpower reserves) provides an example of that odd Western knack of finding an excuse or justification for something they condemn in their own country.

André Fontaine also notes that many Russians are nowadays turning to "moonlighting" to complement their income "from the official job that receives less and less of their efforts." The first generation of Bolsheviks would never have dreamed that idle supernumerary workers and organizational inefficiency might become the justification of socialism. The apparently paradoxical but undisputable fact, that must be underscored, is this: *the secret of productivity and labor discipline belongs to Europe—* Europe the "decadent," the Europe of trade unions and industrial strife.

A paradox, or a profound truth? It seems to me that the greatness of modern civilization is bound up with the never-quite-fulfilled attempt to

*André Fontaine, *Le dernier quart de siècle* (Paris: Fayard, 1976), p. 66.

educate the whole population and to enable everyone to take some part in the national culture. Industrial labor, so wrote Auguste Comte, replaces military command with cooperation. The Russians seem to have retained a thoroughgoing sense of hierarchy, and to have preserved the "authority of the top man" (this applies to their delegations of intellectuals or scientists at international congresses, as well). But nothing runs more against the grain of our civilization than the "military style" of order. Men like Kapitza and Sakharov see, in the Soviets' lack of free and open communication, the major cause of the inferiority of Soviet science as compared to that of the Americans.

The "idleness" of the Russian worker is not an expression of national character, as some people would have us believe. The first generation, fresh from the countryside, may have trouble adjusting to the constraints of industrial work, but that sort of explanation is no longer acceptable today. In reality, that which creates "idleness" and overstaffing is the absurdity of the system itself—the determination to control all enterprises from the center rather than grant them the autonomy privately (and sometimes even publicly) advocated by the country's own theoreticians. *Kolkhozniks* are idle when they are toiling in the collective fields for ludicrously low wages; they exhibit quite a different attitude on their private plots, where they labor freely, on their own behalf, with the prospect of normal payment for their efforts.

Let me add that, although I cannot prove this proposition, I am inclined to regard the classic interpretation of the Russian low living standard (in terms of the state's enormous accumulations of capital and the size of its budget for armaments) as inadequate. Certainly these two factors ought never to be forgotten—ordinary mortals do not consume tanks or machinery. But one must also consider that, during the early Five-Year Plans, millions of Russian country-dwellers were forced to migrate to the towns, and no houses were available for them to live in. Only during the last fifteen years or so has the earlier rate of construction increased, thereby making it possible for more favored towns like Moscow to reduce the number of apartments in multiple occupation.*

As regards both investments and distribution, allowance must always be made for the system's built-in defects. What use are tractors if spare-parts shortages cause them to be out of action as soon as a break-down occurs? In the final analysis, there are only two kinds of end products: consumer goods and armaments, which either feed, clothe, and house people, or protect the homeland and kill its enemies. Whether it is turning out steel or

---

*According to Jerry F. Hough's study, "The Brezhnev Era: the Man and the System," *Problems of Communism,* March-April 1976, living space per urban dweller expanded from 109 sq. ft. in 1964 to 127 sq. ft. in 1973. In 1975, 70% of blue- and white-collar workers' families had their own accommodation.

tractors, heavy industry produces only intermediary goods, and the figures for the national product should be reduced by the amount of investment wasted (the many projects started simultaneously and left unfinished for years and years, or the trucks which finally emerge from the giant factories built with Western help, but which do not improve the movement of goods in proportion to their number).

Likewise, in measuring the Russian standard of living, it would be appropriate to deduct* the time lost rushing off to the shop where a new consignment of some product in short supply has been reported. What the statistics do not disclose—but which all first-hand evidence confirms—is the irregularity of supply and the persistence of having to wait in lines. Here again, both phenomena are consequences of the system: of all economic activities, it is probably trade (together with certain sectors of agriculture) that lends itself least readily to centralized organization and that ought, logically, to be left to direct dealings between one enterprise and another and to the development of the greatest possible diversity, as happens in the West, where supermarket and corner store work together, even if not without friction. Compared with the evolution of trade in Western Europe, the Soviet distribution system undoubtedly belongs to another age, or rather another world.

Despite the deliberate brevity of this analysis, it will suffice to illustrate why I have called Part II of this book "Europe unaware of its own superiority," because even now, free Europe does not realize the extent of its advantages over Eastern Europe. I intend to point out the various aspects of the superiority of Western Europe in simple categorical terms.

The French Socialists have published a short book on *la liberté* and *les libertés*, and the French Communist party is filing a bill on "the freedoms" (Georges Marchais affirms, "*la liberté, c'est notre forte*"). Yet every Soviet subject has to be in possession of an internal passport. Citizens may not settle in the town of their choice and do not have the right to travel abroad without authorization. Usually, scholars who are allowed to travel must go alone, without their families. The Soviet leadership is still obsessed with its fear of defection by the very persons to whom it grants the greatest material advantages. Relations with foreigners are not forbidden, but they are viewed with suspicion. Similarly, quite a large amount of Soviet territory is still out-of-bounds to journalists. In this century of television and computers, the *praxis* of Marxism-Leninism is a dazzling illustration of the resistance of the political régime to the logic of technology.

The ever-present secret police commands extensive forces (hundreds of thousands, both professional and amateur). Compared with what it was under Stalin, the Gulag has lost its monstrous dimensions. Nobody knows

*Also to add on the value of free or low-cost social services.

for certain the number of prisoners in the camps (a million?), and there is no exact count of the number of "deviationists" in the care of the state's psychiatric hospitals. But these repressive practices do persist, even if Western protests occasionally manage to save a man like Plyushch, or if a few tens of thousands of Jews finally do get permission to emigrate.

On this point, the contemporary historian hesitates between the fear of saying either too much or too little. It is not enough that it is now a thing of the past that each social category be required to provide its quota of criminals to the secret police—it would take more than that to prove that the nature of the régime has changed. Even in the days of War Communism, the terror under Lenin never attained the Ubuesque perfection of the Great Purge. Leonid Brezhnev has manifestly not terrorized his colleagues in the Stalin manner; for upward of ten years, there has been no wholesale replacement of personnel observed in the ruling organs of party and state. A collegial power is operating at the top; a "bureaucracy of old men" rules and administers the empire; the No. 1 seems secure in his superiority over his potential rivals. Soviet citizens, subject to permanent checks of orthodoxy, exercise no direct influence on the decisions made by their oligarchs.

Almost half a century after the initiation of the first Five-Year Plans, these oligarchs cling loyally to the principles of what Stalin called "building socialism" and what I have called "socialist capital accumulation." The planners, despite their huge bureaucracy, cannot follow what goes on from one end of the Soviet Union to the other, and cannot trace the paths taken by the tens of thousands of different products. Otto Sik once told me that in Czechoslovakia the planners had effective control over about 1200 out of 40,000 products.

The planning of certain "priority sectors," a partial expression of the ambition of achieving Total Planning, does not involve the regular, constant setting of higher growth targets for Sector I.* The one exception to this rule, the 1965-70 plan, did not make itself felt in the results: once again, the "means of production" progressed beyond the pace of consumer goods. Why this obsession with planning? Today this question is more pressing than ever before, and no certain answer is forthcoming.

Especially since 1962, the Soviet leaders have undoubtedly transferred to the realm of armaments the intention (often stated, since 1930) to "catch up and overtake the United States." And one must not forget the discrepancy between the current targets or projections for 1980 and those set for the same date in Nikita Khrushchev's Twenty-Year Plan. Counting the Khrushchev target as 100, today's Brezhnev target would be 48 for electricity, 66 for steel, 60 for natural gas, 67 for coal, 62 for cement, 29 for plastics,

*I sometimes use the Marxist concept of "sector I" to designate the heavy industries or, more generally, those which do not work *directly* for consumption.

48 for synthetic fibres, 73 for cereals, 49 for meat (carcass weight), 54 for milk, 53 for eggs. Today's projections approximate Khrushchev's for only a small number of products—chemical fertilizers (110), crude oil (90), cotton (86), and beets (94).

Soviet growth rate, though still high, is falling, and it is increasingly dependent on Western growth. In the world's fastest-developing industrial sectors over any given period, the Soviet Union consistently lags behind—backwardness of the chemical industry was exposed by Khrushchev, slowness in electronics by Brezhnev—and it is standard Soviet practice to buy up ready-made factories or to have giant auto and truck factories constructed by Western consortiums. In the peak sectors, despite all its efforts, the Soviet Union finds itself being outperformed by the United States.

More generally, all direct evidence and first-hand observations reveal the enormous *irrationality* of socialism, Soviet-style. The irrationality is twofold: centralized authoritarian planning with arbitrary price-setting results in a waste of capital, and in a duplication of grandiose, complex plans, to be left unfinished—for months or years—for lack of a particular raw material.* There is irrationality also within the enterprise itself, in the planning schedule's allocation of various kinds of products which are not actually needed, in the workers' responding to their poor living conditions and authoritarian organization by their "idleness." It is Western capital, technology, and manpower which will build the hotels required for the Moscow Olympics in 1980.

Nevertheless, let us not deny the rise in the Russian people's standard of living over the last fifteen years. Food consumption per capita has changed as follows:† meat consumption has risen from 79 lbs. in 1958 to 117 lbs. in 1973; milk and dairy products from 525 to 677 lbs.; eggs from 108 to 195 (units); vegetables from 156 lbs. to 187 lbs. But potato consumption fell from 331 to 273 lbs., and cereal consumption from 379 to 315 lbs. The increase in high-grade foodstuffs and the decline in other foods (bread and potatoes) follows the Western pattern. All the same, the disastrous harvests of 1972 and 1975 are a keen reminder of the vulnerability of Soviet agriculture to natural hazards.

Similarly, with respect to consumer durable goods, whose expansion was

---

*Cf. Vassily Vassilev, "Rationalité du système économique soviétique" (unpublished), pp. 79, 93, 95. The author uses only Soviet sources. He casts light on the idleness of capital (in other words, the nonemployment of accumulated capital) owing to uncompleted projects or un-availability of manpower on the spot. At the same time, the socialist countries are caught between the high repair costs of obsolete plants and the cost of new capital investment. "So for the USSR, uncompleted construction as a percentage of total annual investment has risen from 69% for the period 1960-65 to 77% in 1973, after a peak of 80% in 1969." Delays in putting projects into action constitute a *new form* of technological unemployment.
†Figures taken from Hough, "The Brezhnev Era," p. 11.

a feature of the 1950-70 phase in Western Europe, the Soviet Union has followed suit but has lagged some distance behind. In 1965, 24% of Russian families owned television sets; by 1974 the number had grown to 70%. The percentage for refrigerators went up from 11 to 56; for washing machines from 21 to 62. Automobiles are still the preserve of a restricted minority. Statistics indicate an improvement in housing conditions, but these still seem rudimentary to observers, even in Moscow.

Estimating in terms of rubles, the real income of urban and rural (*sovkhoz*) wage-earners surpassed the 1913 level probably between 1960 and 1965, rising by 1975 to 165 (1913 = 100), not counting various services provided free or at low cost by the collective.* As for the real income of the average *kolkhoznik*, even today it probably amounts to less than it did in 1913 (not to speak of 1928). These figures are taken from a book written in a neutral style by an economist who, incidentally, foresees a narrowing of the gap between the Soviet and Western European standards of living, and who draws a distinction between real income and standard of living.†

Whether one judges according to technological progress, labor productivity or the standard of living, the Soviet Union does indeed provide object lessons—by demonstrating what *not* to do and by dissipating illusions. Economic success cannot compensate for the loss of freedoms, far from it; this loss has in fact proven itself to be counterproductive. The apparent disorder of the liberal democracies can exist without threatening industrial discipline; bureaucratic despotism, however, cannot: it causes disorganization in the economy as a whole as well as within the individual enterprise. Let us emphasize once again: the essence of the modern economy is *exchange* and, thus, the freedom of individuals; production, on the other hand, involves hierarchy, a partially authoritarian organization. All the régimes of our day involve a tension between freedom (of the market) and discipline (imposed on the workers). The historic aberration of Sovietism stems from the extension of the authoritarianism (partly necessary for production) into the *entire* economy, to the point of elevating it to the position of being a principle of the régime, whereas it ought to constitute only one aspect of the institutional system.

*Figures taken from Jovan Pavlevski, *Le niveau de vie en URSS de la révolution d'octobre à 1980* (Paris: Economica, 1975).

†The real wage per person is not an accurate gauge of the standard of living. The number of salaries per household also has to be taken into account. Man and wife both work in the Soviet Union, which was not the case in tsarist Russia. The *kolkhozniks'* income from the nationalized sector is supplemented by earnings from their private plots (the same goes for a large number of urban workers). The industry of 1976 offers millions of supplementary jobs more differentiated, demanding, and better paid, than did the industry of 1913. Some social services are provided free, others (such as housing) at low cost. In the towns, living conditions have changed too much over the last half century for the comparison of the real wages of 1913 and 1976 to make possible any rigorous evaluation of the rise in living standards.

Inequality and the evolution of the régime

The superiority of the Mixed Economies over Sovietism gives rise, it seems to me, to two objections and to one misunderstanding. It will be objected that *justice* and *equality* have no place in the foregoing analyses, and that my conclusions are based on the latest findings rather than on evolutionary trends; and, on the other side of the coin, that the mediocrity of the Soviets' performance does not necessarily herald the collapse of the Soviet régime (as Emmanuel Todd has suggested*) or the disintegration of the Imperial Zone.

Let us say, for the sake of argument, that the two notions of justice and equality coincide (although I take their identification to be a denial of justice). Do Soviet-type régimes have within themselves less equality, either actual or potential, than do market societies, or even mixed régimes?

Social differentiation—between peasants and urban workers, blue-collar and white-collar workers, party members and nontravelers, the upper levels of the state bureaucracy, the party, the intelligentsia, and the majority—is found in the East just as in the West, in spite of features peculiar to only one type of society or another. Private accumulations of inherited wealth—those of the Rothschilds, the Rockefellers, the Dassaults—do not exist on the far side of the line of demarcation. The privileged own *dachas,* not *châteaux.* In the absence of private ownership of the means of production, and of direct or intermediary ownership of real property, the fortunes of the founder capitalists or the *anciens riches* cannot be restored.

The criterion of inequality most commonly used at present is to compare the average wages of the highest-paid 10% with those of the 10% at the bottom of the hierarchy. This ratio, which in the Stalin era would have been upwards of 7 to 1, is reckoned to have fallen from 4.4 in 1956 to 3.7 in 1964 and 3.2 in 1970.† After taxes, this ratio can be reckoned at 6.7 to 1 in the United States in 1968, as against 3 to 1 for Eastern Europe as a whole.

However approximate these figures may be, there seems to be no doubt that the Soviet leadership, partly for ideological reasons, has set its sights on reducing inequality—or perhaps one should say, on closing the salary range which Stalin had thrown wide open in the period when he was denouncing the "petit bourgeois cult of egalitarianism." During this same era the gap between the average wage of the *sovkhozniks* or *kolkhozniks* and that of urban blue-collar or white-collar workers has also narrowed: the

---

*See Todd's lively, refreshing book *La Chute finale* (Paris: Laffont, 1976).
†These figures are taken from Peter Wiles, "Recent Data on Soviet Income Distribution," *Survey,* Summer 1976. The *kolkhozniks* and *sovkhozniks* are not included.

average wage of *sovkhozniks* has been estimated to have risen from 59% of the average urban wage in 1960 to 77% in 1973; the equivalent rise for the *kolkhoznik* over the same period was from 31 to 56%.*

In addition to the disparity between rural and urban workers' incomes, there is a further disparity in the earnings of *kolkhozniks* from one republic to the next, and still more between different districts of the same republic. The pay per working *kolkhoznik* varies from 188 rubles in the Turkmen Republic (USSR = 100) to 64 rubles in Belorussia.† In 1965, the daily wages on *sovkhozes* had the following distribution: 11.1% of *kolkhozniks* received less than 1 ruble; 3.8% received 1 ruble; 10.2% from 1 to 1.5 rubles; 19.1% from 1.5 to 2 rubles; 55.8% more than 2 rubles (in other words, more than $2.30 a day).

This trend towards reducing the wage range does not involve reducing the material and moral advantages enjoyed by party members, especially of the top managers. Their accommodation, their cars, their access to shops reserved for the dignitaries of the régime, all create a gulf between the privileged and the many. The income difference does not fully reflect the difference in living conditions. The isolation of the elite, in the strict sense of that term, the concentration of these VIPs in particular neighborhoods, and the closeness of the *dachas* where they gather together again when they go outside the capital—all these factors prompt many writers to employ the notion of *caste* rather than class. In the structure of Soviet societies, two distinctions appear to be crucial: between rural and urban workers, and between the mass of the population and the Power Elite (an expression which I prefer to that of Djilas's New Class).

Since the early 1960s, the Soviet leadership has made pronounced efforts to lessen the gap in living standards between blue-collar and white-collar workers, on the one hand, and *kolkhozniks* and *sovkhozniks,* on the other. Today, in spite of everything, the gap is almost as great as it was more than sixty years ago, under the tsarist régime—1.8 (instead of 2) to 1.‡ Add to this the fact that, even now, about 27% of peasant earnings is derived from work done on their private plots (although the authorities have been trying, by paying more for collective labor, to reduce the amount of private work). Also, two fifths of non-farmworkers own individual allotments and account for almost 50% of private fruit and vegetable production.

The heterogeneity of the Soviet republics which, together, make up one great continuous terrestrial empire is also, and quite naturally, reflected in differences in ways of life and—to express it quantitatively—in inequality. The main feature of the post-Stalin period is that the state and party

*These figures are taken from Pavlevski, *Le niveau de vie en URSS*, who uses mainly the official (and therefore dubious) Soviet statistics.

†Ibid., p. 155.

‡Ibid., p. 163.

leadership has been observing a policy of reducing the inequalities among the various working categories (blue- and white-collar workers, non-manual workers, and various grades of technicians), without, however, so much as touching upon the many material and moral advantages of the small minority, between a half and three fourths of a million, which constitutes the elite in the strict sense used by Pareto.*

Compared with the equivalent minority in the Western countries, that of the Soviet Union appears less wealthy, and also more remote from the masses. The members of this elite have the benefit of supplementary incomes over and above their salaries: they have access to exclusive commercial channels selling luxury goods, usually imported; they are better housed; they are cared for by special doctors; they have the best chance of buying a car for their private use, of taking a vacation or getting a room in the best hotels. Having said all that, the rich of the United States (two thousandths of the taxpayers) enjoy incomes which in absolute or relative terms far exceed those of the Soviet "rich," whose wealth, being a function of their position and their orthodoxy, is less secure and less transferable. Not that there is equal opportunity in the Soviet Union—the few available statistics on the social background of students dispel that illusion. The differentiation of primary and secondary schools in town and country and from province to province rules out any "equality of opportunity" as between the son of a Central Asian *kolkhoznik* and a Central Committee member—and that is not to mention the inevitable influence of "recommendations" from VIPs when it comes to the university entrance exam which will decide those sons' future.

Egalitarian ideology and the absolute power of the party are reconciled in this way: the ratio of the average income of the upper and lower decile, which was greater than 7 to 1 in 1946, has been brought down to about 5 to 1 (3.2 in 1970, according to Peter Wiles).† This is appreciably less, by about a half, than the same ratio in the United States (6.7 to 1 in 1968), or in Italy and Canada (5.9 to 1 in 1968 and in 1972, respectively). The regional inequalities in the USSR may well be due to the size of families. Thus, although incomes per *kolkhoznik* unit seem greater in the Asiatic republics, the "net material product"—a Soviet term comparable in meaning, but not identical, with the national per capita income—suggests inequality at the expense of the ethnically different republics of Asia. The Russian and Ukrainian republics (111 and 96.9) come after the three Baltic states (112, 131, 133), with the Asian republics showing indices of between 60 and 80 (100 for the entire Soviet Union).

---

*Vilfredo Pareto, "Top Incomes in the USSR. Towards a definition of the Soviet elite," *Survey*, Summer 1975.

†This ratio does not apply to the *kolkhozniks* and *sovkhozniks*.

Together with this effort to reduce inequality of incomes, an attempt is made to raise the living standard of the entire population, including that of the peasants. Certainly it remains undeniable and surprising that the Soviet Union, producing as much or more steel than the United States, should still be housing and feeding its citizens or subjects so poorly. The USSR continues to devote 30% of its national income to investment, some 63% of which goes into so-called productive investment (essentially materials). The defense budget takes a 10-15% share—it is difficult to estimate—of the national product. The division of investment among the various sectors has not changed appreciably between the first Five-Year Plans and those of today, apart from fluctuations in the amount absorbed by agriculture and increased investment in construction.* Heavy industry received 32% of investment during the first Five-Year Plan and 30% in 1972 and 1973, while group B (the Marxist sector II) received only 4.9% in 1973 as against 6.3% during the first Five-Year Plan. The agricultural investment quota has gone up from 15.1% during the first Five-Year Plan to 20.5% in 1973, and the construction industry has increased its share from 0.9% during the first Five-Year Plan to 3.7% today. On the other hand, construction itself (for both industry and housing) is still, at 15.3%, on a level comparable with the 1930s (although the percentage for housing construction should be greater than that for the building of factories).

Likewise, the financing of socialist accumulation continues to obey the same principles. Turnover tax (i.e., the tax paid on all consumer purchases, which the planners raise or lower according to the availability of a given commodity, or their wish to reduce or increase its consumption) still accounts for over 30% of total state receipts, although the percentage has been falling (58.7 in 1940, 40.7 in 1960, 31.5 in 1970). On the other hand, the levy on the profits of enterprises has risen from 12.1% in 1940 to 32% in 1973.† This divergent evolution of the share of the turnover tax and of the profits levy explains the unquestionable rise in the Soviet standard of living.

Twenty years ago, at the time when I was teaching courses on Industrial Society at the Sorbonne, I spoke out both against the optimism of those who were forecasting affluence and liberalization in the Soviet régime and against the pessimism of those who were applying to the Soviet Union a Marxist-derived thesis of pauperization. Up to now, the facts have confirmed these moderate or intermediary expectations: the consumer durables—radios, television sets, to a lesser extent refrigerators and washing machines, and to a still lesser extent private cars—are finding their way into Soviet society. That society is proceeding, some distance behind,

*Vassilev, "Nationalité," pp. 24-25. These figures are taken from official Soviet statistics, so they indicate trends without having any claim to exactitude.
†ibid., p. 37.

along the road laid out by the European economy, just as Soviet industry—in the case of chemicals, electronics, data processing, and most new types of weaponry—is struggling, vainly, to overtake the industry of the United States.

In certain sectors, the gap between East and West has a natural tendency to narrow. When 80 to 90% of Western households have radio, TV, refrigerator and washing machine, this percentage does not increase much further, and additional income is spent on leisure and vacations. Similarly, there is a limit to the productivity of American agriculture, and the progress of Soviet agriculture, slow as it may be, will eventually close part of the gap.* Nevertheless, extrapolation of Soviet progress or the growth rate of the national product, disregarding population movement and the number of people employed, produces results which are meaningless because they are arrived at by an erroneous method.

Soviet growth results from the accumulation of fixed capital and mobilization of the work force. It is quantitative rather than qualitative, extensive rather than intensive. The apparent increase in labor productivity is the product of the increasing value of the capital employed by each worker. By the same token, the productivity of capital is decreasing. The overcapitalization—accumulation of dead labor—in which Marx saw the cause of the declining profitability of capital—is indeed happening, but in the *Soviet* economy. This is understandable, because the Soviet model is derived from a crude transposition of the "expanded reproduction" of *Capital*. According to the model, this was supposed to lead to an excess of constant capital and its declining profitability. In the Soviet Union this decline is explained, not by the fact that surplus value is raised only on dead labor (or constant capital), but by poor allocation of resources, excessive heavy industry investment, and the priority maintained for sector I. Furthermore, the planners have *no valid criterion* of profitability available, because this depends on prices, and the prices, in turn, depend on the planners, through the medium of their control of turnover tax. The meat industry is particularly profitable because the planners want meat to be expensive.

The nature of Soviet growth—accumulation of constant capital and mobilization of workers—affords a simple explanation of the fall of the growth rate in the course of the last Five-Year Plan and the more modest targets set for the plan for 1975-80. During the period 1965-70 the work force (not including agriculture) had grown by 19% and the industrial work force by 15%; the plan for 1970-75 forecast respective growth rates of 13 and 6.5% for these two quantities.

Achieving the plan would therefore have demanded an improved growth

---

*But by using three or four times the manpower.

rate for labor productivity and better utilization of existing capital. That is to say, as manpower reserves dwindled, intensive growth would have to take over from extensive growth, so that the fall in capital profitability could be halted, or else, in nontechnical terms, there would have to be an improvement in the organization of enterprises and the choice of investments, allowing progress to be achieved by means of Western-style rationalization.

The plan for 1980 calls for a 24-28% rise in the national income above the 1975 level, compared with the 38% target and 28% achievement of the previous Five-Year Plan. For industrial production the corresponding figures are 35-39, 47, and 43; for industrial consumer production 30-32, 48.6, and 37; for agricultural production 14-17, 23, and 13; and for the value of retail sales 27-29, 41.8, and 35. The 1975-80 plan is less ambitious than the one for 1970-75, with targets lower than either the targets or the achievements of that plan. Even this more modest plan was to run into obstacles, because it once again presupposed an increase in the productivity of the combined capital-labor factors.

Dubbed the "quality plan" (quality of products and quality of the organization and technique of production), nevertheless it depends yet again on capital accumulation in industry (40% between 1976 and 1980 as against 47% in 1973-75): the forecast annual growth of the industrial work force amounts to 1% as against 1.3% in 1970-75. Similarly, the forecast growth for agriculture amounts to only 14-17% compared with the 23% forecast (and 13% achieved) in the previous plan. The disastrous harvests of 1972 and especially of 1975 (a shortfall of 90 million tons of grain) are reminder enough that the Five-Year Plans have even less influence on Soviet weather than on Soviet enterprises.

The Soviet Union and Eastern Europe

Why is there speculation today about Soviet growth in the near future? Because the absurdness of the régime is waxing and the resources necessary for the planners are waning. Why go on pursuing the kind of growth which means piling up more factories and more constant capital and mobilizing more workers, when manpower reserves are shrinking and the return on capital continually falling? The Soviet planners and their economic advisers keep harping on the theme that it is necessary to replace *extensive* by *intensive* growth, and to make the shift "from quantity to quality." Well, fine, but how do you make that shift so long as investment is confused with growth, and so long as the régime clings to authoritarian centralization of management and refuses to restore freedom to the peasantry and initiative to the heads of enterprises, robbing them of the incentive to work?

The Soviet Union enjoys a great deal of aid from the West—the absence of which, in 1972 and 1975, would have been sorely felt. The Americans provide the missing wheat, and European capitalists fall over each other for the honor of building the factories that make trucks, automobiles, cement or aluminum for the homeland of socialism. Despite the high quality of its scientists and engineers, the USSR finds itself hopelessly behind in the technological progress race—except, perhaps, in the armaments category.

Western aid does not and cannot suffice. The greatest contribution to economic growth, other than the items of capital and labor, comes from what is often called "the residual factor," that is, a better organization, a better combination of the factors of production. Now the very thing that the Soviet system and régime eliminate or whittle down to a minimum is this same residual factor, the *quality of organization and labor*. The over-staffing hailed by the *Intourist* guide as the "achievement" of socialism symbolizes the failure of a system and a régime. These are the elements of that superpower's failure: 1) insufficient business autonomy; 2) authoritar-ian planning from the top, which, in the last analysis, controls only part of the economy but sows confusion throughout; 3) freak prices, which do not allow for rational allocation of resourcs and which encourage the planners to persist in their errors, particularly in overinvestment; 4) the waste and underuse of constant capital, which leads to the "idleness" of the workers; 5) low capital productivity; and 6) a level of technical-economic inefficiency that, were it ever to become known in the world, would become a standing joke.

In Eastern Europe, the Soviet standard of living is at the bottom of the scale, far below that of East Germany, of Czechoslovakia, even of Hun-gary. I have in front of me a study by the *Deutsches Institut für Wirtschaftsforschung* (No. 108, 1975), which gives figures on East Euro-pean living standards for 1972-73. With the GDR equal to 100, the figure for individual consumption stands at 81 for Czechoslovakia, 69 for Hun-gary, 65 for Poland, 56 for Bulgaria, 50 for the USSR, and 44 for Romania. The corresponding figures for monthly wages are 83, 65, 62, 61, 51, and 64; for meat consumption 104, 85, 96, 70, 70, and 70; for television sets 108, 83, 74, 74, 73, and 38; for private automobiles 98, 56, 37, 56, 20, and 18. Never let it be said that the socialist states reject the private car, and that demand for it is artificially created by media which are "slaves to the cash nexus" (as Maurice Duverger would say). In the GDR, 21.4 out of every 100 households own a car; in Czechoslovakia 20.9; in Hungary 11.9; in Bulgaria 11.8; in Poland 8.0; and in the USSR 4.2*.

---

*More detailed figures are provided in the Appendix, Note D.

The most casual visitor to Eastern Europe knows that the social climate in Hungary or Poland is subtly different from what it is in Russia. In Warsaw, a Frenchman feels that he is still in the West, in a country with a different but closely related culture. In Moscow he is somewhere else. To me it has always seemed obvious, although often unrecognized, that only the Soviet Union provides the ideal full-scale model of the *deliberately* totalitarian régime, with a single party and centralized authoritarian planning. It was only in the Stalin period that the Marxist-Leninist parties of Eastern Europe each made their own special effort to turn themselves into small-scale Soviet Unions. The difficulty does not lie in listing the divers causes of the differences, but in giving each of these its true weight.

Not one of the Eastern European countries made a voluntary choice of its fate, its political or economic régime. Except in the USSR, this did not emerge from a national or popular revolution but was imposed by the Red Army and by Communist émigrés returning home in the Red Army's baggage cars. In Czechoslovakia, a country deceived by the West, the masses did play a semi-spontaneous part in the 1948 coup; it took Russian tanks to restore Soviet order in Prague in 1968. The régime of the GDR, economically the most efficient in Eastern Europe, created by the victorious Russians, nevertheless confines all its citizens behind the Berlin Wall which also cuts the capital of the old *Reich* in two.

Since destalinization, the rulers of Eastern Europe have gradually acquired a certain legitimacy, both by improving economic performances and by playing a double game with the Soviet leadership and their own peoples. The Hungarians do not regard János Kádár as another Rákosi, and they worry about who may succeed him. Even Gierek, whose power is backed by Russian tanks, seeks a national legitimacy by responding to the longings of the Polish nation. Neither in Hungary nor Poland can one seriously talk about "totalitarianism," if by that word one means granting a sort of monopoly to an ideology. The economists do not teach Marxism-Leninism, nor do the sociologists replace reality with an official super-reality. They observe, analyze, and explain the social differentiation in the so-called socialist states, while taking care not to overstep the tolerated limits.

The degree of political-ideological liberalization, as well as the extent of economic reform—decentralization, business autonomy, rationalization of the pricing system—varies from one country to the next. Economic efficiency appears to depend not so much on political liberalization as on managerial reforms. It might be objected that Czechoslovakia, Hungary, and the GDR had a head start (which is undeniably true of Czechoslovakia, but not of the other two) but, on the other hand, *every one* of the countries of Eastern Europe has manifold advantages over the Soviet Union. None of them went about collectivizing agriculture by such cruel and ruinous methods. Only the Soviet Union physically eliminated the *kulaks* and thereby, inevitably, many of the most active and educated peasants. Only the Soviet Union spent thirty years enforcing low-paid work for the collective. Only Moscow's Marxist-Leninists have waged virtual war against the peasants, and still today they saddle the *kolkhozes* and *sovkhozes* with an administrative staff more representative of the Enemy State than of the rural workers' aspirations.

Secondly, planning a small country does not involve the same difficulties as planning an immense multinational empire. The overall figures for the Soviet Union as a whole are not fully comparable with the figures for Hungary or Czechoslovakia. If the rulers of the empire have been trying to prevent too great a disparity of development between the various republics, this might go some way toward explaining performances inferior to those of homogeneous European states.

Thirdly—and this seems to me to be the major reason why the USSR lags behind its comrade states—the Soviet planners have locked themselves into a kind of vicious circle. For half a century, they have known only one method of growth: more and more permanent productive capital, more and more workers. They are not unaware of the declining profitability of their investments and the importance of increasing the "residual factor" and of improving the profitability of enterprises. Probably they are even aware that the solution lies along the road indicated by the reforms associated with the name of their own Professor Liebermann—decentralization; greater autonomy for enterprises; and reinforcing the role of the monetary indicators. But the reforms attempted in the 1960s have been lost in the shifting sands of bureaucracy. For the period 1975–80, the planners are stressing the priority of capital accumulation more strongly than they did for the previous five years. The distributed buying power will grow faster than the goods available, at imposed prices, and disorderly distribution and shoppers' waiting lines will exist, as before.

What are the lessons to be drawn from the contrast between the Soviet Union and the People's Democracies? Is it the Russian tradition—ideological blinkers and the "will for empire"—which must bear the blame for that caricature of socialism, Sovietism? Let us once again recall the uncertainties of the historical accusation.

The People's Democracies definitely enjoy a threefold advantage over the Soviet Union: by their size they make the planners' job easier; it is the Soviet Union that pays the costs of supermilitarization and the maintenance of the international order; and the leaders ("slave-princes," to use the Reverend Father Fessard's term) do not seal themselves off from the lessons of experience: they innovate more readily, precisely because their orthodoxy has been imposed on them from abroad.

Sovietism therefore definitely contains elements some of which date back to the heritage of Stalinism, others to the specific experience of the Bolshevik movement. In all the socialisms of the European East we find the same minority of party dignitaries or the social elite—a minority which tends to keep aloof from the mass and to reserve certain "caste privileges" for itself (in addition to the advantages guaranteed for all ruling minorities by their higher incomes). But in none of the People's Democracies, so far as one can tell, is the sense of socio-bureaucratic hierarchy taken to such an extreme. Anyone who has had the slightest dealings with Soviet Russians (at international conferences, for instance) cannot fail to have been struck by the pervasiveness of hierarchic differentiation. Everybody gets a reception geared to the person's rank in the eyes of the Soviets. This obsession with one's rank, and with that of others, diminishes as soon as one leaves the Soviet Union. These notions, crude and approximate though they may be, do suggest one major fact: while Poland and Hungary were, and still are, a part of European culture, it was not until the early eighteenth century (and then by decree of its sovereign) that Russia entered the family of European states. On the eve of World War I, most of the social and intellectual elite (to which the Bolsheviks did not belong) were looking to Europe for inspiration for the reforms needed by the tsarist empire. Although Lenin was outwardly a Westernizer, his victory meant the *withdrawal* of Holy Russia into itself. The new masters borrowed Western technology as best they could, but they rejected as "bourgeois" or "capitalist" the virtues of European civilization—freedom of persons and ideas, and the continual reexamination of theories and practices—which are responsible for the instability, but also the richness, of that civilization.

The aberration which gave rise to Marxism-Leninism—the simultaneous rejection of private ownership and of market forces—represents (together with the illusion of eliminating poverty and inequality) the extreme caricatural form of Western self-criticism. Europe has always had its true believers. It has them still today. A few Germans paved the way, in deadly earnest, for bolshevism; a few Parisian intellectuals, in levity or ignorance, have been tending the dying flame for the past twenty-five years. Viewed in the intellectual context of Europe and the West, the Marxism-Leninism of strict observance, despite a few spectacular individual converts, does not rise above the scale or dignity of a sect—and one which is more bizarre than impressive. The electoral successes of the Italian Communist party and the entrenchment already under way in some towns and provinces are reminders of the danger. All the same, I doubt whether the Italian people, or even the party leadership, could claim the fifty years of blind faith and unflinching loyalty to that system of thought and action which are professed by the Marxist-Leninists of Moscow.

Having said all that, and after making the most generous allowance for the effect of specifically Russian factors, there are no grounds for thinking that the leadership of the Hungarian, Polish or Czech parties, once freed from the influence of Soviet Russia, would convert to freedom of their own accord and give up all or even part of their power. As long as the Red Army's tanks are there to assure their rule in perpetuity, they improve their brand image in the eyes of the governed, acquiring a partial legitimacy through a few concessions to the popular will and a few ideological violations. What would happen once they were left to their own devices is anybody's guess. What is beyond doubt is that none of the Marxist-Leninist parties of Eastern Europe would cling so tenaciously to a model of growth which, in the long run, is self-paralyzing. In this sense—this limited sense— Sovietism is not identical with socialism, not even with the socialism sired by Marxism-Leninism—which does not, however, mean that we can ignore the heritage bequeathed to us through the exploits and crimes of Lenin and his partisans.

Social democracy and the nondoctrinal socialisms

Socialism, as a concept, has lost all precise meaning, and some of its opponents replace it by the word *collectivism,* a term more likely to provoke feelings of fear and hostility. Whatever the intentions of such a choice of vocabulary, it seems to me that the ambiguity of the word *socialism* is quite undeniable.

The first ambiguity, as I have frequently stated, concerns the failure to distinguish between *ownership* (public or private) and the *régime* (planned or market). Here a further ambiguity arises, which has to do with the number and diversity of the societies and régimes claiming allegiance to socialism. Because of this, there is *no working model* of society which can be called "social democratic," any more than there is one which can be called "socialist." There does exist a Soviet growth model whose main features I have outlined in the foregoing chapters, a model historically inseparable from one-party rule and Marxist-Leninist ideology. There also exist countries, in Europe, which have been governed by social democrats for some time, and which continue to belong both to the world capitalist market and to the sphere of liberal civilization. Lastly, there exist any number of Third World countries which style themselves "socialist" and whose institutions are extremely heterogeneous.

Of the two characteristics that define a national economy—the modes of *ownership* and of *administration*—economic thinking has long given priority to the former, because it has not truly understood the constraints of economic calculation and the complexity of allocating resources. Opinion, which is sometimes the prisoner of prejudices stemming from an outdated climate of thought, often continues to give pride of place to the legal or substantive formula of ownership.

If we address ourselves to the modes of *administration*, we shall search in vain for a "social democratic" economy. French opinion, both of the Left and the Right, tends to refer to the "Swedish model." Now Sweden affords what is probably the most highly developed example of a fiscal system designed to redistribute the national income and of social legislation protecting the individual against every risk from cradle to grave. Some see this as an example of the "tutelary despotism" described with horror by Alexis de Tocqueville. * Others take the opposite view and see it as an effective, if as yet unfinished, liberal revolution. † Neither side denies or overlooks the fact that the Social Democrats who governed uninterruptedly for forty-four years did not proceed with any nationalization of the means of production out of *doctrinal* principle, that it was mainly concerned with *technical efficiency,* and that it respected the authority of private management and kept open frontiers. Putting it briefly, the Swedish price system retained close ties with that of the world market. The tax system was aimed more at individuals than at businesses. Furthermore, Sweden's spearhead industries (those which are influential abroad, which create subsidiaries, and which bring in foreign currency) are more concentrated than in most other Western countries. In Marxist-Leninist terminology, Sweden's is a "monopolistic capitalism," since a dozen or so families, with worldwide influence, control the firms.

For the rest, the originality of Sweden derives from a *consensus* which critics regard as *conformism*, with socialization starting in primary school and ceaselessly, endlessly, proceeding. The concept of life or the value system—adaptation to the community, rejection of the tragic and the sacred, rational pragmatism, sexuality reduced to a biological function to be duly shorn of its charm and mystery, in other words, removal of the world's enchantment (but with comfort and security)—gradually filters into the general consciousness. The trade unionists and monopolists share the same concern with efficiency, and both are organized into confederations run by a handful of people. The progressive transfer of business ownership to the trade unions, which was part of Olof Palme's program, was momentarily averted by the defeat of the Social Democratic party in the 1976 elections. Various modes of participation—for instance trade union representation on boards of directors—have become customary without arousing protest or conflict, so readily do the representatives of the various classes or class organizations think within the same categories.

New Left critic Gabriel Ardant is quite entitled to find fault with the

*Roland Huntford, *The New Totalitarians* (London: Allan Lane, 1972).
†Gabriel Ardant, *La révolution suédoise* (Paris: Laffont, 1976).

Swedish Social Democrats' continued display of trust in "market mechanisms" and to deplore the persistence of a class structure*—features that define so-called consumer societies.

Cardiac illnesses, more widespread among members of the ruling classes, are the sign of a society generating constant tensions. Is it any consolation for a man threatened by heart trouble to tell himself that his widow's coat will be mink? To sum up, to *destroy class society* it is necessary to destroy *the consumer society which is at the same time a society of waste, frustration, tension and inflation.* †

The question is, why does a society without tension or conflict appear to Gabriel Ardant to be a human ideal? And does the elimination of the socially recognized hierarchy of values among various sorts of work and the reduction of all objects to a strictly pragmatic function, devoid of all symbolism, accord with the natural order of societies, or even with a desirable order?

Conversely, Roland Huntford is entitled to stigmatize a non-violent, non-torture-using totalitarianism.

The Swedes have demonstrated the power of that form of semantic manipulation Orwell called Newspeak: the changing of words to mean something else . . . "freedom" does not yet in Swedish, as in the brainchild of Orwell's Ministry of Truth, mean exactly "slavery," but it already implies "submission". . . . The ultimate crime in *Brave New World* is to deviate from a norm. That norm is innocent of ethics and morality, and decided on grounds of expediency alone. The situation is already a doctrine of Swedish law. Gone is the idea of right or wrong, or the moral content of an action. Crime is now defined as social deviation. . . . Sweden, like Soviet Russia, belongs to that group of countries in which "individuality" has a derogatory ring.‡

I have no firsthand knowledge of Sweden, and I leave it to the reader to choose between the Frenchman who records and deplores the arrested halfway development toward leveling (up to the highest level, of course) and the English journalist who presents Sweden as a medieval relic, extraordinarily backward except in the technological field. Certain features of the Swedish mentality (for example, the "abolition of history") occur as trends elsewhere. In any case, there is no avoiding the comparison imposed by the similarities between the tutelary despotism described by Tocqueville and the Swedish reality described by even well-disposed observers, albeit with some reservations.

The term "social democracy" thus designates no definite economic or social model. The distinction between social democracy and socialism has

---

*Of the young people of twenty undertaking higher studies, 80% belong to social group I (the "highest"), and only 10% to social group III (working-class backgrounds). Ardant, p. 226.
†Ibid., p. 233.
‡Huntford, *The New Totalitarians*, p. 12.

lost all precise significance, in that one of the two terms no longer has any significance at all. What sort of vague idea is being put forward when someone asserts, as did Mario Soarès, that social democracy is not suitable for a relatively underdeveloped country like Portugal?

As far as I can judge, social democracy is credited with redistribution of the national product by fiscal means, the Welfare State, and generous social legislation. Now all these measures presuppose a national per-capita product on which to raise the sums necessary for transferring social wealth without impeding investment. Perhaps the Portuguese prime minister was alluding to the divergence between a policy of distribution, characteristic of worker movements, and the productivism required by poor countries for "takeoff." Perhaps he also has in mind the more or less extended functions of the state and the nationalization of some firms.

None of these characteristics suffices to indicate a clear, distinct contrast between two ideal types. Of the states of Western Europe, the France of the Fifth Republic, a pluralist democracy, remains economically the least liberal and the most *dirigiste* and bureaucratic. Every plan for stabilization provides the opportunity or excuse for a price freeze. Public ownership covers a greater area of industry and the public services than in West Germany. The rulers follow an industrial policy—concentration of firms, development of growth sectors—which is more determined, if not more effective, than in West Germany. The Swedish governing powers who managed capitalism for forty-four years never neglected efficiency of labor and organization; furthermore, the quasi-moral value they attached to adapting the individual to the requirements of the community may be taken as a way of increasing productivity as well as constituting a social end. France, on the other hand, combines a tradition of centralized quasi-authoritarian bureaucracy with a citizenry permanently up in arms against the state.

We are dealing here with a diversity of style and of culture, with the particular stamp impressed by each of the nations of Europe on relations among individuals, and between individuals and institutions. If one singles out only the two major characteristics of an economic régime in a developed Western European economy in the course of the last thirty years, one will labor in vain to find a contrast between the countries dominated by social democracy and those seeking or finding socialism. All the countries of Western Europe are open to the outside world and subject to market mechanisms more or less manipulated by the state and the big employer and trade union oligopolies. All the governments accept their responsibilities as regards the world balance of power, the handling of the economy (combating inflation or depression), social legislation, and the alleviation of damage done by haphazard circumstances of any kind to the interests of a given group. Differences from one country to another depend more on the degree of success or failure than on doctrine, and possibly on the priorities which governments allocate to one target rather than another (the West Germans emphasizing stable prices, the French expansion).

Does the term "socialism," applied to most Third World states and usually proclaimed by its spokesmen, designate any definite economic, political or social system? I think not. Just as most of the developing countries like to call themselves *nonaligned,* they readily call themselves *socialist.* By nonalignment they display their determination not to side with either the Soviet or the Western bloc. But it is hard to see why the countries of Africa, Asia or Latin America should in fact take sides in this historic rivalry, unless threatened from within or without by the United States or the Soviet Union. Their professions of socialist faith are like the declarations of nonalignment: they express, or are meant to express, the twofold rejection of liberal capitalism and democratic pluralism on the one hand, and Sovietism on the other.

In actual fact, the so-called socialist régimes of the Third World do not belong to either of the two types which continue in spite of everything to oppose and vie with each other in Europe. Only the states ruled by Marxist-Leninist parties—North Korea, Vietnam, Cambodia, probably Laos, and Cuba—practice what has to be termed Sovietism. All these states have in common various features derived from the Soviet model: military labor discipline is present in the Cuban sugarcane fields just as much as in the factories of North Korea. Ubiquity of ideology and of police control occurs in every climate, among peoples previously known for their easy-going way of life just as among those who—like the North Vietnamese—have displayed their fighting spirit and fierce resistance to outside pressures all down the centuries. There is no doubt that the countries conquered by the Marxist-Leninists, or converted to the faith of these New Believers, will gradually develop in accordance with their own nature. The differentiation observable in Eastern Europe will also emerge on the other continents. The fact remains that the first phase of a Marxist-Leninist régime always seems to follow various similar, if not identical, patterns. The single party, armed with its own ideology, utterly expunges any other way of thinking and any other account of the world; the truth is vested in the party; reeducation or concentration camps absorb a greater or lesser number of the old upper class, deviationists, and counter-revolutionaries; the planners draw on the Soviet model for their target of faster growth and often for the granting of priority to heavy industry. Yet, after the break with Moscow in the early 1960s, China popularized a different model of economic growth based on the same politico-ideological régime model. So it may be that the "export version" of economic Sovietism no longer entails the same priorities, or at any rate no longer applies these priorities with the same rigor as in the USSR.

In some African countries, Sovietism lends the model a language rather than a practice. Guinea had none of the human or material means necessary to economic Sovietism. Similarly, it is hard to see Angola building an economy or even a state comparable to those of Vietnam or Korea—unless the institutions of Soviet Angola are to be built, if not by the Russians (which would probably cause rejection symptoms), then at least by the Cubans, who stand a better chance of gaining acceptance by the people and leadership of the former Portuguese province.

The non-Marxist-Leninist socialism of the Third World is not tied to any doctrine and displays none of the features ascribed to the post-capitalist system by the prophets of the nineteenth and twentieth century: not Tocqueville's tutelary despotism, nor Huxley's brave new world, nor Trotsky's reign of abundance, nor any egalitarian liberal community. Politically, the socialisms of the Third World reject institutional pluralism, more by necessity than principle. With a very few exceptions, none has succeeded in maintaining a system based on competition between parties. (France is having a hard enough time doing that, even today, so that we cannot look down, with a superior attitude, in passing judgment on what some regard as a failure, others as a rejection.)

In most of Africa, Latin America, and Asia the state and its privileges are more or less monopolized by a party composed of either civilians or soldiers, based either on a privileged group or on a rising class. The transfer of power from one group to another is more often the outcome of a *coup d'état* than an election. The masters of the state nearly always see themselves as "modernizers"; in this sense, they take their inspiration from one of the ruling Bolshevik ideas. On the other hand, they do not invoke any all-embracing ideology, and the future they unveil to the faithful—national greatness or higher living standards—does not affect the whole of humanity and promises no transfiguration of historical destiny.

In the same way, in economic terms these self-styled socialist states tend neither toward wholesale Soviet-type planning nor toward the modern liberalism of Western Europe. They exercise direct control over an area of industry, operate a "voluntarist" development policy, and protect their home market to a varying extent in the interest of fledgling industries. Depending on the country or the moment, these states encourage more (or less) foreign investment, restrict (or enlarge) the area open to private enterprise, refuse (or accept) integration with the world economy. South Korea stands at the liberal extreme, Algeria—to judge by its leaders' statements and the role of state decisions in economic development—at the other. But does the Egypt of President Sadat warrant the "socialist" label much more than the Korea of General Park? The one is more successful than the other, but its circumstances are quite different, and more favorable, as well. Putting it briefly, there is no single model typical of the

Third World, only a multitude of compromises between the various development strategies and the various administrative methods.

Let us take a flight of fancy and imagine that tomorrow, to everyone's surprise, the First Secretary of the Politburo of the USSR announces a new economic policy: not a forced retreat, as Lenin's NEP was, but a stage along the road to communism allowing individual initiative and administrative self-government within the collectives.

The sacred principles—"collective ownership of agriculture and industry"—remain intact and inviolable, but the "associated producers" grant each other freedom of entrepreneurial action and commercial exchange. The *kolkhozniks* elect their own administrators who, being trusted by everyone, determine the division of labor between the collective and the private plot. Dealers buy all or part of the harvests, legally, and the state, as a representative of the people as a whole, participates in the market merely as one buyer among many. In the same way, businesses—now recognized as "associated producer units"—enjoy a broad degree of autonomy with respect to organization, prices, and investment, within the guidelines set by the party. "Planning schedules"—heretofore a permanent cause of dispute among managers and bureaucrats—disappear. The state receives most of the business profits, with a portion being set aside for the party personnel, all the way up and down the ladder. The commercial mode, justly condemned by Marx when it allowed the proletariat to be exploited by the owners of the means of production, changes its nature when it works in favor of the flourishing of socialism—"to each according to his work." And producers associate for the purpose of increasing their contribution to the common task and being paid in proportion.

I do not doubt—and I know scarcely a single analyst of the Soviet economy who does—that within ten years after this happened, Soviet industry would overcome its technological lag and the consumer would be at the forefront of the socialist community, with better to come.*

In other words, the Soviet Union—after sixty years, and untold hardships—has today the material and human equipment necessary to provide butter as well as guns, a higher living standard as well as power. With the present régime, it is not doomed to any "final fall," and will continue to advance, but more and more slowly, and—except in a few favored sectors (particularly armaments)—it will not overtake the West, which goes on innovating despite, or because of, its crises. Prosperity (in the absence of abundance) is now within reach, but also unreachable: it would require the Kremlin leadership to take a "leap in the dark," to

---

*It goes without saying that the foregoing sketch of economic liberalization does not define a particular régime. All sorts of versions would be possible.

sacrifice some of its prejudices, and to upend the power of the settled bureaucracy.

At the point now reached by the Soviet economy, capital accumulation in the primitive form of the Five-Year Plans is becoming absurd. The official economists themselves are saying that giving up certain plans, completing some unfinished ones, and conspicuously reducing accumulation would all accelerate growth. Similarly, the politicians as well as the experts keep repeating that the 1975–80 plan must strive for quality, for the application to production as a whole of what "the other Europe" calls the *scientific-technical revolution*.

But why should the order of tomorrow be different than the one of yesterday? The "plan for quality" calls for an official reassigning of priority to heavy industry, to that which produces the means of production. Indeed, the heavy industry which turns out fertilizers for agriculture does work, in the final analysis, for the consumer. But would it not be cheaper to give the *kolkhozniks* an incentive for not leaving part of the crop to rot where it lies? In the state enterprises, that which slows down technical advance is the absence of risk-taking, the risk firstly of not fulfilling the plan, secondly of having the scheduled quotas raised when the planners discover the greater efficiency of the new machinery. An economy which is at once modern *and* bureaucratic suffers from a major contradiction: all bureacracies fear change, but a twentieth-century industry can only keep ahead by innovation. The Soviets, even with Western aid, are not resolving this contradiction.

Certainly, apart from the drastic jolt that would result from changing the commercial "minus" to a "plus"—partial reforms in the direction of business autonomy and a bigger role for money and monetary data appear possible, even probable. The Soviet émigrés provide an interesting explanation for the fast ebb of the Russian reforms: the Soviet economy, they say, is much less centrally planned than is realized by the Western experts who, in spite of themselves, are more or less the prisoners of the Soviets' own fictions. The economy would not function, were it not for the "grey" markets, unofficial exchanges between enterprises, and the operations of middlemen. What is the volume of this market, which the authorities have to tolerate (because they recognize its usefulness) and express approval of, from time to time? What profits does it involve? Some insiders give the substantial figure of 25% of the national product as the turnover of this "grey" market—an example of human nature "getting its own" against dogma, and an indispensable complement to a planning system always in arrears of real life. This is what paralyzes reforms, the émigrés say, because it *stands in their stead;* this is the individual's investment in the operation of state enterprises and the régime itself; and this is what turns, occasionally, into corruption or crime.

Of the two bureaucracies—that of the economy and that of the party—the principal fear of the latter is a change which would cast light on its own parasitic character. A régime which gives normal rewards to the associated producers has no need of special police, of an extra ideological framework. As to the economic bureaucracy, at its upper levels, when it draws up its plans and takes note of depleted manpower reserves on the one hand and untapped productivity reserves on the other, it proclaims the new objective: the Quality Plan. This objective may not be fully implemented, but neither will it remain a dead letter.

Every society can live with its own contradictions for a long time, and Soviet society in particular. It would only be threatened by what is at present an unlikely conjunction of the various conceivable crises: serious disagreements within the power elite; massive popular dissatisfaction; active nationalism among the different ethnic communities; and open demands on the part of the intelligentsia. The outside observer would exhibit a strange arrogance if he thought he could predict the short- or medium-term future of Sovietism. But he can, and must, give warning of an *illusion* to which generous spirits succumb: of supposing that *history* is the tribunal before which men and peoples appear. For history has never given a verdict on justice or morality. Its verdicts have always been ambiguous, the justice of which only the victors have been prompt to acclaim.

6
Imperialism without empire

The Third World and the theses of Lenin

The notion of the Third World is now a part of the language, it tends to replace that of "nonalignment," this last being a political or diplomatic idea, whereas the "Third World" notion alludes rather to underdevelopment. The régimes of the two parts of Europe are in opposition to each other—capitalism against socialism or democracy against totalitarian despotism. But the countries of both sides have reached a relatively high level of development, or at least of industrialization. On the other hand, the peoples of South America, Africa, and Southeast Asia—some two billion human beings—remain, so to speak, on the *fringe* of modern civilization.

This inequality between nations which has gradually sprung up in the last two centuries was not really known to Marx, because poverty was so prevalent in the countries now called rich, and particularly in the England which he observed. His Europocentric vision welcomed the spread of capitalism across the other continents. (He tended to overestimate the impact of the capitalist mode of production which British rule transferred onto the traditional society of India. Railways and cotton goods did not, even after some dozens of years, overthrow the caste system or the traditional village way of life.

More than *What Is To Be Done*, it is *Imperialism, the Final Stage of Capitalism* that marks the birth of Marxism-Leninism. The critical analysis of capitalism and its operation is still maintained, but the abstract, ideal-typical history of the mode of production is replaced by a *concrete history,* a theory of the history of Western capitalism; colonial expansion and capital exports are fitted into the same process of development as are the conflicts among the states of the Old Continent. Marx was not unaware of the link between capital accumulation in England and the export of cotton goods to India but, as we have said, he explained Russian, French, and English diplomacy in much the same style as did the classical historians: as territorial ambitions, calculations of relative strength, concern with the balance of power or as the more or less aggressive behavior, on the part of various states, as a function of their political system. He continually castigated Russian imperialism in the ordinary sense of an appetite for expansion and conquest, but how was he to attribute this to a Russian capitalism which had not yet come into existence?

It was during the last decade of the nineteenth century that the various ideas later synthesized by Lenin in his pamphlet—which was as poor scientifically as it was effective as a piece of propaganda—became widespread. Lenin lumped together an explanation of the colonial conquests and conflicts of Europe in terms of the needs of capitalism; he explained European "wealth" in terms of the "exploitation" of the other continents; and he shifted the meaning of the concept of imperialism from the standard one of *conquest and domination* to a vague and grandiose meaning, by equating it with a *world economic system* into which the industrialized countries integrate the other countries, subjecting them to the will of the industrialized nations.

This brings us to the present juncture, where the Third World indicts the Western countries at the same time it asks them for aid. Whatever their past "crimes" may have been, the Western countries do not owe their standard of living to the low cost of raw materials; labor productivity, which is expressed in the GNP per capita, has nothing to do with the gold or diamonds which the invaders removed as the spoils of victory.

The inequality of nations will not disappear because of any negotiations for a new world economic order. It will fade out, little by little, as does inequality within nations. Furthermore, the rise of Japan and the fall of the United Kingdom are reminders to the shallow-minded (who cannot think in terms other than of some determining "system") of the inconstancy of fortune, in both its senses. Wealth, like the favor of destiny, is never permanent.

Lenin, monopoly, capitalism, and imperialism

The ideas adopted by Lenin belong to the spirit of the time. Toward the end of the nineteenth century it became obvious, even to some Marxists, that industrial wages were tending to rise, not fall. Unlike Bernstein and the revisionists, Lenin did not accept that the facts disproved the Marxist thesis of absolute pauperization, but he did, in spite of his attitude, acknowledge the improved condition of a working-class aristocracy, which had a leaning toward reformism and trade unionism, and which was represented by the opportunists within the social democratic parties. Other Marxists, admitting the improved condition of the workers, had put it down to colonial exploitation. Lenin took the same line, arguing that the colonists, by over-exploiting the colonized peoples, were able to reduce the exploitation of a "thin upper crust" of the proletariat.

The scramble for Africa, in the last twenty years of the nineteenth century, struck contemporary observers even more deeply because, simultaneously, the capitalist countries of Western Europe—Great Britain, France, and then Wilhelmine Germany—stepped up their export of capital. Colonization in Africa, the sharing of spheres of influence in Asia, Europe as the world's banker*—these three orders of events appeared to be all of a piece, and bourgeois writers dealt with it quite as much as did the Marxists.

The book which provided Lenin with the greater part of his documentation† was J. A. Hobson's *Imperialism,* first published in 1902. In it, the English economist linked together the themes of colonial conquest and overseas investment. The returns on these investments enabled a growing proportion of the bourgeoisie to live as rentiers. The colonies offered their sons well-paid posts as governors, administrators or officers, while the upper class was becoming parasitic. England carved out its own private preserves, eliminating its competitors; it based its expectation of lasting prosperity on a short-term calculation, assuming the possibility of living off other people's labor and its own investments. By this alone, England was paving the way for decline—without even envisaging the likelihood of military conflicts brought about by imperial monopolizing and the reactions of the other industrial and commercial powers to such brassbound egoism.

In the same pre-1914 era, socialists and sociologists both were debating the same problems: the economic causes of diplomatic and military confrontations; the causes and social consequences of protectionism and the violation of the rules of free trade; and the mechanism of capitalist expansion around the world. Schumpeter analyzed the activities of interest groups, landowners of the East who asked the state for protective tariffs (and got them), and agreements between industrialists who set out to conquer the foreign markets by dumping cheap goods—after sharing out the home market among themselves. But if he saw these contraventions of

*To borrow the title of H. Feis's famous book, *Europe As World Banker,* 1930.

†Together with R. Hilferding's *Das Finanzkapital* (1909).

the rules of free trade and fair competition as the source of certain conflicts which were apt to shift from the economic to the political sphere, it was *not* capitalism as such that he blamed, but rather the survival of ways of thought and behavior which were *contrary* to the spirit of capitalism.

While the sociologists took the ideal type of liberal capitalism as their point of reference and questioned, not capitalism, but the violation of its principles, the socialists took the opposite tack of impeaching certain features of the capitalist system as it had become—in particular, finance capitalism; the domination of the banks over industry; and the quest for surplus profit and opportunities for profitable investments. The socialists Kautsky, Hilferding, and Bukharin were agreed on certain themes, such as that the earth was being shared out among the big financial groups, but they differed on whether this division would lead to inevitable war or to an amicable compromise among national financial groups. Kautsky did not rule out compromise (ultraimperialism), the others leaned in the opposite direction.

Lenin's pamphlet bears the same relation to the literature of imperialism before 1914 as the *Communist Manifesto* does to the socialist or even liberal literature of the first half of the nineteenth century. It does not add a single original idea, but collects some current ideas into a synthesis which stamps certain processes of development with the seal of historical necessity. What was striking for observers in 1848 was the contrast between the development of the productive forces and the extreme poverty of the masses. In the *Manifesto,* Marx and Engels sang the greatness of the conquering bourgeoisie—Prometheus triumphant—and, at the same time, gave notice of the liberating catastrophe to which that "grand adventure" must inexorably lead. Similarly, Lenin—on the outbreak of World War I—took up all the themes of his liberal and socialist predecessors (the export of capital; colonial conquests; spheres of influence; finance capital; industrial cartelization) and knitted them into an historical schema. First, he presented the breakdown of competitive capitalism into monopoly capitalism; then the necessary outward expansion of this "putrefying" capitalism, no matter whether this expansion took the form of outright conquest or economic exploitation; finally, he showed war breaking out in Europe, by chance in the Balkans, with the division of the world as the stake among the principal players. It is the structure of "monopolistic capitalism," involving overseas expansion in the territories (then called colonies and today called the Third World). It is this same structure, combined with the "law of uneven development," that rules out any friendly accord between national interests, and it is the incompatibility between these economic interests that ultimately brings about war to the death—war that is imperialist from every angle, since it is a continuation of the internal policies of the states involved, thus deserving to be lumped together with those imperialistic policies. The states had conducted an imperialist policy before 1914; they continued to do so during the hostilities.

Lenin, following Marx, uses mainly the literature of bourgeois authors. He amasses figures and statistics with the design of demonstrating: 1) the concentration of production, the new role of the banks, the development of finance capital, and the power of the financial oligarchy; 2) the export of capital, seen as the necessary outcome of the structure of monopoly capitalism and finance capitalism, and so the dividing up of the world among the great powers, from which arises the thesis that imperialism constitutes a particular stage of capitalism, turned parasitic and doomed to decay; and 3) the impossibility of a peaceful division of the planet and the fallacious character of the Kautskyite theory of ultraimperialism as well as of the petit bourgeois reformism of J. A. Hobson.

The first part of the argument requires little comment, inasmuch as it confines itself to listing numerical data taken from "bourgeois" economists. But Lenin transforms the facts by presenting them as proof of the transition from the competitive to the monopolistic phase. Not that he was wrong to stress the concentration of production or the new role of the banks (in certain countries), but he lumps together cartels, trusts, monopolies, and financial oligarchy, taking his examples haphazardly from Germany, England, France or the United States, as if the structure of capitalism were the same from one country to another, and as if the concentration of production and agreements between financial groups involved *ipso facto* the elimination of competition and the rule of the monopolies. In other words, he identifies the capitalism of large units with monopoly capitalism, without any analysis or preciseness—an identification which persists to this day in Marxist-Leninist literature. (François Mitterrand seems to believe that France is held for ransom by the monopolies).

In the second part of the argument (the transition from monopoly capitalism to imperialism), one much-quoted passage gives Lenin's main ideas:

It goes without saying that if capitalism could develop agriculture, which today is everywhere lagging terribly behind industry, if it could raise the living standards of the masses, who in spite of the amazing technical progress are everywhere still half-starved and poverty-stricken, there could be no question of a surplus of capital. This "argument" is very often advanced by the petty-bourgeois critics of capitalism. But if capitalism did these things it would not be capitalism; for both uneven development and a semi-starvation level of existence of the masses are fundamental and inevitable conditions and constitute premises of this mode of production.*

---

*Lenin, *Imperialism, the Final Stage of Capitalism* (Moscow: Progress Publishers, 1975), p. 59.

This text is surprising in many respects. It speaks of the masses condemned to semi-starvation, during the early twentieth century, in the
advanced capitalist countries, including the United States, England, Germany, and France; but what Lenin sees is that which the theory of pauperization implies, not the reality before his eyes. "Starving masses" and
insufficient buying power are then utilized to explain why an internal
development of capitalism is impossible and why there is a shortage of
favorable ways of investing.

For the rest, if Lenin launches an idea which Keynes later took up in a
different context, namely, the lack of opportunities for profitable investment as a consequence of capitalist maturity,* he does not work the theory
out, he takes as self-evident the inability of capitalism to raise the living
standard of the masses, and he does not compare the various possible
interpretations of European exporting of capital: the higher yield on capital
invested abroad; the distribution of incomes within the various European
countries; or the actions of the public powers and the banks (as in France) in
favor of the investment of foreign loans on the Paris market, etc. In his
view, the English or German investments which financed the construction
of railways in Argentina or Asia constitute a manifestation of imperialism,
although he notes in passing that these exports "may tend to a certain
extent to arrest development in the capital-exporting countries."†

Lenin relates capital export and colonial conquest, both of them out-
standing features of the last twenty years of the previous century, but the
replacement of free capitalist competition by capitalist monopolies‡ is seen
by him as the ultimate root and sufficient explanation of the two phenomena, which both illustrate the partition of the world among the national
capitalisms.

Colonial possession alone gives the monopolies complete guarantee against all
contingencies in the struggle against competitors, including the case of the adver-
sary wanting to be protected by a law establishing a state monopoly.§

It was indeed easier on the colonial market (sometimes even the only place
where the thing is possible at all) to eliminate a competitor by means of
monopoly, to secure control, strengthen the necessary "contacts," and so
on. But he does not ask himself whether in fact the French government
determined to conquer Morocco in order to shut out foreign financial

---

*Lenin writes (ibid., p. 59), "The need to export capital arises from the fact that in a few
countries capitalism has become 'overripe' and (owing to the backward state of agriculture
and the poverty of the masses) capital cannot find a field for 'profitable' investment."
†Ibid., p. 61. But he also notes that capital is looking for raw materials and sources of raw
materials, p. 78.
‡Ibid., p. 82.
§Ibid., p. 77.

groups, and whether the French banks pushed the government and wanted this private preserve. A few quotations from foreign authors are all the proof he needs.

The partition of the planet among the financial (and industrial) groups and its partition among the great powers appear to Lenin as two faces of the same reality, two expressions of the same structure, namely, monopoly capitalism. He does not go so far as to say that the latter is the *cause* of imperialism; it is imperialism by its very nature, since it *necessarily* expands abroad and *necessarily* gives rise to squabbling over the division of the spoils, and to quarrels which are sometimes economic and sometimes political, and alternately peaceful or warlike. To Lenin's way of thinking, the distinction between colonies and semicolonies is meaningless, since in both cases capitalists oppress and exploit in their quest for profits and surplus profits. Similarly, the distinction between rivalries among financial groups and real wars is meaningless because, in the final analysis, the capitalists cannot share out the planet peacefully. Why is peaceful partition impossible? Because partition is now reaching the limits of a finite world?* Because the different national economies are developing at different speeds? Lenin does in fact put forward these two reasons.

He gives, for example, the fact that in 1892 Germany produced 4.9 million tons of pig iron compared with Britain's 6.8 million, but by 1912 was producing 17.6 million as against 9 million.

"The question is: what means other than war could there be *under capitalism* to overcome the disparity between the development of productive forces and the accumulation of capital on the one side, and the division of colonies and spheres of influence for finance capital on the other?†

Lenin clearly considers this proof to be irrefutable, although in fact the modification of the relations of economic forces (which he calls the *law of uneven development*) is a permanent factor in modern economics and probably in all periods of history, and it constitutes one element of diplomatic instability but is in no way a cause of explosion or of military confrontation.

Another text is equally revealing of the Leninist way of thinking:

. . . the only conceivable basis under capitalism for the division of spheres of influence, interests, colonies, etc., is a calculation of the *strength* of those participating, their general economic, financial, military strength, etc. . . . Peaceful alliances prepare the ground for wars, and in their turn grow out of wars; the one conditions the other, producing alternating forms of peaceful and non-peaceful

*One feature of imperialism in its full development is that "the territorial division of the whole world among the biggest capitalist powers is completed" (ibid., p. 83).
†Ibid., p. 92.

struggle on *one and the same* basis of imperialist connections and relations within world economics and world politics.*

Spheres of influence and colonies, financial power and military power, economic rivalries and political conflicts, temporary alliances and wars— all these Lenin looks upon as so many simultaneous or successive expressions of imperialism, otherwise known as "monopoly capitalism." Given this sort of account of the world, what is the good of asking whether exporting capital *necessarily* involves assuming sovereignty over colonies, whether an imbalance between financial and military power *necessarily* results in a trial of strength, or whether the directorates of monopolies *consciously* want or *inevitably* bring about wars between states? These questions are of no significance for Lenin because, in the last analysis, the division of the planet arises out of the relation of continually changing forces and because—in this pamphlet, at any rate—Lenin rejects any essential distinction between economic and military power.

What is all the more striking about Lenin's pamphlet is that it assembles facts and arguments which are common knowledge, without thereby proving the theses which set out to explain the transition from one phase to the next: from accumulations of capital to colonies, from spheres of influence to undying rivalry among nations, and from the partition of the planet to World War I. In spite of everything, Lenin's pamphlet is still in the line of descent of the Marxism of the Second International and of the thinking of Engels, if not of Marx.

Lenin's disregard of any possible mediatory factors between monopoly capitalism and World War I foreshadows the arbitrary nature of Stalin's interpretations: there is no more bothering about studying historical reality, its meaning is decreed by referring to an alleged structure but is, in fact, tied to a broad concept—monopoly capitalism—which, supposedly, defines an historical stage and, in so doing, explains the most assorted collection of events: peace and wars; compromise between "monopolies" as well as refusal to compromise; political alliance between economic rivals (Great Britain and the United States) as well as wars between rivals and between economically interdependent countries. In the end, imperialism designates not so much a form of behavior as it does *monopoly capitalism*.

Surplus value and exploitation; the center and the periphery

The Marxist-Leninist *theory of imperialism* (formulated in 1915 and conceived in the light of Hobson's and Hilferding's books) tied together, in a

*Ibid., pp. 110–11.

general interpretation, three series of events attributable to various individual or collective actions: the export of capital originating from the Western European capitalist countries (Great Britain, France, and Germany); the scramble for Africa, and colonial conquests in the late nineteenth century; and World War I. Lenin located the source of these events in a particular structure of capitalism: in the concentration of the units of production and finance capital. This structure of capitalism *caused* imperialism, in the form of colonies, or of spheres of influence but, in the Leninist view, it already had, by its very nature, an inbuilt tendency to display an imperialist character.

In 1945, as a result of its World War II victory, the Soviet Union—which was absolved, by definition, of the sin of imperialism—annexed what previously had been Romanian, Czech, Polish, and German territory. The two big socialist powers, Russia and China, call each other imperialists, as if, by their "dialogue," to refute their common theory. On the other hand, Great Britain, the Netherlands, Belgium, and France have, in the space of twenty-five years, either lost or liberated their colonies in Africa and Asia. Only weakly-developed Portugal, poor in spite of its African territories, prolonged its resistance to the tide of history for a dozen years longer. A revolution in Lisbon then brought to power soldiers and civilians who made haste to negotiate the liquidation of the Lusitanian empire. Straight away two Leninist notions collapsed, so to speak, of their own accord. First, capitalism does not imply colonial conquests (or, if an even more cautious formula is preferred, it does not imply resorting to colonial conquest and the seizure of sovereignty in order to exclude competitors: colonialism is *not* the indispensable tool of the monopolistic ambitions of a national capitalism eager to shut out its rivals. In addition, as demonstrated by rising living standards in the parent nations which "fell victim" to decolonization, the Leninist thesis which says that the labor aristocracy alone benefits from surplus profits extorted from dependent populations while the mass of the population is impoverished to the point of semi-starvation, is likewise contradicted.

Ideology, fortunately for itself, never has much trouble about incorporating into its system events or evolutions apparently incompatible with its own principles. Moreover, the Lenin-inspired theory of imperialism has undergone a process of rejuvenation and universal diffusion. Taken up by non-Marxists, it now constitutes the nucleus of the Vulgate adopted by a Left which starts with the right wing of the socialists and embraces the leftists proper. Imperialism no longer stands for a particular kind of action by a state or group of states, but for the system of the international economy *per se*. J. Galtung's so-called structural theory of imperialism marks the ultimate possible, if not inevitable, conclusion of the Leninist way of thinking.

Let us go back to Marx and *Capital*. One model, inspired by Ricardo, indicated a considerable discrepancy between the value produced by the worker and that of the wage paid by way of reward. Nearly all the numerical examples accumulated by Marx himself involve an exploitation rate of 100% (equality between wage and surplus value).* The Marxist model can seduce economists, or it can repel them: some reject the very notion of value as metaphysical; others see it as a gratuitous and arbitrary complication of the theory of prices. But this model is wonderfully useful as a propaganda weapon. If any private ownership of the means of production involves the exploitation of man, all it requires to eliminate at once the economic exploitation is to replace it by public ownership.†

Furthermore, private ownership in a foreign country involves what might be called "second-degree exploitation," since it carries the risk of the surplus value not being reinvested in the country where it has been extorted from the workers. From this angle, the Marxist theory of exploitation leads logically to the theory of imperialism, this being nothing more than the exploitation of the workers by foreign capitalists.

Hence, under capitalism, imperialism becomes as "structural" as "exploitation." This leaves the theorists with a perplexing number of ways to deal with the theme, with intricate variations. Just as foreign investments become imperialistic as such because they involve exploitation to the power of two, so transactions between industrialized and developing countries are imperialistic because they are unequal; because of the higher productivity of labor in the wealthy countries, they usually exchange a lesser amount of labor for a greater.

To complete the structural analysis of imperialism, one almost indispensable element is still lacking, namely, political domination. In every society, there exists a dominant minority which we shall call the "center." In the industrialized nations this center ensures a relatively high standard of living for the periphery, the population (or the "dominated") as a whole. This standard of living in turn requires a smooth-running economy, international trade, and the transformation of raw materials some of which come from outside. The "center" of the industrialized countries therefore strives to maintain "centers" (ruling minorities) in the underdeveloped countries whose allegiance is toward the upkeep of the dual internal-and-external system of private ownership at home and unequal trading abroad. If one assumes that the American center backs the centers favorable to the capitalist system and the market economy to an extent everywhere, one is

---

*Marx uses this rate without justifying it or stating that it is consonant with reality. But the constant equation of variable capital with surplus value, in other words, an exploitation rate of 100%, eventually acquired a sort of plausibility. Some Soviet textbooks persist in this practice.

†This same model is equally applicable to the critique of the Soviet economy.

forging the last link in the chain, which is the idea that the domination of the rich over the poor and of the industrialized over the developing nations is no longer exerted by the crude method of colonies or even of spheres of influence, but by the backing given by the centers of the dominant nations to the centers of the dominated ones—who are only too ready to knuckle under, in order to keep themselves in power and serve their own class interest.

The domination of the industrialized country's center over the center of the dependent or underdeveloped country is not obvious, nor does it constitute a constant factor. In today's world, all ruling minorities pay lip service to nationalism, although some of them seek the support of the dominant country in order to keep themselves in power. In order to present the structure of domination as a fact of experience, it is necessary to make a series of assumptions—that the ruling minorities of all countries (except the socialist countries) oppress the masses, that Third World countries remain a part of the world economy only out of class interest, and that the ruling minorities of the industrialized countries play on the class interest of the ruling minorities in the dependent countries. Given this schematic analysis, the exploitation and subjection of the Third World by the combined industrialized countries go hand in hand. The twentieth-century world capitalist economy consequently becomes in itself imperialistic, this word denoting the two inseparable relationships of *domination* and *exploitation* of the periphery by the center, of the developing by the industrialized countries. (In the old days, this would have been called the domination of the raw material-producing countries by the countries which transform these raw materials.)

This so-called structural theory is based on two clever devices—first, the choice of a special vocabulary ("exploitation," "domination") with heavy ideological overtones and, second, a pessimistic interpretation of the relations between countries in the framework of a world economy which is controlled, more or less, by market mechanisms. All vocabularies are attached implicitly to a theory. In spite of everything, the vocabulary of developed/developing countries (or raw material-producing/industrialized countries) is justified by facts or figures; it suggests that all countries are on the road to development. In other words, it does not attach any major importance to distinguishing between the régimes of capitalism and socialism. This implicit theory has no dogmatic character. There is nothing to prevent distinctions from being drawn between degrees of development (per capita production), or between modes of ownership and of management.

On the other hand, to put the imperialist label on industrialized countries which have no colonies amounts to twisting the ordinary meaning of words, and to ordaining, without any examination, the oppressive and spoliatory character of the relations between the industrialized and industrializing sectors of the world economy. The diversity of this economy is a legacy of centuries, and it derives from a historical process in which conquests by force mingle with exploitation by exchange. That the Europeans often extended their own civilization by fire and sword, from the sixteenth century onward—that they were the "aggressors"—is a fact which no one ignores and no one contests. The Spaniards devastated the pre-Columbian civilizations in Mexico, Central America, and Peru; the Spaniards, British, French, and Dutch colonized North America, forced the Indians onto reservations, and pursued their habitual Old World antagonisms overseas.

If European "aggression" led to the destruction of the Aztec and Inca cultures, it caused a mutation in Japanese society, which today is an archetypal industrialized society and, hence, "imperialistic" according to fashionable theories. The example of Japan reminds us that, in the nineteenth century, every country remained to some extent the master of its own fate. It answered or resisted Western aggression in its own style. Access to the center was not barred.

More generally, three kinds of question arise on the subject of the "inequality of nations," questions which cannot be answered by the theories of imperialism sired by Lenin. The first concerns the past: did the development of some nations have as its condition or cause the *under-development* of others? Did Great Britain derive its wealth from the impoverishment of India? Or again, according to a toned-down version of the same thesis, was it to their colonial possessions that the European nations owed the wherewithal for their economic takeoff and subsequent rapid development?

A second category of questions has to do with present-day reality: does the development of the industrialized countries *paralyze* the development of countries that wish to follow the same path? Does the world economic order established and dominated by the United States and Europe hamper the progress of the underdeveloped nations?

Third and last, one may ask whether this order can be called "imperialism" as such. Or to be more precise, exactly what does such a description mean, once all nations have regained or won their independence? Can the relation between the United States (the center of the world's center) and Brazil (which is on the periphery but near to being the center of a peripheral sector of the world) properly be called an *imperialist* relationship?

The conquering West

I shall not linger on the first category of problems—not because it lacks interest, but because it would take us too far out of our way.

Among the European countries, three cases are immediately apparent: Spain and Portugal; the United Kingdom; and France and Germany. The early conquerors, the Spaniards and Portuguese, gained precious metals and a period of power and glory from their distant possessions, but no lasting wealth, nor any lasting capacity to produce wealth. It is not our concern to comment on the historical interpretations of the role played by Portugal and Spain in the sixteenth century.* The first of these countries belongs to the periphery of the European center, the second to the fringe of the center. Neither of them is now a target for antiimperialist propaganda. If they did once contribute to the formation of the world market or the capitalist economy centered on Europe, they have long since lost any central position. In today's imperialism, they no longer have a place.

I have put Germany and France together because one of them was a latecomer to the partition of Africa and the other made haphazard conquest of a dispersed and not very profitable colonial empire. Nobody will argue that Germany's industrialization in the later nineteenth century was at all indebted to the few African territories which the Wilhelmine Reich, finally infected by the spirit of the time, felt obliged to remove from the reach of its European rivals. As for the second French empire—Indochina, North Africa, and black Africa—it made profits for a number of businesses and enabled some additional administrative posts to be created, but it made no substantial contribution to the industrialization or wealth of the parent country.

A small percentage of French overseas investments—about 10%—went to the empire before 1914. The protectorate over Tunisia lasted for three quarters of a century, that over Morocco for less than half a century. In each of the three countries of North Africa, a "French minority" became established. To a great extent the empire constituted a "closed preserve" for the mother country's wares (except for Morocco). The growth of production and of overseas trade after the loss of the empire suggests that the system benefited not so much the entire community as it did certain private interests. In any case, the African and Asian colonies had no substantial influence, in a direct way, on the development of the French economy in the nineteenth and twentieth centures.†

That leaves the case of Great Britain, whose fortune—in the double sense of political greatness and of wealth—is inextricably linked with trade, with the Indian Empire, and with the opening of overseas markets to the

*See Immanuel Wallerstein, *The Modern World System, Capitalist Agriculture and the Origins of the European World Economy in the Sixteenth Century* (London: Academic Press, 1974).

†The human and raw material resources of the empire were put into the service of the parent country during both world wars, but everything depended on the freedom of communication guaranteed by the British and, later, by the American navy. Of course, it can also be said that all Europeans profited from the world economy created by the power of Great Britain.

products of the parent country's industry. To my knowledge, no one has attempted a *counterfactual history** of the Great Britain of 1750–1850 by assuming the absence of imperial hegemony, maritime trade, and the East India Company. It would be a pointless, sterile exercise: it is quite obvious that Britain used its naval supremacy to draw on the resources of the other continents in the course of its struggles with France. Trade left considerable surpluses, and India was opened up to British cotton goods at a time when such goods would not have found easy outlets at home, nor even on the Continent.

More than a century ago, at the time of the Indian Mutiny, members of Parliament in the British House of Commons did not hesitate to declare that the United Kingdom ruled India in its own interest—as earlier conquerors all had done. Conquest was its own justification, to the extent that strength proved the superiority of culture. Even at the start of the twentieth century, the French still had a sincere belief in their "civilizing mission." Nowadays—officially, at least—Westerners refrain from laying down a system of hierarchy among cultures in the ethnological sense of the term. The consequence is that the expansion of the last five centuries, once seen as a succession of achievements, today becomes a chapter of violence and pillage.

There is no disputing the violence and pillage—the Europeans were no better, morally, than the conquerors of the past—but this does not constitute the sole or major cause of the wealth or development of Europe and North America, any more than it constitutes the sole or major cause of the poverty of Africa and Southeast Asia. Western aggression did indeed upset the traditional conditions of life (although, among the Japanese and Chinese, an increase in population had begun even before these countries were opened to the West in the nineteenth century). The *character* of the present-day poverty of nations *is* the outcome of Western aggression: I have in mind the resultant contrast between the "modern" sectors and "the others"—the cancerous cities, the shantytowns, the *bidonvilles* and *favellas* huddled up against wealthy business or residential districts—and the comparisons, on television, of the misery of some and the ostentatious high-living of others. Anyone can add further examples.

While creating the "industrial civilization" condemned by some, exalted by others, the West also created the inequality of nations, it paved the way for the rise of Japan, it touched off a century of civil warfare in the Chinese empire before Mao Tse-tung established a new dynasty. Is this historic *responsibility*, which nobody will deny, to be equated with the *culpability*

---

*That is, reconstruction of the past by supposing an alteration in one important variable. For example, how would the American economy have developed if there had been no railways?

alleged by counsel for the underdeveloped countries? In what sense are development and underdevelopment related—as front to back, cause to effect, master to slave, rich to poor?

In one sense (which might be called strictly verbal), underdevelopment exists only because of development: the two words, and the realities they designate, are the result of a comparison. Neither the Papuans of New Guinea nor the Chinese, with their ancient empire, would consider themselves underdeveloped or be seen as such if it were not for the industrialized countries in which the GNP per capita amounts to several thousand dollars.

In a second and, historically, more significant sense, China (if not New Guinea) became an economic and in part a political dependency of the developed countries in the late nineteenth and early twentieth century. More broadly speaking, the countries which sold raw materials to the industrializing European countries, without using their surpluses to industrialize in their turn, were condemned *ipso facto* to underdevelopment.

The same historical process, the formation of the *world market,* resulted in the inequality of nations and the contrast between the rich countries and the poor ones. On this point, I see little ground for heated argument. But when the causes and agents of this process are called into question, the debate commences.

The first accusation asserts that it was colonialism that prevented—or, at any rate, slowed down—development and, therefore, engendered underdevelopment. As a whole, this theory does not stand up to examination. Would Morocco have modernized more rapidly if France had not exercised a protectorate there for half a century? Would Algeria be more advanced if the French—partly by chance, and not without some bloody battles—had not imposed their rule? Although any categorical answer is bound to cause debate by its very nature, one has only to observe some comparable countries in order to be convinced that underdevelopment necessarily went *with development,* because some states set out early along the path to economism and industry, and other states or peoples came late.

It is possible to ponder the history of the last two centuries as it would have been without colonial domination. Suppose that the Western nations, responding to the advice of the liberal economists or of men such as Auguste Comte—who wanted Western culture spread without the violence of conquest—had abandoned the Indian Empire a century sooner than they did, and had not shared out Africa. Imagine, also, that the peoples of Southeast Asia had borrowed the techniques of production and administration needed for development without having had to experience the humiliation of foreign rule and the spoliation that goes with it. (Japan did in fact manage to avoid this humiliation and now belongs to the center of the world economy, sharing its unpopularity. The example of Japan is at least proof that the dialectic of development and underdevelopment depends partly on the responses of non-Westerns to the Western challenge.)

This counterfactual meditation, on a history which never happened, is ultimately pointless, to my mind. As conquerors in accordance with age-old custom, the Western nations were not always less cruel than their predecessors along the Via Dolorosa of mankind. When they ruled foreign peoples directly, they brought them certain elements of their own civilization—railways, machinery, administration. Would India have been unified and modernized earlier, without the British? Nobody knows. No one can say whether the spread of Western culture could have been brought about without violence, nor whether it would have been faster or slower.

So the debate can now be left to the historians, especially since the *political wrongdoings* of colonialism are supposed to be less serious than the *economic wrongdoings* of neocolonialism. Latin America, a part of the Third World, consists of countries whose independence was achieved during the first third of the nineteenth century: it nevertheless considers itself a victim of "imperialism," first British, and then American.

The Third World in the world economy

To lay the main—if not the only—stress on GNP per capita inevitably leads to making comparisons in time as well as place, so that a given country will emerge as having the same degree of development today as the United Kingdom had in 1780 or 1830. In international organizations, the very notion of the Third World as a body of nations regarded as distinct from two bodies of developed (socialist and capitalist) nations is defined only by the statistics of GNP per capita, all expressed in dollars. These statistics are sometimes utterly meaningless: a national product per capita of 100 dollars or less would be impossible to live on in the United States; when living conditions are radically different, accurate figures distort the economic and human reality, and their only function is to shore up the case for defense or prosecution. The poverty of millions of Indians or Africans is not an invention of statisticians; the life of these "poor" people in the village or the bush bears little resemblance to the misery of the shantytowns on the fringes of the prosperous districts of Rio de Janeiro, or even Paris.

In fact, let us bypass these extreme, absurd forms of comparison: classification by income per capita bring together countries which have little in common and where the problems of development are, therefore, altogether different. Only a statistical fiction or a community of interests and demands could make a single unit out of the ancient empire of China, or the

countries of Latin America—created by Spanish and Portuguese colonization and governed by ruling classes of colonial or mixed descent—or the
peoples of Africa, who owe their written language to their ex-masters. In
fact, the heterogeneity of these "pressure groups" reduces their effectiveness as soon as they attempt to go from words to actions. The non-oil-
producing Third World may perhaps derive some satisfaction from the blow
struck against the rich nations by nations which once were poor, and it may
identify itself with the oil-producing states or dream of matching the feat of
OPEC, but—in the short term and for some time after that—the Third
World will pay more dearly for it than the Western nations; it is in the
industrialized countries of Europe and North America that Iran and
Algeria, Indonesia and Algeria, spend the billions of dollars paid into their
accounts by the oil corporations.

In this era of extreme inequality between nations, it is as if the claims of
the underdeveloped nations were in themselves justified, because our
official ideology pays lip service to the equality of individuals and nations,
as well as to the unity of the human race.

One initial justification for the Third World demands is based on the
West's crimes committed in the past. These crimes are never explicitly
formulated and, if not unfounded, are not completely provable. Indians
and blacks were the victims of the crimes imputable to the ancestors of
United States citizens. The South Americans were no such victims; they
drifted into underdevelopment in the nineteenth century, without falling
under the heel of conquerors, at least as much through their own fault as
through the ingress of English (and, later American) capital and capitalists.
It is the American Indian peoples who could indict their present masters,
the descendants of their original invaders, in the name of a distant past.

The Western nations will not give way, because of any bad conscience, to
the demands of the Algerians, the Indians, the Angolans, or the Peruvians,
solely in order to atone for their fathers' or grandfathers' crimes. The only
argument likely to impress the leaders of the wealthy states is the one
inspired by the philosophy which gradually persuaded the privileged
classes of the capitalist democracies, namely, that it is *consonant* with rich
nations' interests, *not* contrary to them, to raise the overall standard, both
in order to encourage growth and to forestall social explosions. The argument is more convincing within nations than from one to the other, but it
still is the best argument available.

If it is useless to ask the rich countries to atone for their past, can the
advocates of the underdeveloped countries not express valid grievances
against the rules and operation of the international economy? Certainly
they can. But it is still important to distinguish between two kinds of
wrongs: those directed against the situation of the world market in its late
twentieth-century shape, and those aimed at the deliberate, conscious

policy chosen by the rulers of the industrialized states. It is this second category that we shall next consider.

Development comes about today through technological means of production originating in industrialized countries, with incomparably more expensive equipment, therefore, than was used in the factories built in England during the nineteenth century and observed by Marx. There is a vast gap between the pioneer and the late traveler along a path already beaten by others; this makes the task a totally different one, but is it easier or harder?

Development—on this point there is general agreement—consists of a total transformation of society, which can, however, be expressed quantitatively. An economy can produce commodities by using other than technological methods, but is not apt to be content with producing more of the same commodities in the same way. The changes brought about in people's lives—in their equipment, their organizations—can be measured by looking at a country's GNP. The risk is that, in contributing to such change, the developed countries may teach bad lessons: neither the United States not the Soviet Union nor France constitute an example for Zaire to follow.

The immense literature devoted to what is called "development" makes a distinction between the necessary human and economic changes, which are bound up together, the latter involving the former without the former necessarily involving the latter. It is not enough to educate a few thousand students, in a little African country, to guarantee this development. In some of the countries which are called underdeveloped—in Latin America for instance—the general level of education and the qualified personnel are sufficient. In the African republics, on the other hand, the mass of the population goes on living the traditional life and the towns expand without thereby creating a volume of wealth proportional to the number of urban dwellers. If education were a sufficient cause or even, simply, the first condition of modernizing an economy, there would be no grounds for pessimism at all. National governments or international organizations have never made so many efforts or spent so much money in order to teach everyone to read and to provide secondary education for many, and higher education for some. These efforts are costly, and yet there is a risk of their remaining unproductive *in relation to the objective of development,* if graduates crowd together in the towns and do not find jobs adapted to their qualifications.

In the developed countries, illiteracy has practically disappeared, but it had not disappeared in the England of the early nineteenth century, or the France of 1850. It is not enough to eliminate illiteracy in order to start up economic growth, or to accelerate it. This remark does not mean to say that, in the early stages, a proportion of the masses must be neglected in order to concentrate the educational resources on a minority. All it means is that it is not enough to borrow one or another feature of the developed countries in order to start up the kind of developmental machinery that will keep going after a certain point, of its own accord.

Just as it is not enough to build schools or universities, it is likewise not enough to buy machines from abroad, to hire engineers and erect factories. For if it stopped there, the outcome of such a transfer would be to establish a measure of quantitative statistical growth but to accentuate the gap between the two sectors generally labeled "traditional" and "modern." Heterogeneity may, perhaps, represent an inevitable stage which can in any case be found in all economies, even developed ones, but there is a point beyond which it becomes *pathological* and *paralyzing*.

In the last analysis, the obstacle which the rich countries put in the way of the developing countries by the very fact of their own prosperity is what economists have called the "imitation effect." The economists have extended this concept to mean more than the arousal of consumer desires, throughout the world, by the level of consumption attained in Europe or the United States: it has to do with the unavoidable and dangerous tendency of the rulers of poor countries—the extreme example is that of the countries of Black Africa—to imitate the practices of the former parent country in certain spheres.

In this sense, the imitation effect has repercussions even on the economic variables. The Industrial Revolution was preceded in England by an increase in agricultural output. The first industrial enterprises did not require large amounts of capital, nor refined techniques. These factories grew up on a supply of artisans and skilled workers. The products which emerged from the factories, in what then seemed like mass production, found markets at home and abroad and, if need be, the British navy could open them up with broadsides. The Continental nations which followed in the footsteps of England borrowed its relatively simple techniques and, occasionally, bought English technicians. Western industry profited from the outlets which the Western nations afforded to one another and from those opened to the early industrialists by the peripheral or fringe countries which provided food or raw materials.

Times have changed now, or so it is said. The leading industries of developing countries have not so much to substitute themselves for imports as to bring in foreign currency. They have to export, which means not being too far below the technical or organizational level of the advanced countries' industries. They require big investments, the general shortage of which makes mobilization difficult. They remain vulnerable both to economic fluctuations and to decisions made by foreign governments and, in either event, to external variables which the governments of poor countries are utterly unable to control.

In other words—so the argument goes—the gap between developing and developed countries has grown so wide that (unlike the Continental countries which set off in England's footsteps) neither Black Africa nor Latin America can now hope to gradually catch up on the leading nations. By its very structure, it is said, the world economy of the late twentieth century has become ruthless toward latecomers and stragglers; it offers a chance, at best, only to those who break with the world market that was organized and dominated by the wealthy nations.

Although this thesis enjoys some favor, I do not regard it as very plausible. To go by the available statistics of national products, the overall growth rate of the Third World has been superior to the growth rates achieved by what are now the developed countries at comparable stages of their development. Even if we say that the growth rate calculated for the Third World as a whole means nothing, the fact remains that certain countries—for example, Taiwan, South Korea, Singapore—are achieving high growth rates by taking advantage of the characteristics of the world market.

With agrarian reform followed by a continual rise in agricultural output, Taiwan and South Korea have acquired what is probably the indispensable basis for modernization: the two countries managed to attract foreign capital by creating, first, labor-intensive industries such as textiles and electronics and, then, the more capital-intensive industries financed by the profits of these exporting industries. South Korea's growth rate, in the last fifteen years, has been almost as high as Japan's, with only moderate inflation. There are no grounds whatever for supposing that this typical combination—agrarian reform and increased agricultural output, labor-intensive (and low-wage) exporting industries, and industrial expansion toward the capital-intensive sectors—cannot be made to work elsewhere. I do not claim that this liberal strategy can or should serve as a general model. In theory, each country would find a model suited to its own specific situation somewhere in the literature. But the leadership still has to seek it out, and agree to apply it.

In Black Africa it is, quite clearly, agricultural improvement which is the essential prerequisite of all development that would be capable of embracing entire economies or countries. In its absence, the most that can be expected is the establishment of *pockets* of modernism—a few industries in cancerous towns, an intellectual class turned out by Western or Western-imitating universities and incapable of returning to the bush and doing useful work there.

Latin America appears to be quite a different case. In his *Philosophy of*

History, Hegel imagined the United States entering world history and tragedy through conflict with South America. The rivalry between the two Americas has more to do with verbal than military warfare or, if a Hegelian expression is preferred, the conflict is being argued before the United Nations, and not in the court of History.

It is not our concern to look for the reasons—political, economic, moral—why the countries of Latin America, which were richer and more populous than those of North America at the start of the nineteenth century, have fallen so far behind by the beginning of the twentieth.

It may be argued that the industrialized countries have a spontaneous tendency to reserve for themselves the peripheral markets of the marginal countries in which they sell their industrial output and buy their raw materials. In the last century, Latin America belonged to the periphery of a world market whose center was London, not New York. (The United States remained a net importer of capital until 1914.) English capital was invested—in Argentina, for example—to finance railroads or ports. This infrastructure answered the needs of the United Kingdom, of course, but there was nothing to prevent the Argentinian ruling class from undertaking industrialization.

It will be said that the ruling class preferred to *spend* its income instead of investing it in industry, and that the ruling class of the central economy thrived on the subordination of the raw material-producing countries. True enough, but the leaders of the central economy put up with the industrialization of the continent of Europe, of France, and of Germany, and participated—with their capital—in the industrialization of North America, which was to take over their leading position in the twentieth century. In other words, the relative nondevelopment of Latin America is accounted for by a variety of circumstances; it is the outcome neither of causes independent of the will of the local leaderships nor of the policy consciously pursued by the masters of the dominant economy.

In the Caribbean area and in Central America, the United States has made frequent interventions to support "friendly" governments or overthrow hostile ones, but not in South America itself. There, the mainland nations have been devastated by wars of liberation and half-paralyzed by civil strife and unstable governments which have been sometimes despotic, sometimes representative, but never fully legitimate. Since 1945, Britain has been totally replaced by the United States as the dominant influence, and the idea that South American underdevelopment is simply the negative side of North American overdevelopment consequently has been an automatic propaganda weapon, but that does not mean that it is at all probable.

What is true is that the United States had invested capital in mining, oil, and the production of raw materials. The sum total of these investments is trivial compared with the GNP or total capital of the United States,* but whether or not they are deemed to be a form of "exploitation" (this subject is discussed below), they were not enough to stop the process of development any more than to start it. Up to 1945, neither Great Britain nor the United States *determined*—either by conscious policy or the economic context they created—the course of the political or economic history of the principal countries of Latin America. Naturally, they were not upset by the nonindustrialization or slow industrialization in that area (it would be surprising if they had been). Here and there, the Americans sent in the Marines to protect their investments or their citizens, but it would be hard to prove that the governments they threw out would have achieved more than the governments they installed in their place.

In conclusion, today's world economy creates both opportunities and hazards for the developing countries. Clearly, the conditions of development are, for them, not at all the same as they were for France after 1815 or Germany around 1850. The technical methods of the twentieth century and the *effect of imitation*, in the broad sense of the word, saddle national leaderships with political as well as economic tasks which are sometimes contrary to the spontaneous aspirations of the people. There are no grounds for asserting that these tasks require a clean break with the world economy centered around the developed countries. The duality of center and periphery has grown up a little at a time; the ruling classes of the peripheral economies have often turned it to their own advantage and found themselves in agreement with those of the central countries.

Since the last war, this duality has been as visible to those who are subjected to it as to those who profit by it, and the former blame the latter for its existence. This brings us to the third theme mentioned above: do the ruling powers of the developed countries maintain the peripheral countries in their state of poverty and subordination, either through deliberate policy or the habit of exploitation?

North-South dialogue and the myth of the new world economic order

The word exploitation has at least two meanings, one of them neutral: putting to use a piece of land, a mine or an oil field; the other carrying a political and moral connotation: making unfair profits from some transaction or economic activity. Similarly, the notion of dependence has at least

*The cash value of direct U.S. investment in Latin America in 1975 was $22.2 billion, or 16.6% of total U.S. world investment ($133.2 billion). Investment in Latin America amounts to 0.18% of the GNP of the United States ($1516.3 billion).

two meanings. No individual or state can do everything it pleases, because other individuals or states exist. In this sense, no one is independent, not even the president of the United States, who needs the support of the Congress at home and who cannot simply force his will upon other powerful heads of state abroad. If total independence is by definition ruled out, the relations of dependence are, also by definition, asymmetrical. An officer cannot order a private to carry out any command whatsoever (except possibly in a concentration camp); but the subordination of private to officer, or worker to foreman, secretary to boss, sanctions the inequality of dependence.

It is a dependence which, in turn, has either a legal, organizational character or an effective but not juridically sanctioned one. When Algeria was made up of French *départements*, the dependence of the Algerian people with respect to the decisions of the French government or the governor of Algeria was sanctioned by law and imposed by police or military force. The government of what is now the "independent" nation of Algeria shares the fate of all governments: it runs into obstacles created either by the will of other governments or as the unwilled results of a multitude of different or conflicting actions.

Domination, whether *de facto* or *de jure,* amounts to a more or less extreme form of asymmetrical dependence. The master gets the servant to work as he wants, while the servant seldom gets the master to do the same. Modern societies contain so many specific organizations, each with its own hierarchy and, thus, with its own system of asymmetrical dependence, that there are times when even the head of state may end up in a position of subordination—for example, within the fiscal system. Richard Nixon found this out for himself.

Between the developing and the developed countries, there exists, in fact, a *reciprocal* dependence. The former have the benefit of borrowing or buying technical know-how, expert personnel, and machinery from the latter. On the other hand, the developed countries cannot—or cannot easily—do without the raw materials and energy provided by the developing countries. Is this reciprocal dependence asymmetrical? In what sense? To what extent?

After a long period of trenchwork operating as a cartel, the oil-producing countries quadrupled the price of their products in the space of a few months. Asymmetry of dependence worked in favor of the producing countries and at the expense of the consumer countries. As expressed by the classic joke, the Arabs would be happier to remount their camels than the Westerners would be to descend from their cars. Did the cartel commit the crime of "exploitation"? And did this crime amount to a *legitimate* reply to the earlier exploitation for which the Westerners had made themselves responsible through their big corporations?

These questions admit of an answer only to the extent that the interlocutors—those who say yes and those who say no—are ready to accept the same criterion: in the case of any buying or selling transaction, what is the fair price, in the modern sense of the word—the *nonexploitative* price? The answer varies according to the theoretical schema used and the nature of the product under consideration.

Let us straightway dispose of the "theory of unequal exchange," according to which all exchanges involve an intrinsic unfairness because the quantities of labor bought or sold are unequal. The proposition is not only true but obvious. The inequality of labor productivity between one country or area of a country and another implies that the less developed country or area receives less labor than it gives. No international trade, either in the world capitalist or socialist market, is carried out in accordance with calculations of the quantity of labor (calculations which are almost impossible in any case). In this sense, all transactions are unequal, and the rich—if labor is referred to as a constant—receive more than they give. Otherwise, no exchanges would be transacted, at least in the sphere of manufactured products.

With this theory out of the way, what criterion of exploitation remains? It is feasible to revert to the "Marxist" theory which is identified with the theory of surplus value but, in that case, it turns out to be impossible to find any example of exchange without surplus value. According to the current interpretation the entrepreneur, buying labor power and paying it the cost of its reproduction, retains an amount of surplus value—which is the difference between the cost of the labor incorporated and the sale price. But, according to the ideology, this "exploitation" characterizes the *mode of production*—which applies also to public enterprises—and has no relation to international exchanges.

Exploitation, in the latter category of exchanges, is defined in relation to a fair price, not in the medieval, but in the *market* sense of the word. The arguments leveled by the underdeveloped countries against "exploitation" are usually aimed at the actual mechanism of the international economy, without the accusers always being aware of the basis of their indictment.

Let us first consider the direct foreign investments in a developing country. Normally the firm—American, German, Dutch—will put up a factory in the place dictated by its interests: let us simplify the matter and say the place where it pays the work force less than it has to pay in its home country. Since the production technique is not markedly different from the technique used at home, the surplus value will normally be greater. The average level of wages being proportional to the average productivity of the country concerned, the wage level of an underdeveloped country will be below the wage level of the developed country where the investor is based. Firms react to wage fluctuations so sensitively that during the period

1975–76 the capital flow from one side of the Atlantic to the other tended to reverse itself: Volkswagen built a factory in the United States, not Ford in Germany.

In any case, an American corporation offshoot could not pay Pakistani or Brazilian workers a wage equal to what it paid workers in Detroit without creating imbalances as fatal to the host country as to the firm itself. The variation in wage levels according to the different degrees of development from one country to another—in other words, according to the average productivity of the workers—is what fuels the movement of industrial investment capital all over the world. It is also what explains the present tendency of multinational firms to invest in the socialist countries (where they also have a guarantee against nationalization).

So there are two choices: either the word exploitation or overexploitation (surplus profit) is applied to all investment by multinational firms in developing countries, or the word is restricted to those offshoots of multinational firms which do not reinvest their profits on the spot. In reality, gross profits include a sizable percentage of surplus value set aside for replacing and expanding the means of production. If this percentage is transferred elsewhere, instead of being reinvested on the spot, then the host country of the subsidiary company is, in a way, financing the investments made with the transferred profits. Nowadays, the host country tends—quite rightly—to require guarantees regarding the destination of the gross or net profits of multinational offshoots.

Are these subcompanies gaining a position of dominance over the host country's native enterprises, or over its government? Is the relationship between government and offshoot asymmetrical and, if so, to whose advantage? The answer depends not only on the respective economic power of the bodies involved but also on the political power of the multinational corporation's parent country. Switzerland or Holland do not give the same backing to Nestlé or Philips as the United States has been known to give to ITT. In fact, in the developed countries of Western Europe, the branch companies of multinational corporations are more dependent on the national governments than the governments on the branches. And these companies usually contribute more to the host country's economic growth than they compromise its diplomatic independence.

The main theme of the controversy between the industrialized countries and the others during recent years has been not so much "exploitation" through investments as "exploitation" through prices, and in particular through the terms of exchange between raw materials and industrialized products. The ability of the oil-exporting countries to quadruple their prices has confirmed the already widespread notion that the rich countries "rob" the poor ones by buying their raw materials at low prices.

The arguments relating to the fluctuation of the prices of raw materials, on the one hand, and the movement of manufactured goods, on the other, go around in circles in the absence of one essential piece of information, namely, the date when the relation between the prices of raw materials and of manufactured goods was ever fair. Furthermore, the "raw materials" category is not at all homogeneous. The markets in cereals, metals, coffee or tea, cotton and wool, are not subject to the same influences. Some of these materials may have a long-term tendency to rise or fall. The utmost that can be said is that, in the short term, most of them vary in accordance with the economic situation of the developed countries.

This indubitable fact illustrates the *asymmetry of dependence* between the buyers and sellers of raw materials. In most cases, there is nothing the seller can do about falling prices. In depression periods, demand for raw materials declines and the markets' structure may cause violent fluctuations disproportionate to the quantitative oscillations of supply and demand. The generalized inflation of 1973–74 brought with it a general and massive rise in the raw materials index. The recession caused the same index to fall at the very moment when the non-oil-producing developing countries were suffering the backlash of OPEC's victorious action.

This action promptly produced another thesis. What the raw material exporting countries now blame on the industrialized countries is not only the instability of the market and the fact that export receipts are dependent on variables which the exporters are powerless to control, but the actual level of prices. Morocco has trebled the price of phosphates. Here and there, the exporting nations have made serious efforts to organize cartels for other raw materials, in the hope of extracting advantages like those which transformed the situation of the oil-bearing states. None of these initiatives has gotten very far nor achieved any great success.

Oil was unique in a number of respects. The dependence of the importing countries on this sort of energy constituted a unique instance; in the short term, there was no substitute. In addition, the limited numbers of exporting countries, the political and economic advantages of coalition, and the decisive importance of one of them (Saudi Arabia) guaranteed the cartel's cohesion, in the short term at least. Lastly, over the previous ten years, the big companies—and in particular the seven giants which dominated the market—had allowed the real value of oil prices to decline, in spite of the annual increase in consumption of more than 10%. The market price, in this case, was a matter for endless politico-economic debate.

With reference to the marginal price of Saudi Arabian oil, if it is admitted that the rationale of the world market requires that the oil cheapest to produce should be the first consumed, with market prices tending to rise as rising demand make it necessary to open up the less easily developed fields, then there is nothing exceptional about the low prices of the 1960s, and they do not imply any overexploitation of poor producers by rich consumers. But the producers, who control a wasting asset (because fossil energy, once consumed, cannot be reconstituted), have what they see as a legitimate desire to make the maximum possible profit out of their oil before it is burned away. To achieve that aim was enough, at first, to take control of production (which did not even entail nationalization), then to agree among themselves not to put more oil on the market than prices would bear. In this respect, the cartel itself was basically dependent on Saudi Arabia, where the marginal production cost is lowest and potential further output at marginal cost is greatest.

After three years, the asymmetry of the dependence between producers and consumers has lessened: producing countries like Iran, Algeria, Indonesia, and Nigeria have launched so many development projects or programmed so many investments that they are as dependent on their oil revenues as the consumers are dependent on their oil. The cartel's dependence on Saudi Arabia has increased.

Let us recapitulate the grievances which emerge from the foregoing analyses of the position of the developing countries:

1. The direct investments of the industrialized countries cannot be held to be a form of exploitation in the culpable sense of the word. The example of the United States, which gained so many advantages from foreign investment in the nineteenth century, is in itself enough to refute this thesis. But there are numerous ways in which a multinational firm can make a poor country pay more than it can afford for the capital it receives: by repatriating profits, refusing to submit to the host country's economic strategy, hiring away potential business leaders, adding to the corruption of the ruling class, and so on. The balance of advantages and inconveniences varies from country to country. Independence now enables governments to refuse foreign investment or to lay down conditions for accepting it. Experience proves that it is in fact possible to make good use of the multinationals—or so the Soviet leadership, for one, undoubtedly believes.

2. The *terms of exchange* are a permanent theme of an argument which will never be resolved. The socialist states themselves refer to the prices of the world capitalist market to settle the conditions of their transactions, since their own price systems, because of their arbitrary character, have no transnational meaning. Once market prices are ruled out, there is no way of knowing how to organize trade in goods and services between economic entities with unequal productivity and using different currencies. Even if bilateral exchanges are built up, it is still necessary to find the unit which will serve to express the relative values of qualitatively different goods. Bartering oil for tanks still requires a unit of value.

Raising the prices of raw materials relative to manufactured goods—by what procedure? in what proportion?—involves one major objection, which is that around 50% of raw materials (cereals, metals) come from the industrialized countries (the United States, Canada, Australia, the Soviet Union). Would the European countries, which are poor in raw materials, accept an arbitrary increase in their prices?

To my mind, a generalized pegging of prices of raw materials to the prices of manufactured products would be unacceptable to the industrialized countries. On what indices would the pricing be calculated? Some exporting countries would benefit from reference to a general index, but others would suffer. Furthermore, to raise the prices of all raw materials in accordance with an index of all manufactured products would accentuate the deficiency of demand on several of the raw materials markets. I shall refrain from speculating on the consequences of a generalized indexation: it comes too close to economics as propaganda or economics as delirium.

On the other hand, one can envisage the possibility of compensating certain countries in the event that their export revenues decline. With respect to key raw materials, it is also possible to envisage a stockpiling system to soften the impact of sudden upward or downward movements (although initiatives of this type have seldom succeeded: it is hard to distinguish between the short-term fluctuations which need to be eliminated and the long-term trends that must be seen as inevitable).

3. What remains, then, to be settled? In the last analysis, three questions: reduction of the debts of certain small countries; stepping up unilateral financial transfers, in other words, the amount of aid granted by the industrialized countries; and opening up national frontiers to the manufactured goods of the Third World. The first two questions are simply a matter of dollars and cents. They are only a matter of generosity and enlightened self-interest. After all, the West does grant huge credits to the Soviets. The opening of frontiers—toward which "generalized preference"* would represent a first step—might run into opposition from certain production· sectors in the industrialized countries. All the same, those countries are heading that way, and they will do so more and more.

What, then, is the meaning of the "new world economic order"—a catchphrase which has been much in use since 1973 and the oil-price boom? To put it bluntly, it means nothing. Neither the monetary régime of generalized fluctuation, nor the validity of market prices for international exchanges, nor the ratio between the prices of raw materials and manufactured goods are going to be transformed overnight by universal accord. For the time being, it looks as if the rules of the monetary and the commercial game are *nonnegotiable*.

These rules do not in the least prevent the countries of the periphery

---

*The name given to the idea of reducing customs duties on the whole range of goods imported from the Third World.

from protecting their infant industries, nationalizing the subsidiaries of so-called multinational corporations, or setting their own conditions for direct investments. The volume of aid supplied to the Third World depends on the good will or uneasiness of the industrialized nations. It remains to be seen in which countries the volume of aid might be used, in any substantial way, to influence the prospects for development.

Within the international system (both political and economic), the reciprocal dependence of states contains an asymmetry in favor of the strong and the rich. However, if the word *imperialism* is used to describe the dependence of the raw materials exporters on the economic ups and downs of the industrialized countries, then that word will lead, finally, to a confusion between this inevitable dependence and the dispatch of Soviet tanks to Prague (or if one prefers, of U.S. Marines to Santo Domingo). Propaganda makes deliberate use of this confusion in order that the Soviet Empire cease to appear imperialist and that the European countries—including Switzerland—continue to be regarded as such, despite their decolonization.

With all this tumult taking place, one may forget, in the end, that the fate of the Third World remains bound up with the Atlantic alliance, not with the Soviet bloc. It is in Europe, Japan, and North America that the underdeveloped countries sell their raw materials and buy their capital equipment, and it is the industrialized capitalist countries that provide almost all the aid they clamor for. What do they get from the Soviet Union, apart from the ideology of imperialism—which is an *indictment* of the nations from which they demand everything, and a *justification* of the ones who give them nothing?

The weapons of peace
or Western aid to the USSR?

In 1973 a lesser Western Europe, one fragment of a minor headland of Asia called capitalist by the USSR and imperialist by the Third World's intellectuals, was showing all the signs of an historical success and a spectacular recovery from disaster. Nations that had fought a deadly war were reconciled to the point of virtually obliterating frontiers. Empires grown too costly and condemned by the spirit of the time had been, more or less graciously, relinquished. The challenge of Soviet growth—always more fictitious than real—had been countered by outrageous prosperity. There had been a broad integration of the world market, the result of an annual increase in the volume of trade by some 12%. Together, the Europeans who people the Western fringe of the Eurasian landmass from the far North to Sicily and from Istanbul to Stockholm appeared to have embarked on a new adventure—freedom for *all*, not only for themselves; greater wealth less unevenly distributed, first within individual states and then, by degrees, between them.

At the time of this writing (in the fall of 1976), crisis casts its menacing shadow over this recent past. The miraculous quarter century of triumphant and popularized Keynesianism now strikes one merely as the prelude to the "stagflation" in which the Western economies are floundering, causing the precarious unit among the industrialized economies, and between them and the assorted nations of the Third World, to break apart. The next part of this book is devoted to this polymorphous crisis. It is proof of the continuing vitality of a civilization which progresses through self-criticism. Or is it, quite to the contrary, proof of the exhaustion of societies that are fearful of the future and will not bear children anymore?

I have looked for the superiority of Europe in a field where many will not let themselves see it, in economics, and by speaking of productivity and efficiency. Not that I see the productivity of capital or labor, or productivity in general, as the index of the quality of a society or a civilization, but Western superiority in the sphere of freedom or *joie de vivre* could only be doubted by minds captive to fanaticism or prejudice. Those societies which call themselves socialist claim to have introduced a socio-economic régime worthy of succeeding the mixed systems of the West and destined to take over from them. All the clever thinkers who carp at the declining return on capital in the West have not yet perceived that it required the quantitative growth through accumulation which has characterized the *Soviet* economy to illustrate one of the projections made by *Capital* and to make possible an accelerated decline of the yield on capital. Such a decline presupposes a self-fueling accumulation which has no need of the buying power of the masses in order to maintain itself.

The "convergence theory" which drew the same barrage of protest from the theorists of Sovietism and of the Mixed Economies (or, if one prefers, of capitalism) was already outmoded even before the crisis erupted. It required a quaint misunderstanding of history to imagine that the systems which we call democratic—based on interparty competition, the legal status of the opposition, and permanent involvement of the power minority—represent either the necessary culmination or the normal mode of government. Quite the reverse: it is as a rare, precious, exceptional achievement of the art of politics that these systems deserve to be preserved (even if it runs counter to the "natural" course of events) by the will of man.

Of course, if it was naive to expect democracy in the USSR to advance at the same speed as the index of output or consumption, it was no less naive to put forward the choice of Stalinism or Westminster, the Kremlin or the White House. There are more things in heaven and earth than are dreamt of in our philosophy. One can imagine the Soviet oligarchs becoming more sensitive to popular demands. Except in the frantic periods of ideological tyranny, the oligarchs cannot isolate themselves from the bureaucracy and the people in any modern society. The Brezhnev team has been doing its best to meet the needs of Soviet consumers, first because (unlike Stalin) it would rather give its subjects what they want, secondly because, in the long run, consumer satisfaction is translated into the will to work, and lastly because Marxism-Leninism has never adopted the Spartan version of socialism except as a stopgap remedy.

By virtue of its standard of living, its cars, its gadgets even, Europe inevitably weighs heavy in the scale against the *other* Europe, a reluctant convert only barely resigned to the fate imposed upon it by Soviet dominion. This dominion cannot raise the Iron Curtain, nor itself evolve toward democracy solely under the influence of better living conditions: the maintenance of Soviet politico-military domination requires that the allied states not depart too much from the Moscow model. Twice already, in thirty years, the Kremlin has had to resort to the bayonet in order to remind the Hungarians, then the Czechs, of the limits to its tolerance of deviation.

The ideas expressed by one of Henry Kissinger's colleagues and which the press at once christened the "Sonnenfeld doctrine" did not altogether deserve the hostile reception they received but, even in the most favorable light, they suffered from naivety and/or inconsistency. The head of the State Department was saying something like this:

Soviet Russia's domination of Eastern Europe still comes down to crude military strength. We Americans cannot "liberate" the East Europeans and push back the Red Army. So we are prepared to recognize the Great Power interests which justify a Soviet presence or dominance in the so-called buffer zone, but that zone should at least change its character.

Let us overlook the unfortunate expression *organic character* applied to the Soviet presence by the American diplomat, who clearly wanted— without damaging the interests of the Great Power next door—that the East Europeans be able to regain some at least of their freedoms. In fact, they already have won back a few of them. The naivety and inconsistency of the diplomat's words derive from his misappreciation of the indissoluble link between Great-Power interests and the safeguarding of a minimum of institutional and ideological conformity.

The buffer zone protects the Soviet Union only to the extent that it contains régimes related to the Kremlin régime. Without them, it does not protect, but threatens. If the conflict between Europe and the Soviet Imperium were strictly a military matter, the Hungarian or Czech mode of government would hardly matter, or at any rate loyalty to the alliance would count for more than the payment of lip service to dialectical materialism. Now, militarily speaking, the men in the Kremlin are well aware that they no longer need to fear invasion from the West in the foreseeable future; it is rather the heartland of Old Europe which, with good reason, has to fear the deployment of the thousands of tanks that pour out of the Soviet factories, year after year. And yet, through its ideas, and even more through its way of life, Europe is able to call into question the foundations and the practice of Sovietism.

Going back to the self-evident proposition which I have mentioned several times already, there are only two kinds of end product, two kinds of output: armaments and civil consumption. People do not consume machinery, fertilizers or tractors; they do consume bread, meat, cars, and refrigerators. Of the Soviet annual GNP, 30% goes into investment, at least 10% (between 10% and 15%) into defense, and from 5% to 10% to public expenditure. That leaves about 50% for private consumption. It is the absurdity of its ideology (party power = democracy) and the irrationality of its economy (accumulation of the means of production = progress) that make the Soviet régime vulnerable. From this vulnerability arises the policy of the Kremlin: peaceful coexistence between states, war to the death between ideologies. In our own language, this means that the Russians want to keep the community of socialist states together and bring about the disintegration of the "aggressive" NATO bloc. They reject the West's ideas but buy its technology. Like many Third World governments, they buy bits and pieces of a system without grasping its spirit; they acquire a machine, not the human relationships which it presupposes or implies.

The much-debated question of East-West trade relations appears within this context. At first glance—and this is generally the reaction of the Soviet dissidents—the West is betraying its own death wish by providing enemies bent on its destruction with the means to deprive it of its remaining superiority: technology. To quote Lenin, "they will make the noose we hang them with." Conversely, some people see trade as a weapon of peace. If the capitalist and socialist markets become interdependent, a decisive step will have been taken along the road to the reconciliation and reunification of the two halves of Europe.

If one takes an overview of the zones which the Marxist-Leninist vocabulary calls the "capitalist world market" and the "socialist world market," one cannot conceive that the initiative for a break would come from the former. The capitalist world market contains one dominant entity, but *not* an imperial power. The states of Western Europe would not submit to a U.S.-dictated embargo against the USSR or the socialist states. Far from criticizing the occasional restrictions imposed on American exports to the Soviet Union by the government in Washington, they tend to rejoice at the opportunity this affords them to make a profit and increase their share of East-West trade. In the Cold War era, trade was reduced to a minimum, because the Soviet Union wanted to reorientate the trade of the satellite states so as to integrate them into a system where it retained control. For its part, the United States drew up a list of military items which were forbidden to be sold. According to later American studies, this "selective embargo" ultimately proved to be sterile or "counterproductive." The Russians filled the gaps through their own industries; they even made various technical advances in response to the challenge posed by the embargo.*

Apart from certain items of advanced technology (for instance, the latest generation of computers), the selectivity of the American embargo becomes increasingly meaningless the more one seeks a rational basis for it. According to the law of comparative costs, what is most profitable for the Russians to buy from the United States or abroad generally is grain, because production in the Soviet Union is so expensive in terms of both capital and labor input. Yet for a number of reasons, not least of which is pressure from its own farmers, the United States will not refuse to sell grain unless there is a worldwide shortage, when sales to the Soviet Union would reduce the resources needed by the underdeveloped countries.

The objection will rightly be made that the purchase of equipment, unlike the purchase of wheat or corn, enables the Russians to improve the productivity of their factories and compete more strongly with the West. In some spheres, the proportion of Western-derived equipment is considerable—a third of the sugarbeet crop is processed in factories bought from the West, and a third of all beer comes from breweries built by European firms. Overall, foreign industrial equipment is thought to account for 15% of the Soviet total.

It is striking to observe that the Russians bought only 130 Western licenses during the 1950s, whereas the Japanese bought 2500.† Here again, the nature of the régime explains the preference for buying complete ready-made factories rather than obtaining licenses. First, in any case, the Russians can imitate foreign models in many fields. But thereafter—and this is the crucial point—they have trouble overcoming the obstacles put up by their method of management, and in coordinating the activities of different factories and of several branches of industry. The priority aim of Soviet enterprises is to meet the quotas laid down by the "indicators," the central operational orders. Introducing a new procedure or an improved machine does not necessarily promote the fulfillment of the plan, not at first, at any rate.

By giving a Western firm overall responsibility for building a production unit—capital, engineers, sometimes even workers—the Russians reduce

*Cf. *Soviet Economic Prospects for the Seventies,* pp. 638–89, in particular pp. 662–64. In response to the embargo on natural rubber and diamonds, the Russians built a synthetic rubber industry and discovered vast diamond fields in Eastern Siberia.
†*The Economist,* April 17, 1976, pp. 50–51.

or eliminate the bottlenecks, the difficulty of inserting foreign machinery and organization into the Soviet system. This does not mean that they are catching up on the West, however, for the simple reason that the equipment sold is not necessarily the latest technology and, without replacement and modernization, quickly becomes obsolete.

After all these arguments, however, uncertainty does persist. For industrialists to be reluctant to give up deals with the Russians, particularly during periods of reduced activity, is understandable. According to the *Financial Times* of July 29, 1976, West Germany accumulated a surplus of 22 billion marks out of its trade with Eastern Europe in the period 1972–75. Eastern Europe absorbs a sizeable fraction of West Germany's capital exports and provides the greater part of its overall trading surplus. On the economic level this may be called reciprocal dependence—one side needs orders, the other equipment, and everybody benefits. From the political point of view, the advantages are not so evenly balanced, since the West is selling some of the secrets of its continuing superiority. But as the West is incapable of refraining, and a lot of these secrets remain nontransferable, it is best to accept what cannot be prevented and to investigate the long-term consequences.

Since the Soviet plan for 1975–80 anticipates a 20–25% annual growth of trade with the West—which assumes increased resources to finance imports—we come to what is ultimately the decisive question: does growing Soviet dependence on Western technology, balanced by growing Western dependence on the markets of Eastern Europe—mutual dependence, in fact—constitute a step along the way to reunification and, therefore, to genuine peace?

In our present state of knowledge, the answer to this question must be no. It is true that the Soviet Union and the countries of Eastern Europe are feeling the effects of the capitalist market's inflation. As providers of raw materials, they are feeling the impact of the rising prices of the goods they import. Furthermore, the Soviet Union benefits from the price of oil, while the petroleum-importing countries of Eastern Europe suffer from it. From this angle, so-called socialist Europe probably has a vested interest in the survival and restored health of Western capitalism. The Poles and Hungarians make no secret of this fact, but then they belong to the Soviet bloc only by compulsion, not by choice.

If the socialist economies continue to increase their purchases in the West, and if, in order to repay their debts, they have to export manufactured goods (not just raw materials) to their creditors, what appears on the horizon is a growing symmetry of mutual dependence between the two world markets and between every East European state and the two world markets. In this sense, and in the long term, commercial exchange would contribute toward bringing the two worlds closer to one another. In the short and medium term, there is a different prospect: the Soviet Union is multiplying its efforts and is borrowing more and more, in an attempt to close a gap in technology and productivity which is constantly being recreated by its own political and ideological régime.

All the same, the USSR is less threatened by ideological competition than by the example of the West. Its frontiers remain relatively leakproof, but not those of Poland or East Germany. Millions of West Germans have visited East Germany as a result of the Helsinki agreement. In Poland, there is resistance from workers against falling living standards and from intellectuals against Soviet domination. Even in crisis, Western Europe continues contrasting its color with the bureaucratic gray, its easy bearing with regimentation, the life of individuals with the imperatives of the Plan.

part III
Europe its own victim

The great fear of 1973;
themes of self-criticism

Since 1945, the capitalist or Western economies have suffered no crisis in the sense used by nineteenth-century economists and still more between the wars. The alternation of phases of boom and slump have not disappeared and, in the United Kingdom, there was talk of "stop-go," meaning the recurrent need to take restrictive measures to combat inflation or a negative balance of payments following strong expansion. Despite these alternations, which were not synchronized throughout the world market as a whole, the terms used were no longer "depression," or "crisis" but, at the very worst, "recession."

Since the fall of 1973, everything has changed. All the Western economies were then the simultaneous victims of an inflation whose average rate of 15% was the highest ever observed in peacetime. The brutal rise in oil prices spread a great fear, that of an energy and raw materials "famine" which would bring the wheels of industry to a halt. In response to these two events—steep inflation and the increased price of oil—Western governments once again adopted a concerted policy of deflation. A recession affecting the entire world economy was the natural outcome.

This recession would probably not have made such a deep impact on world opinion had it not succeeded the widespread social and cultural criticism of the 1960s. Today, when the French refer to crisis, one does not know whether they have in mind the 15% fall in industrial output between mid-1974 and mid-1975, the concurrence of a drop in output and a persistent rise in prices or, lastly, the criticism of modern civilization. This criticism—another expression of "the Crisis"—was expressed in France by the events of May 1968, tumultuous, absurd or exhilarating, according to taste. The student rebellion—a kind of "cultural revolution" which fell just short of true revolution—popularized themes which had been cropping up in just about every sphere of sociological and journalistic literature both in France and, even more, in the United States.

The ecological theme. *Industry is devastating nature and polluting the air, the rivers, and the seas. With new and often valid arguments, the indictment of ecologists echoes that of the conservatives or counterrevolutionaries who detested technology and its ugliness, machines and their artificiality, and the severing of the link between human beings and their original environment.*

The neo-Malthusian theme. *For two hundred years, ever since the Industrial Revolution in England and the demographic revolution that accompanied it, the optimists and pessimists have pursued an endless debate, with first one side, then the other, winning the battle of public opinion. In the late 1960s, the pessimists got the upper hand, and the first report of the Club of Rome—an almost ideal model of pseudoscience and pseudoexactness—scored an immense success. Playing with five variables* without specifying the relations postulated between them, it claimed to prove that "wild" growth—the growth of population, consumption of nonrenewable resources, and agricultural products—led inexorably to physical impossibilities. The temporary embargo on oil exports to certain countries and the quadrupling of oil prices have absolutely nothing in common with the forecasts, or rather the forebodings, of the Club of Rome. Inevitably, a confusion grew up in the public mind between eventual shortages of nonrenewable resources and the immediate scarcity of energy. The effective action of a cartel became the alarm bell, the harbinger of an apocalyptic catastrophe; unless a change of pace*

---

*Population, nutrition, industrial output, nonrenewable resources, pollution.

or direction occurred, the world would see "panic in the year 2000."

The indictment of productivism. *Productivism (whose alleged "cult of growth" is only a phase) has never been unanimously accepted in the West. It still has to defend itself against the hostility of nostalgics who may equally be called traditionalists or romantics, descendants of Jean-Jacques Rousseau or of the counterrevolutionaries. The ideological or existential critique of industrial society prolongs a current of thought which goes back at least as far as the late eighteenth century. Freudo-Marxism, as well as the denunciation of technology, mass culture, and impersonal relations enriched it without adding anything fundamentally new.*

The European growth performance in the period 1947–72 came in response both to the haunting memory of the Great Depression and to the Soviet challenge. One kind of propaganda presented growth rate as the major criterion of the quality of a régime. Why be surprised if the governments of Paris, of Bonn, of Rome, set out to let themselves not be overtaken and to avoid the mistakes of the interwar period?

Hindsight showed, not the limits of growth, but the limits of the benefits it could be expected to provide. Growth itself is not enough to transform the established order; society reproduces itself in its own image, and differences in pay, prestige, and power between classes or individuals remain essentially what they were. Even improvements in the general level of education have only a slow effect on changing the respective prospects of promotion for young people from different social classes. Furthermore, competition for position and privilege intensifies, and envious comparisons of living standards start up an endless marathon which no group can ever win.

Crisis, in the sense of criticism or self-criticism, seems to me to be typical of Western civilization, which owes its own originality and its centuries of creativity to this perpetual reexamination of every question. Separation of the temporal from the spiritual power prevented the sacralization of ephemeral institutions, fostered disquiet, and actuated the quest for an accord between the virtues to which all régimes lay claim and those (more modest) to which they have access.

Neither recession, nor stagnation, nor unrest in church and university, imply or foreshadow any economic or moral decline of Western Europe. The 1947–73 period, the brightest in the economic history of the West, could not continue indefinitely to produce such high rates of growth with no interruptions or temporary setbacks. In a long-term perspective, even the Great Depression was only a brief episode for the United States, barely visible on a graph of GNP per capita. But out of that episode came millions of unemployed, Hitler, and World War II.

In the next three chapters, I discuss the present crisis, *in its three dimensions: economic, political, and cultural. The time of "economic miracles" is over, and the climate promises to be rougher for the next few years, at least. All the same, an observer from the nearest inhabited planet would hardly see a 10% drop in living standards as a catastrophe. The 1974–1975 recession did not produce any such hardship for the French people, but if a 5% unemployment rate and the grievances of workers and managers bring the Communists to power—in Italy, or in France—the "brief episode" suddenly becomes a momentous event.*

Greatness and vulnerability go together: the Western societies pay for their liberalism with instability, and for their complexity of organization by crises. We certainly do not envy the bureaucratic despotisms their polished façades; we want to preserve freedom itself.

It is up to the Europeans to ensure that the crisis remains a passing episode and does not become a step toward decline.

7

No more miracles

Structural or conjunctural crisis

More than a century ago, each time a crisis of overproduction broke out, often in a single industrial sector (in those days it was cotton goods), Marx and Engels feverishly asked one another whether it was a cyclical or a structural crisis, a temporary crisis or the "final crisis" of capitalism. The world crisis of 1974–75, as if it were a matter of course, revived the debate: once again, with a gravity that was at bottom comical, Marxists, economists, and journalists debated which adjective ought to be applied to the recession.

I say that the debate was comical, because it is meaningful only in the context of a philosophy of history which most of the crystal-gazers do not share. What makes a crisis "structural"? It is the fact that the causes of crisis are a part of the system itself, and can be eliminated only by a radical alteration of the system. Nationalization of this or that company does not constitute such an alteration, therefore we are back at the same old theme of "structural crises," namely, the falling profitability of capital. This is, indeed, a likely hypothesis: owing to a number of circumstances—inflation, among others—it may be that the profitability of capital in most of the big industrial nations has fallen, on the average, during the last decade or so. To transform this fall (which jogs Marxist memories) into a necessary and sufficient cause of a structural crisis, and one which capitalism is incapable of overcoming, it takes the imagination of a true believer and the everdisappointed trust of a Marx or Engels in a "final revolution around the corner."

Like any crisis, the one of 1974–75 had certain unusual features, but these did not make it a mystery. As the first crisis after a quarter century of continuous fast growth, it shook public opinion, principally, because neither the governing circles nor the commentators or opinion-makers had any direct experience with the phenomenon. One day, I heard the French premier make an off-the-cuff speech in which he spoke the following words (I am quoting from memory, not verbatim): "Last year something exceptional and unpredictable happened. There was no growth. There was even *negative growth.*" (The latter is modern jargon for a decline in the national product.) I turned to my neighbor and whispered: "He's young." A man of forty has not lived through any crisis. If he was educated at the Institute of Political Studies or the National School of Administration, he has received only a superficial introduction to the theory of crises and of short and long cycles. Of course he knows that, in theory, the same Keynesian therapy cures too little aggregate demand as well as too much; all it requires is reversing the remedies. But, in 1974–75, stagflation (the combination of high prices and unemployment) did not reproduce the economic situation on which Keynes's *General Theory* was based.

Expansion, inflation, and the dollar

Before 1973, the economists were wondering about the causes of an apparent structural transformation of the Western, and particularly the European, economies.

I have in front of me a working document drawn up for the "1985 Commission," which sat in the early 1960s. In France, the annual increase in productivity per man-year for the period 1950–60 was 4.7% for agriculture, 4.5% for industry, and 3.3% for services. For the period 1960–85, the commission projected rates of 4.7, 4.2, and 3.3%. Now the French rates of 1950–60, which were higher than those of the United Kingdom and the United States per man-year, would have given France a growth rate of GNP per capita more than twice as high as the 1.8% rate which took the United States to the top of the league. Until 1973, the projections of the 1985 group looked likely to be confirmed by the facts.

Why this exceptional success? In common parlance, a variety of causes combined to make a European "miracle" understandable (although who would have seen this sort of divine surprise coming in 1947?). The needs of reconstruction, followed by the general spread of consumer durables through every social level, created both the demand necessary for full employment and good opportunities for profitable investment. In Italy and France, there was a substantial shift of manpower from agriculture into industry and the tertiary industries, and from low-productivity into high-productivity jobs. Businesses financed investment out of their own profits or with the help of the banks. The magical (25%) percentage of investment in the national product which was supposed to characterize centralized economies able to impose all kinds of sacrifices on consumers was achieved or surpassed by some decentralized or capitalist economies without resorting to any method of compulsory saving. Wages rose faster than prices and kept the boom going. Liberalization of trade and monetary convertibility, from the late 1950s onward, created a world context favorable both to exchanges of goods and transfers of capital.

Should this be called a "mutation" of the capitalist economies, to be explained in terms of greater experience in handling economic ups and downs, or a superior capacity for management or organization? Several scientific studies set out to establish the precise importance of each factor (capital, manpower transfers, etc.). They all put their finger on the influence of a residual factor, in other words, the difference between the growth rate resulting from adding up the various quantifiable factors and the growth rate actually observed. The difference was christened "the residual factor" and attributed to what may be called economic progress: better coordination of the means of production, and better management.*

However that may be, the period 1948–70 saw the simultaneous appearance of major innovations (e.g., electronics, computers), the general spread of goods previously available only to the few, and the opening of frontiers to goods and capital—in short, a favorable historical constellation of the principal macroeconomic variables. There was no need to postulate any radical, permanent mutation of the capitalist economies. Those of the European nations had fallen behind the American economy and were simply narrowing the gap, running fast before a friendly wind.

Only a few years later, the direction of the debate was switched around. Instead of speculating about the "mutation" which permitted or guaranteed annual growth rates for GNP per capita of 4 or 5%, other economists (but sometimes the same ones) were asking themselves what structural cause condemned the same economies to choose between inflation and unemployment, and perhaps soon to take the brunt of both these economic evils.

This type of speculation does not in fact date from the 1973 recession itself, for the wave of prosperity had been accompanied by a certain amount of worldwide inflation. There again, without going into specialist theories, observation of the real world provided at least the beginnings of an explanation. Western governments—with the sole exception of the U.S. government until about 1961 and the West German government after 1965—had given growth and full employment priority over price stability. Keynesianism, a system devised to counter low levels of aggregate de-

*See Appendix, Note E.

mand, served to fuel the machinery of expansion. Of the "magic trinity"—price stability, full employment, and a high growth rate*—they unhesitatingly sacrificed the first term to the second, which was the priority objective, and to the third, which they considered to be an historical constraint. The simultaneous upward movement of output and prices now seemed inevitable, and businesses were inclined to devote the gains due to improved productivity to raising wages, rather than cutting the price of their goods. The wage increases agreed to by businesses with rapidly rising productivity were communicated to all sectors and, in consequence, the average growth of wages overtook the average growth of labor productivity.

Of course, this socio-economic mechanism assumed the tolerance of the monetary authorities. Only a lax credit policy allows businesses to gamble permanently on growth and inflation, and to give wage boosts compatible with the stability of prices within the business itself but not inside the economy as a whole. Governments very often encouraged the permissiveness of banks and the transformation of short- or medium-term deposits or investments into long-term investments.

The French and Italian "miracles" had a rational explanation, one that did not require any such extraordinary hypothesis, such as a mutation of the decentralized economies. Nor was it any different with the last phase of the big expansion of 1965 to 1971 or 1973, with the big inflation of 1973, and the recession of 1974–75.

After 1961 the American leadership, struck by the difference between their own growth rate and that of the Europeans, also decided on a voluntarist growth policy. The first two years of the Kennedy era, 1962–63, stand out as a kind of Golden Age. As forecast, tax cuts made in step with growth boosted the buying power necessary for the pursuit of growth. Business devoted part of the productivity gains toward a lowering of prices, so that higher wages across the whole economy did not outstrip higher average productivity. During those exceptional years, there remained a margin between the state of the economy and full employment; and experience perhaps might have confirmed the optimism of the advocates of the "new economics." But in 1963, J. F. Kennedy was assassinated; in 1965, Lyndon Johnson took the United States into the Vietnam War almost surreptitiously, and did not have the courage to ask the Congress for the means to finance it. The United States thus got bogged down in both the rice fields of the Mekong and in the quicksands of inflation.

American inflation has an altogether different effect on the world economy than any other country's inflation, and for two reasons: the sheer

---

*Sometimes it is free wage bargaining which constitutes the third term, since full employment and growth are assumed to be indivisible. In fact, apparent full employment does not always imply a high rate of growth.

volume of the American economy and the role of the dollar. This was not and could not be "just another currency." Like the pound sterling in the last century, after World War II the dollar became the ideal international currency. As an accounting and working currency, and a reserve currency as well, convertible into any other currency anywhere in the world, it freed the United States from certain constraints by which other countries are bound.

Suppose that France has a balance-of-payments deficit: we are spending more foreign currency to buy goods and services abroad than we are earning by the sale of our own goods and services. Without foreign currency, we can no longer buy the raw materials and energy we need, and without which the economic machine runs down like a car with an empty gas tank. In order to balance its foreign account, the government will inevitably slow down the development of the economy at the same time it tries to restrain inflation. In other words, since the external deficit is imputable to a domestic imbalance, the measures taken to correct this imbalance will in fact usually slow down growth as much as (and sometimes more than) the upward trend of prices.

It is different with the United States, as issuer of the international currency. In the 1950s, it readily accepted a deficit of between 1 and 2 billion dollars on its balance of payments. These deficits involved a redistribution of the gold supply, as intended by the various Washington administrations. But with the arrival of President Kennedy in the White House, a new era was ushered in: the volume of deficits increased, causing the president—President Kennedy and, after him, Johnson—to become uneasy about it and to take measures against the deficit: limitation of capital exports, bank lending, and equalization tax to discourage the acquisition of foreign securities and restrict foreign access to the U.S. capital market, etc. None of these *ad hoc* measures reduced the external deficit, which was swollen by Vietnamese inflation. In 1968, the institution of a free market in gold marked the end of the convertibility of the dollar into gold. In August 1971 this convertibility, which now existed only in theory (the principal central banks had agreed not to insist on their dollar holdings being convertible into gold), officially ceased. At the same time, President Nixon imposed on the Europeans and recalcitrant Japanese a devaluation of the American dollar against the currencies of countries which were political partners and commercial competitors. A year and a half later, in March 1973, after a second devaluation of the dollar, it officially became a floating currency, freely convertible into any other currency at a rate determined by the market, but not into gold at a fixed rate. The foreign central banks resigned themselves (or decided) to cease maintaining the dollar exchange rate by buying dollars at a fixed rate. After holding out against it for a long

time, the American authorities made up their minds to accept the devaluation of their own currency, and not only the revaluation of the mark and
the yen.

The transformation of the Bretton Woods international monetary system
and the transition from the gold exchange standard to a general float was
the subject of an impassioned polemic in governing circles as well as among
economists. Undoubtedly, the dollar's status as an international currency
enabled the United States to pay its foreign debts, not in foreign currency,
but in its own. The low contribution of foreign trade to the national
product* dissuaded the American leadership from trying to use a slowdown
of economic activity as a means of balancing its external account. American
firms continued to invest abroad;† as for the banks, they got past the
restrictions legally imposed on their foreign loans, by means of the
Eurodollar market. But if, with hindsight, one may regret that the analysis
of the situation given to Kennedy by some economists (by Professor P.
Samuelson in particular) did not lead him to conclude that devaluation of
the dollar was a necessity, the fact remains that, whether it is convertible
into gold or not, whether its exchange rate is fixed or floating, the dollar
remains the standard international currency, even if it is no longer in such
general use as a money of account. The pound occupied a comparable
position in the nineteenth century, it was no less linked to gold, and
throughout the century Great Britain kept its accounts in surplus (thanks to
returns on capital invested abroad).

1965, the start of Vietnam-based inflation; 1968, *de facto* severance
between gold and the dollar; 1971, official devaluation of the dollar; 1973,
liquidation of the Bretton Woods system and installation of a system (or
non-system) of generalized currency floating. These four dates mark the
stages of a monetary and inflationary crisis which resulted in the Great
Inflation of 1973, with an average rate of 15% across the whole world
economy. Among the industrialized nations, inflation in Great Britain and
Italy exceeded 25%, while West Germany kept its own inflation down to
half the average rate.

There is debate among economists about the degree of responsibility
which should be attributed to the transformation or dislocation of the
international monetary system. They do not dispute the spread of American inflation after 1965, when the central banks were buying all the dollars
put on offer in order to maintain the rate of exchange. The world economy
had already entered upon a process of endemic inflation before the explosion of 1973. This was preceded by an abnormally rapid expansion of the

*U.S. exports accounted for about 5% of the GNP.

†In 1975–76, a certain reversal was observed in the flow of capital. Volkswagen wanted to
build a factory in the United States, and various American towns competed with each other
by bidding up the concessions accorded the foreign investor.

money supply in the United States,* after the restriction of 1971 and a number of bank failures, with a view to the presidential elections of 1972. To cap it all, developments in the main industrial countries were rigorously synchronized. On the world scale, a surplus of credit appeared, produced more by electoral considerations than the desire for growth at all costs. Some random events—poor harvests, massive grain purchases by the USSR—caused a rise in food and agricultural prices which, in turn, had effect on the cost of living and, therefore, on wage claims. The simultaneous world boom has caused a massive accumulation of stocks in 1973; a stock clearance crisis followed inevitably, as if to confirm the excess.

Let us not even consider the fourfold rise in oil prices. An average inflation of 15%, affecting all the industrialized countries, was bound to force governments to take action against inflation. In the present state of available counter-inflationary measures, such action stops *growth* more quickly than it stops price-rises. That it should have provoked a recession and a certain amount of unemployment without also stabilizing prices does not seem to me to contradict the lessons of economics.

There is no need whatsoever to speculate about structural crisis and cyclical crisis. The last years of the great expansion had paved the way for the inflation of 1973. This inflation, in turn, together with the synchronization of similar economic developments, provoked a backlash, a recession, involuntarily triggered, with the purpose of putting an end to inflation. What requires study and reflection, here, is the manner in which the Western economies reacted to this first postwar recession, and the way the decentralized economies with democratic régimes have tended to react toward inflation. If such a tendency is admitted, should we not also fear that inflation itself tends to accelerate? This raises, once again, the notion of a structural crisis, but in a positive and, so to speak, empirical sense: the internal tensions in a partly state-regulated market economy reach the *threshold of rupture* or, to put it more simply, they reach a point where they do not permit expansion without excessive price increases or price stability without intolerable unemployment.

Crisis politics and living on credit

In 1974 and 1975, the principal Western countries pursued similar policies, which were the counterpart of the similar errors they had committed, although on a different scale. All of them were threatened with balance-of-payment deficits because of increased oil costs and inflation, and all of them took more or less severe restrictive measures. Usually, it takes nine months

*The expansion of credit preceded the presidential elections in the fall of 1972; its effect made itself felt during 1973, and governments were slow to take corrective measures.

for restrictions or relaxations on credit to feed through and produce a change in the economy. In 1974, following the superboom and superinflation of the previous year, * came a slackening of activity; then, some months later, prices started rising more slowly. About halfway through 1975, the monetary authorities timidly began to reopen the valves, and halfway through 1976 recovery was well on its way in the United States, West Germany, and also in France (though not without all sorts of reservations and causes for anxiety).

Naturally, the synchronization of deflationary economic conditions in 1974–75 did not rule out disparities between countries, in terms both of inflation rates and a drop in production. The inflation rate fell to 5–6% in the Federal Republic of West Germany, and to 9–10% in France; it remained close to 25% in Great Britain until mid-1975 and decreased to half that rate in the course of the following year. Industrial output fell by 10–15%, GNP by 5–6%.

On the whole, the "built-in stabilizers" appear to have worked satisfactorily and to have prevented a slide from a recession into a deep depression. Social security transfers and other shifts of social wealth upheld the overall level of buying power, despite the decline in production. Governments accepted budgetary deficits. In France, unemployment (calculated according to the number of persons looking for work)† reached about 5% (1 million out of about 20 million wage earners). In the United States, it rose to 8%, although differences in statistical methods account partly for this. As for the industrialized countries' balances of payments, they improved within a year (no doubt as a result of the recession), while those of the poor countries suffering from oil scarcity took the full weight of the inevitable deficits—deficits which were the automatic outcome of the oil-producing countries' surpluses and the billions of dollars these countries earned but were unable to spend.

Let us consider France, for example. To judge by reports of the press, radio, and television, any Frenchman (or foreigner in France) might have thought that the country was going through a tragic ordeal affecting practically the whole population. In reality, the wage policy guaranteed civil servants and public sector employees a wage that was a few (three or four) points higher than the rise in living costs. In the private sector, too, wages continued to grow more rapidly than did the cost of living. Partial unemployment probably meant a slight reduction in real monthly wages for a

*The retail price index in the United States for December–December rose by 3.4% in 1971–72; 8.8% in 1972–73; 12.2% in 1973–74; 7.0% in 1974–75. For France, the figures were 6.9; 8.5; 15.2 and 9.6. For West Germany, 6.5; 7.8; 5.9; 5.4. For the United Kingdom, 7.7; 10.6; 19.2; 24.9.

†This number appears to be greater than the actual number of unemployed.

minority of workers, but the great majority of the French people were unaffected. Where was the similarity to the depression of 1931–36?

If anything, the stabilization machinery worked too well or, to be more exact, the governing circles, apprehensive about working-class reactions to a situation that had been unknown for a generation, took precautions that can quite properly be called demagogic. Workers, laid off for economic reasons, were allowed to receive 90% of their wages for a year;* why should they rush out to find another job? Likewise, even though it was perhaps a very good thing for workers to earn almost as much, for thirty-two hours' work, as they had received, previously, for forty, but should one be surprised that they complained at having to return to a forty-hour week? In general, the French government—the prisoner of its wage policy—lacked the courage to announce, by way of a directive, its objective of maintaining buying power† (instead of the previous objective of raising it), nor its non-use of tax money to finance the measures taken to limit unemployment and reduce its repercussions on people. Part of the cost of these measures fell on businesses which, at the time when recovery was taking hold, were far from having set their accounts in order in the course of the recession, and needed public assistance.

As a percentage of the total work force, foreign workers represent 28.2% in Switzerland, 9.4% in West Germany, 9.0% in France, and 6.8% in Belgium. Even in Holland, which is supposed to be overpopulated, and where population density is extremely high, the percentage is still 3.4.‡ In recent years, governments have restricted immigration, but these millions of foreign workers perform jobs which are distasteful to Western Europeans, to the French in particular. This highlights the cause—call it structural, if you wish—of unemployment which occurs as soon as the growth rate falls: it is the discrepancy between the jobs that are sought and the ones that are offered. The less the French consent to do certain tasks, the greater becomes the number of young people who complete secondary and higher education, causing marginal unemployment increasingly to resist government efforts to provide jobs. Furthermore, the parties in power, encouraged by the opposition, seem to be relapsing into the errors of the 1930s: once again, there is a tendency to reason as if there existed a *fixed quantity* of available work, to be shared out as well as possible; as if, by reducing some people's work, work were created for others; as if the work of some people did not in fact create buying power and, indirectly, work for other people.§

*Only a minority of the jobless benefited from this measure.
†Raymond Barre was the first to reach this decision, in the fall of 1976.
‡Figures for 1973, quoted in *The Economist*, August 9, 1975.
§Cf. the books by the socialist A. Sauvy, who never tires of denouncing this fallacy.

France has thus been through the two years of recession without furore and without undue social agitation. Most people reacted by the wise old course of saving more*—which, in the short term, contributed to slowing down activity. Criticism of "wild growth" has lost a little of its virulence; the experts are asking each other what growth rate would enable unemployment to be permanently eliminated (probably an unattainable target under present-day French conditions); the notion of *slower growth* (for want of a better way of expressing the ill-defined slogan of "a different growth") has become a part of current thinking.

Bearing in mind the agonies of 1973, as well as the apocalyptic prophecies which caused some observers to rejoice, the general world economic situation tends rather to justify equanimity. Recession did not turn into depression; the industrialized nations massively increased their exports to the beneficiaries of the oil-price increases;† the poor countries, deprived of oil, borrowed the billions of dollars they needed, to make up their deficits, from banks which received, directly or indirectly, the oil-rich nations' surpluses. In mid-1976, the Western economies seemed to be showing their capacity for adaptation, rather than their exhaustion.

I suspect that this cautiously optimistic diagnosis will encounter a fairly widespread scepticism. Its motives will vary from country to country, but some of them will crop up nearly everywhere, and I want to enumerate them. In Europe, two countries, Great Britain and Italy, are apparently suffering from a more deep-seated disease which was not caused by the recession and which recovery will not cure. Are these national diseases, or are they the extreme form of the disease which has affected *all* the European countries? We will come to that in the next chapter. The fact remains that, in both cases, the recession was an indicator, but not the cause of the problem.

A second reason to be concerned is economic: the absence of an international monetary system in the ordinary and traditional sense of the term. For the first time, there is no longer any reference to a real good, a metal. The only remaining money of account, or specie, is a cocktail of currencies or a quasicurrency, like the special drawing rights. The floating exchange rate has become the norm, and no government feels obliged, any longer, to defend the parity of its currency. Does not such a system or nonsystem apply permanent instability, permanent inflation?

The consequences of higher petroleum prices still continue, and have been met by stopgap methods. In 1974, the deficits of the oil-importing countries rose to 52 billion dollars and, in 1975, to 35 billion. The industrialized countries—as a result of the recession, their increased sales to the

*The percentage of household income saved rose by several points in 1974.
†Oil prices rose by more than 50% overall, between 1973 and 1974.

oil-producing countries, and the drop in the cost of raw materials (itself due to the recession)—have just about balanced their accounts. The poor countries without oil are living on their borrowings. What is more, the industrialized countries have not as yet redeployed their means of production to bring about the necessary transfer of resources implied by the high cost of oil and other energy-producing materials.

Lastly—and this third reason may embrace all the rest—in the view of many economists, the capitalist societies must henceforward be regarded as torn by an insoluble contradiction: inflation or unemployment, nor is the likelihood to be excluded that greater inflation will cause further unemployment. It is in the nature of the decentralized economies that they contain a labor market in which trade unions (if not individuals) haggle with employers over working conditions. If the trade unions have acquired so much power that they can successfully demand wages incompatible with stable prices, or else if the level of unemployment which would be liable to curb wage claims is socially unacceptable, the only remaining choice is between an income policy negotiated by the government with the unions, or endemic inflation which, in the long run, will involve the paralysis or destruction of the liberal capitalist system of the West.

Before going on to discuss the international monetary system and endemic inflation, let me briefly recapitulate why a cautious diagnosis is so essential. It is essential because there is nothing to prove that the recession is over and that adaptation to the new oil prices has been achieved.

Among the oil-producing states there were some (such as Iran, Indonesia, Nigeria, Algeria) which, with their large populations and a determination to modernize, were willing and able to spend all their oil revenues. To be sure, their investment plans ran into occasional bottlenecks—shortages of ports or roads, means of transportation, or trained technicians—but, despite these holdups, they did not accumulate dollars, or not in large amounts. The industrialized countries received most of their orders and contracts, and these exports therefore paid the oil bills.*

A second category of countries, headed by Saudi Arabia, could not possibly spend its income and, in any case, did not want to. With a relatively small (less than 10 million) population, a traditional form of social organization, and good reason to fear hasty modernization (which would be fraught with revolutionary dangers), the country least able to spend its oil revenues is also the one with the greatest reserves which are, in addition, the cheapest to tap.

OPEC has kept itself together but, as of this writing, has not raised its 1973 prices to adjust to Western inflation and the higher cost of the goods

---

*The resources shifted as a result of the oil price rise represented about 3.5% of the gross world product (GWP).

bought by the member states of the cartel. This moderation is explained partly by the sales difficulties encountered by some exporters during the recession phase, but partly, also, by political decisions of the Saudi leadership. It is in their power to raise or lower the yield of their wells and, consequently, to bring about surpluses or penury. Of all the oil-exporting states, it is Saudi Arabia that holds most of the trump cards and which can decide the life or death of the cartel and the ups and downs of its prices. Only Saudi Arabia can decrease its production in the event of a glut on the market, because it does not spend all its revenues. Only Saudi Arabia can raise its outputs high enough to satisfy all demand at the prices fixed by OPEC.

In the negotiations between the exporting and the importing countries, the position of the latter has relatively improved. The exporting countries have embarked on ambitious development schemes and thus lost their freedom of action. They have become dependent on their higher oil income. Certainly, if all the oil countries found themselves in the same situation and had the same interests, they would, if necessary, reach agreement to raise their prices, even if it meant cutting production. But the contrast between Iran and Saudi Arabia reveals the divergences between the members of the cartel—divergences which do not entail the dissolution of the coalition indispensable to them all, but which compel compromises that are welcome to importers but disappointing to exporters already in external deficit.

Not that the importers have settled the two problems created by the OPEC decisions; the poor countries which have no oil can keep going only on credits granted to them by the international organizations or the banks and it does not look as if the redeployment of the productive apparatus required by the transfer of real resources to the oil-exporting countries has as yet come about.

Does this mean a serious threat to the world economy? It is hard to see how the poor countries without oil are to balance their external accounts again. The burden of interest payments will have to be added to the cost of essential imports. A growing number of countries—socialist states included*—now live on the loans they receive. Some of them will never obtain the means to pay off the interest and repay the loans. Even if the outcome is not a general crisis of the monetary and banking system, does this pyramid of credit not constitute a cause of *inflation on a worldwide scale?*

In the case of the industrialized states, they have settled their oil bill, as a result of recession and improved terms of trade. After a brief panic, the

---

*Eastern Europe as a whole was around 35 billion dollars in debt in the late summer of 1976.

Western economies are back on the same route as before, although, for the time being, at a slower pace.

I subscribe to these views while emphasizing the lessons of recent years. Events confirm the most simplistic chains of reasoning. What happens to extra revenues? Either they are spent through orders for goods from the industrialized countries (which thereby gain the wherewithal to pay for their imports), or else they pile up, and since paper dollars buried in the sand are worthless, they have to be "put to work." Where do you put them, if not into the Western monetary and banking system, which thereupon takes charge of the funds necessary for lending to countries with adverse balances? The *nouveaux riches* provide credits for the poorest countries, even without knowing it, while the *anciens riches,* who are less impoverished than they had feared, go on granting more credits than they receive. The situation is unprecedented, but it does not necessarily finish up in catastrophe.

What appears to be graver than the effects of the oil cartel is the persistence of an annual price inflation of about 6% in West Germany and 10% in France, where in mid-1976 the leadership was still hovering between the brakes and the accelerator. The slow rate of recovery, particularly in the field of investment, suggests a touch of acceleration; the inflation rate of 10–11%* seems to indicate the reverse. In fact, businesses are reluctant to hire because they kept on more workers than they needed during the recession. They are unwilling to invest because they have doubts about the volume of future growth.

To bring inflation down to an acceptable level, it is quite clearly necessary to limit the growth of credit, if not the budgetary deficit, during the first phase of recovery, even if that means being satisfied with a rate of growth lower than what French planners considered normal before 1973 and still regard as indispensable for the next plan. In brief, without venturing to make a prognosis, it seems likely to me that the economic climate of the coming years will differ from that of the phase nowadays referred to, whether in praise or condemnation, as "Keynesian."

What monetary system?

On Thursday, June 17, 1976, in San Francisco, Johannes Witteveen, managing director of the International Monetary Fund, delivered a speech entitled "The International Monetary System Takes Shape." Meanwhile,

*Retail price rise.

most French economic analysts have continued to denounce monetary anarchy, the absence of rules, the arbitrary behavior of the Americans—regarding the United States sometimes as the expression of "American imperialism" and sometimes as the cause of inflation and worldwide instability.

These two accusations must be carefully distinguished. To hear Michel Debré tell it, the United States has sacrificed gold to its "lust for power"; and according to Jacques Rueff, by using and abusing the gold exchange standard, the United States has "radically distorted the rules" of monetary order and contributed to the decline of Western civilization. The first accusation does not imply the second, nor the second the first.

In the aftermath of World War II, when by the Bretton Woods Agreement the international community set up the International Monetary Fund and the ground rules of a monetary order, what was feared by the American leadership (in common with all who remembered the 1930s) was partly the repetition of retaliatory devaluations in the event of depression, and partly the burden which would fall on the fund and, indirectly, on the United States itself, because of the deficits which other states would accumulate. The United States therefore contributed to the creation of a system which imposed severe constraints on states in deficit, and refused to take Lord Keynes's plans to their ultimate conclusion and establish the equivalent of a central world bank. The secretary of the treasury himself took the initiative of informing the secretary-general of the IMF of the U.S. government's intention to guarantee the convertibility of the dollar into gold. By that very fact, he encouraged the equivalence which grew up between gold and the dollar, with the central banks indiscriminately using either metal or paper as reserves. In those days, only a handful of observers followed men like Charles Rist in forecasting a coming movement in reverse, with the gold stock, then concentrated on the other side of the Atlantic, traversing the ocean to return—symbolically—to the coffers of the European central banks.

Apart from any controversy about the adequacy or inadequacy of gold as a foundation for the international monetary system, I think it likely that the dollar would have been considered "as good as gold" in any case, whatever the attitude of the American authorities. In that period, between 1945 and 1949, the United States was enjoying a supremacy comparable with the position of Great Britain in 1850. The Americans combined the advantages of advanced technology, financial power, and an output per capita greater than that of all other countries, either hostile or allied. The currency based on this triple predominance was superior to gold for prestige, the more so because the central banks, which preferred it to metal, drew interest on it.

For a dozen years or so, until about 1961, the gold of Fort Knox recrossed the Atlantic* without arousing the unease of the American authorities or the annoyance of the French. It was after 1961–62 that the controversy took a hectic tone or turn, and Presidents Kennedy and Johnson decided to stop what seemed like a drain on the reserves. (In the United States, only gold constituted a reserve currency, because the Americans had not yet come to the point of proclaiming that the dollar was its own reserve and that, consequently, the American currency could easily do without gold or any other medium of reserve).

I have asked myself, more than once, what would have happened in 1961 if John F. Kennedy had concluded from Professor Paul Samuelson's analysis (a conclusion the professor himself made in private conversation, though not in public) that the real cause of deficits was, quite simply, the overvaluation of the American currency. The exchange rates set in the late 1940s, and influenced by the wreck of the European economies, no longer corresponded to parity of buying power or the ratio of productivity. According to him, two currencies in particular, the yen and the mark, were undervalued. Nearly all economists are now agreed on the accuracy of this diagnosis, but governments on both sides of the Atlantic were reluctant to take notice. In international councils, U.S. government experts haughtily rejected any suggestion of devaluing the dollar. Many of them took refuge behind the assertion of its political impossibility. To this day, they would argue that they were right, because it took extreme measures by President Nixon and the Texan style of John Connally to impose a devaluation of the dollar on America's refractory partners—who are quite as responsible as the Americans for the U.S. refusal to devalue the dollar between 1961 and 1971.

Who benefited by the overvaluation of the dollar? The simple answer is: commercially, Europe and Japan; financially, the United States, which, all through the deficit period, profited by the dollar's overvaluation through investments abroad. The big American companies created subsidiaries or bought up bankrupt businesses. On the other hand, European goods profited from the dollar's exchange rate, both on the home and on the Third World market.

The Europeans had an easy indictment available, and General de Gaulle presented it several times, though perhaps without fully grasping the causes and consequences. No country whose balance of payments is in deficit (or which makes up its deficit by drawing on its reserves, or by borrowing) ought in theory to export capital—no country but the United States, which, all through the 1960s, went on investing two or three billion dollars a year abroad, even when some foreign central banks were buying surplus dollars to keep up the exchange rate. The dollar was therefore a

*Not always in the physical sense.

currency "more equal than others," to adapt Orwell's phrase. What remained at stake was, first, the possibility of divesting the dollar of its privileges, then, the likely cost of such an operation, and, lastly, the odds on or against a return to a system based on metal.

Events since 1973 have proved that even detached from gold, even with a floating rate of exchange, the dollar continues to function as an international currency, an *operating currency,* and even as a reserve currency (but no longer always as a currency of account). Whether it is gold-based or floating, the dollar relieves the government and business community of the United States of some of the restrictions which hamper other countries. If they spend more abroad than they earn in foreign currency, they pay their creditors in dollars and do not dream of taking overall measures designed to alter their economic position so as to correct the external imbalance. In this respect, nothing changed in 1971 except that the Europeans and Japanese lost the former commercial advantage which the dollar's excessively high rate of exchange had afforded them.

Would a devaluation of the dollar in 1961 have prevented an overseas buildup and the substantial deficits of the years 1968–71? Would it have created the conditions for a return to a classical system in which a real good—gold—is the solid foundation and which does not confuse a national currency with a reserve device? The reply to this "counterfactual" question will always remain in doubt. My own inclination would be to answer no.

In a given era, the international monetary system depends, essentially, on two causes, *the way of thinking and the interests of the leaders of the dominant economy, and the characteristics of the world economy.* The Americans have never understood the attachment to gold displayed by the French people, from peasants all the way to General de Gaulle. Even if American economists have hesitated to endorse the Keynesian notion of a "barbaric relic," a "fetish from another age," they always leaned toward the side of Keynes and the British school rather than the orthodox side. If it were up to them to choose, if the Bretton Woods system were no longer working, their choice would be predictable—they would "demonetize" gold or, since the notion of demonetization is itself equivocal, they would reduce the monetary function of gold and would tend to bring it closer to that of an ordinary metal.

The ground of the question thus shifts to asking whether a dollar devaluation in 1961 would have prevented the accumulation of "dollar balances" in the central banks. Would it at least have curbed the so-called Vietnamese inflation of 1965–70? The answer is probably yes. But for one thing, the U.S. government was not in favor of devaluation as a way of restoring the Bretton Woods principles and, for another, it is difficult to see why Lyndon Johnson should have run the economy on less inflationist lines, if the dollar exchange rate had been different. Finally, in order to visualize any return to the 1947 orthodoxy, one has to deliberately ignore the Eurodollar market and the liquid assets held by the so-called multinational corporations, in other words, the entire corpus of what may be called the *transnational economic and financial system*. Certainly the 1961–71 decade contributed to the creation of this transnational ensemble, but the latter is so in tune to the logic of economic evolution that it is hard to bring oneself to believe that a simple dollar devaluation in 1961 would have permanently changed the direction of that evolution.

What do we mean by "transnational ensemble"? By that, we mean a system of monetary and financial markets, of companies which, wholly or partly, can evade the control of national authorities, and where there is a volume of transactions so expanded that no government has reserves great enough to resist the *opérateurs* (or speculators) when they judge, rightly or wrongly, that a modification of the exchange parity must affect a particular currency.

Does the Eurodollar market meet a definite need? Inaugurated by the socialist states investing the dollars they needed for their commercial transactions in banks outside the United States, its growth was galvanized when the American authorities imposed restrictions on the export of capital from the banks and the so-called multinational firms. It thus seems probable that, in one way or another, a "transnational ensemble" would have come into being, inasmuch as it expresses the dynamism of a world economy that links the national economies closer and closer together without creating a concomitant political power or issuing-bank at the center.

Still, hypothetically supposing that there were no such thing as the Eurodollar market, how would it be possible to control the assets of multinational firms capable of emigrating from one country to another and of multiplying "monetary crises," at least as long as the rules require fixed parities? In other words, the overvaluation of the dollar from 1961 to 1971 and the inflation of 1965–71 caused the ruin of the Bretton Woods system and brought about, in its place, the present system (or nonsystem) of *generalized floating*. But the dynamism of the world economy, the volume of international trade, the interpenetration of the money markets and the rise of a transnational ensemble—all these phenomena characteristic of the quarter century which ended in 1973—tended to produce the present situation, if not to make it, perhaps, inevitable.

Must we agree with Michel Debré, who says that the Americans sacrificed gold to their own interests and therefore bear a major share of the blame for world inflation? Whatever the system, the currency of the dominant economy always has privileges. These, in the period of the overvalued dollar, were offset by the commercial advantages enjoyed by America's partners and competitors in Europe and Japan. I have always thought and written that, by working for the fall of the dollar, General de Gaulle was unwittingly playing a game of "heads you win, tails I lose." Whatever system succeeded the gold exchange standard, denounced so passionately by Jacques Rueff, would be even less in accord with French interests, as interpreted by those currently responsible for stating them.

Is theirs a valid interpretation? The answer is not self-evident. The interests of France coincide partly with those of the other industrialized countries to the extent that all the partner-competitors gain by fair rules and a balance in the world economy. It is therefore important to know how far the monetary system bears the blame for world inflation, and then to clarify whether, and to what extent, this system—be it generally good or bad for everybody—works to the particular disadvantage of France itself.

No one disputes the fact that American inflation, or the worldwide circulation of a mass of dollars over and above the funding needs and wishes of private holders and the banks, has contributed to world inflation (although several countries—France, especially—have little right to stand up as accusers when they themselves have raised inflation to the level of an institution). What remains a matter of controversy is the extent of the international monetary system's contribution to inflation and, more significantly, the degree to which floating currencies and price stability are compatible.

What makes the present conjuncture so radically new? It is the abolition of the real good, of the commodity (originally the currency) which, on the world scale, served also as an "ultimate referent." Within individual countries, even if the value of a currency is still expressed by a certain weight of gold, the gold supply no longer exerts any influence on the buying power of the monetary unit. This unit is much more a buying certificate or credit instrument than a good, being meant to work as a universal equivalent for all goods. This buying certificate enables more or fewer goods to be acquired, depending upon the monetary or budgetary policy being pursued by the government. The ultimate referent has not retained even a psychological efficacy.

Until recently, the international position was different. Only governments had the power to mint money—or, if one prefers, to issue "buying tokens," valid solely in the area covered by the laws of the issuing government. Gold appeared to be a *supranational* currency, recognized as such by all nations and safe from the arbitrary decisions of any one government. The *de facto* equivalence which gradually became established between gold and the dollar scandalized General de Gaulle, quite apart from any academic economic considerations, because it set the seal of approval on a kind of special entitlement for the United States to mint money. They paid their foreign debts with their own currency; then, when the dollar was devalued, holders of dollar reserves had to take the consequences.

Scandalous or not, this privilege existed, and still does exist. And yet, General de Gaulle's paeans of praise for gold are not above criticism. As a metal, physically, gold does indeed possess the qualities of immutability which have been ascribed to it. With the passage of time, however, gold has never maintained a constant value. As long as there was only a single gold market, a given quantity of the various convertible currencies could be acquired on it, but this did not produce any stability of the value of gold in commodities. The value of gold was doubly variable: its value in paper money fluctuated, and so did the buying power of this paper money.

One reason why the French favored the use of gold in the international monetary system was, basically, political. If, in the last instance, the convertibility of currencies is related to gold, then no state can contract external debts in excess of a certain amount. It was precisely this constraint which Great Britain, then the United States, refused to accept. The more the London money market received foreign capital which it might trans-form into British investments overseas, the less it could abide by converti-bility into gold, even as a last instance. Similarly, as its gold holdings grew closer to the magic figure of 10 billion dollars (at the price of 35 dollars an ounce), the United States effectively discontinued the application of the convertibility principle. Its official discontinuation occurred in two stages: in 1968, the gold pool disappeared and the central banks pledged them-selves no longer to require their dollar balances to be convertible into gold; in 1971, convertibility was officially revoked. But one has only to compare the United States' gold holdings with the volume of its short-term foreign commitments over a number of years to be convinced that convertibility was already a thing of the past.

The authorities of the United States were rid of the final constraint on their freedom. The trade-balance deficit of the 1968–71* period finally broke down their obstinacy, which had been a blend of egotism, short-sightedness, and unenlightened self-interest. It was not enough to display "benign neglect" toward revaluations of the other currencies orbiting that sun of the monetary system, the dollar; nor could the American currency allow itself to be committed to immobility. Floating, in combination with non-convertibility into gold, assured the U.S. rulers total autonomy of action.

All the same, the outcome of this new autonomy—which the French government, misunderstanding its inevitable character, resisted out of political principle—was not *ipso facto* at loggerheads with the interests of the other countries involved in the world economy. With the OPEC price rise, and the accompanying great inflation, the floating of exchange parities

*It was not until 1971 that the American balance of trade was officially declared in the red (by 2.7 billion dollars), but the positive balances of some hundreds of millions of dollars in 1968 and 1969 actually concealed deficits, if tied-loan exports are taken into account.

permitted multiple adjustments in response to unequal inflation rates, and with no major crisis. America's conduct of affairs in 1965–71 was probably much to blame for the inflation of 1973 (although excessive increases in the money supply, all over the world, were the immediate cause). But since the fall of 1973, the floating system adopted by Washington in March 1973 has served the world economy better than any other.

What are the theoretical objections? What makes it an inflationary factor? I can see two principal mechanisms. Insofar as inflation becomes a worldwide phenomenon, it is the volume of world credit or the growth rate of the world money supply that has to be considered, and no longer the national money supplies or the sum of the national supplies. The transnational markets and the Eurodollar market have a degree of independence with respect to the national markets. The very fact that they are partly free of control by national authorities means that they constitute a standing danger of excessively increasing the world money supply and, therefore, the level of world prices—an effect which national policies may modify here, amplify or minimize there, but which they cannot eliminate.

In fact, since 1973 the French, too, have been using the facilities provided by the system they condemn. The Paris government, like many others, called on the American banks or the Eurodollar market to cover its balance of payments deficit in 1974, and again in 1976, either by borrowing on its own behalf or by inviting public and private enterprises to borrow abroad. Since 1973, it has been as much through the private markets as through the international organizations that the debtor nations have financed their imports. More than ever, the United States remains the *lender of last resort*. The world economy increasingly constitutes an integrated whole, even though there is no responsible authority above the national level, and no coordination between nations of the kind demanded by this unprecedented international ensemble.

The second cause of inflation imputable to generalized currency floating is more psychological than technical. Metal currency is tending to disappear from the monetary system, so bullion, too, is now subject to violent fluctuations, and liable to lose 30 to 40% of its value in the space of a few months: it is a speculative property, with no more inherent value than other currencies. That being so, why should governments feel morally or politically obliged to maintain the parity of the currency exchange rate? They used to resist inflation in order to preserve the currency: now there is no longer any reason for preserving the currency. In the event of external deficit, when domestic prices rise more than in neighboring competing countries, devaluation becomes the normal response—it is bowing to the inevitable.

This utilization of monetary appreciations or depreciations in order to adapt an economy to external circumstances does not imply inflation, but it does reflect a mental state of resignation to permanent inflation. As many as fifteen years ago, the dictum "Don't make more blunders than the others"* testified to a general consent to general inflation.

The present setup is awkward for America's partner-competitors when the dollar falls to an artificially low rate. † It also has advantages for firms able to invest in the United States. The flow of direct investment has reversed itself. As manpower costs tend to become lower across the Atlantic than in Europe, it is in the United States that the Rothschild Bank buys up a business, and it is American towns or states suffering from unemployment that offer special concessions to foreign capital. This is an oddly logical outcome: the overvaluation of the dollar until 1971 encouraged American firms to make direct investments in Europe; the devaluation of the dollar, coupled with rising wage levels in the Old Continent, encouraged European firms, in turn, to make direct investments in the United States. ‡

Can any conclusions be reached in our present state of knowledge and experience? The innovatory nature of this experience was partly a deliberate step by the American authorities and partly imposed by circumstances. The volume of international trade and the transnational monetary and industrial ensemble made it almost impossible to return to a system in which gold was the only exchange reserve. This system does tempt governments to grant easy credit, and it has a potential to produce inflationist credit pyramids (but it does not prevent governments with strict management practices from softening the effects of worldwide inflationary drift through the relative appreciation of their own currency in relation to that of others). It also aggravates the inflation of countries with weak currencies, depreciating their monetary unit and triggering a rise in domestic prices through imports and by psychological contagion.

Does this mean that inflation is bound to accelerate, and that a quarter century of growth has reached a predicament which the world economy will not be able to overcome?

The crisis continues

At the moment, condemnation of Keynes's "fallacious" doctrines is generally replacing the defense and illustration of the "Keynesian revolution." To tell the truth, the ideas derived by postwar governments from the *General Theory* were only vaguely attributable to the author of the book.

*W. Baumgartner.
†In 1975 (and 1978).
‡The total amount of such investment still appears to be fairly small.

This century's most famous economist had been reflecting on the situation between the wars and, in particular, on the 1930s and the low level of aggregate demand. The problem of the last twenty years, and especially the last ten, has been precisely the opposite, namely, how are the excessively high levels of aggregate demand, and the rising prices—caused by permissive monetary policies and the higher costs attributable to the actions of pressure groups, business administrators or labor unions—to be reduced?

Although there are various conflicting theories of inflation, some stressing the purely economic factors (e.g., money supply), others stressing social factors (e.g., the power of the unions, the price policies of big businesses, the struggle among social groups over the apportioning of the national product), the area of agreement among these theories seems to me to be greater than their margins of difference. The growth of the money supply may sometimes be the immediate and direct cause (as in 1971–72) of the inflationary wave; such augmentation of the money supply always sets up permissive conditions for inflation. In the absence of sufficient growth of the means of payment, no business can grant wage raises generally higher than the mean increase in productivity. But, on the other hand, if businesses, under trade union pressure, are forced to grant excessively high wage raises, then the authorities ease up on credit so as not to cause the level of activity to slacken. In other words, the Western economies' endemic inflation is located at the meeting point of three factors: excessive credit (the creation of money by the banks); wage increases supported by the power of the unions, and the consent of big firms to the granting of simultaneous price and wage-increases; and the acceptance by governments of endemic inflation in the hope of accelerated growth and out of fear of unemployment.

The inflation of 1973 and the recession of 1974–75 appear to have taught lessons to authorities on both sides of the Atlantic. There is a point beyond which inflation, far from encouraging growth, actually paralyzes it. Budgetary deficits deprive enterprises of the funds necessary for investment. Wage increases erode profit margins and discourage productive investments. Unemployment itself no longer acts as a brake on wage claims. The Phillips curve* no longer reflects the play of social forces: there is no longer an observable correlation between the rate of unemployment and the rate of wage increases, which go on even when unemployment is affecting 5% of the work force. An unemployment rate which would halt upward wage drift would be socially unacceptable. Furthermore, the measures taken to guarantee a decent living standard to the jobless are liable to

*The economist Alban Phillips thought he had observed that the closer an economy comes to full employment, the faster wages tend to rise.

raise the lowest wages above the marginal level, thereby tending to increase the number of those requiring protection.

The contradiction is expressed, roughly, as follows: the labor market which, in a decentralized economy, should be a market like any other, cannot in fact be any such thing. Not, as antiquated Marxists absurdly state, because the labor force is paid only the price of its own reproduction but, on the contrary, because the collective bargaining pursued by the unions produces inflationary agreements or, to put it another way, it leads to wage levels which are not restricted by the rise in the mean rate of productivity. Which is to say that the capitalist economies suffer, not from treating labor as just another commodity but, on the contrary, from no longer being able to do so. It is as if wages had to be increased or, at any rate, maintained at their real value, in spite of economic circumstances. When Keynes took nominal wages as a datum, he unwittingly foresaw a social fact whose economic consequences are still unfolding.

Two countries, the United States and West Germany, came through the recent recession in the best—or the least bad—shape.* On the American side of the Atlantic, business still has freedom to hire and fire, as well as a certain fluidity of wage options. The restrictive policy pursued by the monetary authorities and their acceptance both of a lower level of activity and a fall in real wages enables firms to stabilize their financial position and restore their profit margins, in other words, to go into the *new phase of expansion* with no handicap of surplus manpower and no excessive level of debt.†

In Federal Germany, comparable results were achieved by the European method of consultation between employers and employees under the aegis of the government. The labor unions are aware of both their power and its limitations. The increased nominal wages which unions can impose under the threat of withdrawing their labor can only be translated into increased real wages on one of the following two conditions: either the increase must keep within the field marked out by improved productivity, or else it must involve a redistribution of the national product among the interested parties. Even so, this redistribution has to affect high salaries or independent incomes, and not business profits, because it only requires these to be cut too far for wage earners to be hit by businesses that cannot (or will not) invest during the next phase.

France has neither the American nor the West German kind of advantage. It has not been capable of accepting the painful process of re-

*Sweden too, at least in terms of eliminating unemployment. On the other hand, it accepted an inflation rate of nearly 10% and an external deficit.

†I do not conclude from this that the United States has solved its long-term problems. Investments still make up a small proportion of the national product compared with the USSR or West Germany.

adjustment as has the United States, nor has it entered into the kind of union-management agreements which the West German government has made and encouraged. France's two main trade union groupings, both of them politicized, both of them professing revolutionary ideologies, have never officially endorsed voluntary wage moderation. Fear of unrest has caused the government to ask business to participate in the financing of the various measures taken against unemployment or in favor of the unemployed, and has urged it not to lay off workers temporarily in excess of requirements.

The present recession has nothing whatever in common with the final apocalyptic crisis envisaged by Marx a century ago and still intermittently expected by Marxists. Even if one agrees with some Marxists that capital profitability has fallen in recent years—which does seem likely—the phenomenon is neither new nor definitive. Inflation tends to distort economic arithmetic and to create the illusion of profits, whereas with a stable currency these profits do not exist, or are a good deal lower than the book figures indicate. A long phase of rapid growth with heavy capital accumulation leads naturally to a reduction in capital profitability.* Wage increases which are tolerable for some firms tend to reduce mean capital profitability, if they become widespread.

Whatever the impact of these different factors on different countries, there is no proper long-term conclusion to be drawn from the often unreliable statistics about the profitability of capital. The development of the world economy is an *histoire*, not a regular process of evolution toward a predetermined catastrophic or paradisiac end. After a quarter century during which the problems of the 1930s seemed to have been solved, the world economy is now entering a new phase characterized by three major features:

1. A general system of floating currencies, without ultimate reference to a commodity, has been tested. This system probably requires close cooperation among national authorities and possibly measures to control the whole transnational ensemble. At the present, national governments have neither the knowledge nor the resolution necessary for administering the world economy in its evolved form. Currencies will continue to float in the coming years, for however much progress is made in cooperation between states, the fate of each country will depend primarily on the actions of its national authority.

In theory, if one reasons from a model, a general floating currency system does not imply uneven inflation rates and therefore frequent profound changes in exchange rates. But the fact is that, since 1971 (or 1973), the

---

*Particularly because this capital accumulation tends, as a consequence of rising wages, to increase the apparent productivity of labor and reduce the number of jobs.

currency float has been accompanied both by general inflation and by an apparently widening gap between strong and weak currencies.* In the present situation, what people fear is not competitive devaluations but the reinforcement of the strong currencies by revaluation and a downward plunge in the weak currencies through depreciation. The advantages which went to Britain's exports with the fall in the pound have been wiped out by the fall in the unit price of goods exported, and even more by the rising prices of imported goods. After a certain point, monetary devaluation continually fuels domestic inflation, unless there are efforts made to bring about domestic deflation. Whether it is the cause or the effect of generally floating currencies, disparity in inflation rates brings with it the progressive disintegration of the Common Market.

2. In none of the principal countries will a further dose of inflation allow restoration of "full employment," or what Western Europe regards as such. On the contrary, full employment and satisfactory growth are much more likely to result from cutting inflation, and from the ability of governments to create conditions which will make it possible for firms to find the resources—and the incentive—necessary for productive investment.

3. Inflation is said to be "an expression of the behavior of social groups," but this behavior results in turn from that of the people in charge of the budget, and especially credit. Depending on the times or the country, the immediately operative cause of inflation seems to be either the power of pressure groups (of trade unions, above all) or, on the contrary, of the expansion of the money supply through excessive credit. This expansion, which is always a permissive condition of inflation, is sometimes the direct cause.

In the history of the Western economies, these novel features, whether they be novel or merely more prominent than in the past, are not as serious as were the troubles of the 1930s. If they are a cause of anxiety, it is primarily for political reasons. The Great Depression brought Hitler to power. Will the 1973 inflation, the 1975–76 recession, and the subsequent monetary disorder bring about the collapse of the democratic societies of Western Europe?

---

*Late in 1976 tourists were still making buying expeditions to London to take advantage of low prices there, just as they used to go to Germany, or to Italy, a few years earlier.

8

Self-destruction by the liberal democracies?

The United States and the historical nations

On the occasion of the bicentennial celebration of the American republic, one British journalist eulogized the United States in these terms: Will Great Britain remain a free society if it does not manage to halt its economic decline? Will Italy preserve its freedoms once Enrico Berlinguer's party becomes a participant in government? What would be the fate of a France ruled by Georges Marchais? On the other hand, who would not venture to bet that the United States *will* elect a president in 1980, and in 1984, and that—in the foreseeable future—it *will* remain a free society?

The contrast between the uncertain fate of three of the principal nations of Western Europe and the sure future of the American republic is not just a matter of differences in economic circumstances or in the way the United States has reacted to the recession and to the events of recent years. Freedom, in the Anglo-American sense of the word, lies at the root of the American experience—political and personal freedoms are basic to it. The citizen of Europe, Japan or China becomes a citizen of the American Republic as soon as the federal authorities make out a passport in his name. In the United States, and there alone, citizenship and nationality are one. In America, the federation was the offspring of a contract signed by the states, and the charter of freedom is as old as the political entity itself. In Europe, freedoms were acquired at the expense of the traditional authorities—in France, at the price of revolutionary violence. Certain ideas belonged to both the American and the French revolutions, but these revolutions—in origin, development, and consequences—are nevertheless fundamentally different.

The American Revolution laid the basis of the Republic and its freedoms. The French Revolution touched off a quarter century of war, and left behind a divided nation. The Jacobins were the Bolsheviks' mentors. The French Revolution was an historical failure transformed by legend into a Promethean feat, and the myth of the Revolution continues to obsess men's minds. The American Revolution was an historical success, now regarded as over and done with, requiring neither repetition nor prolongation.* Its meaning became distorted only when professors began presenting it as "the birth of a nation," of a nation like those which emerged from European decolonization in Asia and in Africa. The American colonies lived and were governed, before 1776, on the English pattern: they protested against George III and his government's taxes in the name of freedom. As a society of pioneers and emigrants making *their own* laws, they did not break with the past as did the French. They constituted an expression of the French Revolution's original principle, and were its crowning achievement.

Present-day Italian democracy dates from the end of World War II. The Fifth Republic is twenty years old. Only the British government can claim a more venerable (because older) descent than that of the Americans. However, Britain, also, faces a threat, albeit a different one from that to which the régimes on the Continent have been exposed. But let us get away from the historical background and try to distinguish the various problems which, together, make up the political crisis of the West.

In the short-term—the immediate future—all Western countries have to meet the same economic challenges. They must restore business profit margins, so as to give the firms an incentive to reinvest. They must gain acceptance of a lower rate of wage increases, or even of temporary stability, in order to allow for the shift of resources imposed by deterioration in exchange rates and, especially by the rise in oil prices. And, to create conditions for powerful growth, they must expand productive capacity. Endemic inflation is inseparable from this challenge; being both a cause and an effect, it has grown to be a symbol of the West's socio-economic crisis.

In France and Italy, the recession is heightening the danger of defeat of the ruling majority and the accession to power of a Communist party. This

---

*The Americans do think of their Constitution as having laid the basis for a right to rebel against a despotic government, but rebellion has nothing to do with revolution in the European sense.

highlights, at the same time, the contradiction inherent in the régimes which we call democratic, where power comes out of the rivalry between parties whose aims are different and, sometimes, incompatible. These countries' constitutions do not forbid parties which, if in power, might possibly abolish such competition. The Nazi party came to power by a process formally quite in keeping with the Weimar constitution. What would happen in the event of the "historic compromise," in other words, a government formed by an alliance between the Italian Communist party and the Christian Democrats? What would happen in France in the event of a Socialist-Communist victory, or of the election, in 1981, of a socialist president?

Looking beyond the challenge of the recession and the built-in contradictions of a pluralist system which tolerates the activities of parties hostile to pluralism, many people are asking a more far-reaching question. Are the liberal-democratic societies still governable? It is an odd and paradoxical question, since there are a good many fashionable ideologies which never tire of denouncing the oppression, alienation, and repression which are supposed to be afflicting the individual; at the same time, other observers put stress on the weakness of an omnipresent state which is expected to be all-providing but which cannot even prevent trade unionism in its own armed forces.

The Western Communist parties

Let me start with the contradiction of liberal democracies which postulate freedom for the enemies of freedom or, to put it another way, of democracies which, in certain circumstances, are brought up against the alternative either of a *coup d' état* or the accession to power of a régime likely to destroy the government which has given it its opportunity.

Quite obviously, I have in mind the Weimar Republic and the conquest of the state by Hitler and his Nazi party. What is at issue, today, is the conquest of the state by the Communist party in Italy. (In France, the Communist party would share power with the Socialists, who on the latest figures would have more deputies than their partner and would therefore hold the levers of power.) The question, therefore, is: what have the Communist parties of Western Europe become, and what do they want?

If one looks at Western Europe as a whole, I think it is not misleading to say that the Communist parties are going through a period of decline. The French Communist party now gets about 20% of the vote, whereas, in the postwar years, its score was as high as 25%. In Portugal, after more than half a century of an authoritarian régime, the Communist party captured only about 16% of the vote in the first elections for the Constituent

Assembly, and even less in the 1976 elections for the first legislative assembly.

If the winning of elections in the West now requires rejection of the Soviet model (and the tutelage of the USSR), this in itself is significant, even if it is only more emphasized, rather than something new. We probably ought not to overlook the contrary proposition that the Communist parties owe some of their special character, influence, and prestige to the links they retain and the relationship they claim to the First Socialist (or so-called socialist) Revolution in history. If Communist parties suffer from a contradiction, it is that of being "damned if they do, and damned if they don't." With the Soviet Union, they are open to the charge of totalitarianism; without it, they fall back upon prosaic social democracy or a dull utopianism. Where are they headed if they simultaneously disown both the régime founded by Lenin and ruled by the successors of Stalin, and the régimes which are run by Social Democrats but which remain integrated into the world economy?

Among the criteria to be used in judging the sincerity of the Western Communist parties' conversion is the nature of their ties with Moscow. In this respect, the Italian party has been well ahead of the French. Togliatti himself seems to have grasped the implications of Khrushchev's 1956 speech straight away; he was not at all satisfied with the meaningless phrase "cult of personality." In short, for some twenty years now, the Italian Communist party has been openly examining and criticizing the real Soviet Union. One cannot say the same of the French Communist party. Even among party intellectuals, debate about the USSR and the "cult of personality" is still conducted *sotto voce*, intentionally or not. The secretary-general and the politburo condemned Soviet intervention in Czechoslovakia, but in a manner which led observers to feel that the French Communists were putting on a show, or bowing to some convention (or compulsion), without the slightest sign of conviction.

Today, the Italian Communists would probably condemn the "normalization" of Czechoslovakia more vehemently than they did ten years ago. Enrico Berlinguer is quoted as having said that it was "easier to build socialism in Western than in Eastern Europe," and this may be a revealing remark. The secretary-general of the Italian Communist party is perfectly well aware that it is the Soviet army that keeps up the discipline of the Eastern so-called socialist bloc. If he genuinely does want a pluralist socialism, it is a fact that he only stands a chance of building it outside the zone controlled by the Kremlin. But how is anyone to believe in the sincerity of Enrico Berlinguer or of Georges Marchais (lately departed along the same road) when they both persist in seeing the world in the same categories as the men in the Kremlin, and their line on international politics outside Europe is identical with that of the Soviet Politburo?

This brings out a principal ambiguity in the position of those Communist parties which are not the pawns of Moscow. Why do they denounce Western "imperialism"? Why do they regularly take the side of Communist countries or movements, if they are fighting for a "pluralist socialism," for the freedom inseparable from pluralism? Let us take up the same question in a different form: according to the Marxist-Leninists, as I have explained in a previous chapter, private ownership of the means of production implies exploitation of the workers by the surplus-value mechanism, which in turn implies imperialism as practiced by the United States and all developed capitalist countries, France included—which are in league with the United States, both as partners and as competitors. This global concept automatically places such Communist parties alongside the Soviet Union and the countries professing Marxism-Leninism. The only time any doubt about this arises is in cases where Moscow Marxist-Leninists and Peking Marxist-Leninists are in disagreement with each other.

The Communist parties' connections with Moscow do not disappear on the day they claim and publicly announce their independence. The Italian Communist party, even though free to choose its tactics, would not necessarily change its attitude toward Israel or Angola. As yet, there is nothing to indicate that the French Communist party looks upon Soviet domination in Eastern Europe as "imperialist" and the American presence on the demarcation line as "nonimperialist." Georges Marchais has not yet followed Enrico Berlinguer in declaring that the West affords better opportunities for socialism than does the East, nor has Berlinguer taken his own remark to its logical conclusion.

The Communist parties of the West—for the sake of simplicity, we may as well call them the Eurocommunisms—are taking up the theme of the "nonviolent road to socialism," but they are putting off the decisive question of where the road ends. In other words, would their socialism (Italian, French or Spanish) resemble that of West Germany or Sweden, or that of the Soviet Union? Do alliances with Socialists or Christian Democrats testify to a lasting tolerance, or are they short-lived tactical maneuvers? Once in power, would they respect the present diversity of religious belief, the existing variety of schools of thought? That which defines "pluralism" (to use a word devalued by misuse) is not solely or, rather, not *essentially* party competition. It is rejection of factitious unanimity, of intellectual conformism imposed by an ideology and embodied either in a party or a man, it is refusal of a principle good only for fanatics and sceptics. On this point, there is nothing to prove that the Eurocommunisms have undergone a conversion, nor have they even begun to do so.

Two obstacles stand in the way of this conversion. For half a century, Communists have defined themselves by their joint allegiance to Moscow and Marxism-Leninism. It is not enough for them to echo the Spanish

Communist Santiago Carillo and say that "Moscow is no longer Rome" or that "Rome is no longer in Rome." There must be a break with the Moscow interpretation of Communist ideology, and also a change in the specifically Communist type of party structure (referred to as "democratic centralism") as it exists in Europe.

The Italian Communist party is different from the French. The latter stood firm, for years, against the impact of Nikita Khrushchev's Twentieth Congress speech, and clung to Stalinism, even after the party in the USSR had officially abandoned it. The Italian party was much quicker to learn its lesson. The infallibility of the party could not outlive that of the man who had embodied it for so long. Even if the Soviet régime had not *necessarily* created Stalin, at least it had made him possible. In the West, criticism of Stalin gradually broadened into criticism of Soviet socialism: after 1956, step by step, with no commotion and no outright breach, the Italian party disengaged itself from the Kremlin. In June 1976, Enrico Berlinguer spoke from the rostrum of the Congress of European Communist Parties in East Berlin as the representative of a national autonomous party, without thereby incurring the wrath of Leonid Brezhnev. On the contrary, Brezhnev received him and congratulated him on his party's success in the recent Italian elections.

It was different with Georges Marchais, who seems to antagonize Leonid Brezhnev quite as much as the men in the Kremlin antagonize Marchais. After Valéry Giscard d' Estaing's success in the presidential elections of May 1974, the French Communist party suddenly began a campaign *against* the Socialist party in the autumn of that year. With occasional polemic outbursts, it subsequently rejoined *"l'Union de la gauche."* Notwithstanding the progress made by the Socialists, as demonstrated by the local elections of 1976, the French Communists are supporting the "united" Left ticket more strongly than ever. In so doing, they have sacrificed one key element of their orthodoxy: they have discarded the sacrosanct formula of the "dictatorship of the proletariat."

For an ideological—and therefore scholastically and theologically inclined—party, changes of vocabulary have a significance barely comprehensible to infidels. By renouncing the dictatorship of the proletariat and agreeing to share power with non-Marxist-Leninist parties, has the French Communist party given proof of a genuine conversion?

Communist collusion with the Christian Democrats in Italy

The Christian Democratic party came out on top, in the elections of June 1976, in the precise and limited sense that its share of the vote was two percentage points higher than the Communist party's. The Communists nevertheless improved their previous vote in the legislative elections by seven points, although they made no advance over their previous year's performance in the provincial elections. The Socialist party did not repeat its score in the provincial elections. The Christian Democrats owe their success mainly to the defensive reflex of electors of the Right or Center who deserted the lesser parties and rallied round the one party capable of standing up to the Communists and of winning more votes than the Communists did.

The gap between the Socialists and Communists in 1976, seen from either side, illustrates and symbolizes thirty years of Italian political history. If the Communist and Socialist parties taken together are termed the Left and all the other parties the Right, the relative strength of forces is considerably changed. In the 1940s, the Christian Democrats could win absolute majorities, or more, by themselves. The Left's score was barely 40%; in 1976, it was about 48%. But this shift in the distribution of votes between Left and Right is not as remarkable as the changes in distribution that occurred within what is termed the Left. Thirty years ago, the Socialist party used to get more votes than the Communist party; now it gets only a fourth as many. The progress of the Communist party is a reflection of its success, but also of the Socialist party's failure.

This reversal of relative strength accounts partly for the bizarre nature of the tactic adopted by the Socialist party. It formed a coalition with the Communists during the worst days of the Cold War, then joined the government at the time of the "opening to the left" when the tension between the Two Europes was slackening. It did not acquire the status of a defender of freedom during the Stalin years, and did not justify its presence in the government during the subsequent years by reforms which might have benefited the mass of the population.

Today, everyone denounces the Christian Democrats—for their weaknesses, their corruption, their nepotism. These reproaches are indeed well founded. But party rule and party graft, as elements of a system based on proportional representation, are deeply rooted in tradition. After thirty years of uninterrupted power, the Christian Democratic party can argue—with justification—that it has presided over a period of exceptionally rapid economic development without thereby compromising the freedom of the individual. I doubt if the Italians—a people with a far greater tendency toward scepticism than toward fanaticism—are deserting the Christian Democrats out of a spirit of moral rebellion against routine nepotism or against political corruption—which in all régimes are endemic phenomena, and common knowledge under democracy.

In my view, that which invites comment and reflection is the contrast— in the aftermath of World War II and the Fascist régime—between the conservative majority and the progress of the Left and of the Communist party under parliamentary democracy. Portugal provides another example of the same phenomenon. It is not true, as some people claim, that authoritarian régimes always open up the way for revolutionary movements and expand their ranks. Often the reverse is the case: it is the free expression of ideas and demands which gradually strengthens extremist movements.*

One initial—and pessimistic—interpretation can be summed up in the following form: despotism drums up enthusiasm, democracy brings out dissatisfaction, or rather it justifies the dissatisfactions which some groups are bound to feel in any society. But this formula does not settle the real question, namely, why does dissatisfaction lead to social democratic reformism in one place and to the Communist party in another? Why has Italy's economic progress encouraged communism instead of being chalked up as an accomplishment of the ruling Christian Democrats?

Social democrats give one of the classic answers: the reduction of inequalities has not kept pace with growth. † That is how the Swedes assess the Italians and, to a lesser extent, the French and the British. With respect to Italy, it seems to me that there are two decisive factors to be considered, one historical and the other contemporary. The development of modern Italy, compared with that of the other European countries, presents certain distinctive features which have repercussions for democracy elsewhere, as revealed by the failure of liberalism, of the parties and the men embodying the philosophy of the Enlightenment. Right-wing critics who reproach Anglo-Saxon liberalism for supporting communism should ponder the Italian experience: when a party which is Catholic both in name and intention comes to be the sole representative of liberal democracy while professing a philosophy which is anything but liberal in its past and in its inspiration, the danger is that socialism or communism may attract many whose allegiance to collective ownership or planning is weaker by far than their opposition to clericalism, if not to Catholicism.

The weakness of the state Center is another distinctive feature of modern Italy. The house of Savoy, which achieved the unification of the peninsula, had no resemblance whatever to the royal house of France. Once monarchy had been condemned by referendum, the republic began to live under an extreme form of "party rule." In France, the traditional centralization and the power and high caliber of the bureaucracy mitigated the consequences of the division of the state between parties equally mindful of their own gain and equally incapable of putting the common good above their partisan advantage.

*It goes without saying that this statement is not always valid. I would only say that it is true in certain cases which deserve consideration.
†Cf. Appendix Note F.

Down the centuries, the political life of Italy has flowered in the towns: the municipal framework is closer to the citizen and has favored the survival of ancient social—if not economic—hierarchies. The Communist party, not so much by any inspired intuition as by a natural tendency, set out to conquer society, first, and only then, the state. By administering towns, participating in the administration of the provinces created by the Christian Democrats themselves, and by its constant presence in the press, radio, and television, the Communist party has become a major landmark in the political geography of Italy under the Christian Democrats. The latter now find themselves negotiating with their opponents in the corridors of the National Assembly to obtain the support or abstention of the Communist group on behalf of bills for which the official majority cannot guarantee the necessary votes. Does the "historic compromise" signal a decisive shift, or the official consecration of a process already enshrined in the practice of the two great rival parties?

What are the reforms demanded of the Christian Democrats, and which they are accused of having ignored? The reforms fall, it appears to me, into four categories:

1. improvement of state administration;

2. fiscal reforms and reduction of tax evasion;

3. creation (or improvement) of an infrastructure of services, without which elevations in the standard of living are either not felt or even constitute a cause of resentment;

4. transformation of interpersonal relations, which still bear the stigma of the tradition of master/servant inequality.

Nepotism has swollen the numbers of an already inefficient administration—on this point, there is universal agreement. But Italy has about a million so-called students. The demand for nonmanual employment surpasses the needs of a rationalized economy, even more so than it does in France.* Italy has engineers, scholars, and civil servants "of international class," as the saying goes, but does not come near the average standard of its Common Market partners. Italians display neither the Gallic sense of state nor the Germanic discipline. Christian Democracy will not supply either quality, even if it does bring off the revival daily entreated by massed ranks of foreign critics.

There are probably no insurmountable obstacles standing in the way of improved public services (health, communications, transportation), and a modern taxation system will gradually take hold, even in Italy. But in 1976—and for the coming years—the fate of Italy's economy and democ-

---

*The official OECD figures do not in fact bring out this harmful distribution of the work force. According to the figures (*OECD Observer,* March–April 1976) agriculture employs 16.6% of civilian labor, industry 44.1%, and the rest 39.3%. As they stand, these gross figures do not reveal the evils currently complained of.

racy together remains dominated by a single question, namely, by whether or not the government will succeed in bringing inflation down to a level comparable with that of the rest of the European Community. In 1975, a rigorous credit policy balanced Italy's current account and reduced inflation.* In 1976, social unrest restarted inflation and fear of communism hastened the devaluation of the currency. The power of the unions threatened to outweigh the authority of the legal government—a phenomenon typical of the liberal democracies of Western Europe, but more pronounced in Italy than anywhere else.

In the short term, the main function of the "historic compromise" is to bring the masses around to accepting unpopular measures aimed at reducing consumption to the level of production. Even in the context of such a compromise, the two main parties together would have no easy task in imposing the necessary measures (which include reform of the wage-restriction policy). Does the Christian Democratic party have any chance of succeeding by itself? Will the Communist party come to the rescue gratuitously?

Italy provides almost as good an example of the contradictions of liberal democracy in the 1970s as the Weimar Republic did in the 1930s. Forty years ago, the combined right- and left-wing anticonstitutional parties outnumbered the constitutional parties. Either the president went on governing with no parliamentary majority, using the powers allowed for by the constitution in exceptional circumstances, or the leader of the National Socialists had to be appointed chancellor. Having come to office by due constitutional process, Hitler obtained dictatorial powers by a vote of the Reichstag, and went on to establish a régime which violated the letter and spirit of the Weimar Constitution. Clearly this was revolution, even though the first step, the führer's appointment as chancellor, was taken in accordance with democratic legality. Once again, the question arises: must freedom be allowed to the enemies of freedom?

The question is always being asked, although there is no general answer. In the extreme form of "no freedom for the enemies of freedom," the negative answer can provide a pretext for terror—one group claiming that it alone embodies freedom (or revolution) and eliminating all the rest. But, at the opposite extreme, it is equally unjustifiable to answer with an unqualified yes. Any régime must defend itself. Representative democracy belongs to our imperfect world, it aims to create a legitimate power based on the consent of the majority expressed by electoral processes. It presupposes a consensus as to the type of régime, if not to the policies to be

*From June 1974 to June 1975, retail prices had risen by 19.0% and wages by 31%; in December 1975 retail price inflation, compared with the twelve previous months, was down to 11.2%, and wage inflation to 20.3% (according to the annual report of the Bank for International Settlements).

pursued by government. In the absence of that consensus, different circumstances reduce it to contradicting itself, either by refusing its opponents the very freedoms it professes, or by endangering its own existence by letting cheats take part in the game. In 1933, the Weimar Republic could have been saved only by the *Reichswehr;* in 1976, the Italian Republic had no choice: it had to quarantine the survivors of fascism or of the far Right. But the Communist party belongs to the constitutional sphere and, sooner or later, it will demand a share in government as the price of its neutrality and its support.

What will happen on that day? It would be a mistake to see catastrophe as the only possible scenario. Already, a sizeable sector of Italian industry belongs to the state, and the big industrial firms that sprang up or expanded during the "miracle" phase are dependent on the civil authorities, even though they are still managed by prominent families. Even if the Italian Communist party were to expand the nationalized sector* a little by taking over firms which call on public funds to make up their deficits, that in itself would not result in an irreversible change.

From another angle, the Italian economy cannot easily part company with the European-Atlantic complex within which it has forged ahead so rapidly for twenty years. The Italians have a Western style of life, not the style of the Eastern European, "exploitation-free" peoples. The Italian Communist party has been much louder than the French in declaring itself in favor of the European Community, to which Italy owes more than any other member of the Six. Short of immediately using violent means, the Italians (or the government of the "historic compromise") would first have to take unpopular measures to somehow restore national consumption to the level of production—measures which the Christian Democrats recognize as necessary, but which they consider themselves too weak to impose.

This picture produces the rather optimistic vision of the debut of the historic compromise, resembling, in its beginnings, what Moscow did not tolerate in Prague, and what Westerners have termed "socialism with a human face" or social democracy. Having arrived in power as a result of a national crisis, the Italian Communist party would take action for the common good, passing the measures which it voluntarily or involuntarily had prevented the bourgeois governments from taking. What price would the party then charge for its contribution toward restoring the Italian economy?

There is nothing surprising about the Kremlin's lack of enthusiasm regarding the Italian Communist party's possible success. Brezhnev does not object to the extension of the Soviet zone but he seeks, more than anything else, to maintain the coherence of the Imperium of Eastern

---

*It claims to have no such intentions.

Europe. A Communist party sharing power with Christian Democrats, or a Communist party in power in its own right but with some respect for individual and intellectual liberty, could have a direct harmful effect on the Soviet ideocracy. For this ideocracy does not confine itself to suppressing civil liberties, it also turns words upside down, it asserts that the party, in its leading role, constitutes both the expression and the guarantee of the freedoms. The Czechs brought retribution upon themselves when they called a spade a spade, loudly proclaiming that freedom of the press meant the right for people to write what they wish, and what they think.

It goes without saying that Washington's apprehension makes as much sense as Moscow's, if not more. Let us accept the first phase of the scenario, in which the Italian Communist party takes part in government and nothing dramatic occurs. Communist ministers sit in the councils of the European Community and the Atlantic Alliance. The link between domestic policy and foreign policy which has characterized postwar Europe is strained, if not already broken. Does the Atlantic Alliance now take on the unforeseen and paradoxical role of protecting the building of socialism by the Euro-Communists against the expansion of the Soviet zone where the Brezhnev Doctrine rules? That Enrico Berlinguer is afraid of finding himself in a situation like Dubcek's, nobody doubts. But why should the president of the United States keep troops in the center of the Old Continent only to assist in the painless collectivization of Western Europe? Would a socialist Italy rely on the imperialism execrated by its rulers in order to keep their former spiritual homeland at arm's length, and ward off the ideocracy which did, after all, give birth and form to their vision of the world?

The Common Program of the Left

Notwithstanding Georges Marchais's numerous efforts to convince public opinion of the profound affinity between the Italian and French Communist parties, in the hope of borrowing the Italian party's reputation for a "liberalism" which the French party clearly lacks, the differences between them continue to outweigh their similarities.

To be sure, both parties have felt the effect of various international currents. It has become impossible, after Solzhenitsyn, to deny certain aspects of the Stalinist past. It is impossible, now that the most famous dissidents come to the West instead of disappearing into camps,* to deny certain positive aspects of the Soviet present. And it is impossible to apply the word "freedom" to the ruling Communist parties' acknowledged monopoly on political debate. In the electoral competition, the French and

---

*Which is not a negligible improvement.

Italian parties both find it necessary to condemn the "negative aspects" or "errors" of the Soviet experience, while naturally reiterating their opposition to any form of anti-Sovietism.

The differences, first of all, concern the structure and style of the two parties. The French party has never regained the membership figures which it proudly published in the aftermath of World War II. Today, it probably has a membership of around half a million and, for many of its activists, it is still no more than a temporary stopping place. Although there is a permanent, almost irreducible hard core, and some of the membership is remarkably loyal (in many families communism descends from father to son), most members leave, after a few years, and give way to others.

After being Stalinist longer than any other Communist party *in partibus infidelium,* the French party has moved clear of Moscow and abjured the dictatorship of the proletariat with a crude abruptness which only served to confirm the persistence of "democratic centralism." In doing so, Georges Marchais seems to have irritated Moscow more than Enrico Berlinguer had done. For a man like Kanapa, reared in the party seraglio, with all the intellectual servility and mediocrity of the prototype Stalinist, to become the spokesman of a party claiming allegiance to France still further weakens the credibility of an inherently unlikely conversion.

More important than the differences between the French and Italian Communist parties is the difference between their respective countries' political situations. In the French presidential election of 1969, the Socialist party hit rock bottom. The candidate it put up, without organizing its forces, came in a long way behind Jacques Duclos and Alain Poher, and observers no longer saw it as a serious rival for the UDR party (the Union de défense de la république). Seven years later the Socialist party, according to opinion polls and by-election results, looked set to become the leading French party. In 1974, François Mitterrand missed the Elysée Palace by only a few hundred thousand votes. He believed—and so did most observers—that the Socialist-Communist coalition was going to win the general election of 1978. In this respect, French and Italian development has diverged: in the first postwar elections, the Communists did better than the Socialists in France, and the Socialists did better than the Communists in Italy; thirty years later, the Socialist vote in Italy had fallen to less than 10% and the Communist vote had risen to more than 35%, while in France, the Socialist party vote was estimated to be more than 25% and possibly as high as 30%, the Communist vote down to about 20% after a maximum of 25%.

One must not forget, however, that this recent climb in the popularity of the Socialist party represents, almost exclusively, no more than an *electoral* success. Outside the unions of government employees—particularly teachers—the Socialist party's influence on the mass of the population is quite limited, although it has been trying to gain a foothold in the private-sector unions. Furthermore, it has a left wing which provides one third of the delegates to the party's conferences, which is close to the Communist party, and which probably would not follow the majority if it meant breaking with the Union of the Left.

The joint program of the Socialists and Communists is a typical attempt to find a socialism halfway between social democracy and Sovietism. The social democratic parties which have achieved lasting success have all subordinated nationalization of the means of production to the priority of efficiency; in other words (knowing that the masses expect a Socialist government to improve their living conditions), they have made it a priority to keep the productive apparatus in good working order. Nationalization of what is often the small industrial sector of an underdeveloped country may be justified but, in the present state of development in France, the nationalization prescribed by the Common Program goes *far beyond* the limit acceptable for a country that wants to stay within the European Community, which is itself an integral part of the Atlantic political and economic alliance.

To use a dictum dear to Marxists, there arrives a point at which quantity turns into quality. Nationalization of Renault has not prevented—in a sense, it has even favored—the expansion of the French automobile industry. The Renault directors, who no longer had shareholders to pay off (and who paid the minimum of taxes), staked everything on the one card: expansion. The Peugeot bosses were more cautious, those at Citroën made fatal errors. Whether or not it is desirable, nationalization of a firm in a sector which remains competitive does not compromise the system as such. The nationalization of gas and electricity presented technical and economic advantages, originally. But the state-run sector has a tendency to overinvest and, thereby, to reduce the supply of capital available for the private sector.

The Common Program for 1978 announced 1) the nationalization of the entire banking and credit system, 2) the takeover of nine large industrial groups, and 3) the threat of nationalizing any business whatsoever.*

There is, thus, no social-democratic perspective here, although the program does reject the Soviet, ideocratic perspective and does seek to be socialist, halfway between the two extreme interpretations of Marxism, namely, Leninism and the Vulgate. Unfortunately, this midway course condemns itself in advance by its internal contradictions. In fact François

---

*"Changing the juridical forms of ownership must allow the workers effective access to responsibility. When the workers in the enterprise express their willingness to participate, and in agreement with the government, new managerial structures will settle the conditions of their participation in the designation of councils of administration, in labor organization, in personnel management, and in relations with the Plan."

Mitterrand, without even realizing it, accepted the slogans of the Communist party and the Marxist-Leninist world view as established truth. Given this assumption, the Common Program acquires a kind of rationality, but a rationality which goes straight into crisis. In all naivety, the program promises stricter control of foreign exchange. No ifs or buts here: right from the start, Mitterrand has committed himself to break with the very essence of the present government: its open frontiers. In theory, exchange control does not rule out the preservation of trade freedom, but in fact this kind of control and freedom make strange bedfellows. Freedom would riddle control with holes, and control would soon extend to trade.

The drafters of the Common Program took as their point of departure the formulas of the Marxist Vulgate, more or less tinged with Marxism-Leninism—monopoly capitalism, the discretionary power of a handful of big industrial and financial groups. On the basis of this pseudoanalysis, they want to restore to the state the power which they see as having been usurped by the monopolies. Yet, in the strict sense of the term, the only monopolies in France are those created by the state itself, on the production and distribution of gas and electricity, and on the railways (though this monopoly is restricted by highway transportation). To call Rhône-Poulenc or the CGE (the Companie générale d' électricité) monopolies is an abuse of popular credulity: as long as frontiers remain open, competition between the various chemical groups, which are all more or less transnational, will remain both keen and expensive. The only chance of Rhône-Poulenc gaining any kind of monopoly position in France will arise on the day when the Socialists and Communists are compelled to close the frontiers.

What the Socialists have failed to understand is that, by endorsing the Marxist-Leninist interpretation of "monopoly capitalism," they bind themselves to follow their allies along a road of upheavals, not reforms. Nationalization of a sector which embraces the entire finance system (insurance, banking, credit) gives the state direct control of all savings and investments, both by individuals and groups. Anybody who knows the attitude of the French toward taxation, tax collection, and public authorities can be in no doubt about their reaction to such a measure. The same Frenchmen who have just apparently displayed their trust in the Socialist-Communist coalition through the ballot box will immediately find themselves defying a state which feels itself entitled to a monopoly on the management of private savings and of capital assets, great or small.

With French politics once again defined by the duel of Right and Left, why shouldn't the Left get its turn? In 1974, François Mitterrand collected ten times as many signatures from prominent people (artists, writers, scientists, professors) as did Valéry Giscard d' Estaing.

The 1958 constitution, revised in 1962 to provide that the President of the Republic be elected by universal suffrage, gives today's majority a strong hand. Once the president has been elected, how can he be refused a parliamentary majority ready to collaborate with him? And once this majority is ensconced in the *Assemblée nationale,* there would be a crisis if the new President of the Republic had to dissolve the Assembly. At each election, the government blackmails the voters by threatening such a crisis; sooner or later, the French people will take a stand against this. (However, in the elections of 1978, they did not yet do so.)

Would they have revolted against *bad* or *unjust* management? Is French management bad? Certainly not, if standards are based on what is feasible, rather than what is ideally desirable. The modernization of the economy begun by the Fourth Republic has proceeded and accelerated under the Fifth. Without taking the Hudson Institute's projections at their face value or setting too much store by reports that French GNP growth rates, in the years before the recession, were higher than those of West Germany, no one can doubt that France changed more in the quarter century between 1948 and 1973 than in the whole of the previous century. Has France made up the ground lost between the wars? It has indeed. Would it have done as well under another type of government? Perhaps, but the Fourth Republic, which had its unacknowledged virtues, has been harshly treated by historians, because it allowed the country to be seen as a caricature, an object of ridicule. During the last years of the Fourth Republic, the French felt rather ashamed of their political system and steered clear of their capital city. Since 1958, they have again recognized themselves in their republic, even if they may want a different majority in power.

The authorities have made their share of mistakes, of course. All states now have industrial policies, and decisions involving large amounts of money fall upon ministers with no special competence in fiscal matters. It cannot be said that the decisions taken on computer technology or aviation have been justified by events. A great deal of construction may have been accomplished, but not much of it has been a source of pleasure to people's eyes or to their sense of fairness. Huge blocks of buildings and "dormitory towns" symbolize the most unpleasant aspects of modern urban planning. Low-cost housing has often been diverted from its proper function, and the people most in need of shelter have not been provided for.

Having said all that, is French society any more "unfair" than others? Any more inegalitarian? Is tax evasion any more widespread? The French fiscal system helps the farmer and the small businessman; it leaves inheritances intact because there is no capital tax* and the maximum estate duty rate is 20%. One can therefore say that, in many ways, this is not a "modern" system—if the standard taxation model is that of the Anglo-Saxon countries, the Netherlands, and Scandinavia.

---

*The tax on capital through inflation is clearly considerable, and cannot be called equitable.

Valéry Giscard d' Estaing's attempt to get a capital-gains tax bill through the National Assembly finally produced a ludicrous document, with tax liability riddled with exceptions. But the very idea of such a tax in a period of inflation was an inadvertent joke; as the Socialist Alfred Sauvy pointed out:

There is a touch of humor in lauding a capital gains tax at a point of maximum capital losses, and in asserting that there is no tax on capital in France. It is playing games with the meaning of the words *tax* and *capital*. *

As for inequality of income in France, the statistics are not adequate, † but it is certainly greater than in the social-democratic countries (Sweden, Norway), but possibly not much greater than in Great Britain. It does not account for the paradox which is best summed up by Alfred Sauvy:

In one generation, the standard of living has more than doubled, giving rise to a startling contradiction: a) progress is the most rapid known to history, and will probably never be equaled; b) discontent is higher than ever, at almost all levels of society. This discontent has increased, stimulated by the professional groups whose function is to create discontent, and even more by the mass media, whose information is designed to gratify and win over the public. ‡

What are we to conclude from this? That the liberal democracies can only survive by modeling themselves on Swedish social democracy? Or that growth itself, as pursued for the past quarter century, contains within itself the promise not (as I and many other have believed) of a "grumbling satisfaction" but of a "devouring dissatisfaction" which, yet again, will turn to socialism in its vain search for equality and community?

The British decline

When the traveler from the Continent sets foot on British soil, he feels that he is approaching a "pinnacle of civilization," a society of men and women who have learned to respect each other, tolerate each other's notions, and live together without violence and without excessive envy or resentment.

Whether this impression is true or false, or is based on memories and gratitude, it cannot conceal the strict accuracy of facts and figures. Not that the intellectual and moral greatness of a nation is measured by the size of its GNP. The Germany of kingdoms and principalities, the land of Goethe and

---

*A. Sauvy, *L'économie du diable* (Paris: Calmann-Lévy, 1976), p. 69. For fixed-interest securities from 1914 to 1974: negative rates of 4.2% per annum. For equities: the sums invested have retained their value if the investor paid no income tax; if he paid even a low rate of tax, the interest rate has been negative. *Idle capital earns nothing*.

†*See* Appendix, Note F.

‡Sauvy, *L'économie du diable*, p. 211.

Weimar, reached heights which the Wilhelmine empire never attained. French literature shone more brightly during the years of decline between the wars than it has since the country's economic recovery. On the other hand, Athens and Florence had their golden ages at the height of their power.

It is possible that London now has the most inventive and creative theater. And judging by the number of Nobel Prizes won by its scientists, the United Kingdom still plays a substantial part in the advance of learning, a much greater one than the size of its population—expressed not as a fraction of the world population (which would be meaningless) but of the population of Europe or North America—would suggest. Oxford and Cambridge, islands of inherited wealth, offer a matchless setting both to teachers and to visitors. But without an economic recovery, how long will the British strengths resist impoverishment?

Anyone who wishes to illustrate the decline of Great Britain with figures has only too many ways of doing so. In the year 1955, the British had a 22.9% share of the world's trade in manufactured products, West Germany a 19.2% share. In 1975, the figures were, respectively, 7.5 and 22.4%. In the same year, the GNP per capita at current prices and exchange rates was $5,060 for France, and $3,370 for the United Kingdom. West Germany's exports (FOB) came to $89,106 million (23.1% of the GDP), French exports reached $45,896 million (16.7% of GDP), and Britain's were worth $38,703 million (20.3%).*

Bypassing the vexing (because insoluble) question of the quality of life, there is no doubt that slow growth has not protected Britain from strife and unrest any more than fast growth has shielded Italy and France. In addition—and it is this that makes the British case interesting—the British unions seem ideologically closer to the Scandinavian and Dutch unions than to the French and Italian ones. A few Communists have filtered into key positions in important unions, but the long-term answer is to take measures to involve the great majority in union electoral processes, reducing the influence of handfuls of militants and activists.

What constitutes, what mechanism explains this sickness, which has come to be called "*le mal anglais*"? On the surface, it manifests itself through an alternation of short phases of expansion which cause higher prices and adverse trade balances, followed immediately by phases of contraction brought about by the government's own attempts to restore the balance of trade. The "stop-go" technique has been seen as typical of the disease afflicting the British economy. It supposedly threatens all Western economies as soon as union power outweighs the labor market.

This commonplace economic interpretation can easily be reinforced by

*At current prices and exchange rates, according to the *OECD Observer*, March–April 1976.

an equally unoriginal social one. Basically, the behavior of the trade unions is a reflection of the feelings, habits, virtues, and defects of organizations formed during the last century and out of tune with the present one. The numerous surviving trade unions tend to get involved in endless demarcation disputes. Their leaders do not want to run British business or abolish private ownership of the means of production (although they are dispassionately in favor of public ownership, in accordance with the Marxist Vulgate). The socialism of the British trade unions stems from the Fabian tradition with its emphasis on redistribution rather than on production.

In the early postwar phase, it became clear that the British economy was not matching the growth rate of West Germany, France, Italy or indeed of the Continent in general.* Various causes were advanced, all of them plausible. It was alleged that the Establishment was under the thumb of the City and was sacrificing industry to finance. In order to reassure the holders of assets invested on the London market, the brakes were hit, it was said, too soon and too hard.

It was also said that, although the unions were impervious to Continental ideologies, they also resisted the changes required by modern organization and the quest for productivity. With the same machines as those of the United States, British factories sometimes use twice the manpower.† During the coalminers' strike, when Britain's industry was working only a three-day week, it managed to produce nearly as much as usual. Did this not prove that, with the same plant, increased output would become possible as soon as the social climate improved and efficiency became a stronger motivation for workers who now tend to cling to familiar conditions and traditional practices?

The discrepancy between the growth rate of Britain's GNP and its industrial productivity and the growth rates of Italy, France or Germany was not enough to bring home to observers the seriousness of the problem. For the British growth rate has been consistently less than the German and the American rate for more than a century and, until the early 1960s, its postwar rate was higher than the long-term average. The UK was making a *slow* advance on its past performance, France and Italy a rapid one.

But here again, some reassuring explanations came to mind. France and

---

*Between 1949 and 1963, the annual growth rate of total productivity was 3.5% in France, 2.3% in the United States, and 1.2% in Great Britain. *See* J.J. Carré, P. Dubois, and E. Malinvaud, *La croissance française, Un essai d'analyse économique causale de l'après-guerre* (Paris 1972), p. 245. According to another table (ibid., p. 246) between 1950 and 1962 the growth rate of total productivity was 3.85% in France, 4.63% in West Germany, 4.78% in Italy, 2.86% in the Netherlands, 2.37% in Belgium, and 1.52% in the United Kingdom. The French growth rate for the period 1950–55 was 3.7% as against the UK's 1.3%; for 1955–62 the respective rates were 4.0% and 1.7%.

†Robert Bacon and Walter Eltis, *Britain's Economic Problem: Too Few Producers* (London: Macmillan, 1976).

Italy had started from lower down on the scale; they had a reserve of manpower in agriculture whose move into the industrial and service sectors was bound to produce a rise in the GNP, since the move meant workers would be switching from low- to high-productivity occupations. Furthermore, the percentage of the United Kingdom's GNP invested remained at about 15–17%, well below the level of German investment, which was between 20 and 25% in the 1950s—the level which France reached in the 1960s. In 1975, gross fixed capital formation at current prices accounted for 25.1% of the French GDP at current prices, and 20.1% of the British GDP.* The social tensions stirred up by the French and Italian "miracles" at least made it worth asking whether a high growth rate was *per se* a good thing or a supreme criterion. A lower level of investment and, therefore, a more moderate rate of growth *might* indicate wisdom, not laziness.

These justifications or excuses no longer stand up, after the catastrophic performances of 1961–75 and 1965–75. The mean inflation rate for 1955–65 was 3.1%; it doubled over the period 1965–75 (7%) to reach 26% in 1974-75. Similarly, the mean rate of unemployment went from 1.9 to 2.6% to reach 5% in 1975. From 1955 to 1965, the pound held its value in relation to the currencies of the principal industrial nations; from 1965 to 1974, it lost 38% of its value. The number of days lost as a result of industrial disputes was multiplied by a factor of 2.1.† The helter-skelter course of prices and incomes is illustrated by figures which follow.‡ The retail increases (for the previous twelve-month period) were 9.0% in December 1971, 7.7% in December 1972, 10.0% in December 1973, 19.2% in December 1974, 24.9% in December 1975. The equivalent wage increases for the same period were 9.0% (1971), 14.0% (1972), 14.7% (1973), 26.7% (1974), and 20.7% (1975). These figures make it impossible to say, with certainty, whether the push came from prices or incomes. Another factor to be considered is that taxation makes wage-earners claim increases that are greater than the rise in prices, in order that their salaries, after taxes, will still have the same buying power.

In other words, during the last ten or fifteen years the nature of the "British sickness" has changed. It is no longer confined to the familiar symptoms—the stop-go tendency caused by dependence on the price level of imported products, as well as by the power of the unions, the priority given to the defense of the pound, the low investment rate, and so on. Although the diagnoses differ, there do appear to be some concrete facts to go on. During the period 1963–74, real wages rose by only 1.9% per annum, not only because the rising cost of living reduced the increased face value to almost nothing, but also because of higher taxation and social

*OECD figures.
†Ibid., p. 5.
‡Taken from the British Information Service report for 1976.

security contributions. In 1963, the average worker earned £18 a week and took home £15.05; in 1974 he took home £17.9 out of gross earnings of £47.7; taxation and social security took £13, the higher cost of living £16.8.*

Robert Bacon and Walter Eltis have produced a thesis which deserves serious consideration in all Western countries. The percentage of nonindustrial employment has increased by one third compared with industrial employment, and this 33.9% shift has been very much faster than elsewhere (in France 18.6%, in Germany 14.2%). Employment in central government has grown by 9.4%, in local government 53.7%, in education 76.4%, in leisure and entertainment 19.0%. Shifts like these are in line with the normal evolution of Western societies but, according to Bacon and Eltis, they have been too quick—to the point of reducing the manpower available for the industrial sector—and also ill-conceived. In addition, according to their assessment, the cost of administration has risen more than has the quality of the social services.

Industrial sector production is split five ways: consumption outside industry; net investment outside industry; consumption by industrial workers; net investment in industry; and net exports. Expansion of the nonindustrial sectors increased the share of the first two categories, and industrial workers tried in vain to keep up their own share, but the most affected were the latter two categories. Net industrial investment and net exports fell, respectively, from 8.2% to 6.3% (as a fraction of total industrial production), and from 15.4% to 6.6%, between 1961 and 1974. These figures were linked with low growth in production capacity and a deficit on the balance of payments.

Clearly, the tendency toward inflation and the stop-go technique are less the outcome of bad management than of the structure of the British economy, the distribution of the work force, and the means of production among the various sectors. As long as, for one reason or another, the industrial sector does not obtain the means for expansion and productive investment, even a rise in labor productivity, which was more rapid at 4% from 1965 to 1974 than from 1955 to 1965 (+3%), does not solve the problem. If the workers released by increased productivity cannot be employed in new factories, either they will stay where they are (which is hidden unemployment), they will be jobless, or else they will find jobs in nonindustrial sectors—particularly in those which do not produce for the market—and will further aggravate the structural distortions of the British economy.

This analysis tells at least some of the story, and it illustrates one of the dangers that beset the liberal democracies of the West. Economic growth

---

*Bacon and Eltis, *Britain's Economic Problem*, p. 7. Cf. Appendix Note G.

tends to increase the number of nonmanual jobs. Rising standards of education tend to increase the number of people seeking nonmanual employment even faster. In theory, in a perfect market, these extra job-seekers ought not to succeed, but in fact the demand has some bearing on the supply. What is more, local government in Great Britain, just as in cities such as New York in the United States, reveals the vicious circle created by *misapplied* social democracy. In New York, the budget has necessitated higher and higher taxes, and companies have reacted to this sort of burden by leaving. In Great Britain, firms cannot move away, but the fiscal burden resulting from state expenditures and from the nationalization of bankrupt businesses comes down on the sector with added force (which is not the case in the industrial sector). In the last analysis, the state can fund its expenditures only by taxing those sectors which sell on the market and make profits. If these sectors do not hold back enough of their profits to keep the pump primed—in other words, if some of the profits are not applied toward *increasing the capacity* to create surpluses—the whole economy will go downhill.

Social democracy in Sweden has, so far, escaped·the British and New York troubles. The state authorities have never forgotten that to finance the social services and redistribute incomes it takes a highly productive industry and a high level of investment, above all in the industrial sector. Whatever the precise mechanism which explains it, the economic catastrophe of the United Kingdom seems to me to carry a lesson and a warning for the whole of the West.

No country can withdraw from competition unscathed. Nobody should fail to understand the priority demands of the productive sector in the broad sense—the sector that works for the market, that produces surpluses and, consequently, finances the expenditures of the state and of firms in deficit. If the state or the unions deprive firms of the financial means or the motivation to invest, then they doom the régime as it is and oblige themselves to assume the burden of investment, growth, and distribution of the work force among the different sectors. The contradiction which is threatening to paralyze the British economy has nothing in common with what Marx predicted. Its roots lie in excessive taxation and redistribution of income, in the truncation of the market economy by the administrative economy of the state and local authorities.

A double threat looms over the West's Mixed Economies. As the level of education rises, the demand for nonmanual work increases more rapidly than the supply. If France did not have three million foreign workers, this disparity would be even greater, but the market might do better. Manual work would be better paid, and this might improve its status. All Western societies are thus tending to become societies of welfare and of income redistribution. Criticism relating to industry and pollution, together with environmental concerns and ideologies that came into fashion after the "miracles" of the 1950s, have accelerated the movement which is a response, in itself, to the logic of our type of system.

But—and this is the lesson of the British disaster—the productive sector in the old sense of the term, in other words, the sector which produces a surplus and works for the market, must remain sufficiently extensive and retain a large enough amount of its own surplus for investment, so that there will be an increased capacity to create further surpluses.* The inroads made by taxation and the social services create the threat of provoking wage claims which, in turn, tend to reduce the funds available to business for investing. Also bureaucratic organization—and here again, the example of New York City is just as instructive as that of Britain—sometimes increases the cost more than it does the efficiency of the social services. The municipal workers' unions, through their power and their role in elections, secure privileges (escalator clauses, pensions effective well before the average retirement age, etc.) which by no means entail comparable advantages for less fortunate social groups. Once again, two social democracies have so far been successful; they are Sweden, which jealously protects the prosperity of its big exporting groups, and West Germany, which has the highest percentage of industrial jobs (47.6% of civilian employment) of any Western European nation. The French percentage is more than eight points lower.

The current notion of the "industrial sector" is not identical, of course, with that of the "productive sector"; an industry which exists only because of subsidies (like that which makes the Concorde jet) is not productive and has to borrow resources from the rest of the economy. The more the state takes over firms which do not stay in the black, and the more the nationalized firms either make no profits or pay no taxes, the more the fiscal burden increases, along with the simultaneous threat of inflationary pay claims and further loss, by the productive sector, of the amounts required for investment.

The City has kept its productive capacity in the sense I have been using the term: banks and insurance companies play the part of an exporting industry. The production of services and intangible commodities is still an industry in the broad sense, and the whole economy, including the currency, must maintain the framework necessary for the operation of these providers of international services. At the end of 1975, London was still the banking center of the world, with nearly half of all European deposits and about one third of the world deposits. The *Economist* entitled one article in its July 3, 1976 issue "Bye-Bye Banks," and did not report (but did foresee)

---

*In theory, public enterprises could create surpluses and make a share of their profits available to the social services. In reality, however, the state tends to take over businesses which are in the red, or to put its businesses into the red.

an exodus of foreign banks apprehensive because of the fall in sterling and of what the British government might do about it. The report read:

> ... the behaviour of sterling, and the effect that it is having on bank balance sheets, highlights an old problem: namely, the ability of a weak industrial nation to support such a large international financial sector. People have argued the pros and cons for years. Now the marketplace is deciding. So far, this year, against.

Once the center of an empire on which the sun never set, in the quarter century following its victory in the last world war Great Britain has been cut down to the size of a second-class nation closely linked to the former colony which has now risen to the rank of superpower. In the words of Dean Acheson's cruel dictum, it has "lost an empire but not yet found a role." When it finally steeled itself to join the EEC, the Community no longer preserved much of its dynamism or ideological attraction. The idea of a United Europe was becoming equated with the Brussels bureaucracy.

It may be thought—though it cannot be proven—that the prestige of the monarchy, the Sirs and Lords, an aristocracy at once traditional and open to outside talent, was altogether greater at the time when Queen Victoria had herself crowned Empress of India than it was on the day in 1948 when the British political genius shone again—but in graceful retreat rather than in insolent pride. Is it North Sea oil, or is it the loss of the old Empire outlets which is giving rise, now, to Scottish nationalism?

Yet in spite of everything, I am hesitant regarding the scope of these historical interpretations. Certainly, one can describe or record the British crisis in Toynbee's terminology. The ruling minority, in which old families mingle with the newly successful, no longer arouses the same respect or obtains the same obeisance. Is this because the nation is no longer great overseas? Workers had a hard life in the United Kingdom of a century ago, when the Royal Navy ruled the waves and the city of London ruled the world market, and when British industry supplied both hemispheres with textiles, shipping cargo, and machines. The last half century presents a two-sided spectacle: the disintegration of an overgrown and vulnerable maritime empire, but also the provision of decent living conditions for the mass of the people, including the working class. In short, the so-called consumer society has more influence on the behavior of the trade unions than the loss of India.

Great Britain has preserved many of its traditions: a "semi-sacred" monarchy (not thoroughly bourgeois, as in Sweden), interpersonal relations still marked by a sense of hierarchy; elitist practices (early selection for the grammar schools, and the slow spread of comprehensive schools), and a handful of universities still laden with privileges—all this, at a time when the movement of minds and events is drawing British society (as it is drawing the Continental societies) toward a *de jure* egalitarianism not very compatible with the spirit of the traditional culture. As for the ruling class—which, even before World War II, tended to put the quality of life before the conquest of markets and the opening of new frontiers—it now seems to have lost the will to fight. It safeguards its own amenities and perhaps is more concerned about the general conditions of life than are the rulers on the Continent. It asks relatively few questions about the causes of Great Britain's relative decline in comparison with West Germany and France; it discusses dispassionately reforms that might restore to parliamentary democracy a capacity for action; and it waits for the manna which will not fall from Heaven but will gush from the depths of the North Sea.

What are the advantages we have attributed to the British system in the past twenty-five years? The government was backed by a workable majority in the House of Commons which, though it did not represent an absolute majority of the electorate, was at least a relative majority and the most sizeable fraction of the voting body. The cabinet governed, rather than Parliament, but it was in the Commons that the politicians were tried and tested, and in the Commons that opposition was expressed, including possible opposition within the majority party. It was the duty of the "shadow cabinet"—in other words, the ministers who would replace the present incumbents if the majority changed—to guarantee the quality of debate; the main speakers spoke as if they themselves held ministerial authority (which protected them from demagogy). None of these merits any longer exist as such; although the parliamentary ritual survives, it is drifting into parody because power has deserted the House of Commons.

Is the government backed by a "workable majority" in Parliament or in the country? The one-vote, one-victor system leads to the formation of a homogeneous government which represents barely a third of the electorate, and even then the Labour government, which represents a minority in the country, is itself divided into a left wing and a right wing, the latter a minority within the Parliamentary group but capable of exercising a kind of veto power over decisions of the cabinet. Keeping the party together has become the principal function of the leader, chosen for his ability to perform this task. The ministers find themselves caught between the civil service and the unions. The civil service advises them and follows the application of their programs, while the unions brandish the strike weapon in order to keep a deterrent in reserve against the government and also to keep a hold on their own troops. When the Chancellor of the Exchequer, Denis Healey, presented a budget in which some tax provisions were subject to an agreement with the unions, the sovereignty of the Commons appeared symbolically limited by another and equally legitimate sovereignty:—the unions.

A different political and economic system will gradually emerge out of the British crisis, in the coming years. Already, by accepting wage-restraint agreements that were concluded with the government, the leaders of the trade unions have recognized that power implies responsibility. Through greater state intervention, probably, and through a restoration of the market and business profits, possibly, industry—the productive sector—will regain the means for growth. In 1980, North Sea oil will assure Great Britain an autonomy in energy comparable only to that of the Soviet Union.

The world recession, which has hit Italy and France as much as it has the United Kingdom, may appear to have been the immediate and direct cause of Britain's political and moral crisis. But the conflict expressed by the events of May 1968 continues to reverberate in France and Italy whereas, beyond the Channel, it has never assumed a violent character or slid toward anarchic disturbances. The crux of the problem in the two Latin countries, both in the short and the long term, has been the question: how can the working masses and the parties that represent them in the national community be integrated?

9
Crisis of civilization?

May 1968, the universities and the students

Some of the most clear-sighted Italian observers have no hesitation about saying in private that, of the three crises—economic, political, and social—it is the third which ultimately governs the other two.

In spite or because of its economic progress, in the wild weeks of May 1968 France went through a curious repetition of the revolutionary days of the last century. As for Italy, although it has not undergone revolutionary days in the French sense of the word, and although the far Left has never been able—and the Communists never willing—to overthrow the established government by force, the nation displays phenomena which French observers designate by the expression "crisis of civilization." It is as if a fraction of the workers, particularly the young, no longer attacked just a system, identified by propaganda as the source of their troubles, but the essence of civilization itself, as if they opposed civilization's urban, industrial framework of rationalized labor with a technical background.

The British and American sociologists took over where the French left off; they in their turn have focused on the *événements de mai* and are trying to explain them. Never has the word *événement** been so appropriate, so marked was the disproportion between the antecedents or earlier incidents, on the one hand, and the widespread turbulence of the four

*I refer to the strong French sense of the word *événement*, as opposed to a plan or an evolution. British and American analysts do not give this strong meaning to the word *event*.

weeks of May, on the other. To this day, all attempts to explain what happened in terms of cause and effect leave a remainder, and a sizeable one. Comprehension is the most that is achieved—meaning that the reader, by an effort of sympathy, is enabled to "relive" the climate of those days and the experiences of the people involved.

Why do those events still attract so much foreign sociological research? What is the mystery, or the mysterious "remainder"? A comparison between the student troubles in the United States and in France will give us the beginnings of an answer. In France and only in France, the wave of rebellion which started out at one university—Nanterre—spread all over the country and affected the whole of the university apparatus. In France and only in France, the student rebellion triggered a working-class movement unprecedented since June 1936 (when a wave of unrest occurred, following the electoral victory of the Popular Front). In France and only in France, worker strikes, originally with no revolutionary objective, destabilized a régime which was headed by General de Gaulle and which had seemed to be the soundest and most popular since the Third Republic of *la belle epoque* (that is, the ten years preceding and the ten years following World War I).

The current version of the first *événement*—the nationwide expansion of a local uprising—and the only one imaginable (without assuming some undisclosed conspiracy), is provided by the conjunction of two causes: the absence of autonomy in the universities (which, in those days, formed a *single* university, strictly subordinated to the ministry of education in Paris); and the existence of a more or less similar state of mind among students in all the university towns, with the same malaise and the same grievances being felt everywhere. By adding to this the "lyrical illusion" of the early days in May and the prevailing resignation among the authorities, one has the classical—and probably the only—possible explanation.

The second *événement*—workers' strikes—can also be readily explained. In the aftermath of the general strike called by the trade union confederations for Monday, May 13, a number of wildcat strikes broke out here and there without instructions from union headquarters but, rather, on the spontaneous initiative of young *gauchistes* (activists holding a wide range of beliefs, farther to the left than those of the Communist party). The Communists responded by using their dominant position in the biggest union group, the CGT (the Confédération générale du travail), to call mass strikes aimed at regaining control of its troops.

The third event, which was even more specifically French, has no explanation in the strict sense of the word, but lends itself to an historical interpretation. In Paris, between the twenty-fourth and the thirtieth of May—between General de Gaulle's speech on television and his broadcast address on the thirtieth—the political class, including the majority parties in government, believed that the régime was on the point of collapse. On the day when General de Gaulle dropped out of sight, leaving the prime minister in ignorance of his whereabouts (he was visiting French army units in Germany), some deputies in the majority called for the resignation of the chief of state, others for that of Prime Minister Pompidou. Functionaries were deserting the ministries; the *polytechniciens*,* despite their military status, were slipping into insubordination; students at the Ecole nationale d'administration† were questioning their privileges and promotion procedures. Everywhere in business and on the factory floor there was talk of reforms and a vision of a different society; here and there, the legal authorities had faded—one could almost say fainted—away, and been replaced by self-managing communes. But these communes actually managed nothing except festivities, traffic, and twenty-four-hour talking shops. General de Gaulle's broadcast of only a few minutes put a halt to the holiday, and within a few days' time the French—like naughty pupils caught misbehaving—were back in class, with all its tedium.

Of their own accord, the French had rediscovered kinds of behavior, words, and states of mind characteristic of the series of revolutions since 1789, with amazing similarities but also with one radical difference: the revolution fizzled out and the French went to the ballot box. All the activist minorities could do was set up a clamor of *élection-trahison*, "betrayal by vote."

In 1956, revolution broke out in Hungary, in what could be called the French style: following miscalculations by the ruling class, the power which seemed unshakeable, one day, was swept away overnight, and an apparently unanimous population celebrated its own liberation by driving out the tyrants. (The fact that Russian tanks later restored the beaten leadership did not change the nature of the event itself.) Perhaps Austria, Germany, and Russia in the aftermath of World War I also experienced days comparable to the revolutionary days in France, which certainly has no monopoly on them.

Yet what is still unique about the experiences in France is the fact that it was *minor incidents* that started the revolutionary process rolling. In the nineteenth century, the blame was usually laid on the monarchies' loss of

---

*Students (but the word also applies to graduates) at the École polytechnique in Paris, one of the official *écoles speciales* which supply most of France's top-level civil servants, a high proportion of French politicians, and the backbone of the French "technocratic" system, a term used by its supporters as well as its detractors. The *polytechniciens* are generally thought of as a conservative, establishment-minded elite; for them to even look like breaking ranks was almost unthinkable.—Tr.

†Another of the *écoles speciales*, located in St-Germain-des-Prés. Its graduates automatically qualify for the best available positions in government administration for their year, and are very often to be found in diplomacy and politics. They are commonly nicknamed "énarques" (ENArchs, after the acronym for their school) because of the dominant position of their "old-boy" network.—Tr.

their legitimacy and on the dominant role of the city of Paris. It was not France, but Paris, that drove out Charles X or Louis-Philippe; but it *was* France, and not only Paris, which fought the workers in June 1848 and the Communards in 1871. In 1968, the world was dumbfounded because the revolt had neither cause nor objectives. For a few days, all authority—in government, the schools, the churches, business—was challenged. In spite of its abortive character (perhaps one ought to say: *because* of its abortive character), the "revolution of 1968" therefore took on a symbolic value. And neither François Mitterrand nor Pierre Mendès-France would have had an answer to the questions put forward by the May rioters.

History enthusiasts will long continue to scour the records and the statements of the protagonists, and to ask themselves: what would have happened if . . . ? Perhaps the sociologists will try to find reasons why the French still retain that extraordinary capacity for revolutionary action and lyrical illusions. But as I see it, this is not the main point. Within the space of a few weeks of brawling and arguing, the French—and especially the Parisians—popularized all the themes relating to the critique of industrial civilization; brought to light the tensions between age groups and the manifold and incompatible objectives of the modern educational system and, particularly, of higher education; revealed the existence and potential strength of a New Left rebellious toward Marxism-Leninism but likewise toward liberalism—in short, the French demonstrated the social *failure* of economic success.

Crisis of civilization was the final diagnosis of a good many of the less committed historians, but there is something equivocal about the idea itself. In the present-day sense it means either the negation of the values and imperatives which are the basis of a given society's cohesion, or (and this would be rather more precise) the inability of the older generation to pass on to its juniors a respect for these values and an obedience to these imperatives. This second meaning at once brings us to the students and their revolt—the origin and symbol of those "events." For what the students did was to show how unsturdy the old university structure was, it revealed the birth of a New Leftism or *gauchisme* (a popular rebellion which refuses to be subject to Communist discipline), and it brought to light the turbulence in all the country's hierarchies.

Student rebellions are not an invention of the 1960s. They have both precedents and pedigrees (if ancientness and a role in revolution make up such a thing). In the United States, they were bound up with a national movement of protest against the war in Vietnam. Everywhere, they constituted a kind of "rite of passage for adolescents," a way of informing the older generation about the identity and special will of the generation already past its infancy but not yet integrated into the production apparatus. In many developing countries, students protest against their own society, despite the privileges they enjoy. Their numbers are too great, and not all individuals can achieve the rank they feel entitled to, with the result that—their ambitions frustrated—they transmute their disappointments into ideologies.

The French example seems to me the most interesting, because it is the most complete and the most complex. The students denounced not only the universities, but the whole social order, together with the beneficiaries of this order in the universities and in the state. They became the heralds of an *ordre nouveau*, in which it would be forbidden to forbid.

The denunciation of the "mandarins" is not without its own quaint charm. Among teachers with seniority and prestige there were, and still are, those who abuse their positions. In some scientific disciplines, research workers or even advanced students sometimes get the feeling that they know more than their masters; in other disciplines, with a political content, students—and also some of the teachers—refuse to make a distinction between knowledge and action. For teachers to have to face losing the security they too often enjoy, for them to feel judged by their hearers, for them to have to answer to those who question or even wish to refute them—such cries for reassessment by the younger generation are a protection against the closed system of academic access to the administration and against stagnation, and they maintain the vitality of the institutions of teaching. Or rather, these beneficial effects come about, provided student "questioning" itself does not fall victim to a crystallization worse than that of the functionaries and pedants, petrified either into Marxism-Leninism or else into a leftism exposed to all winds, but changeless in its empty negativity.

The foregoing remarks relate to the words of the principals in the performance, to the ideologies which they developed or are developing. Sociological inquiries inspire reflections of a quite different kind. The first characteristic of today's French and Italian universities is the enormous size of the student body. In 1976, more than 800,000 students were enrolled in France (only half of whom would be awarded degrees). In Italy, there are more than a million students. In 1968, everyone was talking about the theme which had been expressed in a book by Pierre Bourdieu and J.-C. Passeron entitled *Les Héritiers*, "The Heirs."* It is a fact that opportunities for higher education vary widely according to the socio-professional category and cultural level of the parents. But since the appearance of that book, educational inequality has been a recurrent theme in ministerial speeches, as an injustice to be combated. This does not mean that there is anything new about it: the victims of this "injustice"—the workers' sons who had never gotten further than the elementary or lower

---

*(Paris: Minuit, 1964).

secondary school—never used to complain about it. On the other hand, a good many of the sons of bourgeois parents have complained, and have become leftist militants. But those who rebelled out of idealism did not represent the bulk of the student population.

That population contained a sizeable number of students from the petit bourgeois milieu: artisans' children, boys and girls with working-class backgrounds. "Nondemocratization" can be measured by the persistent inequality of opportunities for higher education according to the parents' socio-professional category, but a degree of "democratization" can also be measured by the percentage of students coming from families farther down the scale. The rebellion of the "heirs," whether based on idealism or on the fear of reduced circumstances, is matched by the anxiety of the nonheirs, who, realizing how great their numbers are, are afraid of having to knock on closed doors, and of not being able to find positions commensurate with their ambitions.

Obviously, it was the anxiety of the many rather than the indignation of the few, the nonheirs' fear of the future more than the heirs' bad conscience, which created a climate ripe for trouble. The authorities' response was to swallow the ideology in fashion, to set themselves the target of eliminating or of reducing what is in fact a more or less inevitable inequality and, last but not least, to take precautions to avoid a repetition of the "events."

The reforms contained in the "Orientation Law" of 1968–69 tended to make a separation between the university authorities and the central state authority. There is no longer any risk that Valéry Giscard-d'Estaing would be directly affected by trouble at Nanterre, as General de Gaulle was in 1968. Each of the seventy-five universities is run by a president elected by a governing council which, in turn, is elected according to complex procedures. The division of the universities into a large number of "education and research units" (Unités d'enseignement et de recherche) is helpful for localizing revolts, although the student movements have gone on striving to give their protestations a national character. The troubles caused in 1976 by a new decree relating to secondary education confirm both the permanence of the crisis and the fragility of the barriers raised by university autonomy.

The crisis has not gone away, and cannot go away: in France and Italy all students who have passed the baccalauréat are entitled to attend the university; there are not many campuses, and students derive some material advantages from enrollment (e.g., social security coverage, use of university dining hall), but many of them live in conditions of hardship; the bachelors' and masters' degrees are devalued by the large number of those who obtain them, and they no longer guarantee a position in education (which was the channel for most B.A. recipients); a relatively small fraction of students and an appreciably higher percentage of teachers (especially in the lower lecturer and assistant-lecturer categories) lean toward parties on the left or far left; "politicized" left-wing students and teachers are more active and better organized than the moderates. These well-known facts point straight to the obvious conclusion that a pretext is all the militant minority needs in order for it to drag in a mass of anxious or passive students, and teachers as well, who either sympathize with the grievances of the protestors or who do not bother to take a stand against them.

The impotence of the authorities occasionally results in striking and almost comical contrasts. The study of law can be pursued in peace and quiet at Paris II (Assas). Why? Because the far-right groups, with their booted and helmeted commandos, rule there. Some left-wing students, enrolled—in accordance with a distribution system (abandoned in 1976)—in Nanterre, asked to be transferred to Assas, in spite of the loathing they felt for its self-appointed "custodians of order." Here, the regular authorities capitulate out of powerlessness or cowardice; there, the private militia rule by the threat of violence.

In Eastern Europe, all countries apply the authoritarian solution, and the number of persons to be seated at the university is settled by those at the top. Candidates are subjected to a rigorous selection system. Perhaps high school graduates who are forced to go into colleges of technology or into industry may resent it, but students escape the anxieties of their opposite numbers in the liberal countries. In France, there is no longer any question of going back to such a rigid system, which General de Gaulle eloquently defended and explained during his visit to Romania in May 1968. The number of seats therefore depends on the demand, with student seats directly dependent on demand, and teaching positions a reflection of student demand; both have the same interest in increasing their numbers. The counterpoint of this growth, even when studies are proceeding normally, is obviously: the devaluation of each degree. Simplifying the matter, one might say that a degree is today the equivalent of the *baccalauréat* a generation or two ago. With the birthrate falling and university expansion slowing down, the present student generations will have a tougher fight for promotion than the postwar generations.

In view of these developments the activism of the Communist and *gauchiste* minority groups seems neither surprising nor pathological. Since France has a large Communist party which collects 20% of the votes cast, it is bound to be represented in strength among the students and lower-grade teaching staff. Similarly, with the Communist party having lost its revolutionary standing and pursuing what is seen as a reformist policy more or less linked with that of the Soviet Union (about which the French now have fewer illusions), there was bound to be a crop of militant minorities to its left—hostile to the Communist party, although more or less Marxist-Leninist—of one stripe or another.

What is pathological in France is not the existence of these minorities but the political and moral capitulation to them. In some French circles, it has become quite common to refer to an antiyouth "racism" (a bad habit has developed of using the word racism for any form of hostility toward any group whatsoever). Personally, I see tolerance of university unrest as a lot more striking and revealing than the actions of the students. I do not feel that these young people—now that the "lyrical exaltation" of May 1968 is over—are condemning our society to death, nor do they herald its collapse by their rebellion.

In all classes of society, there exists among the young a fraction—its size cannot be measured with exactitude—which, being "allergic" to work, refuses to be integrated into society. Probably there has always been a minority of young people whose socialization has been, so to speak, a failure. Today these failures, besides being more apparent, are more plentiful, and for a number of reasons, which are still being debated. Certain social causes spring to mind at once: living conditions in the big housing estates and New Towns; the abrupt transition from one way of living to another; the decline of family "togetherness" when a mother and a father both have to go out to work. For the children of middle-class families, there are other factors involved, such as the parents' abdication of their role, and the lack of any national sense of direction.

All the evidence confirms that totalitarian societies have been encountering similar phenomena—except for student disturbances, which they do not tolerate. Thus, the fundamental questions are not even raised. In contrast, France was allowed to go off on a three-week revel in May 1968, and the university authorities were robbed of the means to impose discipline and to impose a sense of reason upon the agitated student population which, by inclination or design, had become unruly.

Is the collapse of authority not the real and only crisis of civilization? Pareto remarked that history is the "graveyard of aristocracies." Democratic societies also have aristocracies, and their need to believe in themselves is greater than that of hereditary aristocracies, because their power is justified only by the consent of those who obey them. No one obeys anybody who has no belief in his right to command.

Church and army: authority in the institutions

. . . A land so shifting in its changing thoughts and tastes that it ended by becoming an unexpected spectacle to its own self, and remains as surprised as foreigners are by the sight of what it has just done.

Who among the readers of Alexis de Tocqueville did not recall this description—taken from the famous portrait of the French nation at the end of *L'Ancien Régime et la Révolution*—on the morning after the May events? The French had put on a spectacle for one another. Each Frenchman played his part, obsessed by historic memories. In *L'Education sentimentale,* Frédéric hears a revolutionary tell another who suggests abolishing degrees: "No, it is the people who will award them." In 1968, the students dreamed of turning themselves into examiners, in a community where everyone would alternate between the roles of instructor and of the instructed.

These fantasies of the lyrical illusion, these revolutionary stereotypes, engraved on the collective unconscious, would have left no traces or disquiet behind them if the power of speech had not been extended to nearly all organizations, public and private, at least for a few days, and if this power of speech had not been almost indistinguishable from power itself. Vatican Council II, the student rebellions, and the soldiers' trade unions seemed to come together as a system, symbolizing, if not the collapse, then at least the challenging of authority (or the present form of authority) of the three institutions whose roots go back to the *ancien régime:* the church, the army, and the university.

Arnold Toynbee wrote somewhere that the West could avoid decline only by becoming reconciled with the Catholic church, with the faith which gave it its soul. If he was not mistaken, Europe, if not the entire West, will continue its slide toward decline. Not only is the Catholic church now feeling the delayed backlash of a secularized civilization, but it is also breeding various Christian heresies—some are discovering the Holy Spirit in the Chinese commune, others the Messiah in the proletariat, while still others want to ignore transcendence in order to live out the spirit of Christianity more fully, and others are "sacralizing" violence in the service of the right cause—namely, justice. It is as if some Catholics, unable to convert to theism or moralism (unlike the faithful of the reformed religions), were looking to this world to provide another path to salvation with claims to universality.

A century has elapsed since the council of Vatican I marked the extreme extension of the authority principle, incarnated in the pope. Nowadays, even in matters of dogma, the pope tolerates practically anything, for fear of creating or multiplying heresies. If only for reasons of decorum, I shall not enlarge on the case of the Catholic church, but confine myself to a single comment. Once the authority principle had a precise meaning: in matters of dogma the pope proclaimed the truth, and that was that. By extension, in other spheres the faithful bowed to the decisions made at the top. Most Catholics submitted to the Vatican's condemnation of the right-wing *Action* *française* political group in 1926.* That was only half a century ago. . . . A similar condemnation directed at the theology of violence—the *théologie horizontale,*† or the ritual of Pope Pius V—would only come up against either resistance or indifference from the people involved.

In the southern European countries of Spain and Italy, where Catholicism was still part of the everyday life of the nation, the downfall of the old interpretation of the authority principle is shaking the foundations of society itself. Elsewhere, in Protestant countries and also those where the church had, so to speak, withdrawn from the world and concentrated on its proper mission, it is protest in the army which takes on a symbolic character. Are soldiers' unions compatible with what the classic dictum called the principal strength of armies, their discipline?

For the same reason as the church, the army belongs by its origins and many traditions to the *ancien régime*. The social distance between officers and men dated back to the time when the lower ranks were recruited from the lowest classes of society. Ernest Renan explained—and in a way justified—antimilitarism by arguing that a man of culture had no choice but to detest the conditions in which the private soldier lived and died. I was struck by the aristocratic style still prevailing among British army officers in 1940; French officers, or a good many of them, were quick to adopt the British swagger stick. With all its overstatements and injustices, *Mars ou la guerre jugée*‡ expresses the rejection of the systematic domination of man by man maintained by the military hierarchy. Janowitz, the best American sociologist writing about the institutions of the armed forces, declared several years ago that the Western democracies would eventually be choosing between trade unions made up of soldiers and an army of skilled professionals. Events seem to be confirming that forecast: do they also confirm the decline of the West?

Modern politics has laid claim to the two—in a sense contradictory—ideas of *citizenship* and *economism*. In the wake of the French Revolution, the former led to conscription and to people's armies—armies which did not change as much as their new method of recruitment required. The British and Americans resorted to conscription only in wartime. France gave it up after 1815, only to revive it after the disaster of 1870, when the professional army of the Second Empire had been defeated by the larger army of Prussia and the German states. The British have stuck to a career army and, since the war in Vietnam, the Americans have also given up

*But not *l'Action française* itself.

†"Horizontal theology"—looking not upward but sideways, not toward religions but to social and political concerns.—Tr.

‡A critique of war and militarism, published in 1921, under the pen name "Alain," by the philosopher and essayist Emile-Auguste Chartier (1868–1951).—Tr.

conscription in the selective form they used to practice. Like it or not, France is now faced with the question of having a professional army.

Until now, only Federal Germany has managed to find a middle way, namely, an army manned by young conscripts but without soldiers' committees or unions. Part of this success derives from the inspiration of those who created the *Bundeswehr* with the intention of fostering a citizen army. In abstract terms, the reformers can be said to have wanted to lay the main stress on the strictly specific character of the command exercised by officers and NCOs. Left to itself, the army tends to become what Goffman calls a "total institution." In the factory, the worker obeys the foreman as a function of the needs of production (ideally, at any rate). Why shouldn't the same apply to the army? The soldier would leave the barracks in the evening, after his day's work, just like a factory worker; he would leave his uniform behind, and salute officers only in the line of duty.

Auguste Comte compared the industrial with the military system and claimed that the former was superior, since industry replaced command by cooperation. He underestimated the degree of command involved in industrial cooperation, and did not allow for a change in the nature of military command.

The British and Americans have no historic memories comparable to those of the mass conscription of the revolutionary wars, or the *sans-culottes*. Their answer is to recruit soldiers from the lower levels of society with the offer of good wages, and to maintain the social distance between officers and men simply because of their different backgrounds. In the long term, these professional armies—which are expensive, if they have a sizeable establishment—may be emblematic of the destiny of republics which no longer entrust their fortunes to the loyalty of their citizens; in the short term, they avoid trouble and do the job of defense.

The formation of unions in the armed forces can express two intentions (though these are often linked): either a thoroughly political subversive purpose or a wish to compel the military institution to model itself on civil institutions. The young Dutchmen who created the unions they were used to having available in civilian life do not seem to have had any subversive intent; the French soldiers may have half-consciously wanted to force a change of character on the military institution, but all the evidence suggests that their main motivation was political. Their protest was actuated by their hostility to the régime or the government, even if they also wanted to express specific grievances. In theory, and even in some concrete cases, trade unionism may not be a negation of the requirements of the institution in peace and war, but clearly this only holds true provided that military trade unionism has no subversive intention and has no other aim than to "defend" soldiers in the sense that unions defend workers—in other words, to defend their wage levels and living conditions. In barracks, this defense presupposes a very different mental attitude on the part of officers and NCOs; in an attenuated form it would come down, as it does in the *Bundeswehr,* to organized dialogue between officers and ranks through the medium of a trusted representative chosen by the soldiers. (It would take a superhuman effort of the imagination to envisage unions defending the soldiers' living conditions during wartime.) What gives the soldier's "trade" its somber grandeur is that he gives death, and receives it. It is the commanding officer's decision that presents his subordinates with the more or less great, more or less justified risk of death.

In France, the politicization of the unions and the strength of tradition among officers and NCOs precludes that form of Western democracy which is generally gaining ground, namely, the organized challenging of the "teachers" by the "taught," of business heads by works committees or unions, of the Catholic hierarchy by the clergy or laity. The armed forces can and must recognize that young people all over Western Europe will no longer agree to obey the holder of some titular authority solely because that individual has the right to command. Obedience to reasonable orders justified by the technique of arms, the means of production, the necessities of physical or moral training, and obedience to a charismatic personality who shares his subordinates' hardships and leads by example are considered, by many observers, to be as easy to obtain today as ever—and possibly easier, if the rebellious or nonsocialized minority is not taken into account.

Why should one be surprised if the young choose one or another means of protest against conscription (which is no longer conscription because, of those liable for the draft, half of them—and especially the reluctant sons of middle-class parents—are not called up). In any case, so it is argued by the "nuclear deterrent" school of thought, the Europeans will never mobilize conventional forces on the scale of the Soviet bloc, and a few more or a few less hardly matter. The balance of power results from the presence of one of the superpowers and, with it, thousands of nuclear warheads, on either side; who can know how far hostilities will go, once they have begun? Even apart from the nuclear threat hanging over everybody's head, both sides share the wish not to settle their historic conflict by force of arms. Some will say that the extension of the Soviet Imperium as far as the Atlantic would decisively strengthen its power. To be sure, Western Europe would provide an enormous surplus of material resources, but what would happen to the moral unity of the Eastern bloc and the authority of the Kremlin? Already, the men in the Marxist-Leninist bunker have twice had to use the Red Army to bring to heel Marxist-Leninists tempted by national and even individual freedom. What means would they have to use to restore to Paris the order which rules in Warsaw? How long would they be able to prevent Western "corruption" from infecting the Soviet Union itself? A half-free

Europe—a Europe on probation, one might say—contributes to technological efficiency without shaking the Soviet ideocracy to its foundations.

Having said all that—and there is no shortage of arguments along this line of thought—the historian cannot repress a feeling of uneasiness. In the Soviet Union, strict Prussian (in the French sense) discipline is still the rule; in the West, we are debating the question of unions for the armed forces. In the Soviet Union, all scientific and literary organizations have a hierarchy in which the top place is occupied, not by the most qualified person, but the party hack, the time-serving academician. In France, the magistrates' unions have been hitting the headlines, and one of them boasts of rendering "political" justice. Where is the decline? Where is the future? In Soviet ideocracy, or in the generalized controversy of the West?

The answer is not self-evident. In the field of scientific research, rigid organization does not favor progress, it retards it. It is competition between centers of research, and the challenging of scholars and scholarship by the young, which give the United States its intellectual inventiveness. Russian towns do not suffer any less than Western towns from petty crime, gangs of young toughs, and alcoholism. The elected rulers of Western Europe can rightly proclaim themselves to be "legitimate." The almost universal acceptance of the elections which followed May 1968 symbolized rejection of "revolutionary legitimacy" and ratification of electoral or representative legitimacy. No Eastern European Communist party, not even the Soviet Communist party, would dare to submit to such a test.

What is more, it is in strife-torn Western Europe that productivity grows most rapidly and workers submit to the exigencies of rationality. It is in the Soviet Union—where a few men at the summit of the state settle the fate of tens of millions of their fellow-Russians, without having to account to anyone—that factories employ twice the manpower of German or American factories, even when they are using the same equipment. Once again, what is there to fear? In order to play host to the Olympic Games, the Soviet Union has asked Western capitalists and engineers to build the hotels it needs, and the foreign firms will even import workers to hold down the anticipated delays.

License and repression; Tocqueville's Law

Perhaps the Soviet conjunction of political and intellectual despotism and its scientific and economic inefficiency goes some way toward explaining one of the paradoxes of our time. By what aberration or ignorance of history do so many intellectuals denounce as "repressive" the societies that legalize abortion, that tolerate homosexual relationships, that give consideration to unions in the armed forces, that have, for the most part, abolished the death penalty, and that do not refuse freedom of speech to anyone, whether it be to speak in favor of pornography, or the Baader-Meinhof gang, or the wildest of possible extravagances? Unless all the signs are deceiving us, what threatens liberal Europe is not excessive repression, but license. Or is this license merely a deception? The West testifies to its productivity; but does the Western production system not imply a permanent constraint and, therefore, a kind of repression?

The conjunction of *paraded license* (which in certain countries is the practice, and not pretense) and of *denounced repression* is due primarily to what I call Tocqueville's Law, which can be formulated in all sorts of ways. It is when societies have been weakened by reforms that they are brought down by revolution. Despotisms become vulnerable when they "liberalize" themselves. The last surviving privileges are resented all the more bitterly because of the elimination of others that were abolished. Whereas the victims of a system put up with a fate they judge themselves incapable of changing, those who glimpse the summit but cannot reach it are prompted to rebel.

These different formulations are not equivalent. One of them applies to peasants who already owned their land and took up arms against feudal rights, which were all the more intolerable because they were on their way out. Another applies to a bourgeoisie impatient for elevation to the same status as the nobility and for access to all state offices. Yet another applies to the *ancien régime* as a whole, whose ruling principle (in Montesquieu's sense) was undermined by the movement of ideas, and whose privileged elements—failing to foresee, or even to fear, the collapse of the whole structure—wanted to reform it.

Let us apply these commonplace or classic notions. When it comes to morals, "liberalization" is not to be denied; take sexuality, abortion, or what once passed for normal or abnormal, and Western societies display what, in the light of history, can be described as *extreme tolerance*. This tolerance, which varies from one area of society to another, is not and can never be total. The law punishes the corruption of minors. If man is defined as a "machine with desires," Western society, like all known societies, remains repressive (the socialist societies of Eastern Europe are much more so).

"Antipsychiatry" is another application of Tocqueville's Law. Some people see that "total" institution, the asylum, as the despotic institution *par excellence*. But "despotic" is not quite the right word; constraining, or totalistic, would be more appropriate. In a sense, the protests on behalf of criminals in prison and the insane asylums testify to a more scrupulous moral conscience and an effort to respect the individual, even when he is no longer a whole person, or is paying for a crime. All the same, the pessimistic sociologists—of whom Pareto is the most famous voice—would have detected several symptoms which they would have viewed as omens pointing to the fall of the established order: greater sympathy toward criminals than to their victims or their judges; fewer and lighter penalties; the indictment, not of the criminal, but of society, which is considered to be guilty by definition; in brief, the mental attitude which has been called "humanitarianism."

The present state of affairs or, at any rate, certain aspects of it, would have surprised Pareto and would probably have angered him. In one fashionable view, the isolation of criminals or the insane becomes an example, not of bourgeois humanitarianism, but of a cruel and subtle kind of repression. Prison is worse than the galleys; the distance between classes greater than that between the prerevolutionary "estates"; the medieval *cour des miracles* (the Parisian thieves', beggars', and madmen's quarter) more civilized than the mental hospital; and bands of mercenaries less repugnant than the barracks and the discipline imposed on soldiers in the eighteenth century. Who does not discern an element of truth in each of these assertions? What we are observing today, in fact, is a revolt against "total" institutions—asylum, barracks, jail—which deal with the whole man in terms of a specific feature of his being or activity, treating the mad, for instance, as if their madness extended to their entire personality, and as if they no longer possessed any of the reactions and feelings of so-called normal people. In this sense, our own century—the century of Verdun, the Holocaust, the Gulag, and systematic torture—displays, simultaneously, an extreme solicitude for the outcast, to the point of rejecting the very concept of madmen or criminals, on the argument that there has been no consistent definition of it throughout history. With respect to morals, Tocqueville's Law obviously applies, with the ambiguous results always observed in such cases.

Among intellectuals and in the upper classes, it is the survival of taboos which is most readily condemned; among the middle classes—and even in the working class—it tends to be open, aggressive liberalization (e.g., pornography) which provokes disapproval. Occasionally, alliances take shape between the upper class and the most underprivileged: in the United States, the wealthy upper middle class comes out in favor of mixed schooling for blacks and whites (but sends its own children to private schools), while it is the lower middle or working class which has to submit to having its children "bused" to schools which are sometimes quite distant, and which has to accept the deterioration of educational standards in some of these "mixed" schools.

Likewise, in France it is the intellectual class or bourgeoisie that detests the death penalty, that condemns the prison system most harshly, and denounces what the French have taken to calling the "racism" of discrimination against the young. This is the usual division of roles: the middle or lower classes, who profit less from the established order than the upper classes, incline toward a simpler and sterner morality than do the intellectuals and the privileged—nowadays, at least. The Victorian bourgeoisie displayed no such feeling, any more than does the Catholic bourgeoisie of northern France. In the United States and France, the majority of the upper class and higher officialdom is on the side of the progressive intellectuals, and favors tolerance in all its forms, rather than the prohibitions and obligations handed down by tradition. Is this progress toward freedom, or does it mean loss of the virtues needed for the privileged class to retain its traditional role? What makes the answer all the more uncertain is that the two interpretations do not necessarily conflict. Moral progress does not exclude historical decline.

To Soviet dissidents—to Solzhenitsyn and to Sakharov, probably, as well, if he were forced to emigrate—some aspects of Western freedom, such as pornographic films and magazines, and the press's pursuit of information and scandal deserve no respect and call for no imitation. They are expressions of license and are, at best, the price to be paid for the more worthwhile rewards of freedom.

In spite of everything, Tocqueville's Law does not account for the success of the contemporary theme of the "repressive society." Or the Law has to be at least interpreted differently. We were saying that "total institutions" tend to reduce their scope of activity and concentrate on specific problems. The barracks occupy only a portion of the soldier's activity and time. An early breach in the prison system was the granting of permission to prisoners to go outside the jail now and then. The man with a five-year sentence does not spend five years in his cell, and the parole board may allow him days or weeks of leave. Similar advances have been made in the mental institution system. At the same time, the authorities are making occasional attempts, within total institutions, to create activities or amusements parallel to those of the outside world, so as to lessen the sense of exclusion from it as much as possible. The logical conclusion would be for the insane or the criminal to have to take only the direct, specific consequences of their illness or crime. Working outside and returning to prison every night would be the extreme form of "nonexclusion" of the prisoner.

The same kind of development is occurring in the nontotal institutions, particularly in businesses, at the place of work. Studying the eastern provinces of pre-World War I Germany, Max Weber noted that Germans preferred even lower-paid factory work to working on the big *Junker* estates, and he had no difficulty in analyzing their reasons. In the vocabulary I have been using here, people who worked for the big landowners felt personally dependent on their boss, even if he exercised his authority in a benevolent paternalistic manner. In factories, the wage earner obeys not so much a person as an anonymous organization and, in any case, he spends his free time outside his place of work, away from the owner of the means of production. The "servants" of big landowners greeted industrial proletarization as a liberation. What creates a problem—one which grows in step with this dissociation of social roles—is the reaction of people to the "depersonalization" of all their activities.

I use the term "depersonalization" in a specific sense, of course: no one commits his whole person to his job. A modern system breaks down quite readily into a considerable number of partial systems, and every flesh-and-blood individual can belong to several systems, with nobody defined by a single role, or even by the sum of these roles. Does not such a society, in some dimly perceptible way, become as intolerable as the last traces of a nearly humanized prison system?

The Weberian typology of the forms of domination allows the idea toward which I myself incline to be formulated with what is probably excessive rigor. Traditional authority—by father, king, bishop, teacher (of which the pope's unconditional authority in matters of dogma is a kind of symbol)—is being eroded by the progress of ideas and events. Not that it is disappearing entirely, for no society can do without it but, within the family, school, and university it does not go as far as it did in the past, and in the church it has been shaken. Boys and girls who have reached the legal age of majority pursue their high school studies, but they no longer automatically accept orders from their teachers or the administration. Teachers have to win their pupils over; they must interest or convince their classes by their grasp of the subject and force of personality. In other words, they have to possess some of the qualities of charismatic leaders, within a system based on knowledge and, therefore, on rational authority.*

In the United States where universities—*in loco parentis*—used to have some of the features of total institutions, the 1960s brought some irreversible changes. Students do not do less work: at present, they are working harder than ever, because of the tough competition they expect. They flock toward some courses and steer clear of others (in a way which is not confined to the United States). It is true that they have always paid for their studies and thereby acquired the right to choose and assess their teachers;† what has gone is the kind of parental authority which had belonged, particularly, to the private universities. In various ways, students participate in the management of the universities, or at least they exercise a vague

---

*The reader may object that this has always been the way, and this is true in one sense, but, in the old days, traditional authority kept the organization together, even if the teacher did not possess the necessary qualities.

†Max Weber believed that this mediation by money was already observable in the relations between American teachers and students.

right of veto on some appointments and on the content of syllabuses. Here too, the weakening of tradition gives greater authority to some people and simultaneously removes it from others.

Not all modern organizations are based on traditional authority; on the contrary, the main ones profess the rule of reason, but they do not permit recourse to charismatic authority, and are in danger of becoming oppressive through their very rationality. I shall not work through the over-rehearsed examples of repetitive assembly-line work which appear in all indictments of the capitalist economy, when these indictments should instead be aimed at productivism *per se*, as Simone Weil clearly recognized. It is the whole enterprise that the individual feels to be oppressive, because he is subjected to its rationality without knowing, usually, the purpose of it; society, too, is oppressive, because of its fluctuating economic conditions and price movements, which are a burden to everyone. The oppression is anonymous and depersonalized, like the social role played by the individual in the production process. Ideological myths, such as monopoly capitalism or secret service interference in people's lives, perform a psychological function. Philosophers may possibly abhor abstractions such as capitalism, imperialism, and productivism, but the popular imagination needs these villains, it has to see them in the flesh. The notion of monopolists, the sight of string-pullers exploiting and manipulating the people, gives a shape and form to the *anonymous oppressor*.

One segment of the left-wing intelligentsia reluctantly acknowledged that the oppressiveness is largely a product of society itself, of the system of production, and that public ownership of the means of production is not in itself enough to alter the condition of individuals, either at or away from work.*

Another section of the intelligentsia of the Left has been working to isolate the specifically capitalist features of Western economies: "the rule of money" (the cash-nexus); the treatment of human labor as a commodity; the deciding of status according to wealth. But it is a fact that, in societies of the Soviet type, it is the state managers who enjoy economic and financial privileges. They do not owe their wealth to success in economic competition, but to their position within the administrative or party hierarchy. The intellectual, artistic, and scientific elite, too (provided that it knuckles under to ideological conformism), gets all that money will give in the USSR, where it is only the privileged who have access to the shops where the goods most in demand are available at the most favorable prices. In other words, in *both* systems the powerful are rich and the rich powerful,

*Some ideologues—Marcuse, for example—continue to insist on public ownership of the means of production, although their anticapitalist indictment applies just as strongly to Soviet productivism.

although on the one side, it is wealth that leads to power and, on the other, power that leads to wealth. This picture is a little overdrawn, of course. In the West, administrative or political success does not lead to great wealth on the Rockefeller or Rothschild scale, but it does guarantee a privileged way of life. In the East, economic success, in the Western sense of the term, does not exist, in the absence of a free market, but does exist in the sense in which one refers to the success of a given manager in running an enterprise.

Whether in the field of morals, or of subjective, material or immaterial rights (freedom of opinion, or freedom to travel abroad), of trade unions or voluntary defense or pressure groups, any observer of good faith will agree that "oppression" is much more characteristic of the Soviet type of society than it is of the Western type. Among the tireless detractors of "Western oppression," I distinguish several categories:

1. those who condemn Soviet oppression even more vehemently (a section of the *gauchistes*);

2. those who ought to denounce the Soviet régime but do so hesitantly because they remain attached to the Marxist Vulgate and, particularly, to the intrinsic merits of public ownership of the means of production (e.g., Herbert Marcuse);

3. those who, at heart, do not detest oppression as much as they do the liberties enjoyed by individuals and groups in the West;

4. lastly, of course, those who still cling to the "Communist utopia," despite all the recorded experiences of the twentieth century.

To conclude our analysis: there are two major explanations for the simultaneity of the apparently incompatible phenomena of *license* and *revolt*, namely, Tocqueville's Law and the quasi-oppressive character of modern civilization itself (which, in the context of the enterprise, imposes an anonymous discipline and, in the context of the world economy, seems to obey a runaway dynamism). And it may be that many people find it easier to put up with a traditional leader (or customary form of authority) than with an authority which professes to be a "simple necessity" or which justifies itself by a rationality which eludes the majority. Perhaps the cult of movie or TV stars and the personalization of the political scene are testimony that people feel the need of a charismatic authority in the absence of the traditional authority which has gradually been undermined in every sphere: the family, the church, the university, the state.

This raises one last but fundamental question: to what extent do individuals consider themselves "oppressed" because of doubts about their government's political and economic legitimacy? Is the decisive factor—which would explain the behavior of the unions and the relative strength of the various Western Communist parties—the acceptance or rejection of democracy as a legitimate form of government, the acceptance or rejection of a system which allows private ownership of the means of production?

Political and economic legitimacy

Of all the countries of the West, the only one that seems safe from the threat of revolution, the only one where freedoms appear not to be at risk from any party or interest group of importance, is the United States. And with good reason.

Before federation, the Anglo-American states called upon "the rights of man," basing themselves on their nonconformist faith. But freedom in scriptural interpretation did not entail a similar freedom in the field of custom and morality. What struck Tocqueville was the link between democracy *(le sentiment égalitaire)* and political liberty, with religion operating as the intermediary. It was a strict, sometimes puritan, religion—at the opposite pole to the permissiveness of the present age.

If religion has lost its hold on a sizable fraction of the population of the United States without the society having been shaken, it is because since the early nineteenth century it has played a role that the French aristocrat could not have foreseen. The observer Tocqueville was studying the Anglo-Americans; since his time, however, peasants from Italy, from Poland, the Ukraine, Catholics, Jews, have emigrated to the promised land by the tens of millions. They were given citizenship and U.S. passports, and citizenship was inseparable from respect for the Constitution. A person is born German or French; one *becomes* American; and one ceases to be American by betraying the very essence of citizenship, which is respect for the Constitution.

None of the historical nations of Europe give the press as much freedom as does the United States, none of them put laws above men, judges above governments, human rights above actual laws; and none of them has a Supreme Court comparable to the American model. Nowhere else is the *legitimacy* of political and economic institutions so deeply rooted.

In France, nonpartisan political writers from Tocqueville to Renan have deplored the never-ending conflict as regards the country's form of government—does the state claim to be *monarchie* or *république*, is it legitimate monarchy *(monarchie légitime)*, or cadet-branch monarchy, or some other royal form of government between *république* and *empire?* The revolutions of the nineteenth century are explained by the divided passions of the privileged classes on this question. Only Napoleon III had the good sense to found his reign on universal suffrage. In the era when France was still a rural nation, it was enough to guarantee the advances made by the peasant class to be assured of an enormous majority. The descendants of forty kings were never willing to base their rule on a formula of legitimacy incompatible with their tradition.

Democratic, representative, electoral legitimacy now enjoys unanimous assent among the French. The last bid by counterrevolutionaries, the

Vichy régime of 1940, did not last even until the total occupation of France. The followers of Maurras and other counterrevolutionaries of a nineteenth-century cast had lost their influence before Pierre Laval's return to government in April 1942. A kind of monarchist or Maurrassian press has survived on the fringe of the political or intellectual class; but there has been nothing comparable to *l'Action française* as it was from the end of the nineteenth century until 1941.

It is a very different situation in the economic field. Neither private ownership of the means of production ("free enterprise," as the British and Americans call it), nor the market mechanisms, nor the present distribution of incomes enjoys the same degree of assent as that which supports representative democracy. Max Weber was one of many who have underlined the elective affinity, the stylistic connection, between the economic free market and electoral competition. Political observers readily use economic schemas to analyze political life, leaving it to the radical economists to make use of socio-political concepts in order to interpret phenomena such as exploitation. And, in fact, the more the progress of democracy and the claims of groups and individuals develop, the more shocking—or, at any rate, the less and less tolerable—seems the contrast between the *political* equality of citizens and the *economic* inequalities that are inseparable from the free market.

At the same time, the notion of private ownership—to which, when it comes to their inheritance, or their house or apartment, the vast majority of the French remain attached—becomes suspect in business, especially big business. The liquidation of a bankrupt firm occasionally turns into a national problem when a few hundred workers lose their jobs; the occupation and takeover of the Lip factory expressed and symbolized a widespread attitude. To put it briefly, although political power derived from elections is still legitimate in present-day France, the legitimacy of power in business, and consequently in the whole economy—is controversial and uncertain.

The employers plead for free enterprise, and make efforts to convince public opinion that this liberty is no different from any other. The fact that they only half-succeed may be explained by the circumstances, during recent years (but there are deeper reasons, if one takes a longer view).

France has one of the most state-controlled economies of any Western nation, in every sense of the term. A sizable fraction of the productive sector is in public ownership, and governments do not confine themselves to general measures (budgeting, credit control) intended to strike an overall balance, but take particular individual decisions—for instance, regarding the choice of a telephone exchange model, or the formation of a large-scale industrial group. Civil servants often move over to the private sector at a given point in their career. The administrative minority which runs French capitalism is recruited among the *polytechniciens* and *énar-*

ques, with no precise distinctions drawn between civil servants, the managers in the nationalized sector, and the so-called monopolists (the latter being the sole villains, according to Communist propaganda, which sees them as the embodiment of the principle of evil). The nationalization of any given group would not in itself disturb anyone, as long as the public thought in terms of one more Renault or another Electricité de France.

Aside from the specific features of the French economy, the "private" structure of large corporations is no longer justified by the "right of ownership" because, usually, the legal owners, that is, the shareholders, have hardly any influence on the management of the business, and only rarely on the choice of managers. Private ownership of giant corporations is justified on the grounds of efficiency, the advantage of separating political from economic power, and reluctance to give too great responsibility to government. But conditional utilitarian legitimacy is no firm foundation for the established order and does not inspire strong opposition to those who may, perhaps, wish to overthrow it.

The European societies are probably bound to evolve toward some sort of socialism in a broad indefinite sense. Reduced to the minimum imposed by political democracy, this entails: state intervention to keep a general balance and manage the overall economic situation, as well as to iron out the effects of localized or worldwide fluctuations on particular groups; the passing of legislation to guarantee the basic rights, especially in regard to health and education; a system of direct taxation based on the progressive, not the proportional principle. In addition, this list should probably include a more or less extensive public sector.

Minimal socialism does not interfere with the operations of an economy that is open to the outside world; the exceptional postwar phase made such socialism compatible with rapid growth. On the other hand, the events of recent years show the difficulties encountered by representative democracies in controlling the "class struggle" with respect to distribution of the nation's income in periods of crisis; they also reveal the danger that the inflationary process might become accelerated by the fact that anticipation of higher prices by some tends to precipitate the movement foreseen by all. Without pronouncing in favor of any particular theory of inflation, I see three major trends standing out in a country like France, all of which spell danger to the government.

In the first place, the more extensive the functions which the state attempts to assume, the weaker it becomes. In Britain the Labour government secured the cooperation of the unions only when a total currency collapse seemed imminent. In France, between 1974 and 1976, neither Valéry Giscard d'Estaing nor Jacques Chirac even tried to keep wage rises down to the level of price rises. In 1975, wages in the public and nationalized sector rose by about 16%, retail prices by about 10%.

Secondly, freedoms are no longer defined, as they were in the eighteenth century, as being *against* the state but as being at once against *and in favor* of it. The Communists themselves swear to high heaven that they will protect citizens *from* the police, *from* computers, *from* censorship, *from* arbitrary interference . . . in other words, that they will uphold the sphere of personal independence, safeguard the principle of participation in public life through elections and, at the same time, extend individual and collective freedoms. What constitutes these new freedoms, if not the extension of social rights (in the areas of health, education, promotion, etc.) and expansion of the powers given to organized interests, to working men's unions and works committees for use *against* managements, and to people's parties *against* t ose in authority?

The possible tension between egalitarian aspirations and libertarian imperatives belongs to the classical tradition of political philosophy. In one sense, experience does not confirm the thesis of a contradiction. Soviet-style socialism—even if, according to some people's reckoning, it reduces inequality in the matter of income distribution—digs a deeper trench between the party machine and the ordinary worker than the one that separates a French worker from his employer. On the other hand, it is arguable that the least inegalitarian Western societies—let us say the Scandinavian ones—are eluding the totalitarian menace, while France and Italy, where income distribution is regarded as deing *more* unequal, are both exposed to the threat of a Communist party coming into power.

I do not deny these facts, although the relationship between inequality and the strength of the Communist party in France does not seem to me to be either as direct or as necessary as social democrats suggest. Despite appearances, it seems to me that, in the long term, the verbal ideological obsession with equality is contrary to the survival of a liberal-spirited society.

We all construct our own hierarchies among people and their actions and merits. Nowhere does inequality of incomes reflect the hierarchy of values, whether as put forward by the dominant social or moral doctrine or by any particular group. Western societies are blamed, with a certain amount of exaggeration, for subordinating all hierarchies to the sole hierarchy of incomes. They could just as well be blamed for going over from a just idea of equality—the right of every human being to be treated as a human being—to a false and even absurd idea—the equal worth of the good and the vicious, creator and imitator, the few whose work or qualities raise them above the rest, and the countless herd of the mediocre.

It would be absurd to claim that the hierarchy of incomes in a liberal society reflects that of merit or values, and this is not in fact the liberals' argument. They assert that this inequality does exist, that it is not opposed to the element of justice contained in the idea of human equality, and that no society can ratify a single hierarchy consonant both with the differences in services rendered to the community and with the disparity of values. Within certain limits, the liberal accepts the verdict of the market, and does his utmost to preserve *plurality of hierarchies*. He is not outraged if the thriller-writer makes a fortune and the poet sells only a few hundred copies. His greatest fear is that a particular group might set itself up as the supreme arbiter both of income distribution and of literary and artistic quality. The liberal must have the courage to affirm that he does not reject inequality, or rather inequalities, but he does strive to eliminate abject poverty.

As for freedom or ability for group action, a more accurate term would be freedom *powers*. They can be asserted only at the expense of other powers. Within business organizations, workers' representatives serve on some committees which have more or less extensive functions, depending on the country. This freedom to "participate" at the place of work runs into two different obstacles, namely, the requirements of efficiency and the refusal, on the part of some unions, to play the game according to the rules within the framework of the existing system. Here again, the trend is against personal initiative which does not stem from authority.

The third trend—which, in my view, is observable in the universities and the church—seems to confirm an idea of Joseph Shumpeter. He predicted the decline of capitalism not because of its failures but because of its successes. He wrote that the social context in which liberal economies thrive is created by relics from the pre-industrial *ancien régime*, and from a social order based on attitudes and convictions radically different from those of tradespeople, entrepreneurs or economists. Neither the profit motive nor cost-benefit analysis, Shumpeter said, instills in civil servants and police and tax officials the *morality* required by their function. Disinterestedness, self-sacrifice, and public spiritedness relying on nothing but a good conscience are all virtues which belong to a world of tradition. They seem alien to the motives of the typical agents of modern civilization, whether one thinks of the consumer's pursuit of enjoyment or the producer's Promethean ambitions.

Must we conclude, with Edmund Burke, "The time of the sophists, economists and calculators has come and the glory of Europe is extinguished for ever"?

Crisis and creation

The Europe of the Six or the Nine does not constitute a political entity and, as far as the eye can see, it will not constitute one. Even supposing that a United States of Europe had been possible in the first decade after World War II, the opportunity disappeared with the European Defense Community. The loyal supporters of Jean Monnet accuse General de Gaulle of having given integration the *coup de grâce*. As I see it, it was already too late. The nation states had recovered and, in the final analysis, their collapse, in the bombed-out ruins of the towns, was only outward.

As a recent book* has forcibly demonstrated, the formation of a world market without a world empire is one of the most original aspects of modern civilization. France, Germany, Italy, and the Benelux countries belong to this market (whether or not they are unified in a Common Market or a European State). The least "Atlantic" of French presidents in the last thirty years, General de Gaulle, contributed more than any other to the integration of France into this international and transnational ensemble. Why? Because he saw, in open frontiers, the means of achieving more rapid growth and industrialization. The greater the role of exports in industrial output, the more France became both European and Atlantic.

General de Gaulle did fight at least a verbal battle, in his press conferences, against two aspects of Atlanticism,† namely the "privileges" of the dollar and direct American investment in France, particularly the taking over of bankrupt companies. Whether he was right or wrong, he fought in vain; the gold standard system of exchange, as the American authorities maintained it until August 1971, afforded commercial advantages to the Europeans which matched the financial advantages enjoyed by American conglomerates ambitious to expand abroad. Under the generalized floating system, the dollar still retains its "privileges"—in other words, the United States pays for its purchases abroad with its own currency and, if need be, it is able to give its exports the benefit of a lower exchange rate.

As for direct investment by foreign firms in France, all governments finally gave them a provisional welcome, though with some ups and downs of mood. Jacques Chaban-Delmas made much of laying the first stone of a Ford factory in the Bordeaux region, which was, besides, a logical policy, since investors usually bring capital, technical innovation, and a method of organization. The French economic revival is at once the effect and the cause of participation in the Atlantic world market whose center is the United States.

"An economic giant, but a political dwarf": that is how diplomats were describing West Germany fifteen years ago. Today, it is the whole of Western Europe which deserves that description. Not that it does not possess the men, the technology, and the financial means to balance the power of the Soviet Union. It has chosen to stay under the protection of the United States, a choice made by Gaullist France, too, even if dressed up in bold language. A European defense system—which Valéry Giscard

---

*Immanuel Wallerstein, *The Modern World System* (London: Academic Press, 1974).
†This is true only of economics; in politics, he had other aims in view.

d'Estaing does *not* regard as being "on the order of the day"—would require, at the very least, close cooperation between West Germany, the United Kingdom, and France. West Germany, admitted to NATO in 1955 but not permitted to possess nuclear weapons, feels, almost physically, that its security depends on the strength and resolution of its alliance with the United States. Good relations with France are welcome, of course, since France is a close neighbor and a part of the European area to which the Bonn republic, by geographical decree, belongs. But only the American republic can guarantee security, as long as the Soviet Imperium survives and its thirty armored divisions—in the center of Europe, East Germany, and the neighboring People's Democracies—reveal the capacity, if not the intention, for aggression.

Here again, General de Gaulle made a vain effort to swim against the tide. No West German government would have preferred common action with France to solidarity with the Americans. By withdrawing from the NATO military command, General de Gaulle hardly altered the basic situation at all. He drove his country's partners in the Community into the full-scale Atlanticism toward which they were naturally inclined. In return, France gained a certain amount of autonomy—possibly more theoretical than real—in the event of military operations in the center of Europe. A good deal of optimism is required for one to believe that, if war broke out on the central front between the armies of the Warsaw Pact and NATO, the Warsaw Pact troops would voluntarily halt at the French frontier.

The postwar economic "miracles" brought Western Europe out from under the ruins, enabling it to build up its moral (if not its political) unity, and causing it to challenge the Soviet Union to open its frontiers to the men and the ideas of the "decadent" nations and to rediscover a perspective on the future. For five years, this Europe—whose difficulties seemed minor compared with the living conditions provided, in the so-called socialist states, for the liberated "proletariat"—has been starting to doubt itself again. In the last analysis, that doubt will prove to be either creative or fatal.

The history of nations does not proceed in a straight line on a plane surface. A nation asserts itself by surmounting the ordeals imposed by its setbacks as well as by its successes; it progresses from crisis to crisis. The excesses of a vulgarized Keynesianism have resulted in endemic inflation whose rate differs from country to country, which threatens to break up the European Community and, possibly, even the Atlantic alliance. The "British disease"—not so much public expenditure as such, but insufficient productive investment and the protection of sectors in deficit—lies in store for all Mixed Economies which wind up sacrificing the production of wealth to its redistribution.

As for the self-criticism (which some see as a sign of crisis), there is nothing to prove that it does not testify to the *vitality*, rather than the decline, of the West. In its haste to rebuild, to be aligned with the United States, and to safeguard itself from the "totalitarian temptation," Europe in general and France in particular have more than once sacrificed quality to quantity. They have built a lot, done much building, but often badly; they have industrialized, but polluted as well. Concern for labor productivity has not always been balanced by equal solicitude for the worker. Westerners are questioning the achievement of the previous period. They want alternatives to New Towns and massive housing estates, they are seeking new forms of communication and participation. This *creative dissatisfaction* also reveals divergent, if not contradictory, aspirations; it shows Promethean pride, but also respect for the person.

By two roundabout routes, social criticism is threatening, however, to turn into a crisis of civilization. These routes are: rejection of inbuilt economic constraints and rejection of the imperatives of collective action. Recession, aggravated by the massive increase in price of oil, was a sudden reminder to the large numbers of people who had been forgetting that Latin motto, familiar to millions of French schoolchildren: *primum vivere,* "living comes first." Maintaining the standard of living and reducing unemployment to a minimum once again became priority objectives, reestablishing a hierarchy of urgency which a quarter century of continual expansion had made it possible to forget. Growth is neither a gift from heaven nor part of the inevitable nature of things.

The enthusiastic reception given to the first ridiculous report by the Club of Rome hinted at a strange taste for apocalyptic visions, a kind of fear of the future. When I incline toward a pessimistic diagnosis, I remind myself of what are, nowadays, the two most striking features of the attitude of individuals toward "society," namely, expecting everything from it and giving nothing to it—at any rate, nothing which might deprive them of any pleasure and cost them any sacrifice. For some years now, this contradiction has become symbolized by the falling birthrate in France, Western Europe, and the United States. Nobody—or hardly anybody—has worried about the possible, if not probable, consequences of two of the ideas so warmly advocated by President Giscard d'Estaing: legalization of abortion and the movement toward equal status and equal conditions for men and women. Both these notions correspond to the aspirations of the majority. It remains to be seen whether, when births have been reduced to the desired number, there will be enough of them to replace the previous generation. Biology does not forbid it, and justice demands that there be legal and professional equality between the sexes, but how is equality to be prevented from bringing with it a gradual identity of roles? For the career woman, children are becoming a nuisance and a contretemps.

The link between armed forces unions and a reproduction rate of 0.7

(appreciably less than 2 children per couple, when it would take 2.2 to keep the population level) may seem indirect and remote, but both phenomena may proceed from one and the same cause: the hypertrophy of individualism in its utilitarian, selfish form. In the Eastern bloc countries, despotism camouflages the trouble but does not cure it; the institutionalized Big Lie is undermining the secular faith and, here and there, it has produced and energized the revival of a transcendental faith, or deeply felt rebellion. In the West, the collective organizations, whose claims echo around the market place, neglect anything that lies outside the short-term interests of their memberships and constituencies. It is as if distribution of the national income among those entitled to it used up all the resources of politics, as if the state kept its eyes exclusively on the volume of the national product, and the individual on his or her due share—an obsession ultimately incompatible with the ends such a part is intended to serve. Humanity finds satisfaction only when, aiming beyond its own ephemeral existence, it surpasses itself and goes out toward others.

The civilization of self-centered enjoyment condemns itself to death when it loses interest in the future.

10
Two specters are haunting Europe: freedom and the Red Army

Ernest Gellner recently wrote an article, "From the Revolution to Liberalization,"* which contains a kind of historical diagnosis. It argues that the myth of The Revolution which grew out of the French Revolution has dominated the past two centuries, and that the myth of Liberalization is on the way to replacing it.

The claim which is being made is that *the* liberalization is now becoming a generic and indeed a crucial phenomenon as *the* revolution has been; that, for good and in the main obvious reasons, it is replacing the earlier myth as a central political preoccupation or category; and that its basic assumptions are not merely more pertinent to our time, but probably also rather sounder by any criterion and at all times.

According to Gellner, Liberalization applies just as much to Eastern as to Southern Europe, and calls for analyses which cannot at present be found in the literature of political science.

Government and Opposition 2, no. 3 (Summer 1976).

Gellner's thesis—which I would like to see come true—is based on an indisputable fact. In Greece, democracy was restored without its going through a period of revolutionary transition. Portugal spent two years living through a revolutionary celebration of the "lyrical illusion" only to end up—through disputed elections—with a parliamentary system, a general as President of the Republic, and a homogeneous minority socialist government. In Spain, the king himself took the initiative in instituting what was rightly christened "liberalization"—amnesty, *de facto* legalization of political parties, tolerance of public demonstrations, etc. In Eastern Europe, on the other hand, there are no clear grounds for assuming that liberalization has become the order of the day. It is a Western term. Juan Carlos has adopted it, but not Brezhnev. Less than a year after Franco's death, his die-hard followers were already edged out. Twenty years after Nikita Khrushchev's speech at the Twentieth Congress, *A Day in the Life of Ivan Denisovich* was still unobtainable in the USSR. In other words, if we accept that the category "liberalization" covers both the events in southern Europe and those in the East, then this category contains two subcategories which are, to say the least, remote from one another.

In Greece, the "dictatorship of the colonels," for which the monarchy was largely responsible,* claimed no ideological allegiance. The despotism of the Greek colonels succeeded the corruption of democracy, which had taken over from a played-out dictatorship paralyzed by its own mistakes. What rightly arouses admiration is the skill of the former prime minister, who, after his return from exile, succeeded in guiding the nation's transition from a despotism with no popular base to a representative democracy, in reintroducing all the freedoms with no costly interlude of anarchy and, lastly, in scaling down repression. The Greek experience, a masterpiece of the political art, characterizes not so much an era of world history—the exhaustion of the myth of revolution after two hundred years—as a cycle already described by ancient Greek philosophers. The tyranny of the colonels is distinguished only by the mediocrity of the tyrants and the poverty of the demagogic measures with which they hoped to consolidate their power.

The case of Portugal does not fit into the liberalization schema any better. It began with a military *coup d'état* against a régime which the army itself had installed in power, and which had been suffering the threefold attrition of time, modernist influences from outside, and colonial wars which, on the ground, could neither be won nor lost. The régime could not be called fascist without distorting the meaning of the word—at least, if fascism as a species is considered as containing Italian fascism, and German National Socialism as a subspecies. Salazarism was authoritarian, but not

*First the queen forced Constantine Karamanlis into resignation and exile, then the king rejected the leftist régime which had won the elections.

totalitarian. It was mainly defined by rejection of modern civilization, stubborn resistance to decolonization, loyalty to the "Lusitanian dream," prolonged indifference to economic development, and a Christian conception of austerity and poverty.

The Spanish experience is not yet out of its initial phase, and I shall refrain from making any prognosis on the further course of events. Yet, this first phase does offer a confirmation of Ernest Gellner's thesis: none of the opposition parties—with the sole possible exception of the far Left and the advocates of violence for its own sake—claim to be in favor of revolution, and all of them (including the Communist party, under the leadership of Santiago Carillo) see themselves as democratic and liberal. All of them, even those which are opposed to the monarchy on principle, place the restoration of freedoms ahead of the form of government. It is as if the extremism of the Portuguese Communist party and Alvaro Cunhal were an exception, or even an aberration, imputable to the personality of a secretary-general home from Eastern Europe after a long exile and, thus, a stranger to his own country.

It seems to me that there is no doubt about the strength of the longing for civil liberties in southern Europe, any more than there is any doubt about the rejection of a revolution which would signify or threaten to signify civil war. But, before substituting the category of "liberalization" for the myth of revolution, we should recall the characteristics of Salazarism and Francoism which set them apart from ideocracy. Students and intellectuals in Franco Spain did not pretend to be pro-Franco in the way that students and intellectuals in Eastern Europe have to make a show of allegiance to Marxism-Leninism. Students in Madrid made no attempt whatever to conceal their more or less Marxist views, and the works of Marx and his disciples were on sale in all the bookshops (it was different in Portugal).

Spaniards and Portuguese, workers as well as students, moved freely between their home countries and the countries of Western Europe. Quite a few of them adopted the more or less leftist opinions fashionable among the workers and intellectuals, but even the converts to Marxism nearly all interpreted this in the liberal sense, as professed by socialists in the West. Both workers and students regarded the absence of trade union freedom and intellectual freedom as a deprivation of a natural right, as a national humiliation. Certainly the two régimes of the Iberian peninsula based themselves on traditional values and were backed by privileged minorities, but economic progress in Spain, combined with the spread of ideas from modern Europe,* gradually undermined the historical foundations of Francoism. It was some former Francoists who took the initiative for

*In Part III, I examined whether certain liberal aspirations in Western Europe might not threaten the democratic societies. In the Appendix, Note H, I discuss a book in which some French Socialists outline a philosophy which they mistakenly believe to be liberal.

liberalization and who see no future for their country except in Western Europe and participation in the EEC, despite its present state of crisis.

An examination of Eastern Europe is now in order, to confirm or invalidate the Ernest Gellner thesis. In fact, none of the three régimes of Greece, Spain or Portugal deserved the adjective *ideocratic*. In none of these countries did the state tend to ingest civil society into itself; social and ideological pluralism was suppressed by the threat of sanctions or the police, but it did subsist, and was not denied by the national ideology. Even before the death of Franco, some of the Spanish universities were hotbeds of Marxism and leftist politics. The liberalization began, upon the termination of the Civil War, through a reintegration of the beaten militants of 1939 into the nation; then the frontiers were opened to exiles, permitting public expression of opinions already known and barely concealed, and giving official approval to trade unions and to parties which, previously, had led only a tolerated clandestine existence. None of these conditions of pluralism is to be found in the Soviet Union.

The humiliation felt by the Spanish or the Portuguese student, when comparing his or her country with France or West Germany, is not shared by the Soviet intellectual, who can take pride in belonging to one of the world's greatest powers. (There is no need to quote the Marquis de Custine's saying that "the slave on his knees dreams of ruling the world.") The evidence as to the Soviet citizen's way of looking at things is quite plentiful nowadays: it reveals a strong desire for freedom, security, higher living standards—but it offers nothing to compare with the expectant mood, the irresistible pull of liberalization which the people felt in Spain on the eve of Franco's death.

The dialogue between the two former labor camp occupants, Solzhenitsyn and Panin, illustrates Ernest Gellner's Revolution/Liberalization antithesis. Solzhenitsyn chooses the latter term, Panin the former.* Although Solzhenitsyn does not manage to give any articulate expression to his political conception, it seems to me that he is clearly heading toward a separation between liberalism and representative democracy. The *Letter to Soviet Leaders*, a letter-program addressed to the nation and the world—and which aroused Panin's indignation—explicitly restates an old thesis that has always been argued by liberals of the Hayek persuasion: that individual freedoms matter more than democracy as such, inasmuch as democracy is defined by the electoral origin of the rulers' mandate. Let us take a step further and say that a traditional monarchy occasionally offers a better guarantee of freedoms than the processes of mass democracy which typify our own era.

What does Western democracy mean, not in theory, but in practice? It

---

*Dmitri Panin, *Soljenitsyne et la réalité* (Paris, 1975).

means the emergence of the government from a fight between parties or between people closely linked to parties. The paradox or contradiction is that the man elected by half the French nation is also supposed to be president of the *whole* population. Or it means that the coalition which has collected the most votes in a propaganda battle, against one or several other parties, takes charge of the entire country and, in the name of the principle of majority rule, is obeyed by the very same citizens who voted for the out-of-power group.

Alexander Solzhenitsyn manifestly dislikes the lack of restraint, the exhibitionism, and the vulgarity of Western electoral warfare.* Simone Weil felt much the same way. The Russian writer states that he is hostile to revolution for two reasons: he fears that revolution would simply lead to another kind of despotism, not to the freedoms he longs for; and he could put up with an authoritarian régime, in other words, with the continued rule of the Communist party, if it would only renounce compulsory lying or, to use Western terminology, if it would get rid of ideocracy and would guarantee human rights. Panin, on the other hand, argues *for* revolution, either because he considers that liberalization is impossible without it, or because liberalization is not enough for him.

In the aftermath of Stalin's death, in the early 1960s, the thesis of a coming "liberalization" or "democratization" (the two notions were not clearly distinguished) enjoyed some favor. Setting out from the indisputable fact that there is a correlation between countries with high living standards and those with representative democracy, some commentators reached the conclusion that the effect of prosperity would be to make the USSR itself democratic. The prognosis was hedged with various reservations, and was usually delivered with no set time scale. Events have encouraged optimists to revise their forecast or to think in terms of an abbreviated time scale.

It may be that the tolerance enjoyed by writers and artists evolves in cycles of expansion and contraction and, in spite of everything, the overall drift of the Soviet Union is away from the Lysenko Affair and the Great Purge. All the same, I am far from affirming that nothing of the kind is possible anymore. As long as a small group of people are the sole arbiters of the fate of all, in the name of a party that holds a monopoly on political truth, the régime will bend according to the inclinations of the clique at the top. But the fact remains that this same clique *will* do its utmost to keep any one man from engrossing power in the Stalinist manner, and that it no longer will have to deal with such "Stalinist" tasks as agrarian collectivization. The Great Purge came after Collectivization, it is true, but whatever

---

*I shall not go into a discussion of Solzhenitsyn's critique of the whole body of modern civilization since the Renaissance, his adherence to the theses of the Club of Rome, his "Slavophilism."

its causes may have been (and the debate is still open), it presupposed a No. 1 like Stalin. A clique would not decimate the party the way the Father of the Peoples, in all conscience, had done.

Does it follow that the "hour of liberalization" has struck in the Soviet Union? Is it possible to imagine anything like the process which has started in Spain? The straight answer must be: *no*. Francoism set out to be a unifying principle and a mediator between classes, doctrines, and social and ideological conflicts; it made no claim to have created a New Man or a state of the whole people, identifiable with society. Sixty years after the seizure of power, the Communist party is continuing the revolution of which Marx was the prophet and Lenin the standard-bearer. It cannot, without endangering its own safety, tolerate any challenge to the ideology in whose name it has spilled so much blood, built so many factories, and liquidated so much of the past.

The Soviet ideocracy can certainly limit the domain of its application, and, compared with the lunatic policies of Stalinism, such restrictions have already taken place. There is no longer a Marxist-Leninist mathematics, physics or biology. On the other hand, there is still only *one* official truth in politics and history.

Here again, various limitations are conceivable. Atheism is an integral part of Marxism-Leninism; without officially dropping it, the Kremlin leaders could do what was done during the Great Patriotic War: tone down their antireligious propaganda and, in any case, their persecution of believers.

I do not deny the existence of a kind of liberalization, even in the Soviet Union, but I hesitate to use the same word to designate what the king of Spain and his advisers have done in a matter of months and what the successors of Stalin have allowed to go on for twenty years. In Spain, the leadership said what it wanted to do, and began to do it. In the East, the same old story continues: there is no question of accepting peaceful coexistence of ideologies, in other words, of removing the Marxist-Leninist ideology's claim to universality; no question of recognizing that the régime founded by Lenin is one among others and does not go beyond the dictatorship of the proletariat to represent the people as a whole; no question of officially tolerating another ideology or even the legitimacy of a transcendental faith by reducing Marxism-Leninism to the prosaic level of a mere opinion. Is this a difference of pace within a common process of liberalization? For the time being, the differences outweigh the similarities, both in the intentions and the actual reforms produced by the principal actors.

Reforms in the East tend to *eliminate* pathological growths from the system, rather than to liberalize it. Whether the concentration camps were meant to provide cheap labor or get rid of active or potential dissidents, neither of these purposes then required—in any case, neither of them any longer requires—a prison-camp population in the millions.

Similarly, the revival of genetics and the downfall of Lysenko denote a return to normality. An exhibition of abstract painting denotes a concession to a Western fashion, but also to practices which were commonplace in the early days of the revolution. The alliance between the artistic and the political *avant-garde* proved precarious and fragile; political intransigence entailed literary conformism, and this could not adopt a style which only book lovers could understand. As the novelist Jean-Richard Bloch once remarked, with all the enthusiasm of the neophyte, the return to the use of columns in architecture, an artistic retreat, nevertheless constituted a dialectical advance.

Without denying the ground covered since 1953, it seems to me that the main point (and characteristic of the régime) is that the men in the Kremlin have been trying hard to fend off the danger inherent in economic relations with the West by ordaining vigilance and ideological struggle. You buy computers from the corrupt West, and maybe you consider it *all the more corrupt* because it sells computers. You get rid of incorrigibles—Jews, intellectuals, particularly Jewish intellectuals—by banishing them to the West instead of sending them to Siberia. This is certainly progress *per se* (from the perspective of the dissidents), but it still expresses the same state of mind: there is no place in Soviet society for those who do not pay lip service, at least, to the Creed, and nowadays that only rarely inspires true faith.

At the same time, I discern the seeds of two kinds of pluralism, one of them rooted in both civil and official society, the other in the ideological world. One characteristic of the Stalinist and, possibly, the Soviet style of government is that minor problems go straight to the top. The Politburo had to make decisions which, in other societies, would have been handled lower down. Such concentration reinforced centralization. According to some Western observers, the Brezhnev team has been leaving a narrow but widening margin of autonomy to some subsystems, hence encouraging decisions which the experts consider to be rational.* Also, despite all ordinances and watchwords, the West—with its cars and Beatles, abstract painting and analytical philosophy, drugs and pornography, permanent unrest and abundant crises, sexual freedom and love of life—is penetrating the closed frontiers and gradually winning a place within the world which the men in the Kremlin wanted to keep free of "harmful effluvia" from the West.

Whatever scope is to be ascribed to these phenomena, all historians

---

*Jerry F. Hough, "The Brezhnev Era, the Man and the System," *Problems of Communism*, March–April 1976.

ought to accept one simple but, in my view, fundamental idea. *Political time does not elapse at the same speed on both sides of the demarcation line.* A régime in the line of descent from Asiatic despotism—or, if you prefer a less ideologically resonant expression, a military empire under a centralized bureaucracy—is one of the most durable and stable political forms known to history *as long as the ruling class sticks together and the masses are kept conscious of their helplessness.* The ruling class of the Soviet Union, unlike the pre-1917 one, does not vow allegiance to a No. 1 designated by birth; it has not produced, therefore, any institutional solution to the "succession" problem. Furthermore, it is threatened by the excesses of gerontocracy. All the same, it has managed to organize the transition from one team to another, from Nikita Khrushchev to Leonid Brezhnev, by a subtle combination of voting and conspiracy.

A century elapsed between the Decembrist Plot and the tsar's abdication, itself the direct consequence of a war too big and too long-lasting to be borne by an empire shaken by economic development, Western ideas, and the monarch's weakness. There is no reason why the Soviet ideocracy should turn out to be any less vulnerable to the spirit of the age or the erosion of time than the other régimes down through the centuries. Nor is there any reason why the Soviet ideocracy—the tsarist empire in new clothes—should come to rest in Western democracy as if that were its secret home. As long as Russia goes on ruling the various non-Russian ethnic groups which today make up more than 50% of the Soviet population, democracy will spell danger to the empire and threaten it with disintegration. Even liberalization will have to set limits on the expression of "bourgeois nationalisms." The exiled Soviet dissidents often clash on the subject of "national freedoms." Solzhenitsyn is a Russian, Plyushch a Ukrainian; the latter does not demand independence for the Ukraine—but give the citizens a voice in their own affairs and let national groups express their claims, and where will autonomy end? Except in the unlikely event of an accident—such as war with China or a war of succession—for the foreseeable future (as far as the end of the century), the European West will be faced with a Soviet Union that refuses ideological coexistence and keeps the corrupting influence of Western freedoms under close restraint.

There is a different situation in Eastern Europe, between the Soviet frontier and the demarcation line. Three countries—East Germany, Bulgaria, and Romania— seem to be neck and neck with the Soviet Union in ideologico-political rigor. The first has made planned economic management work more efficiently than anywhere else, and enjoys the highest standard of living in the whole of the Eastern sphere. A fragment of Germany, doomed to eternal friendship with its conqueror of yesterday, the GDR exists as a state or political entity only because of its régime. Like it or not, it has to condemn itself to ideocracy in order to exist as something other than an occupation zone. Romania's ideological rigor is Ceausescu's insurance for a foreign policy which demonstrates its independence with an occasional spectacular decision; Romania has not broken off relations with Israel and has not bowed to the decisions of COMECON and the division of labor within the Soviet bloc, as advocated by the Kremlin and Pankow. In return, the party is particularly ruthless in its hold on power and truth. Of all the Eastern European countries, Bulgaria has been rightly considered to be the most favorably disposed to the old Russia *and* to the new USSR. It imitates Big Brother.

In Poland, Hungary, and Czechoslovakia, the liberalization question is definitely a live issue. The working masses put an end to the Gomulka team by rioting, and went on to exercise a kind of veto right over the Gierek team when it decided to raise the price of staple foodstuffs—an economically justified decision, but involving a sharp drop in the standard of living. On top of the intermittent resistance of the working masses, but not in step with them, comes the mutinous attitude of the intellectuals—which also turns into outright rebellion, from time to time. When the party wanted to write eternal alliance with the USSR into the constitution, the intellectual class made a public protest, which had an effect upon the party. Both workers and intellectuals are well aware that geography does not allow their country a choice of sides. All the same, at heart they are still Poles, Catholics, and rebels against ideological discipline, especially when it comes from Communist Holy Russia, and in 1976 they united, for the first time, against authority.

The uprising of 1956 taught Hungarians the permissible limits of liberalization as decreed by the Kremlin. And yet, the Hungary of 1976 remains the most liberal of the socialist countries: more people are allowed to travel abroad, and discussion of Western theories is more openly conducted at the universities. The Kádár government protects the Hungarians from Soviet domination while guaranteeing loyalty to the Muscovite Imperium. The men in the Kremlin lay down the frontiers of the liberalization they can accept.

After Hungary, it was Czechoslovakia which suffered a temporary lapse of judgment. The Dubcek team made the same mistakes—in word, if not in deed—and these were equally fatal. Leonid Brezhnev did not accept the "Prague spring" any more than Nikita Khrushchev had accepted the "Hungarian autumn": without a shot being fired in Prague, a change of majority in the party's central committee took place, in accordance with "socialist legality." The revisionists considered themselves to be Marxists, nay, Marxist-Leninists; they had wanted to change the way the economy was run, and had proclaimed and practiced freedom of speech and freedom of the press. That was probably the unforgivable crime, which provoked intervention by the armies of the Warsaw pact because, in fact, they were eliminating the guiding role of the party when they defined press freedom in terms of the right of all citizens to say what they believed to be true. The famous 2000-word statement and the phrase about "twenty years of lies" probably did more than any planning reforms to bring on Brezhnev's and the other top people's decision.

One could thus paraphrase Marx, in a way, and write that a specter is haunting Europe today: it is the *specter of freedom*. But one must add that there is another specter, which haunts Europe still, and that is *communism*—better known, today, as the *Red Army*.

As I have kept reiterating in this book, even more than Marxism or *sinistrisme*, it is military might that gives the Soviet Union its present-day stature. Whether we like it or not, it has the largest army and the most modern navy, if not the most sophisticated weapons. Two years of military service are obligatory in the army, two to three years in the navy and the frontier guard corps. And there are 845 ballistic missiles in 78 submarines, 1527 ICBMs, 600 medium-range missiles (mostly on the country's western borders); 50 armored divisions, 111 infantry divisions, 7 airborne divisions, 41,000 tanks; in Eastern Europe, 31 category I divisions (of which at least three quarters of the personnel and equipment are on a war footing).* The United States still leads in terms of nuclear weapons, and—having introduced the MIRV technique—it also has more nuclear warheads. The Soviet Union, with a national product amounting to some 60% of that of the United States, has a military machine on a par with that of its rival.

I do not subscribe to extreme hypotheses such as the one which argues that the Soviet régime, unable to raise the level of popular consumption, is making a kind of "forward retreat" into the only sector where it excels, at least relatively, and where it concentrates its best brains and a considerable share of its resources. I confine myself to the interpretations most favorable to the Kremlin leadership which report that the Soviets maintain an army of more than two million men, as a matter of standard practice, in order to keep a numerical superiority on the central front (facing Western Europe) and technical superiority on the eastern front (facing the People's Republic of China). Their nuclear and naval efforts are a reflection of the Russians' awareness of American superiority which became apparent at the time of the Cuban missile crisis; a "structural" explanation is the Soviet ambition to catch up with and overtake the United States. This ambition—which dates back to Stalin and which was frequently expressed by Khrushchev—was directed toward economic equality, that is, equality of overall production or production per capita. That aim turned to superiority in military might

*Figures quoted from the pamphlet *The Military Balance 1976–77*, published yearly by the International Institute for Strategic Studies.

and armaments, the more the Soviet economy's intrinsic weaknesses became exposed.

There is a growing contrast between ballistic missiles, armored divisions, and that brand-new fleet, and the living conditions of citizens for whom the daily shopping expedition is still an ordeal or an adventure; there is a worsening contradiction between the evident wealth of the state and the relative poverty of the masses. After being deaf and dumb for decades, the West's left-wing intellectuals have finally accepted what had been staring them in the face. If they remain prisoners of *sinistrisme*, it is despite—and not because of—the Soviet experience.

Why do the Kremlin leaders reject reforms which have bettered living conditions in Eastern Europe?

All the evidence proves that men like Stalin and Beria, who had the power and knew how to operate the party machine, were revealing their innermost thoughts when they made remarks such as "How many divisions has the pope?" The only relations they could see between classes and states were relations of force—and, in this, they were not betraying one of Marx's basic ideas.

Pride of Empire probably counts for more, in the thinking of the Politburo, than the millenarianism of Karl Marx. Even in Lenin's time, the Bolsheviks took charge of the tsarist empire's heritage to the point of using armed force to conquer a republic (Georgia) which had appointed a Menshevik government. Quite possibly, Brezhnev and his colleagues tend to despise the "decadent Europe," in which armies tolerate the bohemian attitude typical of the younger generation. Why do they not broaden their diagnosis, as we do: if it is in the West that the discipline of collective civic action seems most shaken, it is also in the West that workers' productivity is the highest.

And should the Soviets not entertain doubts regarding their own success, along with their doubts about the West? Sixty years after the seizure of the Winter Palace, the Bolshevik party presides over the destinies of an immense empire reaching from Vladivostok to Weimar, and its ideology has spread across five continents. Which of Lenin's circle, in 1917, could have foreseen such a triumph? Yet, sixty years after a proletarian or socialist revolution, that same party keeps the population shut up inside its frontiers and, in spite of proletarian internationalism, forbids it to go outside to look and compare. How humiliating! "Soviets and electrification," Lenin used to say; not one trace remains of the soviets, and though there is no shortage of electricity, wheat does have to be imported from the Midwest. Where does the "obvious superiority" of socialism manifest itself?

Why is the Kremlin so very afraid of economic reform and intellectual liberalization? No question is harder to answer. In the area of agriculture, I am tempted to point to the power and the dogmatism of the bureaucracy. In the sphere of the mind, I believe that the main cause is the difficulty in marking the limits. The repercussions of Khrushchev's speech on Eastern Europe revealed, to the men in the Kremlin, the danger of saying aloud what used to be said in a whisper: of admitting what they know. An ideology cannot easily dispense with the institutionalized lie, even if most people recognize it as such. Lastly, the Soviet leaders—unlike those of the People's Democracies—have to ponder the impact of *any* kind of liberalization, economic, political or intellectual, on the unity of the empire.

Both now and in the foreseeable future, the USSR's leaders will remain fiercely hostile to the West because they envy and, simultaneously, despise it. As ideologues, they envy its productivity and standard of living; as men in power, they despise its permanent unrest and its rulers condemned to paying court to the masses and, at the same time, they continue to suspect the rule of a minority of "monopolists" under the democratic surface. They have trouble believing that Richard Nixon was ultimately overthrown by the press, itself alerted by the curiosity of two unknown journalists. Such an episode does not fit in with their vision of society.

Détente or Cold War, it hardly matters. Failing a favorable opportunity, such as the resignation of the United States, the men in the Kremlin will not rush into any open military aggression* against decadent, fascinating Western Europe, which disappoints the dissidents by its frivolity but, nevertheless, constitutes a standing accusation of a régime which is so unsure of itself that it is afraid of its own citizens.

More than the hundreds of thousands of Russian soldiers in Eastern Europe or the thousands of nuclear warheads (why destroy nations that you want to enslave?), in the short term it is the Europeans themselves who are their own worst enemies. Not that they are deeply affected by *la tentation totalitaire,* and in fact they are making a slow recovery from *sinistrisme,* although numerous intellectuals, great and small, have not renounced their prejudices or their ideological "drug addiction." But rejecting servitude is not enough: one must also recognize the dangers, and face up to them.

---

*It goes without saying that Soviet armaments still influence the course of diplomacy and that Western Europe could be threatened by events in Africa and the Middle East (a fact which its governments appear to overlook).

Notes

Note A

There are various well-known difficulties about evaluating the USSR's national product and defense budget, and I cannot go into detail about them here. Instead, I shall confine myself to the following deliberately simple observations. To the extent that the Soviet Union, with a national product of about 60% that of the United States, maintains a military machine of the same magnitude, clearly the defense budget—all paradoxes aside—must represent a greater drain on the national resources.

The following rough but fairly reliable estimates are taken from *Soviet Economic Prospects for the Seventies. A Compendium of Papers Submitted to the Joint Economic Committee*, Congress of the United States, June 1973. The Soviet Union, with a population 18% greater than that of the United States, provides less than half the number of goods and services consumed or utilized by the American population, although it uses 45% more labor and invests just as much. With such a massive input, the Soviet economy's growth rate should be almost as rapid as that of the Japanese. In reality, it has been at around the American level (p. 106).

Soviet defense spending is particularly hard to estimate. Reliance on the official figures means leaving out what may be a sizeable amount, because arms production can be hidden in the budgets of the metallurgical and manufacturing industries, and in the research and development budgets for space and nuclear physics. In the absence of a key to this riddle, the American experts use a different procedure and calculate the cost, in dollars, of the Soviet military machine. This is a rough and only minimally significant calculation, because the Americans do not produce the same weapons as do the Russians, and the same weapons do not cost the same amount in both countries. Obviously, the ratio of the Soviet defense budget to the American one will be greater if American prices are used to calculate the dollar equivalent of Soviet defense expenditure than if Soviet prices are chosen to fix the ruble equivalent of American defense expenditures.

The difficulties and uncertainties do not diminish if the cost in rubles of the Soviet defense budget is used to calculate the percentage of the Soviet national product (or *net material product*, a Soviet concept which eliminates most services). What value should be used for the NMP, and what value in rubles for the defense budget, when a fraction of it appears under different headings from the official defense heading?

Thus, estimates depend partly on assumptions of the amount concealed and partly on the cost, in rubles, of military spending. According to the military system's efficiency in producing and maintaining weapons, the percentage of military spending in the NMP or GNP will be higher or lower. Greater efficiency means a lower percentage of the national product. Some American experts have arrived at accepting an equivalent percentage of the national product devoted to defense on either side, owing to:

a) the extreme inefficiency of all the civil sectors, and

b) the relative efficiency of the military sector in the USSR.

Recent information about the volume of the military machine, the amount of concealed spending, and the cost of weapons in rubles (in other words, on the lesser efficiency of the military sector) have involved an upward revision of previous estimates. The pamphlet published by the London International Institute for Strategic Studies, *The Military Balance 1976-1977*, concludes that Soviet spending has definitely been underestimated, and that it comes to 10-14% of the GNP.

Stanley H. Cohn's study in *Soviet Economic Prospects for the Seventies*, pp. 147-204, analyzes the ambiguities in these comparisons and explains the various estimates, which range from 10 to 15% of the national product. The American defense budget and its percentage of the national product have diminished in recent years ($120 billion, out of a GNP of about $1500 billion).

There are other arguments about the effective burden on the Soviet economy— for instance, how would the Russians employ the engineers, scientists, men, and machines which they now use in the military sector? All subtleties apart, the fact is that the application of the USSR's best human and material resources in arms production cannot fail to work against the country's other sectors.

The CIA estimates that the USSR spends 150% more than the United States on defense (in dollars), about 200% more on ballistic missiles (or intercontinental attack missiles), about 175% on conventional forces, 175% on investment, and 125% in upkeep costs. The CIA adds the cost of "strategic defense" (probably civil defense): Soviet spending, under this heading, is thought to be 900 times as great as American spending (but this is insignificant).

Note B

Table 1/ Changes in average wages and pensions in the USSR, 1965-1973

Professional Groups	1965	1973	Increase (%)
	In rubles		
Administration, civil service	106	126	19
Industrial personnel, engineers, technicians	148	185	25
Education and culture	94	121	29
Trade and services	75	102	36
Industrial white-collar workers	86	119	38
Industrial blue-collar workers	102	146	43
State farm workers	72	116	61
Collective farm workers	49	87	78
Workers and employees (excluding collective farms)	97	135	39
	Billions of rubles		
Total budgetary expenditure for pensions	101	184	82

Note C

Comparisons of GNP growth rates are both not very meaningful and technically difficult. The Russians use a different aggregate from the one used in the West, and do not include most services. Also, results vary widely according to the price index chosen. Table 2 reproduces the best Western estimates alongside the official Soviet estimates. Soviet growth rates have in fact gone up, although they are not exceptional. They are higher than the American rates, and this is perfectly normal, for two reasons. First, like periods of development should be compared with like; from 1834 to 1868 the American economy progressed faster than 4% per annum; West Germany and Japan had growth rates of 7% or more during the 1950s. Second, growth rate is largely dependent on the volume of investment and manpower. The growth rate of inputs (capital and labor) and outputs (production per capita) is a measure of economic efficiency.

Table 3 points out the contrast between the Soviet and Western modes of growth—on the one hand, a massive increase of capital and labor with diminished capital productivity; on the other, increased capital productivity with a limited increase in inputs. These tables make it impossible to compare the contribution of the different factors to overall growth.

Table 4 deals with the growth rate per person employed. This eliminates the effect of increasing the number of workers on the overall growth rate.

Tables 5 and 6 take into consideration the share of the increased overall production which comes back to the consumer. They clearly show the two periods 1950-55 and 1965-69, during which the Soviet authorities were trying hard to partially satisfy the demands of Soviet consumers.

Table 2/ Long-term growth of the GNP in the USSR and USA
(*Annual percentage growth rate*)

USSR	Bergson-Cohn Estimates of GNP	Official USSR Estimates *Net material product*	USA	GNP 1958 Prices
1928-40	5.4[1]	15.0[4]	1929-50	2.8
1950-60	7.0[2]	10.0[5]	1950-60	3.2
1960-72	4.7[3]	6.7[5]	1960-72	4.1
1928-72	5.1[2]	9.3[6]	1929-72	3.2
1928-72 (war period excluded)	5.5[2]			
1950-72	5.8[2]	8.3[6]	1950-72	3.7

1. At 1950 prices.
2. Combined index: at 1950 prices for 1928-55, at 1959 prices for 1955-69, at 1968 volumes for 1970-72.
3. In 1959 and 1968 volumes.
4. At 1926-27 prices.
5. At 1955 prices.
6. Combined index: at 1926-27 prices for the period 1928-40 and 1955 prices for the period 1950-70.

Sources: Abram Bergson, *The Real National Income of Soviet Russia since 1928* (Cambridge, Mass.: Harvard University Press, 1961), pp. 180, 210, 261; Stanley Cohn, "General Growth Performance of the Soviet Economy," in *United States Congress, Joint Economic Committee, Economic Performance and the Military Burden in the Soviet Union* (Washington, D.C.: US Government Printing Office, 1970), p. 17; P. R. Gregory and R. C. Stuart, *Soviet Economic Structure and Performance* (Harper and Row: New York, 1974).

Table 3/ Annual growth rate of the factors of production and productivity in the USSR and USA

(a) Long-term trends

	Factors				Productivity		
	Output	Labor (*man-hours*)	Capital	Combined Factors	Output per Combined Factor Unit	Apparent Labor Productivity	Apparent Capital Productivity
USSR (GNP) 1928-66	5.5[1]	2.2	7.4[2]	3.5[1]	2.0	3.3	−1.9
USA (GNP) 1929-57	3.0	0.5	1.0[2]	0.6	2.3	2.5	2.0

(b) Post-war period, 1950-62

	Factors				Productivity		
	National Revenue	Labor	Reproducible Capital	Combined Factors	Output per Combined Factor Unit	Apparent Labor Productivity	Apparent Capital Productivity
USSR	6.2	1.4	10.1[2]	3.6[4]	2.6	4.7	−3.9
USA	3.4	0.8	3.9[3]	1.5	1.9	2.6	−0.5
Denmark	3.4	0.6	3.9[3]	1.4	1.9	2.8	−0.5
France	4.7	0.2	3.4[3]	1.0	3.7	4.5	1.3
West Germany	7.3	1.7	5.4[3]	2.7	4.5	5.6	1.9
UK	2.4	0.4	2.3[3]	0.8	1.6	2.0	0.1
Italy	6.0	0.8	2.5[3]	1.3	4.7	5.2	3.5
Norway	3.5	−0.1	3.4[3]	0.8	2.7	3.6	0.1
Netherlands	4.6	0.9	4.0[3]	1.7	2.8	3.7	0.6

1. At 1937 prices.
2. Total fixed capital (average between net and gross stock for the USSR).
3. Reproducible capital (average between gross and net stock).
4. Combination of labor and capital in the proportions of 0.75 and 0.25, respectively.

Sources: (a) Moorsteen and Powell and A. Becker, *Soviet Capital Stock: Revisions and Extension, 1961-1967* (Newhaven, Conn.: The Economic Growth Center, 1968), pp. 11, 25, 26; (b) Abram Bergson, *Planning and Productivity Under Soviet Socialism* (New York: Columbia University Press, 1968), pp. 53, 94.

Table 4/ Annual mean growth rate of real national income and real production in selected countries, 1955-70[1]

	Real National Income per person employed (%)	Real Material Product per person employed (%)
USA	2.1	2.5
France	5.0	5.4
West Germany	4.8	5.2
UK	2.6	3.0
Italy	5.9	6.8
Japan	8.8	—
USSR	4.2	4.9

1. The *real national income* calculated by A. Bergson corresponds with the *real gross domestic product*. The *material product* corresponds with the *gross domestic product excluding the product of certain services,* principally defense, public services, education, health, and accommodation; the product from cultural and leisure activities and from various other sources is also omitted.

In calculating the gross domestic product per person employed, the volume of employment corresponds, essentially, with the production sectors examined. But in the case of the real material product per person employed, workers engaged on the production of accommodation services are included.

For Western countries, the product is evaluated at "constant" market prices or at "constant" factor costs. For the USSR, the evaluation is made at "constant" factor costs. Employment is adjusted to the variations in the hours worked in the industry, although not proportionally.

Source: A. Bergson, *Soviet Postwar Economic Development* (Stockholm, 1974), p. 69.

Table 5/ Annual mean growth rate of real national income and
consumption in selected countries, 1955-70 and
1960-70

	Real national income[1] (%)		Consumption[2] (%)	
	Per capita	Per person employed	Per capita	Per person employed
1955-70				
USA	2.0	1.9	2.3 (2.5)	2.2 (2.4)
France	4.3	4.9	4.0	4.6
West Germany	4.2	4.5	4.5	4.8
UK	2.0	2.3	1.9 (2.0)	2.2 (2.3)
Italy	4.8	5.7	4.7	5.6
Japan	9.3	8.8	7.6	7.1
USSR	4.3	3.9	3.8 (3.9)	3.4 (3.5)
1960-70				
USA	2.8	2.2	2.9 (3.1)	2.3 (2.5)
France	4.7	5.0	4.6	5.0
West Germany	3.9	4.4	4.1	4.6
UK	2.0	2.5	1.7 (1.8)	2.2 (2.3)
Italy	4.6	6.2	5.2	6.7
Japan	9.9	9.6	7.9	7.6
USSR	4.2	3.3	3.8 (3.9)	2.9 (3.0)

1. Real national income and employment correspond to the concepts used in the preceding table, but employment has not been corrected to take account of variations in weekly hours worked, and this explains the minor differences between the two tables.
2. Consumption is expressed in "constant" prices. The figures without parentheses apply to private consumption only. Those between parentheses include public education and health.

Source: A. Bergson, *Soviet Postwar Economic Development*, p. 72.

Table 6/ Changing uses of the gross national product in the USSR and USA
(*Annual growth rates*)

	Home Consumption	Gross Investment	GNP	Consumption/ Investment Ratio
USSR				
1928-37[1]	0.7	14.5	5.5	0.05
1950-55[1]	8.7	8.7	7.6	1.00
1958-64[2]	4.8	7.4	5.9	0.65
1965-69[6]	6.2	6.8	4.9	0.91
1928-55[1]	2.8	7.9	4.8	0.35
USA				
1834-43 to 1879-88[3]	4.0	6.5	4.4	0.62
1879-88 to 1899-1908[4]	3.8	3.8	3.8	1.00
1899-1908 to 1914-23[4]	3.1	3.0	3.1	1.03
1929-50[5]	2.7	2.6	2.6	1.04
1950-70[5]	3.6	2.0	3.6	1.80
1929-70[5]	3.2	2.3	3.1	1.39

1. At factor costs in rubles 1937.
2. At factor costs in rubles adjusted 1958.
3. At 1860 prices.
4. At 1929 prices.
5. At 1958 prices.
6. At 1955 prices.

Sources: Bergson, *The Real National Income of Soviet Russia Since 1928*; Abraham Becker, *Soviet National Income 1958-1964* (Berkeley: University of California Press, 1969), p. 256; Simon Kuznets, *National Product Since 1869* (New York: National Bureau of Economic Research, 1946), Table II-16; Gallman, *Output, Employment and Production in the United States After 1800*, pp. 26-34; *The Economic Report of the President*, 1971, p. 198; Stanley Cohn, "The Economic Burden of Defense Expenditures," in *Soviet Economic Prospects for the Seventies*, p. 151; P. R. Gregory and R. C. Stuart, *Soviet Economic Structure and Performance* (New York: Harper and Row, 1974).

Note D

The statistics below are taken from a study carried out by the *Deutsches Institut für Wirtschaftsforschung* (case study 108, 1975). *Die Entwicklung in den osteuropäischen Ländern*. The study confirms that the USSR is lagging some way behind the East European countries, at least in terms of living standards.

Table 7/ Rankings of the East European countries 1972-73 (GDR = 100)

	Personal consumption 1975	Mean monthly wage 1975	Per capita savings 1975	Per capita consumption			
				Meat	Eggs	TV	Cars
GDR	100	100	100	100	100	100	100
Czechoslovakia	81	83	56	104	117	108	98
Hungary	89	65	34	85	108	83	56
Poland	65	62	30	96	81	74	37
Bulgaria	56	61	54	70	54	74	56
USSR	50	51	23	70	78	73	20
Romania	44	64	—	70	—	38	18

Table 8/ Development of the consumer goods industry 1960-75
(*Gross production, comparable prices*)

	Percentage annual increase			
	1956-60	1961-65	1966-70	1971-75
Bulgaria	14.0	9.4	9.8	8.4
Czechoslovakia	8.6	4.6	6.4	—
GDR	9.0	4.9	5.0	—
Poland	8.7	6.5	6.3	8.2
Romania	8.4	10.4	9.9	10.3
USSR	8.5	6.3	8.3	8.3
Hungary	—	8.5	7.2	6.8

	Percentage share[1]			
	1956-60	1961-65	1966-70	1971-75
Bulgaria	52.8	47.7	45.3	43.6
Czechoslovakia	40.8	39.4	38.4	—
GDR	33.5	31.9	29.8	—
Poland	43.0	39.4	36.4	35.8
Romania	37.2	30.1	29.6	29.0
USSR	27.5	25.9	26.6	26.7
Hungary	34.0	34.6	36.1	36.7

1. Total industrial production = 100 (average of the five years of each plan).

Table 9/ Mean average growth rate of personal consumption (%)

	Nominal value		Real value	
	1961-70	1971-73	1961-70	1971-73
Bulgaria	8.7	7.4	7.0	6.9
Czechoslovakia	5.0	4.9	4.2	5.0
GDR	3.6	5.2	3.3	5.5
Poland	6.1	9.7	4.8	9.0
USSR	6.6	5.3	—	—
Hungary	5.8	7.1	5.2	4.6

Table 10/ Structure of private domestic spending (%)
(*Aggregate expenditure = 100*)

		Goods	Services	Savings	Other
Bulgaria	1960	75.6	10.6	6.8	7.0
	1968	74.2	12.3	6.4	7.1
Czechoslovakia	1960	80.9	13.7	1.4	4.0
	1970	75.1	14.3	5.1	5.5
GDR	1960	78.7	11.6	7.1	2.6
	1970	80.8	11.1	5.9	2.3
Poland	1961	88.8	3.4	2.7	5.1
	1970	87.6	4.6	2.6	5.2
USSR	1960	83.0	10.3	0.8	5.9
	1970	80.7	12.0	4.0	3.3
Hungary	1960	85.2	10.2	1.9	2.7
	1970	78.6	15.5	3.9	2.0

Table 11/Rankings of East European countries in terms of living standards: comparison with West Germany 1972-73

Textile fibers (lbs.)		Synthetic fibers (lbs.)	
GDR	40.3	Bulgaria	7.2
Bulgaria	37.5	GDR	6.6
Czechoslovakia	35.9	Czechoslovakia	6.2
USSR	31.7	Poland	5.5
Poland	27.6	Yugoslavia	4.9
Romania	22.3	Romania	3.5
Hungary	21.6	USSR	2.6
Yugoslavia	17.4	Hungary	2.2
West Germany	43.4	West Germany	16.8

Refrigerators per 100 households (%)		Washing machines (%)	
GDR	75	Czechoslovakia	94
Czechoslovakia	66	Poland	82
Hungary	53	GDR	67
Poland	42	Hungary	59
USSR	41	Bulgaria	59
Bulgaria	36	USSR	50
West Germany	98	West Germany	76

TV Sets (%)		Automobiles (%)	
Czechoslovakia	84	GDR	21.4
GDR	78	Czechoslovakia	20.9
Hungary	65	Yugoslavia	14.3
Poland	58	Hungary	11.9
Bulgaria	58	Bulgaria	11.8
USSR	57	Poland	8.0
Romania	30	USSR	4.2
Yugoslavia	28	Romania	3.8
West Germany	93	West Germany	80.0

The next table is taken from Keith Bush's study, *Retail Prices in Moscow and Four Western Cities in May 1976*, Radio Liberty research supplement, June 1976, p. 32. It shows the time required in Moscow, Paris, Munich, London, and Washington—taking incomes and prices into account—to buy the various goods which go into the household shopping basket. The incomes considered are the average wages of industrial workers, after deduction of direct tax and compulsory social contributions and addition of family allowances.

Table 12/ Retail prices of goods and services expressed in units
of working time (May 1976)

Items	lbs.	Moscow	Paris	Munich	London	Washington
				Minutes of work		
Wheat flour	4.4	60	18	17	17	12
White bread	6.6	61	54	67	29	64
Pasta	2.2	42	14	29	28	23
Beef	2.2	144	166	115	147	66
Pork	2.2	137	120	91	107	50
Chicken	2.2	216	48	37	56	26
Ham	1.1	133	72	70	77	64
Minced beef	1.1	104	50	29	38	17
Sausage	2.2	158	84	67	60	71
Cod	2.2	56	113	52	98	49
Fishcake	1.1	44	50	20	39	22
Sugar	5.5	163	34	30	38	22
Butter	1.1	71	39	31	29	23
Margarine	2.2	130	35	27	37	29
Milk (quarts)	10.6	213	81	92	108	66
Cheese	2.2	216	84	71	72	89
Eggs (units)	24	156	56	39	28	21
Potatoes	15.4	49	94	53	160	58
Carrots	2.2	72	6	12	10	10
Tomatoes	2.2	216	27	23	48	17
Apples	2.2	325	19	13	24	16
Oranges	2.2	101	13	13	19	7
Tea	0.4	150	36	58	12	18
Coffee beans	1.1	163	43	75	69	32
Instant coffee	0.4	288	72	74	50	42
Beer (liters)	3.0	96	21	12	69	39
Gin/Vodka (liters)	0.2	168	42	18	59	19
Cigarettes (units)	120	996	48	108	162	60
				Hours of Work		
Weekly shopping basket (composed as above)		78.8	25.7	22.4	28.2	17.2
Monthly rent		9.9	35.6	32.0	48.5	46.5
Color TV		780.0	327.3	191.5	221.6	85.6
				Months of work		
Car: Fiat 131/ Zhiguli VAZ-2101		37.5	10.6	7.7	11.1	6.9

Note E

I have already referred, while dealing with the Soviet economy, to scientific studies which aim to clarify the particular share of each factor in the growth of the national product, hence in the growth of production per worker. On France, the standard work is J.-J. Carré, P. Dubois, and E. Malinvaud, *La croissance économique française, Un essai d'analyse économique causale de l'après-guerre* (Paris, 1972).

The most striking findings are on p. 275. For the period 1951-69, the annual growth rate of gross domestic production rose to 5.0%. Of this total figure, the authors attribute 0.4% to the quality of labor (age, education, intensity), 0.6% to professional migration, 1.1% to the volume of net capital, 0.4% to capital rejuvenation, 0.1% to capital intensity. The residual factor therefore amounted to 2.5% per annum, although, in the long term, it comes to only 1.1%. This residual factor reflects the aggregate of what may be called technical or organizational progress and the more favorable combination of the means of production (2.2 for West Germany, 1.3 for the UK, 1.0 for the United States, and 2.9 for Italy).

For the past, the authors shed light on a fact which is often unacknowledged even today, namely, that it is the period 1930-45 which is exceptional and which slowed down the progress of production and productivity which had been developing in France since the beginning of the century at a rate comparable with the postwar rate.

However, that which characterizes and distinguishes French postwar growth is both its continuity and its generality. It affects all sectors, including trade and agriculture. "The speed of the transformations of which agriculture and trade were the subject greatly amplified a movement whose preliminary steps had been fairly timid between the wars." On the other hand, "if only the lag caused by the Depression and World War II had brought about the recovery in the 1950s, then we should have witnessed a certain declaration of growth once the levels corresponding to very long-term trends had been regained. . . . All in all, the rapid growth of the last twenty years has been prolonged well past the point of being a simple return to a normal situation" (pp. 287-88).

The following important remark is also worth adding: "Detailed examination of the trends of productivity by industrial branch, and of the structural transformations of our productive apparatus, suggest that the most pronounced accelerations have occurred in small and medium units of production more often than in the very large ones" (p. 289).

Note F

The OECD has published a study by Professor Malcolm Sawyer which caused a public stir and gave rise to a debate. Opposition spokesmen and some journalists straight away raised the bogey of inequality. The method used consisted of dividing incomes (per person) into ten deciles. The share of the first two deciles (the lowest) in the incomes total, and the ratio between the first and tenth deciles constitute the yardstick of inequality.

Without going into technical discussions which are outside the scope of this brief note, it should first be pointed out that the difference between the countries compared derives mainly from the bottom two deciles and the top decile, in other words, from the ratio between rich and poor. In France, according to Prof. Sawyer's figures, the 10% of poorest households received, after tax, 1.4% of the total household incomes, while the richest 10% received 30.4%, or 21.7 times as much. In Norway, for the same date, the corresponding figures were 2.3% and 22.2%, a ratio of 9.7 to 1. The ratio is obviously very sensitive to the accuracy of the values given for the top and bottom deciles. Only 0.1% needs to be transferred from top to bottom for the ratio to fall to 20.2 to 1.

The results of this international comparison are surprising, not because they reveal that the Scandinavian countries are more egalitarian than France, but because they indicate that Spain and Italy are, too—which is harder to believe. Moreover, there is another study, also by a British economist and statistician, Peter Wiles, which makes a different valuation of the lower decile and therefore puts French inequality at about the same level as in the United Kingdom.

Prof. Sawyer uses figures provided by the statisticians of the Institut National des Statistiques et des Etudes Economiques (INSEE), figures taken from an inquiry into incomes. French statisticians have two basic criticisms of the OECD study:

First, according to the country, the base data are taken either from fiscal investigations or living standard surveys; for France, it only requires the use of data produced by sample surveys of living standards for the ratio between D1 and D10 to come down to about the level of the United States, Canada or Italy; with D1 rising from 1.5 to 1.75 and D10 falling from 31.0 to 25.5, the ratio of D10 D9 to D1 D2 would fall from 10.9 to 8.8, and the Gini coefficient from 0.42 to 0.37. Without at all stating that dividing incomes according to sample surveys gives a more accurate reflection of reality than do figures taken from fiscal surveys, the fact remains that incomes in other countries are mainly based on household surveys. It was not legitimate to compare figures from different sources.

The second criticism has to do with the corrections made for taxation to the totals of the deciles. The INSEE considers that the share of D10 is reduced 2.7% by taxation, whereas the OECD study reduces it only 0.6%. There are other curious difficulties about D7, D8, and D9.

The major difficulty in all these calculations involves D1 and, to a lesser extent, D2. The poorest are mainly found among the idle or among farmers. It is difficult to assign a precise figure to the income represented by the imaginary rent of a man living in his own home, or to the produce grown by poor peasants for their own consumption.

In some respects, France is probably more inegalitarian than countries with comparable levels of economic development, such as West Germany or the United Kingdom. The wage range appears to be wider and the inroads of direct taxation on higher wages are smaller. French business has created the category of the *cadres*—executives, or "salary-earners," but more highly organized and self-conscious as a group—which does not exist in other Europeans in the same form. The *cadres* enjoy a particularly favorable superannuation system.

The reader may also refer to an issue of the quarterly review *Les futuribles* (unnumbered, June 1976) entitled *La croissance et l'inégalité des revenues*, the work of François Bloch-Lainé, Jean Fourastié, Henri Guitton, Jacques Lecaillou, and Pierre Masé.

Surveys by INSEE show that "scatter has been appreciably reduced; in the field of fiscal incomes, it is calculated that the interdecile ratio (i.e. the ratio between the income exceeded by 10% of households and the maximum income of the lowest 10% of households) went from 17.3 to 1 in 1962 to 10 to 1 in 1970; in the course of the same period, the interquartile ratio fell from 3.7 to 1, to 3 to 1, while the value of the concentration coefficient (Gini coefficient) moved from 0.49 to 0.44" (p. 19).

Similarly, according to a study by M. Bandirier, "the ratio of the average income of the most affluent to the least affluent (farm workers) category has dropped from 5.8 to 4.5 to 1 (between 1962 and 1970). Also, the ratio of the average income of upper *cadres* to that of workers has dropped from 3.5 to 3.0 to 1" (p. 62).

Comparisons between West Germany and France have highlighted the relative advantages enjoyed by nonmanual workers in France. One detailed study of nine French and nine German firms produced the following findings: the average ratio of top *cadres'* to foremen's wages is 1.68 to 1 in the first case, 1.33 to 1 in the second. Workers are relatively less well paid and represent a smaller proportion of the staff in France than in Germany. Another aspect of the situation is that nonmanagerial employees in German companies are not much better paid than skilled workers, but in French firms they are appreciably better off. The functions of command, organization, and supervision are more common as well as better paid in French companies.

One last observation (due to M. Jean Lecaillou) is worth making. Between 1962 and 1970, the concentration index was brought down from 0.49 to 0.44—a reduction of 10% in eight years. In 1965, fiscal redistribution is thought to have had the effect of bringing the index down from 0.46 to 0.40—a reduction of 13%. The change in income distribution produced by ten years' economic growth would give a result comparable to all the fiscal measures aimed at redistribution. In fact, redistribution has had hardly any effect on deciles 5, 6, 7, and 8, and very little on deciles 4 and 9. Redistribution tends, basically, to transfer incomes from the upper decile to the two lowest.

Note G

I reproduce below a few of the tables on which R. Bacon and W. Eltis base their interpretation of the "British disease."*

Tables 13 and 14 show the relatively slow pace of growth in the United Kingdom compared to that of the Continental European countries. Table 15 illustrates the gap between the percentage of the national product invested in the UK and that invested in France, West Germany, Italy, etc.

Subsequently, Tables 16 and 17 highlight the excessively rapid decrease in the British industrial work force and the excessively rapid increase in the number of functionaries.

Table 18 confirms the reduction in the British share of trade in manufactured products, and Table 19 illustrates the jump in the change from non-industrial to industrial employment. Lastly, Table 20 shows how small the increase has been in the worker's disposable income, owing to higher prices and tax and welfare deductions, even though nominal wages have more than doubled.

*These tables are taken from the revised and updated second edition of R. Bacon & W. Eltis, *Britain's Economic Problem: Too Few Producers* (London: Macmillan, 1978), pp. 208-15.

Table 13/ Gross domestic product at constant market prices

	1961	1973	1974
UK	100	140	141
USA	100	170	167
France	100	197	205
West Germany	100	171	172
Italy	100	177	183
Japan	100	318	315

Table 14/ Indices of output per man-hour at constant 1963 values

	1961	1974	1975
UK	100	166	165
USA	100	154	157
France	100	218	208
West Germany	100	199	206
Italy	100	236	225
Japan	100	329	319

Table 15/ Share of gross domestic capital formation in gross domestic product

	1961	1973	1974
UK	0.173	0.198	0.205
USA	0.163	0.182	0.175
France	0.215	0.244	0.251
West Germany	0.252	0.247	0.225
Italy	0.278	0.212	0.234
Japan	0.332	0.367	0.343

Table 16/ Number of civilians employed by sector (*thousands*)

		Industry	Agriculture	Other
UK	1961	11,989	972	11,624
	1975	10,096	667	13,812
USA	1961	21,564	5,200	38,982
	1975	24,565	3,381	56,837
France	1961	7,132	4,044	7,540
	1975	8,022	2,351	10,391
West Germany	1961	12,965	3,449	9,824
	1975	11,460	1,822	11,546
Italy	1961	7,646	6,207	6,155
	1975	8,305	2,964	7,549
Japan	1961	13,460	13,030	18,490
	1975	18,550	6,580	26,650

Table 17/ Growth in numbers employed in various service categories in the UK (*thousands*)

	1961	1975	% Increase
Local authorities	1782	3024	69.7
Central government	1776	2246	26.5
Other services	7298	8062	10.5

Table 18/ Shares of world trade in manufactured products (measured in value terms)

	1961	1974	1975
UK	0.164	0.088	0.093
USA	0.205	0.172	0.177
France	0.094	0.093	0.102
West Germany	0.202	0.217	0.203
Italy	0.057	0.067	0.075
Japan	0.068	0.145	0.136

Table 19/ Ratio of non-industrial to industrial employment

	1961	1974	% Change	1975	% Change
UK	0.970	1.299	33.9	1.368	41.0
USA	1.808	2.086	15.4	2.313	27.9
France	1.057	1.254	18.6	1.295	22.5
West Germany	0.758	0.866	14.2	1.007	32.8
Italy	0.806	0.889	10.3	0.908	12.6
Japan	1.374	1.353	−1.5	1.436	4.5

Table 20/ Calculation of real disposable earnings for the average male worker (£)

	1963	1970	1974	1975
Gross earnings	18.00	29.70	47.70	60.70
Tax	2.17	5.84	10.25	14.82
Social security	0.33	0.88	0.84	0.75
Graduated pension	0.25	0.80	1.92	2.83
Rates	0.60	0.97	1.47	n.a.
Net earnings	14.45	21.21	33.22	n.a.
Price index	100.00	133.80	193.40	236.00
Real net earnings	14.45	15.85	17.13	n.a.
Net earnings (before deducting rates)	15.05	22.18	34.69	42.30
Real net earnings (before deducting rates)	15.05	16.58	17.94	17.92

Note H

Some writers and lawyers connected with the French Socialist party have recently published a book entitled *Liberté, Libertés,* "Liberty and Freedoms,"* with a preface by François Mitterrand. The Common Program of the Left for the 1978 elections also contains a chapter on liberty and freedoms, and anyone would think that, in present-day France, under a president who professes a liberal philosophy, these freedoms were being threatened or flouted. R. Badinter's book enables us to understand what the Socialists mean by freedoms, and why—without even knowing it—they are paving the way toward an anything but a liberal society.

The case for the prosecution ranges across several categories. The first concerns justice in the narrow sense of the word, and its grounds for complaint are usually based on a comparison between British or American legal practices and French practices—duration of custody without trial, emergency jurisdiction, subordination of the magistracy to the political power, police violence, the absence of a proper supreme court, etc. The jurists argue that even omitting abnormal periods such as the years of the war in Algeria, liberty as security, the kind of liberty which Montesquieu was first to speak of, is less well guaranteed than it should or could be.

*Edited by Robert Badinter (Paris, Gallimard.)

The second category concerns the protection of individual privacy, now that modern data-processing techniques are giving governments powers which once would have been inconceivable, and *ipso facto* the means to abuse them. All parties have discovered these new or updated problems and have suggested preventive measures.

The third category embraces what is known as freedom of expression or information, but here the debate ceases to be juridicial and becomes sociological. The first two categories of freedom were expressed in relation to the state: today as yesterday, they are defined in terms of the rights of individuals in their dealings with public authority. Freedom of information, in the sense of the elimination of censorship, can be taken for granted; today's demands are aimed not so much at freedom as at the effective capacity to exercise it.

In this sphere, France is presently faced with two problems, namely, how to ensure that radio and television are working as public services, in the service of the public, on behalf of the whole nation and not just on behalf of the government and the social groups it represents. In addition, the economic and financial circumstances of the press are reducing the opportunities for newspapers to express an opinion. Everybody has a right to publish a newspaper, but how many people have the necessary means? In accordance with a typically French way of thinking, most right-wing as well as left-wing commentators support the state monopoly of television, if not radio; they go on dreaming about organizing things so that screen time is shared out fairly among all parties and comment is as close to objectivity as possible. The Socialists are even naive or impudent enough to envisage a system whereby the television networks would be run by "tripartite committees composed of members appointed by the users' associations, trade unions, and parliament." Suppose a Socialist-Communist came to power: it would mean that the present opposition would gain a majority on the committee. Is this an advance for freedom?

Confusion of mind, pure and simple, is displayed in the following remark: "Where there is dependence, freedom fades away. The first principle is therefore *to assure the independence* of the information media vis-à-vis the state, finance, or any pressure group." How could a radio station or a newspaper depend on nothing and nobody? If this nondependence means anything at all, it means unlimited power for those who write or speak. Even then, one should add that journalists depend on their editor, unless each one is expressing his or her own opinion, in which case all newspapers become public platforms.

A fourth category embraces what are now called "social rights." In a limited sense, these now belong to the liberal conception of the individual freedoms. It is no longer enough for everyone to have the right to medical care—in other words, for the state to be unable to prohibit and no individual or group to be able to prevent him from receiving it—because he should also have the financial means without which his "right" would remain empty or "formal." There is no longer any controversy over the principle of these social rights (or practical freedoms)—it was a right-wing majority which voted in favor of social security institutions in the early 1930s. On the other hand, there are some who make an unconscious shift from freedom to equality and do not perceive the consequences of their choice. We read: "Sick people are unequally treated according to their social position. Even if the hospital services guarantee first-rate treatment to all, the fact remains that the most affluent have the time, the money, and the information which make it more possible to prevent or combat illness."*

Liberté, Libertés, p. 174.

Short of all economic and social inequality vanishing away, what kind of miracle could make this particular inequality vanish? In fact, longevity—assuming that it does reflect health—is neither directly nor exclusively dependent on wealth: schoolteachers do better than VIPs, in this respect. The Socialists vaguely suggest a new concept of medicine as a public service. The British experience should be a warning against making health care absolutely free, and against the illusion that equality lies along that road.

By definition, no reform will eliminate that inequality, for two equally obvious reasons: first, some kinds of treatment, such as organ transplants, are so expensive that no society is rich enough to make them generally available; second, not all doctors and surgeons have the same qualifications or the same ability. The best surgeons do not perform all operations. What characterizes and distinguishes Western societies is that a proportion of patients from the least privileged levels have access, through the hospitals, to the best doctors and surgeons.

The tendency of the contributors to the book to confuse freedom with equality recurs in several of the chapters. I admit that the principle of nondiscrimination provides a valid basis for demands for equality between men and women, but is it necessary, even for a "transition period," to reserve the same number of places for women as for men in all establishments where entrance is by selection? Can this rule be reconciled with the universalism of meritocracy? If man and woman are not "alike," is it self-evident that the allocation of roles in society ought to be the same? Can the measures needed to break up the present system of allocation be squared with the rights of individuals?

Similarly, in the chapter on education, equality is explicitly substituted for freedom. After reminding readers of the by now familiar findings of sociological studies—that "the educational system reproduces inequality"*—our reformers propose "to extend every individual's freedom by breaking the old hierarchy-producing model" (p. 129); a few lines previously, these same reformers were advocating the abolition of "free education" and the creation of a "great national public service" whose pluralism would of course be guaranteed. Nationalization or state control, on the one hand, utopia on the other: in a society as intellectualized as today's, knowledge inevitably creates a hierarchy, or even a twin hierarchy, within each branch of learning, and between the various branches. The first appears to be ineradicable; the second capable of mitigation by the growing number of these hierarchies (and Western societies do tend to increase their number). If, on the whole, wealth and power go together, in the West as well as in the other societies known to history, then dissociation between society's activities, social and functional pluralism, and permanent controversy weaken power and remove its all-embracing character. Thus, when our reformers write that "no one can now distinguish the army, industry, science, and police from one another: they are forces compressed into one single force" (p. 60), one wonders if the contributors are living in France or in the Soviet Union.

One last category of freedoms sets out to modify the authoritarian organization of business and the armed forces. There is no question that Western societies, whether democratic or liberal, have not applied their principles of political order to some sectors of society, and least of all to business and the armed forces. Our French reformers intend to "democratize" the armed forces—which involves

---

*This dictum has two meanings which are not usually properly distinguished: the educational system does not modify the nonegalitarian structure of society, and does not modify the holders of the various hierarchized functions. The privileged are still recruited from the same families. The second interpretation calls for a great many more reservations than the first.

recognizing the freedoms of expression and assembly within the various forces, recognizing freedom of association, instituting elected representative committees containing both draftees and officers, having the officers and non-coms represented on the armed forces supreme council elected by their peers, and so on. The text before me is no more precise about business reform, but the few indications given would be enough to make it impossible to run any business, public as well as private. For example: "Ownership cannot be the basis of a private authority over men. . . . The employer can never be sole judge of a measure having repercussions on the men at work" (p. 89). As any step taken by management has some sort of impact on the men at work, the manager cannot make any decision by himself. In that case, can he still manage?

The Socialists' philosophy, as expressed in this book, attempts to synthesize opposites, extending the liberal idea and the democratic idea and the egalitarian idea throughout society with no serious consideration as to whether an army with unions would remain capable of fighting, whether a business where all the boss's decisions were open to debate would still manage to produce wealth, or whether a state which had been entrusted with the ownership of the biggest industrial conglomerates and which organized both a national education and a national health service would remain constitutional and liberal for very long.

In the West, the danger is not so much that of the totalitarian temptation as it is the exorbitance of liberal ambitions, the impetuosity of egalitarian demands, and the blindness of the Socialists. It is true that the workers, in their work place, do not enjoy the same rights as the citizens in the city, and that soldiers do give up some of their rights as citizens. The possible reforms will never achieve all the liberal aspirations; productive and military activity will always be subject to various specific restraints. Freedom, in the sense of actual ability to do or think, will always remain imperfect, in the view of those whose dream is to distribute it equally to everybody. The state, burdened with all the functions assigned to it by this book, would soon be confronted with having to choose between its own professed doctrine and necessity.

The Italians do not feel any trace of the totalitarian temptation; instead, they display keener, more inventive liberal aspirations than all the rest of the Europeans. Perhaps they will resist the Italian Communist party in the near future; for the moment, the far left wing and libertarians are making their own contribution toward spreading the conviction that only the Communist party will create or restore the state—which no society can afford to leave helpless indefinitely. In France, the danger is not so much *gauchisme* as it is the illusions of the Socialists, illusions which threaten to compromise the nation's freedoms, on the pretext of extending them.

Index